Recovering Spain's Feminist Tradition

Recovering Spain's Feminist Tradition

EDITED BY
Lisa Vollendorf

THE MODERN LANGUAGE ASSOCIATION OF AMERICA
NEW YORK 2001

Printed in the United States of America

Library of Congress Cataloging-in-Publication Data

Recovering Spain's feminist tradition / edited by Lisa Vollendorf.
p. cm.
Includes bibliographical references and index.
ISBN 0-87352-273-7 (cloth) — ISBN 0-87352-274-5 (pbk.)
1. Feminism—Spain—History. 2. Women—Spain—History.
I. Vollendorf, Lisa.

HQ1692.R44 2001
305.42'0946—dc21 2001045041

Cover illustration for the paperback edition: *Weaver of Verona* (1956), by Remedios Varo (1908–63). Oil on masonite.

Printed on chlorine-free paper

Published by The Modern Language Association of America
26 Broadway, New York, New York 10004-1789
www.mla.org

In loving memory of
H. Patsy Boyer,
Christina Dupláa, and
Charlotte Lyon Vollendorf

Contents

Eighteenth and Nineteenth Centuries

Twentieth Century

Acknowledgments

This volume would not have been possible without the extensive support of colleagues and loved ones. The Publications Committee and the staff at the Modern Language Association improved the manuscript at every stage. Martha Evans's enthusiasm helped get the project off the ground, and her expertise, along with the marvelous editing of Judith Gardner and Elizabeth Holland, helped shape it into the book that you hold in your hands. Susan Kirkpatrick and the other, anonymous reader for the MLA gave detailed comments that improved both style and substance. Wayne State University provided a small research grant that financed the translation of several essays. H. Patsy Boyer, Anne J. Cruz, Elliott J. Gorn, Amy Katz Kaminsky, Kathleen McNerney, Stacey Schlau, Charles Stivale, Joyce Tolliver, Valerie Traub, Nancy Vosburg, and Alison Weber nurtured the project with kindness and advice. The staff members at the Newberry Library in Chicago and at the Clark Library in Los Angeles were faultlessly generous with their help. Thanks to the contributors, this has been a truly pleasurable, collaborative endeavor from the beginning.

Recovering Spain's Feminist Tradition is about listening to women of the past and laying the groundwork for a feminist future. As the book was going to press, the deaths of H. Patsy Boyer (1937–2000), Christina Dupláa (1954–2001), and Charlotte Lyon Vollendorf (1988–2000) forced me to think once more about the links among women of all ages. Patsy gave me many gifts, but, most important, she taught me to listen across the generations. Christina was a supportive friend and a consummate professional; she will be missed by friends and colleagues alike. My cousin Charlotte Lyon Vollendorf died in a car accident before her twelfth birthday. A vibrant, loving little girl, Charlotte would have grown up to be an impressive woman. May this book honor these and other spirited women's lives.

Introduction

Feminism has been described as a political movement, a social doctrine, an ethics, and a struggle for equality. While contemporary philosophers, scholars, writers, and activists sometimes choose different language to discuss feminism, their definitions share the basic assumption that women are subject to inequality and injustice because we live in a man's world. When feminism is invoked in Western countries—in the academy, in the media, on the street—it is often associated with a fight against gender oppression in industrialized, liberal-minded areas of the world. In particular, discussions of feminism in English are much more likely to be associated with northern and western Europe, Australia, Canada, and the United States than with Africa, Asia, Latin America, or eastern Europe. The move in the 1990s toward international feminism—with its promise of incorporating new voices—marks a positive step toward redressing this relatively narrow scope.[1]

Although we find ourselves in an age of internationalism, some cultures and national traditions continue to be privileged and others subordinated in dialogues about feminism. Spain is one of the countries that remain on the margins of the debate. Despite a growing number of feminists in all regions of Spain, Spanish women do not appear as either authors or subjects in anthologies of feminist thinking and criticism published in English. They are even excluded from those anthologies, such as Robyn Warhol and Diane Price Herndl's *Feminisms: An Anthology of Literary Theory and Criticism* and Sandra Kemp and Judith Squires's *Feminisms*, that claim a commitment to cultural heterogeneity and diversity.[2]

While it might seem odd that Spain does not figure prominently in an international intellectual economy that sees the developed West as the primary producer of feminist thought, this marginalization is part of the larger phenomenon of treating Spain as an anomaly in western Europe. Spain's cultural makeup (Christian, Jewish, Muslim) and geographical location (at the edge of Europe) have contributed to its unique history. This cultural and historical specificity has led to a tendency among non-Spanish academics to treat all things Spanish as separate, different, even disconnected from the rest of western Europe. The twentieth century exacerbated this attitude, as forty years of Franco's fascist rule resulted in Spain's disenfranchisement from its neighbors and potential allies. Adrian Shubert captures the negative depictions of this country in European historiography:

> For most historians of modern Europe Spain barely exists in its own right; it comes into view only on those occasions when it served as the stage for broader European events, as a major theater for the Napoleonic Wars and as the battleground for hostile ideologies in the 1930s. And too many people, Spaniards included, are willing to accept the description of Spain given by W. H. Auden in his poem "Spain 1937" as "that arid square, that fragment nipped off from hot / Africa soldered so crudely to inventive Europe." (1)

More than twenty-five years after Franco's death and the peaceful transition to democracy, Spain continues to be perceived as peripheral to western Europe. Viewed by outsiders as a conservative country with an ideology governed by the Catholic Church, Spain simply tends to be slighted in analyses of European progressive politics or liberal philosophy.

Combined with recent political history, these biases have led to faulty assumptions about feminism in Spain. Indeed, while most non-Spanish academics interested in women's issues can name any number of extraordinary women from the United States, France, Britain, and Italy, many cannot think of one Spanish woman excepting, perhaps, Santa Teresa. Yet Spain has a long history of articulate women committed to feminism, and the last third of the twentieth century saw a veritable rebirth of feminist activity. In an interview from the mid-1970s, the prominent activist Lidia Falcón expressed frustration about outsiders' lack of knowledge of Spanish feminism. Insisting that she and her compatriots were informed about feminist activities abroad, her peers in France, she said,

> no sabían nada de España. En Portugal, no sabían nada de España; en Italia, no sabían nada de España. Que no nos conozcan las amas de casa francesas o inglesas, lo comprendo, pero que mujeres dedicadas al movimiento de liberación de la mujer no sepan nada de lo que pasa en España, no. Porque nosotras conocemos lo que se hace en Norteamérica, en Inglaterra, en Francia, en Italia, en Suecia, en Portugal, en Corea [. . .]. Sin embargo, esta gente está completamente alejada de la problemática española.
>
> (Levine and Waldman 70)

> didn't know anything about Spain. In Portugal, they didn't know anything about Spain; in Italy they didn't know anything about Spain. That housewives in France or England don't know anything about us, I understand, but I don't understand how it is that women dedicated to the women's movement don't know anything about us. Because we know what goes on in North America, in England, in France, in Italy, in Sweden, in Portugal, in Korea [. . .]. Nevertheless, these people are completely alienated from the Spanish situation.[3]

Although outsiders' lack of awareness about Spain continues, current advocacy for feminist causes can be found among Spaniards of different backgrounds and professions, including politicians, businesswomen, lawyers, activists, artists, and scholars.

Falcón is one of many who have been tireless in their efforts to politicize women's issues, to make contemporary Spaniards understand that feminism is relevant to all their lives. For Falcón, a founding member of Spain's Partido Feminista (Feminist Party) and of the 1970s journal *Vindicación feminista* ("Feminist Vindication"), the social doctrine of equality for women requires large-scale political activism for success. In a characteristically direct statement from an interview given toward the end of Franco's regime, Falcón expressed some of the basic tenets of her feminist thought:

> La mujer está sometida al hombre desde que nace. Vive las condiciones que le han sido dadas por sus padres, por su ambiente, por su escuela, por la sociedad entera. Salir de ello requiere lucha y sacrificio y preparación y no la tiene.[4] (Levine and Waldman 74)
>
> Woman is subjected to man from the moment she is born. She lives under conditions that have been given to her by her parents, by her environment, by her school, by the entire society. Overcoming this requires struggle and sacrifice. It requires preparation that a woman does not have.

Here, Falcón protested the institutionalized inequity faced by women in all facets of their lives. And, as in a later article, "Auge y caída del movimiento" ("Rise and Fall of the Feminist Movement"), she recognized the need for a widespread shift in social consciousness before the feminist movement could gain strength and make headway in Spanish society (40). Along with others working toward change, Falcón has sought to dismantle the cultural structures that perpetuate misogyny and discrimination. One of the defining features of nineteenth- and twentieth-century feminisms is precisely this commitment to activism aimed at social reorganization.

The modern women's movement in the West can be traced to the mid-nineteenth century, after which feminism took hold at a varied pace in each country. Because of economic and social factors, Spain has had a unique time frame for its modern feminist movement. Throughout Europe and North America, women's incorporation into the workforce in the 1800s was a major catalyst for change, but Spanish women's entry was delayed by the late arrival of the industrial revolution. Moreover, the restoration of the monarchy after the revolutionary period (1868–74) marked a rise in conservatism that lasted until the end of the century. In effect, conditions were not right for feminist coalition building and large-scale advocacy until the 1900s. And even then Spain had to wait until the 1930s for widespread change. As the historian Mary Nash has described in her analysis of the lack of emphasis on individual rights in Spanish liberal thought, "En definitiva, la cultura política [hasta los años treinta] fue poco favorable para el florecimiento de un feminismo liberal de signo político tal como había sucedido en Gran Bretaña o los Estados Unidos" ("Experiencia" 159) ("The political culture [until the thirties] most definitely was unfavorable for the flourishing of a liberal feminism with a political bent such as that of Great Britain or the United States").

Responding to the disjuncture between women's movements abroad and the Spanish situation, the nineteenth-century reformer Concepción Saiz y Otero (b. 1850) expressed frustration that Spaniards had not embraced feminism as women had in other countries. She wrote in 1897:

> La cuestión del feminismo [. . .] empieza, aunque con timidez, á iniciarse en España. Pocos son en número, pero muy valiosos por la calidad, son los escritores dedicados hasta ahora á su estudio; la masa general permanece por el momento indiferente ó burlona. (248)[5]

> The question of feminism [. . .] is beginning, although quite timidly, to be initiated in Spain. Until now, there have been only a few authors, albeit very good ones, who are dedicated to the study of feminism. For the moment, the general population remains indifferent or even mocking.

Despite what Saiz y Otero calls its timid beginnings, the Spanish women's movement gained significant ground in the first three decades of the twentieth century.

By the 1930s, when the congresswomen Clara Campoamor, Victoria Kent, and Margarita Nelken brought women's issues to the political arena during the Second Republic (1931–39), feminism had taken a decisive turn toward socialism. Nelken lamented the lack of support of the upper classes for women's causes and saw feminism as "[una] cosa de las trabajadoras, de la clase media y de la clase obrera" (36) ("an issue of concern for women workers, for the middle and working classes").

Nelken also highlighted an issue that continues to be important for the consideration of Spanish feminism: women's resistance to calling themselves feminists.[6] Faced with women's lack of active participation in the movement during her lifetime, Nelken adopted a broad definition of feminism:

> Puede asegurarse que, en España, hay aún, con relación a la totalidad, pocas feministas, pero que son feministas todas las mujeres que, por su posición social, por su condición de seres que trabajan, significan algo en el progreso de España. (36)
>
> But one can consider as feminists all women who, because of their social position or their condition as working people, mean something to Spain's progress.

The feminism that flourished before and during the Second Republic was all but extinguished by the Civil War and Franco's dictatorship. Still, the existence of a women's movement before the war provided a frame of reference for feminist activism in post-1975 Spain.

The resurgence of feminism during the late 1970s formed part of the general liberalization of culture after Franco's death.[7] Since 1975, Spain has experienced tremendous political, social, and economic progress. The I Jornadas por la Liberación de la Mujer (First Women's Liberation Days) in Madrid (1975) and the Jornades Catalanes de la Dona (Catalan Women's Days) in Barcelona (1976) marked a shift in the women's movement. In 1978, the new constitution prohibited discrimination based on sex, and contraception was legalized; in 1981, the socialist Partido Feminista became legal; in 1982, divorce laws were liberalized. Women's organizations have proliferated since the 1980s, as has attention to women's issues in the media and in the academy. In addition to an increase in women's bookstores and of women in publishing, three organizations that have played major roles in fomenting discussion on women's issues were formed: the Seminario de Estudios de la Mujer (Seminar on Women's Studies) (Madrid, 1980), the Instituto de la Mujer (Women's Institute) (Madrid, 1983), and the Institut Català de la Dona (Catalan Women's Institute) (Barcelona, 1989). The feminist presence in social and academic institutions has led to what Nash calls "'institutional feminism'—that is, official institutional support, programs, and services designed specifically to respond to women's needs" ("Changing Status" 119). Indeed, the feminist academic presence has solidified in recent years, particularly with the support of publishers such as LaSal, which closed in 1989, and Anthropos, which has printed the work of numerous theorists and critics.[8]

Women's resistance to identifying themselves as feminists persists in Spain today, but questions of terminology fade into the background as more women than ever openly embrace feminist ideas, seek equal opportunity, and reject social restrictions. As Angeles J. Perona and Ramón del Castillo Santos accurately assess, recent feminist debates show a widespread engagement with diverse positions:

> Es tal la producción intelectual feminista contemporánea que exponerla con detalle excedería con mucho los límites de este trabajo. No obstante, no se puede dejar de insistir en la viveza, riqueza y profundidad del debate existente dentro del propio feminismo a propósito de las distintas interpretaciones que se vienen dando de la tradición feminista y de su proyección futura. (348)
>
> Contemporary feminist intellectual production is such that to explain it in detail would greatly exceed the limits of this article. Nonetheless, it is important to keep insisting on the liveliness, richness, and profundity of the existing debate within feminism with regard to the different interpretations of the feminist tradition and its future projection.

As suggested by Perona and Castillo Santos, feminism in Spain is profoundly multifaceted. It does not resemble feminism in France, where an engagement with language and philosophy defined much of the late-twentieth-century agenda; nor can it be defined as generally as feminism in North America, where the concern for the political has remained the primary focus for three decades. Ranging from the rejection of the feminist label to demands for equal treatment of all minorities, from suspicion about the meaning of "women's writing" ("*escritura femenina*") to a celebration of women's difference, contemporary debates about feminism in Spain represent a wide spectrum of ideologies. Like their sisters from previous decades and previous centuries, Spanish women today continue to adopt various positions regarding women's rights and women's roles. The analyses of a wide array of historical antecedents in this volume provide a backdrop for understanding the multiple manifestations of contemporary Spanish feminism.

Historicizing Feminism

Because of the rise of organized feminism during the latter part of the twentieth century, most discussions of the subject rely on an understanding of feminism as a movement aimed at righting social inequality.[9] An unintended result of this decidedly modern frame of reference is the exclusion of women who, over the centuries, have embraced feminist ideologies without participating in organizations or social movements. When such women are studied, their examples frustrate the seemingly easy delineation of the birth of feminism. As the historian Gerda Lerner suggests in *The Creation of Feminist Consciousness*, scholars have had difficulty fixing a date for the starting point of feminist thinking in Europe; the more research we do on women, the more signs of dissent we find. A growing body of scholarship on women in European history has uncovered pockets of resistance, both individual and collective, that suggest we still need to dig deeper to refine our understanding of feminist issues in history.[10]

To this end, Nash has argued for more comprehensive, contextualized research on women's history ("Experiencia" 152). Like Nash, Lerner has taken up the task of contextualizing women's history by tracing the development of feminist consciousness. Rather than search for signs of organized movements, her work emphasizes the historical evolution of feminist thought. This framework allows for the consideration of "the earliest stages of women's resistance to patriarchal ideas and shows that this kind of feminist oppositional thought developed over a far longer period" than generally believed (14). The application of the term *feminist* to oppositional thought (consciousness) and to larger commitments to social reorganization (movements) highlights the historical continuity among women from different time periods. And, as this essay collection argues, we can learn to appreciate the diversity and the challenges of present-day feminisms by examining previous generations' demands for women's rights.

Awareness of women's subordinate status and advocacy for social change have strong roots in Spain's past. Early historical examples of women who defied limitations on female behavior can be found in the figures of the politically savvy queen Isabella of Castile and the Basque cross-dresser Catalina de Erauso. As in other western European countries, Spain's literature often depicts women struggling against societal constraints. This awareness is expressed in a variety of sources dating from the twentieth century all the way back to some of the earliest known literature, such as traditional ballads in Castilian and Catalan.[11]

Expressions of what Lerner defines as a feminist consciousness appear long before the modern women's movements. We can easily compare Falcón's indictment of men's "subjection" of women with seventeenth-century writer María de Zayas's own declaration that men keep women "sujetas desde que nacemos" (*Novelas* 241) ("subject from the moment we're born") (*Enchantments* 175). The ideological and rhetorical similarities between Falcón's and Zayas's statements are striking, particularly when we consider that three centuries separate the two women. This overlap raises the question of why feminism continues to be viewed as a purely modern phenomenon linked exclusively to the industrial revolution and to women's participation in the public workforce.

Since its inception, the modern feminist movement in the West has differentiated itself from previous feminist expression in its commitment to social reorganization or revolution. The ultimate goal of such activism has been to correct the institutionalized injustices facing women and other oppressed groups. Specifically, contemporary Western feminists imagine a world in which everybody would enjoy the privileges of fully democratic citizenship. In a gesture emblematic of the inclusive thought of the 1990s, for example, the philosopher Victoria Camps endorses the inclusion of all groups in her vision of a feminist world, pointing out that inequality is experienced by women and "también [por] los demás grupos que están o estuvieron excluidos de ejercer como clases dirigentes" (41) ("also [by] the other groups who are or were excluded from acting as ruling classes").[12] Ongoing inequality fails to contain Camps's optimism; she is so encouraged by recent progress that she looks to the twenty-first century as "el siglo de las mujeres" ("women's century").

In spite of efforts to articulate and implement a refined feminist agenda, the gap between theory and praxis remains wide. If we in the industrialized West have moved closer than ever to explaining the significance of social justice, we have not necessarily got closer to its achievement. From 1975 to 2000, women in Spain gained ground on many fronts. More women are educated and participate in the workforce than ever before. Women's political representation has increased markedly. Antidiscrimination and liberalized health access laws have improved women's status. Yet, while progress can be seen in several important arenas, the promises of the post-Franco era have had their limits. Continued discrepancies in pay and representation in various professions combine with the conservative backlash of the late 1990s to confirm that equality has not been fully achieved.[13]

While it is disheartening to note that Zayas and Falcón voiced the same complaints about women's subordinate position across three centuries, recognizing this deep-seated problem bolsters the sense of urgency for the feminist cause as the new millennium unfolds. The knowledge proffered by these and other connections that can be made among women throughout history cannot be underestimated. Scholarship from the last three decades of the twentieth century showed that by tracing the historical developments of women's struggles for fuller and fairer inclusion in society, we can learn a great deal about the interworkings of patriarchal society. From those who have protested women's subordinate position openly to others who have worked more quietly for change, our foremothers as well as our contemporaries can teach us strategies for reform and survival, for coping with and combatting the exclusionary practices of Western cultures.

Feminism in Spain: Past and Present

Recovering Spain's Feminist Tradition pays homage to a handful of women who, from the medieval period to the present, have used writing to engage issues that can be called feminist insofar as they critique and challenge patriarchal norms. The nineteen essays contained in this volume trace the development of Spanish feminist consciousness as it emerges and matures. By covering a broad range of genres, topics, and time periods, they search out the historical roots of feminist thought and emphasize women's rich intellectual traditions in Spain.[14]

This volume constructs a genealogy of women who either call themselves feminists or who deal with feminist issues in their work. The essays show the diverse ways women have expressed their desire to improve their collective status and have recognized the accomplishments of their peers and foremothers. Examination of feminism in its historical contexts highlights the strategies women have used to negotiate their status as intellectuals, reformers, and role models.

The contributors to this volume historicize the position of women intellectuals and reformers in both secular and religious worlds, as well as in public and private spheres. Court writers, nuns, mothers, housewives, journalists, and politicians appear in these pages. The essays delineate similarities among women who enjoyed varied success as writers, spiritual leaders, and activists. Some of these women wrote for broad public consumption as columnists or as authors of popular books. Poetry, fiction, autobiography, and cultural commentary figure among the many genres they cultivated. From various social classes, geographical regions, and language backgrounds, the subjects considered here have in common their identities as women writers. And, with the possible exception of the late twentieth century, they lived in a time when women's writing and self-expression were disparaged and controlled.

In her assessment of the current state of women's history, Nash makes the insightful point that scholars tend to disregard women whose struggles for recognition and justice do not coincide with the dominant model of feminism as equality. She argues that we need to incorporate more women's voices into contemporary scholarship by recognizing the plurality of feminist positions taken throughout history: we should not unnecessarily limit our conceptualization of feminist history by rejecting those women who, to the modern reader, do not appear "sufficiently feminist" ("Experiencia" 172). We have attempted to avoid this problem by attending to the historical and ideological specificity of each woman.

We discuss women whose writing is fraught with contradiction and sometimes conflicts with contemporary notions of feminisms (such as Florencia Pinar and María Pilar Sinués). Some, such as Carmen de Burgos, Lidia Falcón, and Montserrat Roig, seem to lend themselves easily to feminist analysis, but others do not. Whether the women are hailed as vocal feminist forces or viewed as more tentative links in the genealogy, they are valued for their contributions to the diverse contours of the Spanish feminist tradition.

The genealogy of feminist subjects in this volume does not purport to be all-inclusive. Rather, the volume offers a mere outline of a profoundly rich tradition that has yet to be sufficiently and programmatically studied. The scope of the volume presented numerous challenges for the selection of essay topics. Many fine writers have been excluded, and minority-language writers are underrepresented. Although we discuss several medieval and early modern women, our selection still leaves out a large number of women who, by virtue of the time in which they lived, impress us with the very fact of their literacy and astonish us with their remarkable literature. Thanks to the efforts of the scholars who have contributed to the collection and of other scholars, research on women writers from all regions of Spain continues to uncover new texts and to open up new areas of study.[15]

Among the choices that had to be made, some of the most difficult were for the twentieth century. The literary giant Carmen Martín Gaite stands out for her absence: her writing undoubtedly has contributed to the larger society's understanding of women's history and literature. The list of other late-twentieth-century writers who might have appeared here is long: Rosa Chacel, Gloria Fuertes, Carmen Laforet, Ana María Matute, Rosa Montero, Mercè Rodoreda, and Esther Tusquets are only a few of the dozens of women who have had a significant impact on the changing face of publishing and politics. The selection of post–Franco period writers only represents Catalonia, but by no means should readers take this as a sign of lack of activity in other regions. Moreover, any number of younger writers who began publishing in the 1990s in all regions of the country might also have been included, as they represent the vitality of women's intellectual and political engagement in contemporary Spain.

The guiding force behind the selection of essay topics was the recovery of a rich tradition of feminist thinking that, for too long, has fallen by the wayside in feminist and Hispanist studies. Some of the writers viewed as forming the backbone of feminism across the centuries in Spain appear here, including Zayas, Pardo Bazán, Nelken, and Falcón. It might be argued that such figures are so canonical that they are not in need of any recuperative efforts. However, by building into our volume some of the women writers who have attained recognition for their oppositional thinking and their activism, we invite a more thorough examination of these particular authors in conjunction with their predecessors, contemporaries, and successors. The consideration of lesser-known or less obviously feminist writers discussed in other essays is aimed at putting the feminist tradition in perspective and at drawing attention to the many variations that characterize the development of feminist ideologies in Spain.

Seven of the nineteen essays in *Recovering Spain's Feminist Tradition* deal with women who predate modern feminist movements. Barbara Weissberger opens the volume with a provocative essay on the problem of discussing feminism in conjunction with medieval authors. Through an overview of recent scholarship on the fifteenth-century poet Florencia Pinar, Weissberger questions the assignment of feminist subjectivity to writers for whom we have very little textual or biographical information. The analysis of contemporary critics' search for an integrated, feminist poetic self raises questions about critical responsibility and methodology. Weissberger's call for historicization and clarity of terminology provides a backdrop for the essays on early modern women.

María Isabel Barbeito Carneiro answers the call for historicizing in her discussion of several women from the sixteenth and seventeenth centuries. Barbeito examines the feminist expressions of several religious women (Catalina de Mendoza, Lucía de Jesús, Marcela de San Félix, Teresa de Jesús, and others) and women living a pious life outside the convent (including Luisa de Carvajal and María de Guevara). Like other scholars of this period, Barbeito wants to recover women's voices, many of which remain understudied. By letting the women speak to each other, this tour of Spain's Golden Age explores a community of women committed to self-expression.

In a nuanced reading of the works of Ana de San Bartolomé, Alison Weber takes us into the world of a seventeenth-century Discalced Carmelite. Caretaker of Santa Teresa de Jesús and successor to Teresian reform, Ana de San Bartolomé presents a complicated case for the critic attentive to gender issues in convents and in convent writing. Ana de San Bartolomé supported stricter male control over nuns, yet she also believed that women should be on the front lines of spiritual leadership. Weber works through these apparent paradoxes and concludes, as indicated in her essay title, that Ana de San Bartolomé exhibited a "partial feminism" that can be deciphered through a consideration of convent politics in conjunction with her personal allegiances.

Anne J. Cruz also examines social change and women's spirituality in "Juana and Her Sisters." By laying out factors influencing women's loss of spiritual self-control during the Counter-Reformation in Spain and Mexico, Cruz suggests that Sor Juana was representative of women's engagement with spirituality, sexuality, and intellectual production during the sixteenth and seventeenth centuries in both Europe and the New World. Cruz argues that Sor Juana's journey from intellectual discovery to forced renunciation of writing is symbolic of women's position in the church and society at that time. The essay pays homage to Sor Juana and others like her while suggesting that many women on both continents faced similar frustrations in their intellectual and spiritual endeavors. Like Barbeito and Weber, Cruz emphasizes the importance of female community for religious women. Her analysis forges connections among Catholic women who staked out their claims on sexuality, intellectualism, and spiritual leadership in a politically and religiously volatile period.

In "'No Doubt It Will Amaze You,'" I examine the feminism of María de Zayas, an author who has enjoyed a recent critical renaissance and whose texts continue to intrigue and baffle scholars. A participant in private literary salons and in the public book market, this best-selling novelist found success in both arenas in the seventeenth century. The essay argues that the representations of the female body in the novella collection provide a key to understanding Zayas's cogent, early modern feminist ideology.

Moving us into the eighteenth century, Teresa Soufas and her co-authors discuss a newly discovered anonymous play attributed to a fourteen-year-old Sevillian *dama.* Soufas worked with her students to answer as many questions as possible about the mystery surrounding the text and its author. The result is a collaboratively written analysis in which methodologies informing literary history are brought to bear on questions of authorship, religiosity, and gender in eighteenth-century Spain. The essay serves as an example of the recuperative work that plays a vital role in the discovery and dissemination of women's texts.

Constance Sullivan's analysis of Josefa Amar y Borbón, the most prominent woman writer from eighteenth-century Spain, also deals with Enlightenment gender ideology. The essay compares Amar's lists of famous women with similar texts written by men and argues that Amar's selective use of female role models strengthens her defense of women's intellectual capacities. Confirming the importance of feminist genealogies, Sullivan suggests that Amar bolstered her own self-authorization as a writer through the appropriation of the genre of lists of famous women. In making this argument, Sullivan delineates the specific techniques that allowed Amar to express a feminist message while avoiding alienation of her readership.

María Cristina Urruela explores the popular genre of nineteenth-century sentimental novels through an examination of the feminist elements in María Pilar Sinués's fiction. Like other authors of this genre (which was extremely popular among women readers), Sinués has been considered second-rate and ultraconservative. Challenging this evaluation, Urruela studies the narrative strategies used by Sinués to criticize the domestication of women in nineteenth-century society. By exposing the difficulties faced by female characters forced to conform to dominant codes of domesticity and femininity, Sinués protested the restrictive norms of femininity. Urruela's analysis of this author (whose fiction is usually interpreted as highly formulaic and ideologically compliant) should motivate scholars to reread women writers whose work has been viewed as conventional, substandard, or reactionary.

"Rosalía de Castro: Cultural Isolation in a Colonial Context" is the first of several essays in this volume to address the issues of regionalism, nationalism, and linguistic difference that play major roles in Spain's past and present. Here Catherine Davies considers the interplay of feminism, nationalism, and colonialism in the life and work of the Galician Rosalía de Castro. A poet who wrote in Galician and lived both in Galicia and Madrid, Castro also held unpopular political views. Taking into account the history of northwestern Spain, the analysis emphasizes the impact, in Spain and abroad, of the large Galician immigration to Cuba in the nineteenth century. Davies casts Rosalía de Castro as a perpetually and paradoxically marginal figure, a woman whose life and works explicitly engaged feminism and nationalism.

Lou Charnon-Deutsch looks at the politics of another major figure of nineteenth-century Spain. Described by subsequent generations as the mother of the women's movement, Concepción Arenal played a significant role in the debate over women's future in Spanish society. Charnon-Deutsch discusses the "woman question" in Spain and examines the success in the public sphere of one of the century's "most avid feminists." Charnon-Deutsch considers Arenal's accomplishments and the sacrifices demanded by her public existence. The analysis lays out the contradictory stances taken by Arenal during her long life as an advocate for women's rights.

A successor to Arenal and publisher of her own Woman's Library (Biblioteca de la mujer), Emilia Pardo Bazán focused her energies on the literary culture of the late-nineteenth- and early-twentieth centuries. Although Pardo Bazán has been accused of individualism and apathy with regard to the general cause of women, Joyce Tolliver reconstructs Pardo Bazán's efforts to break down the barriers of the male-dominated literary establishment, including her support of Arenal and Gertrudis Gómez de Avellaneda for appointment to the Royal Spanish Academy. Praising Pardo Bazán's sophisticated deflection of personal criticism, Tolliver analyzes the strategies used by the author to expose the misogyny in male critics' remarks about women authors. This focus demonstrates Pardo Bazán's uncanny ability to confront her male colleagues with the sexism that operated to exclude women from the intellectual culture of the period.

Author of Pardo Bazán's obituary in 1921, Carmen de Burgos was a lifelong advocate of women's advancement. As Maryellen Bieder discusses in "Carmen de Burgos: Modern Spanish Woman," the ambiguities and contradictions found in Burgos's writings are representative of the complex and sometimes muddled nature of Spanish feminism in the early part of the twentieth century. Unlike her foremother Concepción Arenal and her younger contemporary Margarita Nelken, Burgos supported women's right to vote. But Burgos also exhibited what Bieder reads as rhetorical flexibility: Burgos supported women's suffrage but also disparaged it on certain occasions. In an examination of Burgos's handling of this and other controversial issues, Bieder traces the plurality of feminist stances of this influential journalist, fiction writer, and public advocate.

Nancy Vosburg considers issues related to women's private roles in an analysis of the nonlinear narrative structure of María Teresa León's *Memoria de la melancolía* ("Memoirs of Melancholy"). Overshadowed by the celebrity of her husband, the poet Rafael Alberti, León has received little critical attention. Like so many women of the early decades of the twentieth century, the middle-class León expressed solidarity with working-class women. Yet this commitment also had its limitations, for León remained within the mainstream Spanish feminism of the time. Vosburg disentangles the complex and sometimes contradictory ideology of the burgeoning middle-class feminism that had a significant impact on the politics of pre–Civil War Spain.

Further delimiting the questions of class present in early-twentieth-century feminisms, Josebe Martínez-Gutiérrez examines the political activity and writings of the congresswoman and cultural critic Margarita Nelken. Nelken's beliefs about key issues affecting women were emblematic of some feminist thinking before the Civil War: she opposed women's suffrage, supported divorce, and advocated education to help women free themselves from men's yoke. These commitments to socialist politics were refigured, however, when Nelken was forced into exile and failed to find a place among her cohorts in Mexico. In an analysis of the difficulties facing politically active women, Martínez-Gutiérrez examines Nelken's transition from insider to outsider and from feminist activist to arts activist. In tracing the various roles adopted by this political activist, the essay addresses feminist ideologies of the 1930s and the stultifying effects of Franco's 1939 victory.

As evidenced by the cases of Burgos, León, Nelken, and others, advocacy for working-class women played a singularly important role in feminist ideologies of the first forty years of the twentieth century. With the formation of the anarchist organization Mujeres Libres (Free Women), working-class feminism gained tremendous ground during the Civil War. Despite the high numbers of participants (approximately twenty thousand women), the activity of Mujeres Libres has not figured as significant in either the historical accounts or the popular imagination.[16] In "Feminism and Anarchism: Remembering the Role of Mujeres Libres in the Spanish Civil War," María Asunción Gómez analyzes two sources that have brought Mujeres Libres to the modern Spanish public. She examines the interplay of memory and history in Vicente Aranda's film *Libertarias* and in Sara Berenguer's autobiographical narrative *Entre el sol y la tormenta* ("Between the Sun and the Storm"). As in Martínez-Gutiérrez's essay, Gómez's account of political activity before and during the Civil War highlights the contrast between the liberalization of the Second Republic and the oppression of the Franco period. Indeed, faced with persecution and possible death at the hands of Franco's oppressive regime, both Nelken and Berenguer went into exile.

In an essay on the short-lived 1970s feminist journal *Vindicación Feminista,* Margaret Jones takes us on a journey through the regressive policies of francoist Spain. The bleak Franco period did see some feminist activism, notably on the part of Maria Aurèlia Capmany (see *El feminismo ibérico*) and Falcón, who founded *Vindicación Feminista.* The journal is a testament to the renewal of liberal ideals and feminism that substantially energized political and social reform in the decade following Spain's transition to democracy.

The final essays in *Recovering Spain's Feminist Tradition* examine three contemporary Catalan women. This critical cluster aims to put into relief some of the differences and similarities among late-twentieth-century women writers by focusing on literature from one region of Spain. As in the case of the nineteenth-century Galician writer Rosalía de Castro, nationalism, regionalism, and linguistic difference are central to the identity and politics of many non-Castilians. In "Montserrat Roig: Women, Genealogy, and Mother Tongue," Christina Dupláa pays homage to Roig's rigorous intellectual and political commitments to feminism. Unlike most women writers in Spain, Roig identified herself as a feminist and sought to reconstruct a genealogy of influential women in her critical work. A strong believer in feminist causes, she supported women through her activities as editor and writer. Roig was equally invested in the validation of Catalan, the native tongue of the people of Catalonia and a language prohibited by Franco. Dupláa argues for the contextualized study of Roig and others who write in and support their native minority languages.

Roig's contemporary Maria-Mercè Marçal was similarly focused in her promotion of the language and writing of Catalonia. In her essay "The Passion and Poetry of Feminism," Joana Sabadell examines Marçal's awareness of the sometimes conflicting pressures facing women writers in Spain and, more specifically, in Catalonia, during the last two decades of the twentieth century. Speaking from her "doubly marginalized" position as a woman and a Catalan, Marçal was intensely aware of the presence of these issues in her poetry and in her life. In a description of Marçal's interest in women's political issues and her connections with other writers from Catalonia, Spain, and beyond, Sabadell presents a culturally sensitive reading of gender, nation, and language in the works of one of Catalonia's most prominent late-twentieth-century poets.

In the final essay, Kathleen Glenn reminds us that few women writers in Spain identify themselves as feminists. Among those who reject this label as a strategy to pigeonhole their writing are the high-profile authors Fanny Rubio, Paloma Díaz-Mas, Rosa Montero, Marina Mayoral, and Carme Riera. Focusing on Riera's declaration that she is a feminist citizen but not a feminist writer, Glenn analyzes critical terminology and methodology, issues similar to those discussed by Weissberger in the opening essay. Glenn argues that, despite Riera's refusal to be labeled a feminist writer, she is concerned with the feminist issues of marginality, sexuality, and difference. Respectful of cultural specificity and, in the contemporary scene, of conflicting views about the repercussions of the feminist label, Glenn encapsulates the line of inquiry of this entire volume, in which the contributors weave together the many strands of Spain's feminist tradition.

Despite Falcón's declaration over twenty years ago that feminism has come and gone ("Feminismo" 29), the analyses in this volume suggest that feminism has been alive for centuries and that it is most definitely here to stay. Backed by a long-standing tradition and bolstered by recent, measurable progress, contemporary feminists in Spain have reason to feel optimistic. Some might even dare to believe Camps's prophecy that the twenty-first century will belong to women. Significant progress is more likely to occur, however, if efforts are made to solidify international alliances. To strengthen our collective resolve, feminists need to speak more effectively across cultural, national, and linguistic borders. We hope that this book will encourage readers to listen more attentively to past and present feminist voices from around the world.

Notes

I would like to thank H. Patsy Boyer, Michael Giordano, Elliott J. Gorn, Kathleen McNerney, and Stacey Schlau for reading earlier versions of this essay.

1. All these definitions of feminism appear in contemporary women's writing. María Isabel Cabrera Bosch calls feminism a "movimiento reivindicador de un nuevo estatus personal, social y jurídico para la mujer [. . .] una lucha" (30) ("movement aimed at claiming a new personal, social, and legal status for women [. . .] a struggle"), and the philosopher Celia Amorós calls it an "ethics" in *Hacia una crítica de la razón patriarcal* ("Toward a Critique of Patriarchal Reasoning"). For Anabel González et al. feminism is a social doctrine (1). For Victoria Sendón de León, feminism is the most important social movement of the contemporary era (144). The philosopher Victoria Camps agrees, calling feminism "*el* movimiento social del siglo XX" (13; emphasis added) ("*the* social movement of the twentieth century"). For more on internationalism and feminism, see Gayatri Spivak; Chilla Bulbeck; and Martha Nussbaum.
2. In their introduction Kemp and Squires offer an explanation for the prominence of British, American, and French thinkers in Western feminist debate: "The cultural and economic forces which promote certain national and ethnic perspectives over others are played out within feminist theory as well as elsewhere" (9). For claims on multiculturalism in these anthologies, see Warhol and Price Herndl (x) and Kemp and Squires (1).

3. With the exception of H. Patsy Boyer's translation of María de Zayas, all translations in this introduction are my own.
4. Considered by many to be a controversial figure for her feminist activism and beliefs, Falcón has been called "the most outspoken and uncompromising second-wave feminist writer" (Davies 247).
5. Saiz's essay, "El feminismo en España," was originally published in the October and November issues of *La escuela moderna* ("The Modern Schools"). I quote the excerpts from the more readily available book, *Los orígenes del feminismo en España* (González et al. 175–86).
6. In the final essay of this volume, Kathleen Glenn deals with the disparities between Spanish intellectuals' resistance to the feminist label and North American women's perceptions of this issue. Earlier treatments of the issue of outsiders looking in—of non-Spaniards studying Spanish women's writing—can be found in Elizabeth Ordóñez and in Linda Chown. For a list of self-identified feminists representing various occupations, see Falcón and Elvira Siurana's *Catálogo de escritoras feministas actuales en lengua castellana* ("Catalog of Contemporary Feminist Authors in Castilian").
7. Anabel González hailed the definitive rebirth of feminism: "Podemos, pues, afirmar que el movimiento feminista es ya una realidad" (8) ("We can affirm, then, that the feminist movement is a reality"). One of González's interviewees, Noemí Juantorena, had a more cautious perspective: "El movimiento feminista en España es aún joven y no está consolidado, en el sentido de que no es el movimiento de masas que será en el futuro, ni ha profundizado suficientemente en sus planteamientos" (42) ("The feminist movement in Spain is still young and unconsolidated in the sense that it is not the mass movement that it will be in the future nor has it developed its basic premises sufficiently").
8. Authors published with Anthropos include critics and philosophers such as Lola Luna, Cristina Molina Petit, Alicia Puleo, Rosa María Rodríguez Magda, Amelia Valcárcel, and Iris Zavala. For a brief overview of post-Franco Spain and women's issues, see Pilar Folguera ("Transición") or *El largo camino hacia la igualdad* ("The Long Road toward Equality") from the Instituto de la Mujer. For a discussion of feminism in the 1990s, see Angeles Perona and Ramón del Castillo Santos's "Pensamiento español y representaciones de género" ("Spanish Thought and Representations of Gender"). Geraldine Scanlon's *La Polémica* and Concha Fagoaga's *1898–1998* discuss the development of feminist politics over the twentieth century. See also Juana María Gil Ruiz's *Las políticas de la igualdad en España* ("Politics of Equality in Spain") and Anny Brooksbank Jones.
9. Many scholars writing about Spain attribute feminism to the nineteenth century, as seen in Rosa María Capel Martínez's *Mujer y sociedad en España* (13) ("Woman and Society in Spain"); the selection of primary feminist texts (only one of which predates the nineteenth century) in González et al.; and the title and conceptualization of Folguera's *El feminismo en España: Dos siglos de historia.* The latter study does include an essay on women's status and defenses of women in the ancien régime (see Ortega López). Other exceptions to these temporal limitations can be found in Iris Zavala's series *Breve*

historia feminista de la literatura española; and in Martín-Gamero's *Antología del feminismo.* Like Nash and Lerner, Kathleen McNerney makes a strong case for historicizing feminism ("Women's Organizations").

10. New categories of historical research focused on women have emerged in books such as Mary E. Giles's *Women in the Inquisition,* Judith Bennett and Amy Froide's *Singlewomen in the European Past: 1250–1800*, and Valerie Traub's *The Renaissance of Lesbianism in Early Modern England.* In addition to Nash's extensive work on Spanish women's history, the following list shows the breadth of scholarship that has been done on Spanish women in recent years: Capel Martínez's *Mujer y sociedad en España: 1700–1975*; María Angeles Durán's *La mujer en la historia de España (siglos XVI–XX)* ("Women in the History of Spain [Sixteenth to Twentieth Centuries]"); Mariló Vigil's *La vida de las mujeres en los siglos XVI y XVII* ("The Life of Women in the Sixteenth and Seventeenth Centuries"); Carolyn Galerstein and Kathleen McNerney's *Women Writers of Spain*; Cristina Segura Graiño's *El trabajo de las mujeres en la Edad Media hispana* ("Women's Work in the Spanish Middle Ages"); Jodi Bilinkoff's *The Avila of Saint Teresa*; Electa Arenal and Stacey Schlau's *Untold Sisters: Hispanic Nuns in Their Own Works*; Mary Elizabeth Perry's *Gender and Disorder in Early Modern Seville*; Alain Saint-Saëns's anthology *Religion, Body, and Gender in Early Modern Spain*; Anne Cruz and Perry's anthology *Culture and Control in Counter-Reformation Spain*; María Helena Sánchez Ortega's *La mujer y la sexualidad en el antiguo régimen* ("Woman and Sexuality in the Ancien Régime"); Linda Gould Levine, Ellen Engelson Marson, and Gloria Feiman Waldman's *Spanish Women Writers*; McNerney and Cristina Enríquez de Salamanca's *Double Minorities of Spain*; Serrana M. Rial García's *Las mujeres en la economía urbana del Antiguo Régimen: Santiago durante el siglo XVIII* ("Women in the Urban Economy of the Ancien Régime: Santiago during the Eighteenth Century"); Saint-Saëns's anthology *Historia silenciada de la mujer* ("Women's Silenced History"); Catherine Davies's *Spanish Women's Writing: 1849–1996*; and Iris Zavala's anthology *Feminismos, cuerpos, escrituras.*

11. Many traditional ballads or romances adopt a female poetic voice and narrate women's anxieties about courtship, marriage, and violence. See those dealing with the "bella malmaridada" ("unhappily married wife") and, in the Catalan tradition, the "malmonjades" ("unwilling nuns") in Angel Flores and Kate Flores's *The Defiant Muse* and McNerney and Enríquez de Salamanca's *Double Minorities of Spain.* Catalina de Erauso's incredible story (albeit of questionable authorship) is available in English (*Lieutenant Nun*). Because of the limited numbers of extant women's texts in the premodern period, those seeking to decipher the feminine in history and literature often must turn to the figuration of women in male-authored texts. Iris Zavala eloquently defends "images of women" criticism in "Formas" (1: 67), while her collaborator Myriam Díaz-Diocaretz argues for what Elaine Showalter has called "gynocriticism," the return to women's texts and women's discourse (1: 79). Decades of feminist scholarship have shown that both tasks enrich our understanding of women's position in patriarchy.

12. Perona and Castillo Santos trace the ways in which contemporary feminism

in Spain focuses on "la necesidad de modificar un estado de cosas que sigue justificando y perpetuando la desconexión entre los tres tipos de ciudadanía y la situación de las mujeres" (348) ("the need to change a system that continues to justify and perpetuate the disconnect between the three types of citizenship and woman's condition"). The nuanced definition of citizenship referred to here includes personal autonomy, the right to exercise political power, and the right to participate in redefining citizenship (326). For a synopsis of the development of Western feminist thinking and its engagement with similar issues during the 1960s–90s, see chapter 7 of Nancy Fraser's *Justice Interruptus.*

13. *El largo camino hacia la igualdad* highlights some of the legal and social changes for the period 1975–95, including the sexual discrimination clause in the 1978 Constitution; the 1985 legalization of abortion for cases of rape, incest, birth defects, and danger to the mother's health; the 1980 and 1990 laws prohibiting, respectively, discrimination in the workplace and in education; and recognition that the law prohibiting discrimination in the workplace had been on the books with little practical effect since 1961 (77–86). Marisa García de Cortázar's "Estructura laboral de las mujeres españolas" ("The Labor Structure of Spanish Women") points out the gender gap for workforce representation (over 90% of men between the ages of twenty-five and fifty-five as compared with 50% of women for the same age group) and also demonstrates that women, who work in a smaller variety of occupations than men, are still disproportionately relegated to the lower-paying jobs within these professions (121). At least for the period between 1982 and 1992, women's salaries remained 20% lower than men's, and this difference increased with age (*El largo camino* 81).
14. The scholarship contained in this volume is heavily indebted to the biographical, bibliographical, and analytical work on women found in such excellent reference tools as Levine, Marson, and Waldman; McNerney and Enríquez de Salamanca; Davies; Falcón and Siurana's *Catálogo de escritoras españolas en lengua castellana (1860–1992)*; and Janet Pérez's *Dictionary of the Literature of the Iberian Peninsula.*
15. Recent scholarship on pre-twentieth-century women has uncovered a large body of texts waiting to be studied. See *Escritoras españolas, 1500–1900,* a microfiche collection of the women's writing housed in the Biblioteca Nacional; and *Autoras en la historia del teatro español (1500–1994)*, a two-volume project, directed by Juan Antonio Hormigón, that offers valuable biographical and bibliographical information on women playwrights. For examples of fine scholarship on previously unstudied texts by women, see María Isabel Barbeito Carneiro's *Escritoras madrileñas del siglo XVII* ("Women Writers of Seventeenth-Century Madrid"), Susan Kirkpatrick's *Las románticas,* and Teresa Soufas's *Women's Acts* and *Dramas of Distinction.* Recognizing that the present volume suffers from an underrepresentation of minority-language writers—a problem that is particularly acute in all but the section on the late twentieth century—I refer the reader again to McNerney and Enríquez de Salamanca and to McNerney's "Catalan Women Writers: A Brief History."

16. For figures on the participation in Mujeres Libres, see Gómez in this volume (n9), and Aurora Morcillo Gómez's "Feminismo y lucha política durante la Segunda República y la Guerra Civil" ("Feminism and Political Struggle during the Second Republic and the Civil War") 76–78, especially note 11.

Works Cited

Amorós, Celia. *Hacia una crítica de la razón patriarcal.* Barcelona: Anthropos, 1985.

Arenal, Electa, and Stacey Schlau. *Untold Sisters: Hispanic Nuns in Their Own Works.* Trans. Amanda Powell. Albuquerque: U of New Mexico P, 1989.

Azevedo, Milton M., ed. *Contemporary Catalonia in Spain and Europe.* Berkeley: Gaspar de Portolà Catalonian Studies Program, U of California, 1991.

Barbeito Carneiro, María Isabel. *Escritoras madrileñas del siglo XVII: Estudio bibliográfico-crítico.* Madrid: Universidad Complutense, 1986.

Bennett, Judith, and Amy Froide, eds. *Singlewomen in the European Past: 1250–1800.* Philadelphia: U of Pennsylvania P, 1999.

Bilinkoff, Jodi. *The Avila of Saint Teresa: Religious Reform in a Sixteenth-Century City.* Ithaca: Cornell UP, 1989.

Bulbeck, Chilla. *Re-orienting Western Feminisms: Women's Diversity in a Post-colonial World.* Cambridge: Cambridge UP, 1998.

Cabrera Bosch, María Isabel. "Las mujeres que lucharon solas: Concepción Arenal y Emilia Pardo Bazán." Folguera, *Feminismo* 29–50.

Camps, Victoria. *El siglo de las mujeres.* Madrid: Cátedra, 1998.

Capel Martínez, Rosa María, coord. *Mujer y sociedad en España: 1700–1975.* 2nd ed. Vol. 1. Madrid: Ministerio de Cultura, 1986.

Capmany, Maria Aurèlia. *El feminismo ibérico.* Barcelona: Oikos-Tau, 1970.

Chown, Linda. "American Critics and Spanish Women Novelists, 1942–1980." *Signs* 9 (1993): 93–107.

Cruz, Anne, and Mary Elizabeth Perry, eds. *Culture and Control in Counter-Reformation Spain.* Minneapolis: U of Minnesota P, 1992.

Davies, Catherine. *Spanish Women's Writing: 1849–1996.* London: Athlone, 1998.

Díaz-Diocaretz, Myriam. " 'La palabra no olvida de dónde vino.' Para una poética dialógica de la diferencia." Zavala, *Breve historia* 1: 77–124.

Durán, María Angeles, ed. *La mujer en la historia de España (siglos XVI–XX). Actas de las II Jornadas de Investigación Interdisciplinaria.* Madrid: Universidad Autónoma, 1984.

Erauso, Catalina de. *Lieutenant Nun: Memoir of a Basque Transvestite in the New World.* Trans. Michele Stepto and Gabriel Stepto. Boston: Beacon, 1996.

Escritoras españolas, 1500–1900. Microfiche catalog. Pt. 1: 1500–1800. Pt. 2: 1800–1900. Madrid: Chadwyck-Healey España, 1992–93.

Fagoaga, Concha, coord. *1898–1998: Un siglo avanzando hacia la igualdad de las mujeres.* Madrid: Dirección General de la Mujer, Consejería de Sanidad y Servicios Sociales, Comunidad de Madrid, 1999.

Falcón, Lidia. "Auge y caída del movimiento feminista." *Poder y libertad (Revista del partido feminista español)* 12 (1990): 36–45.

———. "El feminismo ha venido y se ha ido." *Vindicación feminista* Sept. 1978 (nos. 26, 27): 29–42.

Falcón, Lidia, and Elvira Siurana, eds. *Catálago de escritoras españolas en lengua castellana (1860–1992)*. Madrid: Comunidad de Madrid, Dirección General de la Mujer, 1992.

———. *Catálogo de escritoras feministas actuales en lengua castellana.* Madrid: Comunidad de Madrid, Dirección General de la Mujer, 1992.

Flores, Angel, and Kate Flores, eds. *The Defiant Muse: Hispanic Feminist Poems from the Middle Ages to the Present: A Bilingual Anthology.* New York: Feminist, 1986.

Folguera, Pilar. "De la transición política a la democracia." Folguera, *Feminismo* 111–32.

———, ed. *El feminismo en España: Dos siglos de historia.* Madrid: Iglesias, 1988.

Fraser, Nancy. *Justice Interruptus: Critical Reflections on the "Postsocialist" Condition.* New York: Routledge, 1997.

Galerstein, Carolyn L., and Kathleen McNerney. *Women Writers of Spain: An Annotated Bio-Bibliographical Guide.* Bibliographies and Indexes in Women's Studies 2. Westport: Greenwood, 1986.

García de Cortázar, Marisa. "Estructura laboral de las mujeres españolas." García de León, García de Cortázar, and Ortega 121–36.

García de León, María Antonia, Marisa García de Cortázar, and Félix Ortega, coords. *Sociología de las mujeres españolas.* Madrid: Complutense, 1996.

Giles, Mary E., ed. *Women in the Inquisition: Spain and the New World.* Baltimore: Johns Hopkins UP, 1999.

Gil Ruiz, Juana María. *Las políticas de la igualdad en España: Avances y retrocesos.* Granada: U de Granada, 1996.

González, Anabel. *El feminismo en España hoy.* Bilbao: Zero, 1979.

González, Anabel, et al. *Los orígenes del feminismo en España.* Madrid: Zero, 1980.

Hormigón, Juan Antonio, dir. of research. *Autoras en la historia del teatro español (1500–1994)*. Madrid: Asociación de Directores de Escena de España, 1996.

Jones, Anny Brooksbank. *Women in Contemporary Spain.* Manchester: Manchester UP, 1997.

Kemp, Sandra, and Judith Squires, eds. *Feminisms.* Oxford: Oxford UP, 1997.

Kirkpatrick, Susan. *Las románticas: Women Writers and Subjectivity in Spain, 1835–1850.* Berkeley: U of California P, 1989.

El largo camino hacia la igualdad: Feminismo en España (1975–1995). Coord. Instituto de la Mujer. Madrid: Instituto de la Mujer, 1995.

Lerner, Gerda. *The Creation of Feminist Consciousness: From the Middle Ages to 1870.* Oxford: Oxford UP, 1993.

Levine, Linda Gould, Ellen Engelson Marson, and Gloria Feiman Waldman, eds. *Spanish Women Writers: A Bio-Bibliographical Source Book.* Westport: Greenwood, 1993.

Levine, Linda Gould, and Gloria Feiman Waldman, eds. *Feminismo ante el franquismo: Entrevistas con feministas de España.* Miami: Universal, 1980.

Luna, Lola. *Leyendo como una mujer la imagen de la Mujer.* Seville: Anthropos, 1996.

Martín-Gamero, Amalia, ed. *Antología del feminismo.* Madrid: Alianza, 1975.

McNerney, Kathleen. "Catalan Women Writers: A Brief History." *The Feminist*

Encyclopedia of Spanish Literature. Ed. Janet Pérez. Westport: Greenwood, forthcoming.

———. "Women's Organizations and Groups in Catalonia." Azevedo 98–106.

McNerney, Kathleen, and Cristina Enríquez de Salamanca, eds. *Double Minorities of Spain: A Bio-Bibliographical Guide to Women Writers of the Catalan, Galician, and Basque Countries.* New York: MLA, 1994.

Molina Petit, Cristina. *Dialéctica feminista de la Ilustración.* Barcelona: Anthropos, 1994.

Morcillo Gómez, Aurora. "Feminismo y lucha política durante la Segunda República y la Guerra Civil." Folguera, *Feminismo* 57–83.

Nash, Mary. "The Changing Status of Women in Contemporary Catalonia." Azevedo 107–27.

———. "Experiencia y aprendizaje: La formación histórica de los feminismos en España." *Historia Social* 20 (1994): 151–72.

Nelken, Margarita. *La condición social de la mujer en España.* 1919. Madrid: CVS, 1975.

Nussbaum, Martha. *Sex and Social Justice.* Oxford: Oxford UP, 1999.

Ordóñez, Elizabeth. "Reading Contemporary Spanish Narrative by Women." *Anales de la literatura española contemporánea* 7 (1982): 237–51.

Ortega López, Margarita. "'La defensa de las mujeres' en la sociedad del antiguo régimen." Folguera, *Feminismo* 3–28.

Pérez, Janet. *Dictionary of the Literature of the Iberian Peninsula.* Westport: Greenwood, 1993.

Perona, Angeles J., and Ramón del Castillo Santos. "Pensamiento español y representaciones de género." García de León, García de Cortázar, and Ortega 325–49.

Perry, Mary Elizabeth. *Gender and Disorder in Early Modern Seville.* Princeton: Princeton UP, 1990.

Puleo, Alicia. *Dialéctica de la sexualidad: Género y sexo en la filosofía contemporánea.* Madrid: Cátedra, 1992.

Rial García, Serrana M. *Las mujeres en la economía urbana del Antiguo Régimen: Santiago durante el siglo XVIII.* A Coruña: Castro, 1995.

Rodríguez Magda, Rosa María. 1987. *Femenino, fin de siglo: La seducción de la diferencia.* Barcelona: Anthropos, 1994.

Saint-Saëns, Alain, ed. *Historia silenciada de la mujer.* Madrid: Editorial Complutense, 1996.

———, ed. *Religion, Body, and Gender in Early Modern Spain.* San Francisco: Mellen Research UP, 1991.

Saiz y Otero, Concepción. "El feminismo en España." *La escuela moderna* 7.79, 80 (1897): 248–60, 321–34.

Sánchez Ortega, María Helena. *La mujer y la sexualidad en el antiguo régimen: La perspectiva inquisitorial.* Madrid: Akal, 1992.

Scanlon, Geraldine. *La polémica feminista en la España contemporánea.* Madrid: Siglo Veintiuno, 1986.

Segura Graiño, Cristina, ed. *El trabajo de las mujeres en la Edad Media hispana.* Madrid: Asociación Cultural Al-Mudayna, Instituto de la Mujer, Ministerio de Cultura, 1988.

Sendón de León, Victoria. "El feminismo visto por sus protagonistas." Folguera, *Feminismo* 141–46.

Shubert, Adrian. *A Social History of Modern Spain*. London: Unwin Hyman, 1990.

Soufas, Teresa. *Dramas of Distinction*. Lexington: UP of Kentucky, 1997.

———. *Women's Acts*. Lexington: UP of Kentucky, 1997.

Spivak, Gayatri Chakravorty. "Diasporas Old and New: Women in the Transnational World." *Class Issues: Pedagogy, Cultural Studies, and the Public Sphere*. Ed. Amitava Kumar. New York: New York UP, 1997. 87–116.

Traub, Valerie. *The Renaissance of Lesbianism in Early Modern England*. Cambridge: Cambridge UP, forthcoming.

Valcárcel, Amelia. *Sexo y filosofía: Sobre "mujer" y "poder."* 1991. Barcelona: Anthropos, 1994.

Vigil, Mariló. *La vida de las mujeres en los siglos XVI y XVII*. Madrid: Siglo Veintiuno, 1986.

Warhol, Robyn, and Diane Price Herndl, eds. *Feminisms: An Anthology of Literary Theory and Criticism*. 2nd ed. New Brunswick: Rutgers UP, 1997.

Zavala, Iris, gen. ed. *Breve historia feminista de la literatura española (en lengua castellana)*. Vol. 1. Ed. Myriam Díaz-Diocaretz and Zavala. Vol. 2–6. Ed. Zavala. Barcelona: Anthropos, 1993–.

———, ed. *Feminismos, cuerpos, escrituras*. Santa Cruz de Tenerife: La Página Ediciones, 2000.

———. "Las formas y funciones de una teoría crítica feminista: Feminismo dialógico." Zavala, *Breve historia* 1: 27–76.

Zayas y Sotomayor, María de. *The Enchantments of Love*. Trans. H. Patsy Boyer. Berkeley: U of California P, 1990.

———. *Novelas amorosas y ejemplares*. Ed. Agustín de Amezúa. Madrid: Real Academia Española, 1948.

Medieval and Early Modern Periods (Fifteenth through Seventeenth Century)

The Critics and Florencia Pinar: The Problem with Assigning Feminism to a Medieval Court Poet

Barbara F. Weissberger

This essay questions the contemporary critical construction of the work of Florencia Pinar, one of only a handful of named women who share space with some seven hundred male poets in the late-medieval Castilian cancioneros.[1] I first summarize the two main critical approaches to Pinar's poetry, both avowedly feminist in their intention to recuperate a rare and genuine feminine voice for the hispanomedieval canon.[2] I do not deny the importance of these critics' contributions, particularly their elucidation of Pinar's stylistic inventiveness. I suggest, however, that the approaches applied by both schools of Pinar criticism run the risk of essentializing Pinar's poetic persona and, in the process, of reinforcing the traditional masculinist and idealist view of the nature of courtly love and of the role of women in it. This view has never been systematically challenged for medieval Spain as it has been for France, for example, by Roberta L. Krueger and E. Jane Burns (see also Burns and Krueger.)

During the 1990s historians and literary scholars alike became increasingly concerned with the difficulties inherent in the recovery and gendering of the experience and voice of people from the past.[3] Joan W. Scott, for example, eloquently reminds historians that the very production of historical knowledge is inevitably gendered. To take this fact into account requires "analysis not only of the relations between male and female experience in the past but also the connection between past history and current historical practice" (1055). Literary historians must be no less sensitive to these issues. As Sheila Fisher and Janet E. Halley warn, "The muted voice of women's culture and the dominant voice of masculine authority are so intertwined that closely contextual study is required if we are to hear [women writers]" (11–12).

Postmodern awareness of the problems attending the assignment of feminine subjectivity and feminist agency to female writers of the past is relevant to this volume, whose title posits both the existence of a feminist tradition in Spain and the possibility of its recovery. Beginning such a volume with a discussion of the problematic construction of a feminine or feminist voice of a poet working in a period when we cannot rightly even speak of Spain as a national and cultural entity illustrates Scott's point. If this seems to go against the grain, that is my intention, for I believe that the project of "seeking the woman" (Fisher and Halley) in medieval Iberia, as the specific, purportedly foundational case of Florencia Pinar indicates, should raise more questions than it has.

Pinar's lyric persona has been consistently read by contemporary critics as a sincere, autobiographical, feminine subject. The interpretations differ only in that some see Pinar as conforming, either ruefully or resentfully, to a presumably antifeminist courtly love code, while others consider her to be in open revolt against that code. Both these approaches are problematic. To begin with, they apply to the medieval period a distinctly post-Romantic view of the poet as sincere and exalted champion of emotional or political freedom. Second, they do not question the monolithic character of the courtly code or, for that matter, the idealist notion of "love" as an already constituted essence that the code addresses. A related problem is the failure of these approaches to take into account the highly public, rhetorical, and conventional language of cancionero poetry, which makes it difficult to speak of a private, emotional, personal voice with regard to any individual poet.[4] Finally, the exiguous nature of Pinar's corpus and the total absence of biographical information make speculation about her subjectivity extremely hazardous. I suggest that under these conditions, the dominant interpretations of Pinar's work risk reinscribing her in the essentialist, idealist category woman that, as feminist constructionists have noted, precludes any real change.[5] And we must consider the consequences of such a reading for an understanding of medieval Castilian court culture and society that would take seriously the place of women patrons, writers, and audiences or readers within it.

It is to Alan Deyermond, who has done so much to draw our attention to the "lost literature" of medieval Spain (see, e.g., his *Literatura perdida*), that we owe the impetus for the contemporary recuperation of Pinar's production: three brief, vivid lyrics first published in the *Cancionero general.* In a 1978 article entitled "The Worm and the Partridge: Reflections on the Poetry of Florencia Pinar," and its more accessible reworking of 1983, Deyermond proclaimed the triumvirate of Pinar, Leonor López de Córdoba, and Teresa de Cartagena to be "Spain's first women writers," and he declared them worthy of more critical attention than they had heretofore attracted. This call and his own close reading of two of Pinar's poems stimulated a flurry of scholarly interest in the poet throughout the 1980s and 1990s. It is with his groundbreaking analyses that I begin my survey.

Deyermond first notes, following Keith Whinnom ("Interpretación"), that the two poems he chooses to analyze, "Destas aves su nación" ("The nature of these birds") and "Ell amor ha tales mañas" ("Love has such crafty ways") (for texts see app.) are Pinar's most anthologized lyrics because they deal with concrete imagery, "aves" ("birds") and a "gusano" ("worm"), respectively, rather than the colorless abstractions that dominate most courtly lyrics. The dismissal of "¡Ay! que ay quien más no bive" ("A sigh! For there are some who languish"), the third poem definitely attributed to Pinar, as having "no merit beyond that of a moderately difficult puzzle" ("Women Writers" 46), advances the traditional editorial bias against the more abstract lyrics of the cancionero.

Deyermond begins his analysis of "Destas aves su nación" by affirming that it reflects a woman "fairly obviously in love" ("Worm" 4–5), one who, like the partridges she describes, resisted love but now finds herself trapped and caged by it. In reality, his interpretation constructs the poem's persona as belonging to a woman not in love but in lust, since it relies heavily on the representation of the partridge in medieval bestiaries as the most highly sexed of birds.[6] He identifies the play on words "perdiz" and "perder" ("partridge/lose") as central to the poem, a pun that drives home Pinar's sense of betrayal by the man who hunted her down and whose pheromones aroused her lust. A major drawback to this view, as Constance Wilkins (127) and others have noted, is that the word "perdiz" appears only in the poem's heading, most likely supplied by the compiler.

Deyermond then reinforces his highly sexualized reading of Pinar's partridge poem with a phallic interpretation of "Ell amor ha tales mañas." This dark and graphic lyric identifies "amor" with a "gusano" that is physically invasive and destructive: "que si entra en las entrañas, / no puede salir sin ellas" ("if he [sic] enters one's entrails, he [sic] can leave only by tearing them out"). The limpness of a worm presents a bit of an obstacle to the critic's Freudian interpretation, but he readily overcomes it by citing the secondary medieval meaning of "gusano": the more appropriate, because vertebrate, "víbora" ("viper"). Finally, Deyermond warns against a biographical reading of Pinar's poems only to succumb to the temptation: "We cannot know anything of Pinar's life until the necessary archival research has been carried out, but by studying her poems we can reconstruct her temperament" ("Women Writers" 50).

Soon after Deyermond's article appeared, Joseph Snow contributed an essay on Pinar to Katharina M. Wilson's influential 1984 anthology *Medieval Women Writers.* The volume situates Pinar's work in a broad European context, alongside Margery Kempe, Marie de France, Hildegard von Bingen, and other better-known authors. Writing for a more general audience, Snow takes Deyermond's interpretation even further. He portrays Pinar as an assertive advocate for a woman's right to sexual pleasure. He sees her "preoccupation with sexuality" as the sign of a "strong personality, one which found a way [. . .] to convey sentiments the open expression of which was forbidden by the conventions of her age" (322). In this reading, Pinar sounds curiously like a product of the 1970s sexual revolution.

The 1990s saw the publication of a half-dozen important essays on

Pinar. A survey of the analyses of Angel Flores and Kate Flores, Barbara Fulks, Constance Wilkins, Roxana Recio, and Louise Mirrer reveals an interesting concurrence: they all take exception to the Deyermond-Snow view of Pinar's theme. They insist on Pinar's self-representation not as a full, desiring agent in the game of love but as a disabused victim of its male-dominated rules and rituals. None, however, questions the earlier autobiographical and essentialist assumption that Pinar the poet and the poetic persona are one and the same sincere "woman in love."[7]

Angel Flores and Kate Flores were the first to challenge Deyermond's interpretation. They identified the main theme of "Destas aves" as the uniquely feminine sorrow over the loss of freedom caused by love, neatly expressed in the irony of the "gift" made to the poet: caged birds. They use the poem's avian subject to compare it, once again anachronistically, with Alfonsina Storni's 1919 feminist protest poem, "Hombre pequeñito" ("Tiny Little Man"). In their view, Pinar the poet identifies with the trapped birds in order to present herself as a "victim of men's urge to conquer and control; men imprison her and muffle her singing just as they have imprisoned the birds and muffled their singing" (xxiv).

Fulks and Wilkins have provided the most detailed and perceptive stylistic analyses to date of "Ell amor ha tales mañas" and "Destas aves su nación," respectively. Each writer provides excellent insights into the style and structure of the selected poem, pointing out many conceptual and linguistic ambiguities. Wilkins, for example, notes that the antecedent of "la mía" ("mine") in "sin sentir nadie la mía" ("without anyone's feeling mine") has in all English translations of the poem been assumed to be the noun "passión" ("passion") when grammatically it is just as likely "prisión" ("prison") (125). It is not passion but lack of freedom that the lyric "I" laments.

In a desire to gender the poetic persona of Pinar's verses, Fulks, Wilkins, Broad, and, most recently, Mirrer all make a curious linguistic argument. They argue that the frequency of the feminine grammatical gender in Pinar's poetry reveals the poet's feminine subjectivity and her feminist solidarity with a presumably female readership. Their construction of Pinar's voice, while quite different from the one assigned to her by Deyermond and Snow, is similarly modern. For them Pinar's feminine poetic persona is admonitory rather than plangent: a warning to women to beware the destructive effects of love. Fulks is the most explicit in this regard, relying partly on the prevalence of feminine nouns in "Ell amor ha tales mañas" to conclude that Pinar "is a woman speaking to other women" (42). But Mirrer uses a similar argument in her treatment of "Destas aves" to argue for the poem's "focus on sexual division and its enactment of women's struggle for subjectivity" (154), even as she concedes that the symbolic "aves" and "perdices" are textually ambiguous since the biological sex of neither animal can be deduced.[8]

Thus Wilkins, Broad, Fulks, the Floreses, and Mirrer also construe Pinar's poetry as autobiographical by considering "Destas aves" an impassioned political protest against the systematic oppression that women, and therefore women writers, suffered in the late-fifteenth century. But the view of the poet-persona as idealistic and politically engagé is as anachronistic as Deyermond's and Snow's impression of her as a passionate and sexually liberated woman. And what all these critics have in common, a belief in the transparency and idealism of the poet, is simply inapplicable to the medieval court poet, whose corpus often included poems praising the lady alongside others attacking her in the most violent and scurrilous terms.[9]

The major advance in cancionero scholarship in the latter part of the twentieth century was Whinnom's 1968 demonstration (and its later expansion in *La poesía amatoria*) that, even within a single poem, many of the cancionero poets "are more obsessed with physical desire and the tempting possibility of its consummation than with the nebulosity of Neoplatonic, semimystical ideas" (380; trans. mine). Generations of scholars who decried the abstract, cerebral, and repetitive language of the cancioneros had, it seems, failed to see through its self-imposed formal and conceptual restrictions to its underlying eroticism and obscenity. The language of love in the cancioneros turns out to be pervaded by what Ian Macpherson terms a "secret language," clever linguistic puzzles whose bawdy solution is simultaneously concealed and revealed by the pervasive use of the rhetorical device of *ambiguitas* ("double meanings"). Whinnom lists some thirty verbs that recur throughout the cancioneros, including the innocent-seeming *servir, perder, vencer, merecer, cabalgar, ponerse, encontrar* ("serve," "lose," "conquer," "deserve," "ride horseback," "put on," "find") that were documented euphemisms for the sexual act in the fifteenth and sixteenth centuries.[10] Macpherson and others have added to this "secret dictionary" of the cancioneros by cataloging its multiple euphemisms for male and female genitalia: *lanza, cañón, pluma, caverna, dedal, sortijuela, quiquiriquí* ("lance," "cannon," "feather," "cavern," "thimble," "ringlet," "cock-a-doodle-do"), for example.[11]

At first glance it appears that Deyermond incorporates Whinnom's findings in his sexualized reading of the lustful partridges and destructive snake of Pinar's poetry. But Deyermond is more than a little nervous about Pinar's putative expression of sexual desire, as his conclusion makes clear: "I am not, of course, suggesting that this is an admission of sexual promiscuity. What Pinar is telling us is that she feels strong sexual desire for the man she loves" ("Women Writers" 50). The critic thereby mystifies his own provocative portrayal of female sexual desire through an appeal to monogamy. Reading these literary texts autobiographically, Deyermond constructs Pinar as a courtly rebel who dares to speak as a desiring subject instead of a sexual object. Yet in the end, she is reinscribed as a chaste courtly lady. The worm that Pinar lusts after turns out, reassuringly, to be her one true love.

If we believe like Whinnom that the relationships portrayed by courtly love poets are not as unambiguously idealized as post-Romantic scholars would have it and if the humble desire to be ennobled by a frustrated *amor purus* is often a translucent screen for an aggressive desire to gain material (including, though not limited to, sexual) satisfaction, then Pinar may appear to be not exceptional but representative in the way she "convey[s] sentiments the open expression of which was forbidden by the conventions of her age" (Snow 322). The discovery of the polysemy that fifteenth-century poets were intent on achieving on the technical level makes it impossible to continue studying this poetry thematically as the sincere expression of a repressed subject, whether masculine or feminine. Rather, like feminist scholars in their approach to French courtly literature, we must focus on the poetry's material bases and the ideological function of the identities and roles it creates.

An excellent example of this approach is Julian Weiss's analysis of the social uses and unstable persona of the love lyrics of Juan de Mena. In the courts of late-medieval Castile, Weiss argues, courtly love was indeed a game, but a very serious one: it harnessed the force of the imagination to the written word for very material ends. Central to this game, as to any other game, was pretense. This is the meaning of the famous dictum of Juan Alfonso de Baena, compiler of the cancionero that bears his name, to the effect that the noble poet "siempre se precie y se finja de ser enamorado" (1: 15) ("must always boast of and pretend to be in love" [my trans.]). As Weiss notes, "Being in love was both product and proof of nobility. It also entailed what might be called a dialectic of display and dissimulation: love is to be vaunted, yet it is also a pretence" ("Alvaro de Luna" 241). The courtly love poet feigns love seriously to create and manipulate an image of aristocratic masculine power that could pay off handsomely in the second half of the fifteenth century, a time of high social mobility. Any individual lyric is used to reflect not a real self that transcends the poem but one of its guises, a mask that controls both outward signs and inner meanings (254). As Toril Moi notes in a similar vein, with reference to the much misunderstood Andreas Capellanus, "By dominating the word, he [the poet] gains a phallic power that contradicts his seemingly humble stance towards his lady" (24). The masterful control of meaning on the technical level corresponds on the ideological level to the manipulation of self and other that is necessary to achieve material goals: the accrual of wealth and power through aristocratic marriage.

It is important to keep in mind that the means to this end are misogynistic. Any power held by the real women addressed by the poet is deliberately erased in the poetic process that constructs her as a courtly señora. The deployment of the allusive and elusive persona of the courtly lover depends on the total passivity or absence, or, rather, the discursive erasure, of the aristocratic woman whose favor, sexual and social, he seeks (Weiss, "Alvaro de Luna" 249–50).

How is it possible for a woman writer to interject herself into this discourse of masculinity? In view of this volume's collaborative endeavor to recover Spain's feminist tradition, how can we introduce her into that discourse in a way that does not trap her in an essentialized feminine position as either victim or evader of heterosexist ideology? To put it more ambitiously, how might we conceive of her work as creating gender trouble for the institutionalization of that ideology in the courtly aesthetic? I think we must admit that it is an extremely difficult undertaking. We might begin by imagining a variety of scenarios that might free not only Pinar but also the other medieval female poets that Jane Whetnall, in "Isabel González," suggests are awaiting discovery from an idealist or anachronistic critical construction (72; see also her "Lírica").

Why not, for example, entertain the possibility that Pinar's inclusion in the cancionero is the result of her beating the boys at their own game of constructing an identity that is both allusive and elusive in order to gain status and power? If her brother, identified only by his last name and amply represented in the same *Cancionero general* in which she makes the briefest of appearances, can ventriloquize a female voice in his partial gloss to his sister's "Ell amor ha tales mañas" or, more startlingly, given the ethnic as well as gender leap, to the ballad "Yo me era mora, moraima" ("I was a Moorish girl"), why must we assume that she is incapable of the same poetic cross-gendering?[12] Likewise, is it licit to assume that Pinar is "writing as a woman" for other women or "protesting as a woman"—to adapt Jonathan Culler's famous phrase—the injustices of social and cultural conventions that she appears to have mastered? Could Pinar in fact be writing as a man for men? Or could she be writing not as a woman writes but as she thought men of her class expected a woman to write, that is, in the way that Alison Weber has described Santa Teresa's rhetorical strategies? If the humble, suppliant male courtly poet often masks the aggressive sexual predator, why not envision the chaste, rejecting beloved as masking—or, more accurately, veiling—a libidinous, seductive woman? Might Pinar be engaging in a dazzling display of control over "outward signs and inner meanings" (Weiss, "Alvaro de Luna" 245) by creating in her works a simultaneously repressed and liberated, active and passive, feminine and masculine courtly persona? Or might she be accomplishing this contrast like her fellow-poet Alfonso Alvarez de Villasandino in his alternatingly adoring and degrading declarations of "love" (see note 9)?

In each of these scenarios Pinar could be complicit in the masculinist project of Castilian court culture by successfully seeking status and admission to the elite pages of the cancioneros. Or her goal could be more subversive, the kind of strategy of resistance that Luce Irigaray calls "mimicry":

> To play with mimesis is thus, for a woman, to try to recover the place of her exploitation by discourse, without allowing herself to be simply reduced by it [. . .] so as to make visible what was supposed to remain invisible: the cover-up of a possible operation of the feminine in language. (76)

In conclusion, I want to draw attention to the neglected one-third of Pinar's corpus, the poem "Ay que ay quien más no bive." As we have seen, this work has been ignored because of its similarity to the typical cancionero lyric as it continues to be construed by critics pace Whinnom: that is, in its presumed preference for abstraction over concrete imagery. In other words, it is devalued for being the most conventional of Pinar's three poems. Recio, the only critic to focus on this work, uses it to illustrate what she considers the constraining and inhibiting rules of courtly rhetoric, rules that she states were universally restrictive but, for women, a virtual "dead-end street" (337). I suggest that the structuring device of this poem—its insistent and homophonous alternation of the emotive (the interjection "¡ay!") and the declarative (the impersonal verb form "hay" ["there is" or "there are"]—constitutes a tightly controlled display of the instability of sign and voice in the courtly mode.

We must resist the temptation to view "¡ay!" as feminine and "[h]ay" as masculine, or vice versa, or to resolve the many semantic ambiguities the poem presents (more numerous if read in its original form). Even the verses Recio designates as most clearly expressing the poem's message—"[h]ay donde [h]ay penas de amores / muy gran bien si de él gozares / aunque vida se cative" ("There is, wherever bides Love's hurt, great good [should you ever delight in it]. Though life itself be held captive")—present considerable problems. There is the presence of the euphemistic "gozares" ("delight"), preceded two verses above by the equally suspicious "glorias" ("glories"; in cancionero code: orgasms). And there is the ambiguous antecedent of "él" ("it" or "him"): whom or what is the addressee to enjoy, and in what way? In fact, the poem exudes conditionality and plurality. In the first place, there is the repeated "si" ("if") that qualifies the affirmed existence ("hay") of the amorous persona. Second, the splitting of that persona into several different selves or poses (e.g., the "quien" [he? she?] who finds consolation in her or his laments versus the "quien" [she? he?] who does not). What seems to operate in this poem is an awareness of the performative nature of the courtly persona that corresponds to Judith Butler's theoretical construction of gender not "as a noun or a substantial thing or a static cultural marker, but rather as an incessant and repeated action of some sort" (lx).

I have intentionally avoided answering many of the questions raised in this essay, since my aim is to interrogate certain idealist and essentialist assumptions about the literary construction of gender in the Castilian late Middle Ages. If the specific case of Pinar has anything to teach those committed to the feminist revisioning of Spanish literature, it is a warning about the pitfalls that lie along the way. In a laudable desire to uncover a foundational moment in Spain's feminist tradition, Pinar's critics have not avoided these pitfalls: they have assigned to her both a post-Romantic sensibility and a postmodern feminist agenda; they have searched her lyrics for expressive originality in a mode where stylistic conformity is the desideratum; and they have read arbitrary grammatical gender as the socially constructed category of gender. The still-elusive Florencia Pinar stands as a reminder that a feminist critical methodology must be rigorously historicist and avoid the temptations of reflectionism and essentialism in its conceptualization of both literature and feminism.

Appendix
Poetry of Florencia Pinar[13]

Canción de una dama que se dice Florencia Pinar

¡Ay! que [h]ay quien más no bive
porque no [h]ay quien de ¡ay! se duele,
y, si [h]ay, ¡ay! que recele.
[H]ay un ¡ay! con que se esquive
quien sin ¡ay! bevir no suele.

[H]ay plazeres, hay pesares,
[h]ay glorias, [h]ay mil dolores,
[h]ay donde [h]ay penas de amores
muy gran bien si de él gozares,
aunque vida se cative.
Si [h]ay quien tal ¡ay! consuele,
no [h]ay razon porque se cele
aunque [h]ay con que se esquive
quien sin ¡ay! bevir no suele. (folio cxxv^v^)

Song by a lady named Florencia Pinar

A sigh! For there are some who languish because there are none who pity their sighs. And if there is a sigh which is fearful, there also is a sigh with which they—unused to life without their sighs—can counter it. Oh, pleasure! Oh, sorrow! Oh, glory! Oh, endless pangs! There is, wherever bides Love's hurt, great good (should you ever delight in it). Though life itself be held captive, if there is one who finds solace in sighs, there is no need to warn against them; even though there are means by which he who does not live life without sighs can counter them.

(Snow 329; line breaks eliminated)

Otra canción de la misma señora
a unas perdices que le embiaron vivas

Destas aves su nación
es cantar con alegría,
y de vellas en prisión
siento yo grave passión,
sin sentir nadie la mía.

Ellas lloran, que se vieron
sin temor de ser cativas,
y a quien eran más esquivas
essos mismos las prendieron.
Sus nombres mi vida son,
que va perdiendo alegría,
y de vellas en prisión
siento yo grave passión,
sin sentir nadie la mía. (folio cxxv^v^–cxxvi^r^)

Another song by the same lady,
to some live partridges that were sent to her

The nature of these birds is to sing happily and seeing them caged, I feel acute suffering without anybody's sympathizing with me. They weep because they had no fear of being imprisoned, and they were caught by those from whom they were most aloof. Their names are my life, which is losing its happiness, and seeing them caged, I feel acute suffering without anybody's sympathizing with me. (Deyermond, "Women Writers" 46)

Canción de Florencia Pinar

Ell amor ha tales mañas,
que quien no se guarda dellas,
si se l'entra en las entrañas,
no puede salir sin ellas.

Ell amor es un gusano,
bien mirada su figura;
es un cáncer de natura
que come todo lo sano.
Por sus burlas, por sus sañas,
d'él se dan tales querellas,
que si entra en las entrañas,
no puede salir sin ellas. (folio clxxxv[v])

Song by Florencia Pinar

Love has such crafty ways that whoever is not on guard against them will find that once love has entered one's entrails he can leave only by tearing them out. Love, if you look closely at his appearance, is a worm; he is a cancer of nature who devours all the healthy flesh. By his deceits and by his cruelty he arouses such complaints that if he enters one's entrails he can leave only by tearing them out. (Deyermond, "Women Writers" 48)

Notes

1. The other named female poets, represented by even fewer poems than Pinar is, are Mayor Arias, Marina Manuel, María Sarmiento, and, more questionably, Juana of Portugal, Enrique IV's queen. Another, Isabel González,

has been posited by Whetnall on the basis of indirect evidence: her status as addressee in three *Cancionero de Baena* poems written by men. None of her poems has survived. See also Deyermond, "Las autoras medievales."

2. One indication of the success of this recuperative effort is Pérez Priego's recent anthology, in which Pinar occupies a place of honor.
3. On gender and the production of historical knowledge, see Scott. For literature, see Lees and Overing on Latin letters written by women in England and the Continent and Biddick on medieval women mystics. The only studies I know that grapple with the problem of modern critical construction of a feminine lyric voice in the Iberian Middle Ages are Kelley on the *kharjas* and Lemaire on the *cantigas de amigo.* For a nuanced theoretical discussion of the essentialist versus constructionist debate see Fuss.
4. Weiss provides a radical critique of the traditional view of conventionality in the early cancionero genre of the *cantigas d'amor* (late twelfth and early thirteenth centuries). He points out the important ideological function of conventions "in establishing and mystifying a [masculine] social relationship" ("Conventionality" 236).
5. See Mohanty (56) for a similar critique of modern Western feminist interpretations of Third World women. In her view these analyses constitute women across classes and cultures as a homogeneous group bound together by a sociological notion of the sameness of their oppression. Power is thereby automatically defined in binary terms: those who have it (men) and those who don't (women). Such simplistic formulations, she argues, "are historically reductive; they are also ineffectual in designing strategies to combat oppressions" (64).
6. Deyermond cites the relevant entry in White: "Frequent intercourse tires them out. The males fight each other for their mate, and it is believed that the conquered male submits to venery like a female. Desire torments the females so much that even if a wind blows toward them from the males they become pregnant by the smell" ("Women Writers" 47).
7. Peter Broad has a similar view but seems unaware of previous work on Pinar.
8. Recio also states that there is simply no way to know without being told that the poetic voice of "Destas aves su nación" is feminine (334).
9. A good example of the radical insincerity of the cancionero poet is Alfonso Alvarez de Villasandino. Compare the plaintive "Vysso enamoroso" ("Lovable face") with the obscene "Señora pues que no puedo" ("Lady, since I can't") (*Cancionero de Baena* 335; 367–68), which threatens the (same?) lady with rape.
10. For a valuable collection of sexual euphemisms in early modern Spanish verse, see Alzieu, Jammes, and Lissorgues.
11. See Macpherson (62n8) for relevant articles by Francisco Rico, Julio Rodríguez Puértolas, among others.
12. The first gloss appears on folio clxxxvi-clxxxvi^{v} of the *Cancionero general*; the second, on folio cxxxvi. Whetnall ("'Lírica Femenina'") speaks of male ventriloquism of a female voice but only as evidence for putative female poets' ability to express themselves as women.
13. In my transcriptions of Pinar's poetry, taken from the facsimile edition of

the *Cancionero general,* I have regularized the use of *u* and *v* and supplied modern punctuation, accents, and word divisions. In the case of "Ay que ay quien más no bive," to preserve the ambiguities based on the play between the homophones *ay* and *hay,* which in the manuscript are graphemically identical, I have bracketed the latter word's initial h (following Recio).

Works Cited

Alzieu, Pierre, Robert Jammes, and Yvan Lissorgues. *Floresta de poesías eróticas del Siglo de Oro.* Toulouse: U de Toulouse-Miraille, 1975.

Biddick, Carolyn. "Genders, Bodies, Borders: Technologies of the Visible." *Studying Medieval Women: Sex, Gender, Feminism.* Ed. Nancy F. Partner. Cambridge: Medieval Acad. of America, 1993. 87–116.

Broad, Peter G. "Florencia Pinar y la poética de cancionero." *La escritora hispánica.* Ed. Nora Erro-Orthmann and Juan Cruz Mendizábal. Miami: Ediciones Universal, 1990. 26–36.

Burns, E. Jane. "The Man behind the Lady in Troubadour Lyric." *Courtly Ideology* 254–70.

Burns, E. Jane, and Roberta L. Krueger. Introduction. *Courtly Ideology* 205–19.

Butler, Judith. *Gender Trouble: Feminism and the Subversion of Identity.* New York: Routledge, 1990.

Cancionero castellano del siglo XV. Ed. R. Foulché-Delbosc. 2 vols. Madrid: Bailly/Bailliere, 1915.

Cancionero de Juan Alfonso de Baena. Ed. José María Azáceta. Madrid: Consejo Superior de Investigaciones Científicas, 1966.

Cancionero general recopilado por Hernando del Castillo (Valencia, 1511). Ed. Antonio Rodríguez-Moñino. 2 vols. Madrid: Real Academia Española, 1958.

Courtly Ideology and Woman's Place in Medieval French Literature. Spec. issue of *Romance Notes* 25 (1985): 205–390.

Culler, Jonathan. *On Deconstruction: Theory and Criticism after Structuralism.* Ithaca: Cornell UP, 1982.

Deyermond, Alan. *La literatura perdida de la Edad Media castellana: Catálogo y estudio I: Epica y romances.* Salamanca: Universidad de Salamanca, 1995.

———. "Las autoras medievales castellanas a la luz de las últimas investigaciones." *Medioevo y literatura: Actas del V Congreso de la Asociación Hispánica de Literatura Medieval.* Ed. Juan Paredes. 4 vols. Granada: U of Granada, 1995. 1: 31–52.

———. "Spain's First Women Writers." *Women in Hispanic Literature: Icons and Fallen Idols.* Ed. Beth Miller. Berkeley: U of California P, 1983. 27–53.

———. "The Worm and the Partridge: Reflections on the Poetry of Florencia Pinar." *Mester* 7 (1978): 3–8.

Fisher, Sheila, and Janet E. Halley, eds. *Seeking the Woman in Late Medieval and Renaissance Writings: Essays in Feminist Contextual Criticism.* Knoxville: U of Tennessee P, 1989.

Flores, Angel, and Kate Flores, eds. *The Defiant Muse: Hispanic Feminist Poems from the Middle Ages to the Present.* New York: Feminist, 1986.

Fulks, Barbara. "The Poet Named Florencia Pinar." *La corónica* 18.1 (1989–90): 33–44.

Fuss, Diana. *Essentially Speaking: Feminism, Nature, and Difference.* New York: Routledge, 1989.

Irigaray, Luce. *This Sex Which Is Not One.* Trans. Catherine Porter with Carolyn Burke. Ithaca: Cornell UP, 1985. Trans. of *Ce sexe qui n'est pas un.* Paris: Minuit, 1977.

Kelley, Mary Jane. "Virgins Misconceived: Poetic Voice in the Mozarabic *Kharjas.*" *La corónica* 19.2 (1991): 1–23.

Krueger, Roberta L. "Love, Honor, and the Exchange of Women in Yvain: Some Remarks on the Female Reader." *Courtly Ideology* 302–17.

Lees, Clare A., and Gillian R. Overing. "Birthing Bishops and Fathering Poets: Bede, Hild, and the Relations of Cultural Production." *Exemplaria* 6 (1994): 35–65.

Lemaire, Ria. "Explaining Away the Female Subject: The Case of Medieval Lyric." *Poetics Today* 7 (1986): 729–43.

Macpherson, Ian. "Secret Language in the Cancioneros: Some Courtly Codes." *BHS* 42 (1985): 51–63.

Mirrer, Louise. *Women, Jews, and Muslims in the Texts of Reconquest Castile.* Ann Arbor: U of Michigan P, 1996.

Mohanty, Chandra Talpade. "Under Western Eyes: Feminist Scholarship and Colonial Discourses." *Third World Women and the Politics of Feminism.* Ed. Mohanty, Ann Russo, and Lourdes Torres. Bloomington: Indiana UP, 1991. 51–80.

Moi, Toril. "Desire in Language: Andreas Capellanus and the Controversy of Courtly Love." *Medieval Literature: Criticism, Ideology, and History.* Ed. David Aers. New York: St. Martin's, 1986. 11–33.

Pérez Priego, Miguel Angel. *Poesía femenina en los cancioneros.* Madrid: Castalia, 1989.

Recio, Roxana. "Otra dama que desaparece: La abstracción retórica en tres modelos de canción de Florencia Pinar." *Revista canadiense de estudios hispánicos* 16 (1992): 329–39.

Scott, Joan W. "Gender: A Useful Category of Historical Analysis." *American Historical Review* 91 (1986): 1053–75.

Snow, Joseph. "The Spanish Love Poet: Florencia Pinar." *Medieval Women Writers.* Ed. Katharina M. Wilson. Athens: U of Georgia P; Manchester: Manchester UP, 1984. 320–32.

Weber, Alison. *Santa Teresa and the Rhetoric of Femininity.* Princeton: Princeton UP, 1990.

Weiss, Julian. "Alvaro de Luna, Juan de Mena, and the Power of Courtly Love." *MLN* 106 (1991): 241–56.

———. "On the Conventionality of the *cantigas d'amor.*" *La corónica* 26.1 (1997–98): 225–45.

Whetnall, Jane. "Isabel González of the *Cancionero de Baena* and Other Lost Voices." *La corónica* 21.1 (1992–93): 59–82.

———. "'Lírica femenina' in the Early Manuscript *Cancioneros.*" *What's Past Is Prologue: A Collection of Essays Presented to L. J. Woodward.* Edinburgh: Scottish Academic, 1984. 138–50; 171–75.

Whinnom, Keith. "Hacia una interpretación y apreciación de las canciones del *Cancionero general* de 1511." *Filología* 13 (1968–69): 361–81.

———. *La poesía amatoria de la época de los reyes católicos.* Durham Modern Languages Series: Hispanic Monographs 2. Durham: Durham UP, 1981.

White, T. H. *The Book of Beasts, Being the Translation from a Latin Bestiary of the Twelfth Century.* London: Cape, 1954.

Wilkins, Constance L. "Las voces de Florencia Pinar." *Studia hispanica medievalia II.* Ed. Rosa E. Penna and Maria A. Rosarossa. Buenos Aires: U Católica de la Argentina, 1990. 124–30.

Feminist Attitudes and Expression in Golden Age Spain: From Teresa de Jesús to María de Guevara

María Isabel Barbeito Carneiro

Translated by H. Patsy Boyer

When discussing feminist expression in Golden Age Spain, one is confronted with adequately defining two important terms. The *Diccionario de la lengua española* ("Dictionary of the Spanish Language") defines feminism as a "doctrina social favorable a la condición de la mujer, a quien concede capacidad y derechos reservados hasta ahora a los hombres" ("social doctrine favorable to women's condition that concedes to women the capacities and rights reserved until now for men"). Throughout this essay, I use the term *feminist* with full awareness of its possible anachronistic application. However, as this essay and others in the present collection show, in spite of living before modern feminist movements, many women show signs of feminist consciousness in pre-nineteenth-century Spain.

As to fixing precise historical dates for the Spanish Golden Age, the period is generally defined as corresponding with the Hapsburg rule, beginning with Carlos V (1517) and drawing to a close with the death of Carlos II (1700). The death of the great dramatist Calderón de la

Barca (1681) marks the end of an era of remarkable cultural flourishing. During this time, women in Spain were constrained by social imperatives that made it difficult for them to control their own destiny. Nonetheless, many surviving texts attest to some women's vocal dissatisfaction with the patriarchal status quo and can be read as expressions of nascent feminist attitudes.

Two women whose lives frame this time span are Santa Teresa de Jesús (1515–82) and María de Guevara (d.1683). The feminist testimonials of these women are in their own way as forceful as the novellas of María de Zayas (b.1590), an outspoken writer from the first half of the seventeenth century. Teresa de Jesús lived during the rise of Spanish hegemony in Europe, but the expansionist optimism of the period did not distract Teresa from her profoundly focused mission of reforming spiritual life. María de Guevara was a product of much less fortunate times, for she lived when the Spanish Empire slowly began to disintegrate, producing a general feeling of disillusionment and cynicism. The shift in outlook—from the optimism of the Renaissance to the characteristic focus on paradox, extremism, and pessimism of the Baroque period—is evident in the sociopolitical writings of this energetic and committed woman.

The more heavily studied writers Santa Teresa and Zayas and even the less frequently examined Guevara can be seen to a certain extent as spokespersons for many women who did not have the opportunity, or did not dare, to speak out and be heard. Often the actions and writings of many lesser-known women reveal their willingness to transgress the boundaries of established norms for women and to follow a path in accord with their own convictions. A sampling of the lives and writings of some of these women provides a sense of the work yet to be done in the field of early modern Spanish women's history and writing.

Catalina de Mendoza (1542–1602)

When Catalina de Mendoza, from Granada, learned of her husband's marital infidelity just as she had been wed to him by proxy, she retorted, "Si así aman los hombres, necedad será el amarlos" (Barbeito, *Escritoras*

2: 644) ("If that's the way men love, it would be utter foolishness to love them"). As a result, the marriage was never consummated, and she decided to manage the estates of her father, the fourth marquise of Mondéjar while he was abroad serving as viceroy of Naples (1571–80). On his return, she asked him for her share of the inheritance, which she then gave to the Jesuits for the purpose of founding a school in Alcalá de Henares. On 24 June 1600, she dedicated herself to God, publicly taking the three vows of chastity, poverty, and obedience. From that moment on she led a secluded life characterized by austerity, self-mortification, and pious works until her death at age sixty in 1602.[1]

Lucía de Jesús (1601?–53) and Other Urban Beatas

The beatas were highly spiritual and independent women who dedicated their lives to the practice of Christian virtue unregulated by family or religious order. Needless to say, like the mystics and the alumbrados, the beatas often fell under suspicion of the Inquisition. As Angela Muñoz Fernández reminds us, their singular approach to life and the very nature of their commitment to this way of life serve as "la llave de importantes cambios de status femenino, que vinieron avalados por la santidad de vida y los dones proféticos y místicos" (16) ("a key to important changes in the status of women thanks to the holiness of their lives, their gift of prophecy, and their mysticism"). In *Mujeres, conventos, y formas de la religiosidad barroca* ("Women, Convents, and Forms of Baroque Religiosity"), José Sánchez Lora has also addressed the important role of the beatas in the reconstruction of women's spirituality and gender roles in the period:

> ¿Qué mayor transgresión del orden fundado en la supremacía indiscutible de la masculinidad y docilidad femenina que una mujer sin dueño, que no acepta ninguna de sus funciones tradicionales (esposa-madre-prostituta-religiosa) y se encumbra a la categoría de maestra de espíritu, de sacerdote incluso? (345)

> What greater transgression of the established order—which is based on the indisputable supremacy of men and on the subservience of women—than a woman without master, a woman who ac-

> cepts none of women's traditional roles (wife, mother, prostitute, nun) and even ascends to the category of spiritual teacher, of priest?

Lucía de Jesús refused to marry to have a man to support her, as she was often advised, and she did not seek refuge in a convent. Rather, she broke with the constraints that bound her as a servant and opted to become a beata. Despite many hardships, Lucía continued her activities as a beata, including writing her *vida* in 1652, until her death on 10 December 1653.[2]

Other women chose a similar path. Mariana de Jesús fled from her paternal home where they were trying to marry her off and went to live with her servant Catalina de Cristo in a humble shack. Before her death on 17 April 1624, she became famous as a Mercedarian beata. And María Pérez de Ocampo abandoned her family home because of incompatibility with her stepfather. As the *Vida de la benerable sierva de Dios, la hermana María de la Ascension* tells us, she too refused the solution of marriage and set up her own household so she could become a beata.[3] Devoted to this lifestyle until the very end, she died 30 December 1679. These, and many other women like them, lived highly unconventional lives for the times and might even be classified as "urban hermits" for their seemingly eccentric, yet ultimately unconventional choices that allowed them the freedom to avoid marriage and to live out their spiritual destinies on their own terms.

Luisa de Carvajal y Mendoza (1566–1614)

Luisa de Carvajal y Mendoza was not a typical beata. As a missionary she dared to practice Catholic proselytism in England despite the limitations placed on women and on Catholics in the period. After a difficult journey, she established herself in London. She was twice taken prisoner: once in May 1608 as a result of a street fight, and later Archbishop Abbot assaulted her house and took her prisoner because she had supposedly founded a convent for professed nuns that also served as a cover to hide Catholic priests. She did not live long after this second imprisonment:

she died 2 January 1614. Her earthly remains were returned to Spain to rest in the Convent of the Incarnation in Madrid near her dear friend Mariana de San José, founder of the cloistered Augustines. Carvajal is another understudied figure: her religious poetry shows an indisputable mastery of the genre, and her life story figures as an example of self-styled religious martyrdom.

The Convent and Beyond: Marcela de San Félix and Ana de Leyva

Marcela de Vega Carpio y Luján (1605–87) was the illegitimate daughter of the great dramatist and poet Lope de Vega and the actress Micaela de Luján. While one might have expected her to become a transgressor like her father (who was famous for his many affairs), Marcela chose the convent and a calmer life, perhaps to escape the turmoil of her paternal home. Intelligent, clever, refined, and strong willed, she learned through her father about the passions and promises of life outside the convent. And while she recognized her parentage, she also explicitly stated "que se había hecho monja para acomodarse y no perder en el siglo" ("she had become a nun in order to find a comfortable place rather than get ruined in the world").[4] It might seem paradoxical to the modern reader, but the convent allowed Marcela and many other women to engage in activities that would have been harshly criticized in the outside world (cf. Arenal and Schlau, introduction and chapter 4). In the closed circle of the convent she was able to give free rein to the theatricality she inherited from her parents both by writing plays and by performing them. Within the convent walls, she could dress like a man and recite highly unorthodox lines. As was the unfortunate case with many women in the period, Marcela's confessor made her burn at least four handwritten volumes of her writings, and only one, probably the fifth volume, remains to us today. This text, available in the critical edition *Literatura conventual femenina*, prepared by Electa Arenal and Georgina Sabat-Rivers, lets us imagine the pleasure her creativity must have given the sisters. Marcela penned poetic representations of convent life while also showing off her wit and keen sense of humor and taking very daring liberties. An example of her sharp wit is the following parody of the highly politicized purity of blood issue put in the mouth of a so-called scholar, whose role she would have performed:

[. . .] quiero cesar y decir	I want to state and make clear
de mi clara descendencia	my clean lineage
y de mi ilustre prosapia,	and my illustrious ancestry,
que honrar un mundo pudiera.	that would honor the world.
Diéronme muy noble sangre	My parents, may they rest in peace,
mis padres que gloria tengan	gave me noble blood
porque descendió mi padre	for my father descended
y vino por línea recta	in an unbroken line
del más célebre rabino	from the most excellent rabbi
que se halló en toda Judea.	to be found in all Judea.
Mi madre no fue tan noble,	My mother was not as noble,
mas su vida fue tan buena	but her life was so good
que suple bien por la sangre	that it made up for her blood
y excede toda nobleza.	exceeding all nobility.
Volaba por esos aires,	She flew through the air,
penetraba chimeneas,	she came down chimneys,
grande bruja de Logroño	the Great Witch of Logroño
famosa en toda la tierra.	famous throughout the world.[5]

It appears that Sor Marcela found spiritual fulfillment as well as opportunities for creative and literary expression that were often denied to secular women in society. Such dissatisfaction and frustration can be seen in another seventeenth-century woman. Ana de Leyva wrote *Panigírico en alabanza de la Sereníssima Alteza del gran Francisco de Este, Duque Potentíssimo de Módena, quando entró pomposo en esta católica Corte de Madrid con solemne triunfo, por mandado del Rey nuestro Señor Felipe IV el Grande* (1638) ("Panegyric in Praise of His Most Serene Highness the Great Francisco de Este, Powerful Duke of Modena, upon his Grand Entrance into the Catholic Court in Madrid at the Bidding of our King Felipe IV the Great"). Although this laudatory pamphlet might be judged by some as being uneven in its merit, the pamphlet gives great insight into one woman's frustration with the system in which she lives. A devotee of the literary, she is aware that she is losing all that she had learned so painstakingly as a self-taught writer because of the social restrictions imposed on her:

La Emperatriz Eudochia (S.A.) Proba, Falconia, Iulia, Porcia, Tulia, y otras mujeres de veneranda fama, dadas a los estudios, no emplearon lo fecundo de sus ingenios menos que con pintar héroes los más soberanos de sus tiempos. Acordéme entre breves treguas, que me concede la honesta ocupación, el virtuoso empleo que personas de mi porte ejercen en el estrado y almohadilla, en la rueca y aguja, que no se me ofreció menor la ocasión que a las matronas ya nombradas. Tomé la pluma, apenas pude entonar la Musa, porque ya el poco cuidado de las letras, con otros nuevos, disminuye lo poco que había alcanzado en largos desvelos [. . .]. Bien o mal templado, señor, canté dibujando si no en armonioso son, a lo menos en alegre acento, algún encomio breve de V. A. S. en lenguaje castellano mío, con rústica melodía. Si fue atrevimiento, mujer soy, exenta de venganza por la ley de cortesano y del duelo, si acierto, serálo en los ojos de un benigno príncipe.

(fol. 2r)

The Empress Eudochia, Proba, Falconia, Iulia, Porcia, Tulia, and other women of renown devoted to study and writing used their rich genius in portraying the most august heroes of their times. I realized, during a brief interlude granted to me by my everyday work, the virtuous obligation of women of my standing to engage in sewing and spinning in the ladies' parlor, that I had as much opportunity as the matrons named above. I took up my pen, but I could scarcely invoke the Muse, because my neglect of letters among other things had diminished the little I had achieved with such great effort. [. . .] Fittingly or not, Sire, I have sung sketching a brief encomium of Your Highness, if not with harmonious sound, at least with happy accent and rustic melody in my Castilian language. If that was audacious, I am a woman and exempt from vengeance by the laws of courtesy and the laws of the duel; if I have succeeded, it will be in the eyes of a benevolent prince.

Mariana Francisca de los Angeles (1637–97) and Catalina de Jesús (1639–77)

Ana de Leyva's suffocating situation contrasts markedly with the experience of the woman who was to become Mariana Francisca de los Angeles, known mainly as the founder of the Madrid Convent of the Discalced Carmelites of Santa Teresa (1684).[6] Mariana Francisca, a proud, energetic, and impulsive woman, described herself as a person of spirited nature who liked to stand out. She enjoyed handling both the sword and the gun and tells us with some arrogance that she would feel entirely safe among armies and that she had her gun at the ready to punish any impertinent man who pursued her. Mariana's entrance into religious life does not seem to have come from a "true" religious vocation. She opted for this way of life when her parents were trying to arrange her marriage, because she aspired to something more. As she states in her *vida*, which is housed in Madrid in the Archivo de Carmelitas Descalzas de Santa Teresa ("Archive of the Discalced Carmelites of Saint Teresa"), Mariana had decided that men were not trustworthy and that she did not wish to marry when her father flew into a rage one day and pulled her hair out in an act of unwarranted violence.[7] In Mariana's case, the choice of the cloister allowed her to avoid what she perceived as the volatility of a secular union and, perhaps as an unforeseen benefit, to cultivate her intellect throughout her adult life.

The other side of this coin is the experience of Catalina de Jesús y San Francisco, the very antithesis of the stereotype that defines woman as wife and mother. She accepted many kinds of sacrifice but scarcely tolerated the experience of motherhood, and she could never adjust to her husband, as seen in the following lament which appears in her 1693 biography (written by her only son, Juan Bernique). According to Bernique, the text includes excerpts, such as the following quote, that were taken from Catalina's letters and destroyed autobiography:

> ¡Oh, cómo quisiera yo supieran las religiosas que no están contentas con su estado y muy agradecidas a su Majestad por las mercedes que les hizo en habérsele dado, que conocieran los intolerables trabajos del matrimonio, con una sujeción a un hombre con mil mudanzas al día en su obrar [. . .]! ¡Qué intolerable cosa es sufrir la carga de los hijos y de criarlos! ¿Qué ejercicio tan penoso puede haber en la vida espiritual que llegue a esto? Confieso que se me ha hecho poco cuanto he padecido desde que el Señor me llamó para sí. [. . .] ¡Qué esclavitud tan penosa! ¡Qué sujeción tan intolerable a un hombre! (41)

> Oh how I wish the nuns who are not happy with their lot and not thankful to His Majesty for the mercy He has done in granting them their status could know the intolerable travails of marriage, subjected to a man of a thousand moods all in one day [. . .]!

> How unbearable it is to suffer the burdens of carrying children and raising them! What religious exercise in the spiritual life can there be as painful as this? I must confess that since the Lord called me to Him I have suffered very little. [. . .] What dreadful slavery! What intolerable subjugation to a man!

Catalina acknowledged that her reluctance to accommodate herself to motherhood and being a wife made her husband suffer. Juan Bernique stresses that she "tuvo a su marido notablemente mortificado, ya con su aspereza, ya con sus desvanecimientos, galas y diversiones, que le tenían en un continuo martirio" (23) ("kept her husband in a state of great mortification through her harshness, her pride, her galas and entertainments; he lived a continuous martyrdom"). Catalina García Fernández "de Bernique," her secular married name, or Catalina de Jesús y San Francisco in her religious life, was a few months old when her mother died and her aunt, a printer at the University of Alcalá de Henares, took her in. Catalina's precocious physical and intellectual development caused amazement in all the students who frequented the print shop. Her alarmed aunt took the precautionary measure of arranging her fifteen-year-old niece's marriage to a forty-year-old doctor. Nothing could have been further from the young girl's wishes. Although she had to agree to the forced marriage, Catalina never managed to overcome the subsequent trauma.

When she was widowed at age twenty-two, Catalina enjoyed only a few months of spiritual respite, after which she willingly placed herself in the hands of a confessor. She soon took the habit of the Third Order of San Francisco and devoted herself wholeheartedly to founding a school for indigent orphan girls. Although Catalina had found it difficult to raise her own children, Bernique portrays her as a devoted and selfless mother to her adopted religious daughters. After years of self-mortification, Catalina de Jesús died on 7 November 1677.

Santa Teresa de Jesús and María de Guevara

Women like Catalina de Jesús and the others already mentioned have begun to be studied more systematically in recent years, and their writings attest to the emergence of a feminist consciousness that chafes against the restrictions imposed on women by the power structure of Golden Age Spain's patriarchy.[8] If traces of feminist attitudes can be found in these lesser-known authors, we can find sustained and explicitly drawn feminism in the more extensive and widely disseminated writings of Santa Teresa de Jesús and María de Zayas, and in those of the late seventeenth-century writer María de Guevara.

Teresa de Jesús is one of the few writers who with utmost sincerity has laid bare her soul in her writings. Her unconditional desire to conform to divine will overcame any compunction she may have felt as she explored the deepest recesses of her inner life in her *Libro de la vida* (*Book of Her Life*), *Camino de perfección* (*Way of Perfection*), and *Moradas del castillo interior* (*Interior Castle*). A great deal has been written about her; for that reason and because of the limits of this study, we sketch out only the most significant events of her life to situate her feminism within her life and works.[9] She was born 28 March 1515 in Avila to Alonso Sánchez de Cepeda (whose family had converted from Judaism to avoid persecution at the end of the fifteenth century) and his second wife, Beatriz de Ahumada. Of her eleven siblings, only two were girls. When Teresa was seven, she persuaded her brother Rodrigo to run away to the lands of the Moors, where they would try to suffer martyrdom so they could immediately enjoy "los grandes bienes que leía haber en el cielo" (*Vida* 29) ("the fruition of the great blessings which, as I read, were laid up in Heaven" [*Life* 11]).[10] Their attempt failed.

When she was twenty, she ran away again to become a nun. She compared the pain of separation from her family to the pain of separating bones from the body (*Vida* 34). Between 1560 and 1562, the laxity that pervaded the Carmelite Convent of the Encarnación, where she had taken her vows, moved her to seek ways to perfect spiritual life in the convent. Inspired by her love of God, she worked tirelessly to institute reforms for returning the order to its original observance of the Rule of Nuestra Señora del Carmen according to the dictate in 1248 of Fray Hugo, cardinal of Santa Sabina. You can sense the pride and joy the holy reformer must have felt when she referred to the first Convent of the Discalced Carmelites she founded in Avila: "con toda autoridad y fuerza quedó hecho nuestro monasterio del gloriosísimo padre nuestro

San Josef, año de mil y quinientos y sesenta y dos" (*Vida* 161) ("with the full weight of authority this convent of our most glorious father Saint Joseph was founded in the year of 1562" [*Life* 249–50]). Urged on by Teresa de Jesús, who never flagged in her zeal to expand the reform to the male Carmelites, Juan de la Cruz founded in Duruelo, in the province of Avila, the first monastery for discalced friars. In 1577 Teresa wrote letters to King Felipe II in defense of her fellow reformers who had been imprisoned: Father Gracián, Juan de la Cruz, and Germán de Macías. By the time of her death on 4 October 1582, she had established seventeen religious houses, with others projected, and had completed a significant body of writings which would earn her the title Doctor of the Church.

Teresa's opus began to develop only after she reached physical and spiritual maturity as we can see in *Libro de la vida*, drafted during the 1560s when she was in her mid-forties. From that moment on, her pen would not stop until her death.[11] In addition to books on varied subjects, she wrote numerous letters and produced a significant body of poetry. If *Moradas del castillo interior* represents her spiritual or mystical autobiography, *Camino de perfección*, is, in the words of Daniel de Pablo Maroto in the introduction to his edition to *Camino*, "sin género de dudas, la más pedagógica, la más asequible de sus obras doctrinales, la más incisiva, la más maternal" (7) ("without a doubt, the most accessible of her doctrinary works, the most pedagogical, the most incisive, the most maternal"). This practical book sets forth the whole way of life for the Discalced Carmelites, epitomizing Teresian asceticism: the road to spiritual perfection through communitarian living. Teresa's sense of solidarity and her didactic intentions clearly motivate the entire work. Her own experience serves as a guide to help other women follow the road more easily: she teaches them about the difficulties they might encounter in their spiritual journeys.

Given Teresa's deep understanding of the human soul, she comprehended the discouragement produced by an ideal shattered because it was based on false premises. Hence the message of her truth she shared with her nuns: she presses upon them to believe that she is telling the truth and that she is speaking to them to improve their understanding of God and his ways. Teresa's commitment to authenticity moves her to express her deeply held ideas about mental prayer and different kinds of spiritual activity based on her own experience. Teresa was not unaware that she was treading on territory regulated implacably by the Inquisition. But, confident in her truth, Teresa was to uphold it even before the most noted and critical theologians. For Teresa de Jesús, religious life is by nature participatory and perfectionist and is suffused with an energizing sense of renovation.

The social circumstances of that time did not favor the development of strong character in women, and the outlook was discouraging for any woman who sought to initiate change, as Teresa learned from personal experience during her four-year confinement by the Inquisition. But the obstacles also served as a challenge, and she continued to advance her projects in a subterranean way, expecting little of the world and placing herself in God's hands to perform her service for mankind. And even when her proposals for spiritual renovation were appropriate for men, her words seem to reflect a particularly feminine orientation as we can see in the subtle ironies with feminist overtones:

> Sé que no faltará el amor y deseo en mí para ayudar lo que yo pudiere a que las almas de mis hermanas vayan muy adelante en el servicio del Señor. Este amor, junto con los años y experiencia que tengo de algunos, podrá ser que aproveche para atinar en cosas menudas, más que los letrados, que por tener otras ocupaciones más importantes y ser varones fuertes no hacen caso de cosas que de sí no parecen nada, y a cosa tan flaca como somos las mujeres todo nos puede dañar. (Prólogo, *Camino* 196)

> I know that I am lacking neither in love nor in desire to do all I can to help the souls of my sisters to make great progress in the service of the Lord. It may be that this love, together with my years and the experience which I have of a number of convents, will make me more successful in writing about small matters than learned men can be. For these, being themselves strong and having other and more important occupations, do not always pay such heed to things which in themselves seem of no importance but which may do great harm to persons as weak as we women are.
>
> (*Way of Perfection* 2)

Or in the following words from her prologue to the *Moradas*:

> Díjome quien me mandó escribir que como estas monjas de estos monasterios de Nuestra Señora del Carmen tienen necesidad de quien algunas dudas de oración las declare y que le parecía que mejor se entienden el lenguaje unas mujeres de otras, y con el amor que me tienen les haría más al caso lo que yo les dijese[. . .]. (364)
>
> I was told by the person who commanded me to write that, as the nuns of these convents of Our Lady of Carmel need someone to solve their difficulties concerning prayer, and as (or so it seemed to him) women best understand each other's language, and also in view of their love for me, anything I might say would be particularly useful to them. (*Interior Castle* 200)

Teresa tells us that the world needs women to give up their reticence, even though men might refuse to acknowledge women's potential contribution as teachers and thinkers; it is wrong to waste the contributions of one-half of humanity simply because of arbitrary precepts or regulations. Convinced that God accepts the love and dedication of his children without regard to their sex, she looks to him with trust:

> Confío yo, Señor mío, en estas siervas vuestras que aquí están, que veo y sé no quieren otra cosa ni la pretenden sino contentaros; por Vos han dejado lo poco que tenían y quisieran tener más para serviros con ello. Pues no sois vos, Criador mío, desagradecido para que piense yo daréis menos de lo que os suplican, sino mucho más, ni aborrecisteis, Señor de mi alma, cuando andabais por el mundo las mujeres, antes las favorecisteis siempre con mucha piedad y hallasteis en ellas tanto amor [. . .]. (*Camino* 205)
>
> Oh Lord, I trust these your servants who are here, for I see and I know that the only thing they want is to please you; for you they have given up all they had and they would only like to have more to be better able to serve you. You, my Creator, are not so ungrateful as to give less than they pray for, but rather much more. Nor, Lord, when you walked on this earth did you scorn women, instead

> you always favored them with great piety, and you found much love in them [. . .]. (Boyer's trans.)

Santa Teresa, remarkable both in her life's work and in the writings she left, clearly demonstrated women's capabilities and the importance of female solidarity. María de Guevara, who did not become a nun, was also unusual in her refusal to accept the traditional stereotypes of accepted female behavior. As she documented in her carefully tended family archives, she was of illustrious lineage. The House of Guevara can be traced back to the eighth-century hero Pelayo, the first Christian to defeat the Muslim invaders in 718 at the beginning of the Reconquest. Her ancestors had illustrious aristocratic connections. Her father was Pedro de Guevara, her mother Francisca de Mendoza. She was the first daughter following Antonio and José, both of whom died in childhood. After her came two other girls, Luisa and Ana. With the deaths of her brothers, she inherited numerous titles and estates. And, as Guevara herself recounts, her father's elder brother Luis had inherited the Avendaño patrimony from his childless cousin Isabel Angela de Avendaño. The patrimony would later pass on to María, who had no children in any of her three marriages.

Of the many titles Guevara bore, she preferred that of countess of Escalante and was immensely proud of her lineage, of being Spanish, and of being a woman. In fact, she struggled to defend her rights in all three areas. Guevara wielded her pen as a weapon, making many kinds of claims. Her audacity and valor were decidedly unfeminine. Indeed it was even said of her that she was more worthy than two men; certainly she was an exceptional woman.[12] Guevara did not believe that sex determined function, as we see in her claim to the title of Royal Archer, which had long been in her family. In *Desengaños de la corte y mugeres valerosas* ("Disenchantments at Court and Valiant Women"), she advocates women as governors, arguing "que el gobierno de las mujeres a veces suele ser mejor que el de muchos hombres" (2: 10) ("women's governance is usually better than that of many men"). She also defends putting women in the army, considering them as competent in warfare as men and citing the example of one of her forebears:

> Viene Marsidio Rey moro a pedir la Infanta de Navarra doña Urraca. No se la dan. Cerca a Pamplona. Se ve el Rey don García apretado [. . .]. Doña Blanca de Guevara, hija del Conde Pedro de Oñate, y viuda de Ortuño de Lara, como General, prende a Marsidio y liberta a Navarra. Y si ahora una mujer quisiera hacer esto y es varonil, se rieran de ella. ¡Malos tiempos hemos alcanzado! (2: 13–14)

> The Moorish king Marsidio comes to ask for the hand of Urraca, princess of Navarra, in marriage. He is refused. He lays siege to Pamplona. The king Don García is hard pressed [. . .]. Doña Blanca de Guevara, daughter of Count Pedro de Oñate and widow of Ortuño de Lara, rides out as general, captures Marsidio, and frees Navarre. Nowadays if a woman acted manly and tried to do this people would laugh at her. How times have changed!

And again, with regard to relations between men and women, she rejects marriage arranged by the parents: "Como si los padres pudieran forzar las voluntades, que Dios nos deja en nuestro libre albedrío" (2: 11) ("As if fathers could control a person's desire that God has left to an individual's free will").

Guevara also accuses men of special cruelty in making women totally subject to the bonds of matrimony. This arrangement, she argues, enables a husband to commit all kinds of abuse: taking control over his wife's personal jewelry and her dowry, filling her house with children for his gain, and using prostitutes and then infecting her with venereal diseases (1: 6–7). Guevara justifies women's aggression against men as revenge against inequitable treatment:

> Muere el Rey de Nápoles, deja mandado que su hija Juana, heredera del reino se case con el Rey Andrés (como si los padres pudieran forzar la voluntad, que Dios nos deja en nuestro libre albedrío). Viene el Rey Andrés, pónela guerra, y oblígala a que se case por fuerza, y en teniéndola sujeta hace lo que los malos maridos. Ella como valerosa y Reina propietaria, cuélgale el día de San Andrés; y fue la cuelga de veras, pues le envió a que le enviase nuevas del otro mundo. Si hubiera algunas que la imitaran, vivieran los hombres a raya [. . .]. (2: 11)

> When the king of Naples dies, he commands that his daughter Juana, heir to the kingdom, marry king Andrés (as if fathers could control a person's desire that God has left to an individual's free will). King Andrés comes and wages war against her and forces her to marry him and once he has her subject he does as all bad husbands do. She, being brave and as rightful queen has him hanged on the day of San Andrés; and it was a real hanging as she sent him off to find news of the other world. If there were more like her, men would learn to toe the line [. . .].

Guevara believes that men must look at a woman's human qualities rather than her physical beauty and her dowry, given that these are soon ended and then "se hallan con una simple en casa" ("they find themselves with a simpleton in the house"), unable to understand his worries, unable to give him advice; "porque aunque el de la mujer es poco, el que no le toma es loco" (3: 26) ("because even though women's advice seems negligible, the one who doesn't take it is foolish indeed"). Undoubtedly, Guevara had read the popular works of Zayas and shared the ardent feminism that pervaded them, just as she would have been familiar with the writings of Teresa de Jesús.

In different ways, all three writers were reformers who used the pen to change attitudes toward women in Golden Age Spain. Each one addresses her own situation, her own experience, using different literary techniques to express her ideas regarding the inequality of women in society. They particularly denounce the notion of women's "weakness," which, according to all three, is not innate but socially conditioned by their lack of access to education and learning and by laws that privilege men at the expense of women. We see this, for example, in the following words of Santa Teresa:

> ¿No basta, Señor, que nos tiene el mundo acorraladas [. . .] que no hagamos cosa que valga nada por Vos, en público, ni osemos hablar algunas verdades que lloramos en secreto [. . .]? No lo creo yo, Señor, de vuestra bondad y justicia, que sois justo juez, y no como los jueces del mundo que, como hijos de Adán y en fin todos varones, no hay virtud de mujer que no tengan por sospechosa. Sé que algún día ha de haber, Rey mío, que se conozcan todos.

> No hablo por mí, [. . .] sino porque veo los tiempos de manera que no es razón desechar ánimos virtuosos y fuertes, aunque sean de mujeres. (*Camino*, Prólogo 75)[13]
>
> Isn't it enough, Lord, that the world keeps us corralled, that we can do nothing to serve you in public, nor dare we speak the truth that we bewail in secret [. . .]? I don't think so, Lord, given your justice and your goodness, for you are a fair judge not like the judges of this world who, as sons of Adam, are, after all, mere men and they find no virtue in women that they do not consider suspect. I know, my King, that some day they will recognize this. I don't speak just for myself, [. . .] but because I see that it is not right to waste strong and virtuous souls even if they do belong to women.

In a protest that resonates strongly with Zayas's own criticism of male control in "La fuerza del amor" ("The Power of Love"), in the *Novelas amorosas*, Guevara stated:

> Como ellos hicieron las leyes, todas fueron en su favor, queriendo que ellas se contenten con las armas de la rueca y de la almohadilla. Pues a fe, que si usasen las mujeres de las letras, que les sobrepujaran a los hombres; pero esto temen ellos, y no quieren que sean amazonas, sino tenerles las manos atadas. [. . .] Como ellos hacían las leyes y conocieron que muchas mujeres los podrían igualar, procuraron aniquilarlas. (2: 11–12, 3: 21)
>
> Since men made the laws, they made them all in their own favor, intending for women to be content with the weapons of the distaff and the sewing cushion. Well, by my faith, if women had access to letters they would surpass men, but that is what they fear, they do not want them to be strong so they keep their hands tied. [. . .] Because they made the laws and recognizing that many women might equal them, they sought to eliminate them.

Recent interest in women's history has brought to light these and other feminist gestures and attitudes that might be seen to progress in evolutionary fashion. Throughout the centuries women have been making headway in their fight for equal treatment in society, and this struggle involves a struggle to legitimize values that traditionally have been disparaged and disregarded. These women from the Golden Age were well aware of the complexities of this struggle. Their voices provide an important link to Spain's feminist tradition.

Notes

1. For more on Catalina de Mendoza, Lucía de Jesús, María de la Ascensión, and other women mentioned in this section, see Barbeito Carneiro's *Escritoras madrileñas del siglo XVII.* Please note that all Spanish spelling, except for titles, is modernized throughout this article to allow for easier and more accessible reading. With some exceptions, noted throughout the essay, translations are by H. Patsy Boyer.
2. Lucía de Jesús's *vida* is housed at El Escorial: *Vida de la venerable Luzia de Jesus, trasladada a la letra de la que ella escribió de su mano.* For further information, see Barbeito, *Escritoras madrileñas del siglo XVII* (1: 342–45) or *Mujeres del Madrid barroco: Voces testimoniales* (147–56).
3. María de la Ascensión's *vida,* written in seventeenth-century hand is housed in Rome at the Archivo General de la Orden Carmelitana (POST IV, 42). There is also an incomplete manuscript, which includes excerpts from the autobiography as well as from a biography written by Padre Camuñas (*Carmelo místico y campo espiritual*).
4. Sor Marcela never hid her background. In 1641 in a statement about Padre Falconi she declared "ser originaria de la ciudad de Toledo [. . .] y que es hija de Lope de Vega Carpio y de doña Micaela de Luján, que residieron en esta Corte" ("she was from the city of Toledo and was the daughter of Lope de Vega Carpio and Doña Micaela de Luján who had resided in that Court city"). See *Proceso de la vida* (558r–569r).
5. The original version of this poem is in Arenal and Sabat-Rivers (362), and part of the translation is taken from Arenal and Schlau (238).
6. The first Teresian convent founded in Madrid was the Convent of Santa Ana.
7. The full quote from Mariana's autobiography is as follows: "Un día estaba yo como chanceando con una criada, cosa no usada de mí, porque era entonces de modo muy severo. En otra pieza estaba mi padre, y oído, parecióle era de género y en materia que yo la picaba en cosa de sentimiento para ella. Y Dios que lo quiso así por mi bien, permitió que mi padre tomase tal enojo que, como fuera de sí, entró. Yo tenía el cabello tendido, que me estaba tocando. Asióme de él, y de tal manera me lo tiró que gran parte se le quedó en las manos, y a este modo hizo tales extremos que admiró a toda la familia, porque era un ángel en todo. Yo ponderé el caso de modo que en muchos meses no volví en mí. Miraba que si de un padre tan cuerdo había experimentado tal desmán, no tenía que esperar de criaturas [. . .]" (fol. 9r/r) ("One day I was joking around with a servant—quite unusual for me as at that time I was quite a serious person. My father was in the next room, and when he heard, he thought that I was teasing her out of some affection for her. For my own welfare, God willed for my father to become so angry that almost beside himself with rage he came in. My hair

was down as I was fixing it. He grabbed my hair and pulled it so hard that much of it remained in his hands, and he went to such extremes that it amazed my whole family, because usually he was an angel. That event so upset me that I did not return to normal for many months. Then I realized that if I had suffered such extreme behavior from such a wise and gentle father, what could I expect from others [. . .]").

8. For more on women's status in the Golden Age, see Cruz's essay in this volume, as well as Arenal and Sabat-Rivers; Barbeito; and Perry.
9. For more on Teresa and her life, see Madre de Dios; Bilinkoff; Pablo Maroto; Rossi; Slade; and Weber.
10. Source titles of Teresa's quotations are given to differentiate among *Libro de la vida, Camino de perfección,* and *Moradas del castillo interior.* English translations of Teresa's work are from Peers's *Complete Works,* unless otherwise indicated.
11. Works written by Teresa after the *Libro de su vida* include: *Constituciones* ("Constitutions"), *Avisos* ("Warnings"), *Camino de perfección, Conceptos del amor de Dios* ("Meditations on the Song of Songs"), *Exclamaciones* ("Exclamations"), *Ordenanzas de una cofradía* ("Ordinance of the Sisterhood"), *Desafío espiritual* ("Spiritual Testimony"), *Visita de descalzas* ("Visit of the Discalced Nuns"), *Vejamen* ("Satire"), *Moradas del castillo interior, Apuntaciones* ("Notes"), *Cuentas de conciencia* ("Accounts of the Conscience"), *Fundaciones* ("Foundations").
12. Guevara's defense of women in a 1663 letter to Felipe IV speaks to her exceptional views: "Dirá vuestra Majestad, ¿quién mete a una mujer en esto? A que respondo, que harta lástima es que lo lleguemos a entender las mujeres tan bien como los hombres y a sentirlo mejor" ("Your Majesty might ask what does a woman have to do with this? To which I reply it's a shame we women understand as well as men and feel more deeply").
13. Quoted in the facsimile of *Camino* published by Tipografia Poliglotta Vaticana, this passage was excised from the second version of *Camino.* The citation comes from the Vatican edition. The translation is Boyer's.

Works Cited

Arenal, Electa, and Georgina Sabat-Rivers. *Literatura conventual femenina: Sor Marcela de San Félix, hija de Lope de Vega.* Barcelona: PPU, 1988.

Arenal, Electa, and Stacey Schlau. *Untold Sisters: Hispanic Nuns in Their Own Works.* Albuquerque: U of New Mexico P, 1989.

Barbeito Carneiro, María Isabel. *Escritoras madrileñas del siglo XVII (Estudio bibliográfico-crítico).* 2 vols. Madrid: Editorial de la Universidad Complutense, 1986.

———. *Mujeres del Madrid barroco: Voces testimoniales.* Madrid: Horas y Horas, 1992.

Bernique, Juan. *Idea de perfección y virtudes: Vida de la V.M. y sierva de Dios Catalina de Iesvs, y San Francisco, Hixa de sv Tercera Orden.* Alcalá: Francisco García Fernández, 1693.

Bilinkoff, Jodi. *The Avila of Saint Teresa.* Ithaca: Cornell UP, 1989.

Camuñas, Padre. *Carmelo místico y campo espiritual, en la vida admirable de la venerable María de la Ascensión, profesa de la tercera orden de nuestra señora la madre de Dios del Carmen Calçado.* Madrid: Biblioteca Nacional, mss. 6.629.

Diccionario de la lengua española. Madrid: Real Academia Española, 1984.

Guevara, María de. *Desengaños de la corte y mugeres valerosas.* N.p., [1664?].

Leyva, Ana de. *Panigírico en alabanza de la Sereníssima Alteza del gran Francisco de Este, Duque Potentíssimo de Módena, quando entró pomposo en esta católica Corte de Madrid con solemne triunfo, por mandado del Rey nuestro Señor Felipe IV el Grande.* Madrid: Imprenta del Reyno, 1638.

Lucía de Jesús. *Vida de la venerable Luzia de Jesus, trasladada a la letra de la que ella escribió de su mano.* El Escorial: ms. Z-IV-13, 1658.

Madre de Dios, Padre Efrén de. *Tiempo y vida de Santa Teresa.* Biblioteca de Autores Cristianos. Madrid: Católica, 1968.

María de la Ascension. *Vida de la benerable sierva de Dios, la hermana Maria de la Ascension, natural de Madrid y beata.* Rome: n.p., n.d.

Mariana Francisca de los Angeles. *Vida de la venerable madre Mariana Francisca de los Angeles, escrita por ella misma.* Ocaña, 1677.

Muñoz Fernández, Angela. *Beatas y santas neocastellanas: Ambivalencias de la religión y políticas correctoras del poder (Ss. XIV–XVII).* Madrid: I.I.F. Universidad Complutense, 1994.

Pablo Maroto, Daniel de. Introducción. *Camino de perfección.* By Teresa de Jesús. Madrid: Espiritualidad, 1971.

Perry, Mary Elizabeth. *Gender and Disorder in Early Modern Seville.* Princeton: Princeton UP, 1990.

Proceso de la vida, milagros y heroicas virtudes del venerable siervo de Dios fray Juan Falconi de Bustamante. Archivo de la Curia Provincial de Castilla, 1642.

Rossi, Rosa. *Teresa de Avila: Biografía de una escritora.* Trans. Marieta Gargatagli. 2nd ed. Barcelona: Icaria, 1997.

Sánchez Lora, José. *Mujeres, conventos, y formas de la religiosidad barroca.* Madrid: F.U.E., 1988.

Slade, Carole. *St. Teresa of Avila: Author of a Heroic Life.* Berkeley: U of California P, 1995.

Teresa de Jesús. *Camino de perfección.* 1st ed. Facsimile ed. with commentary by Tomás de la Cruz. Rome: Tipografia Poliglotta Vaticana, 1965.

———. *Camino de perfección.* 2nd ed. Teresa, *Obras completas* 192–332.

———. *The Complete Works of St. Teresa of Jesus.* Ed. and trans. E. Allison Peers. 1946. 3 vols. London: Sheed, 1978.

———. *Interior Castle.* Teresa, *Complete Works* 2: 199–351.

———. *Libro de la vida.* Teresa, *Obras completas* 25–191.

———. *The Life of the Holy Mother of Teresa of Jesus.* Teresa, *Complete Works* 1: 9–367.

———. *Moradas del castillo interior.* Teresa, *Obras completas* 362–450.

———. *Obras completas.* 6th ed. Ed. Efrén de la Madre de Dios and Otger Steggink. Madrid: Católica, 1979.

———. *Way of Perfection.* Teresa, *Complete Works* 2: 1–186.

Weber, Alison. *Teresa of Avila and the Rhetoric of Femininity*. Princeton: Princeton UP, 1990.

Zayas y Sotomayor, María de. *Novelas amorosas y ejemplares*. Ed. Agustín de Amezúa. Madrid: Real Academia Española, 1948.

The Partial Feminism of Ana de San Bartolomé

Alison Weber

Ana de San Bartolomé (1549–1626) would appear to be an unlikely heir to Teresa de Jesús, the famous mystic and founder of the Discalced Carmelite reform. If Teresa is a writer whose complex rhetorical strategies, syncretic imagery, and stylistic innovations have challenged generations of readers, Ana often strikes us as an accidental literate, as someone who "speaks through writing."[1] Similarly, if Teresa sought to promote a new model of feminine piety based on an apostolate of prayer, Ana reinscribed Teresa's sanctity within an older, thaumaturgic tradition.[2] It would be possible to dismiss Ana as a theological and artistic primitive, admirable for the simplicity of her devotion if not for her grasp of Teresa's Christian feminism or literary achievements. Yet Ana's simplicity has much to reveal about the sometimes erratic transmission of early modern feminisms and about the complexities of women's leadership roles within Counter-Reformation monasticism.

Ana de San Bartolomé was born in 1549 in the Castilian village of El Almendral, the daughter of *labradores acomodados,* or landowning farmers. She acquired a rudimentary ability to read in the vernacular as a child. Despite the opposition of her family, in 1570 she took the veil as *lega,* or lay sister, in the Discalced convent of San José of Avila. In 1577, during a visit to Avila, the ailing Teresa de Jesús selected Ana as her personal nurse. Ana subsequently became Teresa's inseparable companion and secretary, assisting her during her last four convent foundations. In 1582, Teresa died in Ana's arms. Twenty-two years later, Ana was chosen to extend the Discalced reform into France, where she took the black veil as choir nun. During her sojourn in France she assisted in the foundation of five convents and served as the prioress of three: Pontoise, Tours, and Paris. Despite her humble background, she became a confidante and adviser to Cardinal Pierre de Bérulle, the leader of the Catholic restoration in France, and later to the Infanta Isabel Clara Eugenia, to whom Felipe II had ceded the government of the Spanish Netherlands. Ana's prayers were credited with saving Antwerp when the city was besieged by Protestant armies in 1622 and again in 1624. When she died at the age of seventy-seven, she left behind numerous autobiographical texts, histories of her order, religious guidebooks, over six hundred letters, and a small corpus of religious poetry.[3] She was beatified in 1917.

Teresa as Literary Mother

Ana, like Teresa and many other nuns in Counter-Reformation Europe, is the author of an account of her life in religion. Written at the behest of a confessor or spiritual adviser as part of the process by which the confessor judged the orthodoxy of the nun's spiritual experiences, these *vidas* were seldom produced as exercises in creative self-expression. In fact, the critical term *autobiografía por mandato* ("autobiography by mandate") has to a large extent replaced *autobiografía espiritual* ("spiritual autobiography"), a choice that foregrounds the notion of convent life-writing as a coercive discourse. It is evident that for some women, the mandate to write was distressing.[4] Writing nuns had ample reason to experience an "anxiety of authorship"; they had to convince themselves that by writing they were not succumbing to the temptations of vainglory.

They also had to face explicit prohibitions against women's participation in theological discourse, treading a thin line between recording their experiences and explicating them. Although a confessor's mandate to write could also function as a literary license, the *vida por mandato* nonetheless constitutes a genre in which the addressee exerts an unusual degree of influence over the discourse.[5]

Yet Ana seems to be remarkably untroubled by an anxiety of authorship. Such confidence undoubtedly derived from her conviction that she was the vehicle through whom Teresa's spiritual and historical legacy would be transmitted; indeed, she deemed her very capacity to transcribe the written word a supernatural gift from her Carmelite mother.[6] In Ana's first autobiography, begun around 1607, Teresa is ever present as both spiritual and writerly authority.[7] This double identification allows Ana to appropriate, ready-made as it were, Teresa's solutions to the double bind inherent in the confessional autobiography—the obligation to proclaim one's spiritual worth while demonstrating one's humility. One anecdote in particular illustrates the extent to which Teresa authorized Ana's life and life-writing. Readers of Teresa's *Vida* will remember that one of her most anguished experiences is occasioned when her confessor, who believes her visions are demonic illusions, orders her to "give the fig" (378) every time she sees a vision of Christ. For Ana, the conflict between priestly authority and inner experience is more easily resolved. When Ana's confessor warns her that her mystical transports are the effect of the devil, she writes:

> Yo fue [sic] a nuestra Santa que me dijese si era ansí, y díla cuenta de todo lo que me aví pasado. Y díjome que no tuviese pena, que no era demonio, que ella avía pasado por esa mesma oración, con los confesores que no la entendían. Con esto yo quedé consolada y creý que lo que la Santa me deçía era Dios. (1: 296; *Autobiografía A*)

> I went to our Saint and asked her to tell me if it was so, and I told her everything that had happened to me. And she told me not to worry, that it was not the devil and that she had gone through that same stage of prayer with confessors who didn't understand it. And I was consoled to hear this and I believed that what the Saint told me was from God.[8]

What is a major source of anguish in Teresa's autobiography is quickly dispensed with in Ana's confession. She feels no need to submit her visions and spiritual favors for priestly review since they have already passed muster in Teresa's eyes. Indeed, the confessor as addressee is notably absent from her autobiography, which begins with a simple invocation: "María, Josefe y nuestra santa madre Teresa de Gesús, en cuyo nonbre ago esto que me lo manda la santa obediençia" (1: 282; *Autobiografía A*) ("Mary, Joseph, and our holy Mother Teresa de Jesús, in whose name I write what holy obedience orders me to").

Ana, in fact, was capable of directly challenging the hierarchical assumptions of the confessor-penitent discursive relationship. During a period when her relations with her confessor, Pierre de Bérulle, were especially strained, she politely refused his request for a spiritual account: "En lo que v.m. me manda que le escriva de mi ynterior, suplico a v.m. me perdone y no me lo mande" (2: 236) ("Regarding the fact that Your Grace orders me to write to him of my interior life, I beg Your Grace to excuse me and not to order this of me").[9] In the absence of a compatible authorizing addressee for a text she obviously wanted to produce, she drafts her nephew, a theology student at the University of Paris, to fill the role:

> Zierto que esto, que io no lo escriuiera sino por hazeros plazer, como tanto que emportunás. Yestoime riendo, que me acuerdo de un quento que dezimos en español que "en la tierra de los ziegos el tuerto es rey." I así es esto, que sin ser preste le obedezco a falta de padres espirtuales, ya que todo ba tan atroze en mi soledad y pobreza. (1: 159)[10]
>
> Certainly, I would not write this except to give you pleasure, since you are so insistent about it. I'm laughing, because I remember a Spanish proverb that says "in the land of the blind, the one-eyed man is king." And that's the way it is, for even though you are not a priest I obey you since I lack spiritual fathers, since everything is so wretched in my solitude and poverty.

Here, Ana playfully (and quite audaciously) treats the coercive premise of "writing from obedience" as a formal convention.[11] Teresa's role as literary mother for Ana is, in sum, more than thematic or rhetorical. Teresa's example provided her daughter with the conviction that an account of her spiritual life had a significance that transcended the confines of the confessor-penitent relationship.

Popular Religion or Matriarchal Feminism?

Popular religion is a term that has proved both indispensable and exceedingly problematic for historians. It has been used, with varying emphases, to contrast the religious practices of the elite with those of the people, the beliefs of the learned clergy with those of the laity, and the magic of the medieval church with the abstract tenets of the Counter-Reformation.[12] Ana's religiosity reflects many aspects of popular religion. At the same time, her life illustrates the limitations of the binary oppositions on which this term is predicated.

Popular religion has been described as mechanistic and purposeful, as a system of beliefs and practices that have as their aim the harnassing of supernatural power for specific purposes: curing illness, warding off dangers, securing a good harvest, or assuring a speedy transit through purgatory (Swanson 136–40). In late medieval and early modern Europe, devotion to saints (those officially canonized as well as living men and women revered for holiness) was an important component of this purposeful religiosity. The cult of saints, as R. N. Swanson has explained, responded to a need for "human and humane intercessors" in this world and the next (35). In Ana's portrayals of Teresa, it is evident that her perceptions were shaped by assumptions about what a holy person could and should do. In Ana's eyes, Teresa was a saint with the power to heal, protect, intercede, and prophesy the future, *in vita* and *in morte.*[13]

The miracles Ana ascribes to Teresa may strike the modern reader as naive or even bizarre: Teresa heals Ana of fever; in Burgos, when the nuns are disturbed by the cries of a man whose boils are being lanced in the neighboring hospital, Teresa's blessing allows him to bear the treatment in silence; in need of a secretary, she infuses Ana with the ability to write in one day. Ana also testifies to the uncorrupted state in which Teresa's body was found when exhumed nine months after her death, and she gives detailed accounts of the curative properties of cloths impregnated with her bodily oils and the pieces of her body that were subsequently distributed among her followers.[14]

After Teresa dies, she assumes the role as saintly counselor to Ana. Although most of Ana's visions and locutions come from God the Father and Christ, Teresa comes in a close third, with the Virgin Mary following in fourth place. Teresa consoles Ana, offers her advice, and reveals the future to her, particularly as it pertains to the Discalced reform, reinforcing her decisions in the political struggles between various factions of the order.

This is not to say that Ana's construction of Teresa's sanctity was entirely predicated on ready-made models or traditional expectations. For all her reverence for Teresa's supernatural charisma, Ana was capable of appreciating her humane virtues—charity, patience, humility, courage in the face of physical danger and intimidation, and affability. Of the latter, she writes, "No era amiga de jente triste, ni lo era ella, ni quería que los que yvan en su conpañía lo fuesen. Deçía: 'Dios me libre de santos encapotados' " (1: 11; "Ultimos años de la madre Teresa de Jesús" ["The Last Years of Mother Teresa de Jesús"]) ("She did not take a liking to sad people, nor was she sad herself, nor did she wish those who accompanied her to be so. She used to say, 'God save me from gloomy saints' "). Ana's inclusion of a sense of humor in the catalog of saintly virtues is novel, to say the least.

But what, if anything, does Ana's devotion have to do with her understanding of Teresa's Christian feminism defined—for the sake of brevity—as Teresa's belief in the equality of men and women as witnesses to Christ and bearers of his message?[15] Does recognition of Teresa's charismatic power imply in any way an imperative for women's fuller participation in the church? Does not such an exceptionalist view of female power actually reinforce the notion of women's inferiority?[16]

A passage from a 1605 "Account of Conscience" ("Relación de concienca") suggests not answers but further paradoxes. Here, Ana describes a period in which she was overcome with anxiety about her ability to lead the reform movement in France:

> [E]stando en Pontues diziendo las oras, crezía en mi alma un gran deseo de dar gusto a Dios, si baliera algo; mas bía que no era sino un gusanillo que no sauía ni entendía nada, ni balía nada para Dios ni los hombres. Mas bía que ardía en mi corazón un deseo

> de hazer mis obras como diesen gloria a Dios y a mi santa madre Theresa de Jesús [. . .]. Sentía benía al alma una gran ternura y recogimiento, como que estaua Christo zerca de mí, y díjome: 'Ansí te quiero, sin ser ni sauer, para hazer por ti lo que io quiero, que los sauios del mundo con sus prudenzias umanas no me escuchan, porque piensan lo sauen todo.' (1: 126–27)
>
> While in Pontoise, saying the hours, there grew in my soul a great desire to give pleasure to God, if I was worth anything; but I saw that I was nothing but a little worm who neither knew nor understood anything, and that I was worthless to God and to men. But I saw that there burned in my heart a desire to do works that might give glory to God and to my holy Mother Teresa de Jesús [. . .]. I felt a great tenderness and recollection come over my soul, as if Christ were near me, and he said to me: 'This is how I want you, without being or knowing anything, in order to do through you what I wish, for the wise men of the world with their human prudence are not listening to me, because they think they know everything.'

Though Ana undoubtedly speaks from within patriarchal ideology, two factors allow her to overcome a paralyzing sense of inferiority: her belief that she is the heir to Teresa's apostolic mission to aid a church in crisis, and the conviction that men have failed that church. In a world turned upside down by religious wars, God is capable of doing extraordinary things through inferior vessels. Thus Ana affirms, with urgency, not her self-worth but her infused worth.

We might define these two strands of Ana's thought as "matriarchal feminism," the belief that she has inherited Teresa's mission and, to a certain extent, her charismatic power, and "state-of-emergency feminism," the conviction that God calls on women as reserve troops when masculine forces have let him down. These are, strictly speaking, expressions of a pro-woman rather than feminist argument.[17] That is, they are predicated on women's exercise of power in exceptional circumstances. Such pro-woman positions can, as Ana's personal history demonstrates, lead to confident self-assertion and practical leadership. And exceptions, when multiplied, have a tendency to raise a shadow awareness of the arbitrariness of gender roles.

Ana recounts that as a child she left church one day crying: "[D]ijéronme mis ermanas: 'Por qué lloras, niña?' Yo dije: 'Yo lloro porque no á predicado bien este Padre.' Y dijéronme: '¡Qué sabéys vos deso!' [y yo dije] 'si yo pudiera predicar, yo lo dijera mejor a lo que siento' " (1: 295; *Autobiografía A*) ("And my sisters said to me: 'Why are you crying, child?' And I replied: 'I am crying because that Father did not preach well.' And they said to me: 'What do you know about that!' and I said 'If I could preach, I feel I could have said it better' "). Is this merely a humorous example of Ana's ingenuous childhood piety, or an expression of the woman narrator's desire to do what the priest is doing poorly—to take up the fallen apostolic banner?

The subversive implications of this anecdote were not lost on one of Ana's confessors, Jerónimo Gracián. When he rewrote her autobiography in dialogue form in 1611, Gracián attributed Ana's tears to her inability to understand the preacher's fine points of theology.[18] In spite of Gracián's efforts at containment, Ana's anecdote illustrates how the Counter-Reformation campaign to instill reverence for the church had the unintended consequence of provoking women to question the limitations on their ability to serve that threatened church.

The Discalced Counter-Reformation

Ana's attitude toward feminine authority within monastic governance is similarly paradoxical. She supported the movement to place the Discalced convents more securely under masculine control, yet she defied an aristocratic cardinal over other issues of monastic jurisdiction. She favored restrictions on the nuns' ability to change confessors, but she also defended a quasi-sacramental role for prioresses as spiritual teachers and comforters. The inconsistencies in Ana's positions may well be due to her belief that the ultimate authority in these matters was Teresa's word not only in the written legacy but in Ana's specific recollection of conversations with Teresa in the last year of her life and in communications postmortem. Consequently, Ana's interpretation of the Teresian legacy was often particularist and personal.

After Teresa's death, the members of the newly independent Discalced Carmelite order became embroiled in a series of internecine quarrels over monastic governance. Although the disputes were not lacking in personal animosities and power plays, a fundamental source of conflict revolved around the issue of convent autonomy. Nicolás Doria, who succeeded Jerónimo Gracián in 1585 as provincial of the Discalced, was convinced that the original Teresian constitutions gave far too much autonomy to individual convents and left too many decisions to the discretion of the prioresses. Doria believed that the reform had lost its ascetic purity and was threatened by laxity and excessive familiarity between prioresses and the clergy who ministered to the convents. Several prioresses, allied with Gracián, appealed directly to the Holy See for approval of the "primitive" Discalced constitutions drafted by Teresa, and in 1590 Pope Sixtus V granted their petition with the brief "Salvatoris." But in the following year, Sixtus V's successor, Pope Gregory XIV, revoked "Salvatoris" and approved most of Doria's modifications.[19]

In this turbulent struggle, known by Carmelite historians as "the revolt of the nuns," Ana sided with Doria. As in other moments of crisis in her life, Ana's resolve was strengthened by her visions. In one such vision, Teresa appears before her weeping:

> Y díjome: "Mira, yja, las monjas que se me van de la Orden." Y mostróme muchas juntas en un locutorio que ablavan con seglares. Los de fuera eran rrelisiosos y seglares y qlérigos todos de otras Ordenes y ablando con ellos se bolvían las monjas negras como cuervos; y los de fuera tenían cuernos; las monjas tenían picos, como si propiamente fueran cuervos. (1: 312–13; *Autobiografía A*)

> And she said to me: "Look, daughter, my nuns are leaving the Order." And she showed me many together in a locutory who were speaking with laymen. Those from the outside were religious and laymen and priests from other orders, and as the nuns spoke with them they turned black like crows; and the outsiders had horns and the nuns beaks, just as if they were crows.

Here Ana's vision endorses Doria's conviction that the nuns should be strictly enclosed, protected from corruption by outsiders, whether laymen or clerics from other orders. The rebel nuns believed that Doria's proposals went against the Teresian ideal of a physically enclosed but spiritually open monastic system. Ana's refusal to take part in the nuns' rebellion is initially puzzling. As we have seen she clearly was not intimidated by authority. And she obviously placed Teresa's authority above that of the clergy. Why then did she accept the proposal to amend convent constitutions that had been written by Teresa herself? The most reasonable explanation for her pro-Doria position is that she felt that he was correct on one of the principal points of contention: the move to eliminate the nuns' freedom to choose confessors outside the order. Ana argued that Teresa had told her, one year before her death, that she wished the nuns to confess only with Discalced friars. Ana also believed that Teresa had become disillusioned with the flamboyant Gracián and wanted the more austere Doria to lead the reform after her death.[20]

On other issues, however, Ana took positions opposed to the Dorian counterreform. In her early years as a nun, Ana had been given to severe self-mortification (1: 293–94; *Autobiografía A*), but under Teresa's tutelage, she adopted the Carmelite mother's philosophy of discretion or moderation in penance and asceticism. Doria, as noted above, wished to restore ascetic fervor to the reform, and to this end he had attempted to abolish the hours of recreation after the midday and evening meals, when the nuns were permitted to gather and converse. Ana repeatedly wrote in defense of these temporary respites from the vow of silence as a necessary occasion when the nuns might be able to console one another with spiritual friendship.[21] The hours of recreation, furthermore, provided an opportunity for nuns to engage in a form of mutual spiritual pedagogy. Echoing Teresa, Ana appeals to Christ's conversations with the New Testament women as authorizing a feminine evangelical role (albeit *intramuros*): "[C]omo yço la samaritana, que, en gustando del agua viba, fue confesando el Hijo de Dios. Pues seamos samaritanas y cananeas, y publiquemos a Dios y su divina ley" (1: 555; "Conferencia espiritual" ["Spiritual Address"]) ("Like the Samaritan woman, who, drinking of the living water, went about testifying to the Son of God, let us be Samaritan women and Canaanite women and let us proclaim God and his law").[22]

Ana not only adopted Teresa's moderate stance toward mortification and ascetic rigor, she also assimilated many of Teresa's ideas on spiritual discernment, or the art of distinguishing true from inauthentic charismata. In particular, she subscribed to the Carmelite mother's physiological etiology for pseudomystical states. That is, she accepted that severe penance, in particular extended fasting and sleep deprivation, could produce delusionary raptures and visions.[23] As Ana recounts in her 1622 "Conferencia espiritual," "Oficio de criar novicias" ("The Novice Mistress"):

> En tienpo de nuestra Santa aconteçió que yendo a visitar un convento [. . .], avía allí una rrelisiosa de las que avía sacado la Santa de la Encarnaçión para fundar, y era tan santa al pareçer y sus açiones modestas y su oraçión; deçían los que la tratavan era ángel en la tierra; y casi se pasava sin comer y domir. Ella no tratava sino con aquel saçerdote que las confesava. Tienía [sic] grande espíritu de penitençia, y este saçerdote lo mesmo; púsola en grande perfeçión sus deseos y andavan en ella, y traýa a escusa de la perlada açiendo cosas sin liçençia. Y yendo allí—como digo—nuestra Santa, sospechóse no era buen espíritu. Yçolas algunas pruevas de obediençia, y luego conoçió andava[n] engañadas y que se perderían por aquel camino, y quitólas el confesor y mandólas comiesen y durmiesen. Yanque [sic] el mal espíritu las traý engañadas açiéndolas creer yvan bien y que serían perfetas por aquel camino, la Santa lo conoçió y se lo quitó con penitençias diferentes de mortificaçiones en que se aclararon y obedeçieron, y se quitó aquella santidad tan estremada, y de adelante yva como las demás; y si no fuera por la Santa, se perdiran [sic]. (1: 616)

> In the time of our holy Mother it happened that while visiting a convent [. . .] there was there one of the nuns whom she had taken from the Convent of the Incarnation for the foundation, and she was apparently so holy and so modest in her actions and her prayers that all who dealt with her said she was an angel on earth; she almost got by without eating or sleeping. She only dealt with the priest who confessed them. She had great desires to do penance, and this priest thought her desires a sign of great perfection and without the prioress's knowledge he allowed her to do forbidden penance. And while visiting there, as I say, our holy Mother suspected that this was not a good spirit. She tested their[24] obedience, and immediately realized that they were deceived and that they would be lost by taking that path, and she removed the confessor

> and ordered them to eat and sleep. And although the evil spirit had deceived them making them believe that they would be perfect by taking that path, our holy Mother recognized what it was and did away with it by giving them different penance and mortification which they obeyed and by which they were undeceived, and that very extreme sanctity was done away, and from then on they acted like all the rest; and if it hadn't been for our holy Mother, they would have been lost.

It is notable that Ana not only reproduces Teresa's mystical etiology but also testifies to a woman's capacity for discernment—the art and supernatural talent of distinguishing true from false spiritual desires and favors. Clearly, in this instance Teresa's gift of discernment was superior to that of the priest, who had misguidedly encouraged the nuns' enthusiasm.

If we consider the context within which this anecdote is embedded, however, we can see that its implications extend beyond matriarchal encomium. The subject of this particular spiritual address is the office of novice mistress; in it, Ana sets forth not only prescribed responsibilities of the office but also her philosophy of spiritual pedagogy. Following Teresa, Ana reiterates that one of the most important roles of the novice mistress is to guide her charges in their practice of mental prayer. Consequently, she stresses how important it is for novices to consult with and confide in their novice mistresses regarding the temptations, doubts, and perplexing sensations that often accompanied this practice. Up to the passage cited above, Ana has been writing for an exclusively female audience. But just after that passage she suddenly appears to be addressing both male and female religious:

> [E]n estos prençipios que aora estamos temo las mesmas cosas y veo apariençias dello[. . .]. Pues no es poco ni de poca ynportançia sumeternos al pareçer ageno.[. . .] Y anque tengan confesores, es menester que sean umildes y *abiertos* con sus perlados, que si lo son, *ellas* llevarán su carga y darán cuenta a Dios de sus almas.
>
> (1: 616–17; emphasis added)

> [I]n these beginnings in which we find ourselves I fear the same things may happen and I see signs of it[. . .]. It is of no little importance to seek another's opinion.[. . .] For although they have con-

> fessors, it is necessary for them to be humble and open with their priors and prioresses, for if they are, they will take on their burden and give God an account of their souls.

Although Ana's advice is directed collectively to nuns and friars, as she encourages them to be open ("abiertos" in the masculine inclusive plural) with their "prelados" ("priors" or "prioresses"), the switch to the feminine plural with "*ellas* llevarán su carga" ("*they* will take on their burden") suggests that her concern is that prioresses and novice mistresses in particular retain their role as spiritual guides, in accordance with the Teresian model. This apparently innocuous and grammatically incoherent advice on the role of novice mistresses encodes another example of Ana's selective resistance to the Dorian counterreform. Whereas Doria sought to limit prioresses' roles in spiritual guidance, Ana, like Teresa, insisted that prioresses (and novice mistresses) belonged on the front lines of discernment. Within this context, although the story of the deluded nuns testifies to Teresa exceptional gift of discernment, it serves as an authorizing precedent for a much broader spiritual magisterium for cloistered women collectively.

Ana also comprehended the significance of Teresa's egalitarian reforms. Perhaps her own modest origins and the opposition she faced when promoted from lay to choir nun made her an especially fervent defender of this aspect of Teresa's legacy. She not only ridiculed the class prejudices in the French convent but also insisted on the irrelevance of origins, whether racial or confessional, to those who chose a life in religion. When, in 1605, Bérulle opposed admitting an ex-Calvinist as novice, she protested in a letter to him:

> Sé yo, y las conozco, que desde antes que la Santa murise se rreçibieron algunas de las que llaman yrraelitas, y después también se an rreçibido. Pues si en España y en tienpo de nuestra santa Fundadora se yço por el bien de las que lo pedían con buenos deseos, en Francia ¿por qué no se á de açer con más rraçón?
>
> (2: 146)

> I know that before Santa [Teresa] died, some women (and I know them) called Israelites were admitted [into the order], and afterward some have been admitted as well. If in Spain, in the days of

> our holy Foundress, this was done for the good of those who requested it with good will, should it not be done with more reason in France?

Here Ana alludes to the fact that the Discalced order was originally not only founded but financed and patronized by many conversos, descendants of Spain's converted Jews. Unlike many other religious orders of the time, the Discalced initially had no purity of blood requirements until 1597, when they adopted statutes that would have exluded Teresa from joining the order she founded. In this letter, Ana displays considerable courage in reminding Bérulle of a history the order was doing its best to forget.[25]

Obedience and Authority

How was it that this unsophisticated peasant was permitted to exert such authority within the reform on a par with high-ranking ecclesiastics? Certainly, Ana's close association with Teresa as her nurse and comforter in the hour of her death conferred upon her a special authority. Ana may also have been protected, paradoxically, by her lack of sophistication. We have noted that Gracián, instead of censoring her autobiography, opted to rewrite a theologically "improved" version of it. As he proclaims:

> [Y]o soi vuestro confesor y padre espiritual, io os mando me digáis con llaneza lo que os preguntare; no aiáis miedo que os aga daño, pues bos con obedienzia e io con buen fin prozederemos. Y si vos dezís que sois como la araña, yo soi como el boticario, que sé hazer triaca de ponzoña. Si no azertáredes a dezir quál es berdadera reuelazión o quál falsa [. . .], a mí me toca declarároslo.
>
> (1: 220; "Diálogos sobre su espíritu" ["Dialogues on Her Spiritual Life"])

> I am your confessor and spiritual father, I order you to tell me simply what I ask; do not fear harm, since you will proceed with obedience and I with good intention. And if you say that you are like the spider, I am like the apothecary, for I know how to make the antidote from poison. And if you do not succeed in distinguishing the true from the false revelation [. . .], it is up to me to explain it to you.

Ana's "llaneza" ("simplicity") may have seemed easier to control and correct (and to offer the confessor more opportunities to demonstrate his expertise) than the much more articulate Christian feminism of rebel nuns like Ana de Jesús and María de San José.[26] Nor can we discount the possibility that her visions genuinely moved the elite who had authority over her. Although neither Ana nor the priests who directed her questioned the principle of women's necessary subordination to clerical discipline, on numerous occasions Ana was able to persuade, ignore, or defy male authority.

In sum, Ana's Christian feminism was partial in the sense that it was predicated, to a large extent, on the extraordinary circumstances in which women might participate as active members of the church. But it is also partial in the sense that it is personal, inextricably bound to her particular devotion to Teresa. For Ana, Teresa was a popular saint with the charismatic power to heal, comfort, and assuage anxiety. Yet the purposefulness of Ana's devotion was not spiritually self-centered, but rather infused with caritas, with concern for others as brothers and sisters in Christ. Ana's belief in Teresa as saintly intercessor did not prevent her from using Teresa as a model for apostolic service. In this ecumenical age, Ana's desire to save the souls of heretics for the universal church may have lost its power to compel, but we must recognize that it was this very apostolic desire, so often frustrated, that inspired women like Ana to question the limits of their imposed social roles.

Recognition of Ana's partiality can also serve as a corrective to our current, equally partial, perceptions of Teresa as feminist foremother. Many of Teresa's ideas—her defense of a feminine apostolate of prayer, her insistence on women's equal right to aspire to an intimate knowledge of the divine, her confidence in women's ability to guide and teach each other, her rejection of caste and class prejudice—are indeed signposts toward the future, to a still-evolving liberation of the church from masculinist ideology. Yet Ana's matriarchal feminism foregrounds the fact that many aspects of Teresa's immediate reception and influence were derived from older models of sanctity—models we might be tempted to ignore because of their failure to anticipate our contemporary understanding of Christian feminism. Finally, Ana reminds us that the history of feminism often has "only paradoxes to offer."[27] How else can we comprehend Ana's humble arrogance, her popular piety that captivated France's elites, and her partial awareness that wise men in the church had unjustly limited women's spiritual aspirations?

Notes

1. Ramón Menéndez Pidal's characterization of Teresa as someone who "spoke through writing" has been rejected by many Teresian scholars. I apply the notion of "orality" to Ana's writing with the caveat that writing is seldom a transparent transcription of speech and does not preclude rhetorical strategies, whether these have been absorbed through written or oral sources. Urkiza analyzes many features of Ana's writing—frequent lapsus calami, unconventional word divisions, rudimentary punctuation, phonetic patterns, and lexical idiosyncrasies—that indicate her late and partial assimilation of written norms. See Urkiza 1: 167*–200*.
2. On Teresa's struggle to define an acceptable form of apostolic service for women, see Bilinkoff, "Woman."
3. For the chronology of Ana's life in relation to the history of the Discalced Carmelite order, see Urkiza 1: 39*–73. Electa Arenal and Stacey Schlau provide an excellent introduction to her works and selections from her autobiography and letters in chapter 1 of their bilingual anthology *Untold Sisters.*
4. See, for example, Sherry Velasco's study of a seventeenth-century nun who was nauseated to the point of vomiting when forced to comply with her confessor's command to write. In addition to retrospective accounts of their lives (*vidas*), penitents wrote *relaciones* and *cuentas de conciencia*—accounts of specific spiritual favors or of their religious practices over a more restricted period of time. For discussions on the extent to which convent life-writing was a controlled discourse, see Arenal and Schlau 13–17; Myers; and Poutrin 115–34.
5. The concept of an "anxiety of authorship" is derived from Gilbert and Gubar (45–53). On the applicability of the concept to the writings of women religious, see Arenal and Schlau 14. On the theological climate in Counter-Reformation Spain that limited women's ability to participate in religious discourse, see Weber, *Teresa,* ch. 1.
6. As Ana declared in her testimony for Teresa's beatification proceedings, to help Teresa with her voluminous correspondence, Ana learned to write in one day, at the age of thirty-one, by copying out two lines of Teresa's handwriting (1: 50; "Declaración en el proceso de beatificación" ["Testimony for the Beatification"]).
7. Ana's autobiography exists in two versions; the first, known as *Autobiografía A* (Amberes), is a compendium of texts composed between 1607 and 1624. A shorter version, *Autobiografía B* (Bologna), was written at the end of 1622 (*Obras* 1: 280, 422).
8. English translations from Ana's works are my own.
9. For a concise summary of this conflict, see Arenal and Schlau 30–36.

María Pilar Manero Sorolla analyzes the relationship between Ana and Pierre de Bérulle on the basis of their correspondence. Bérulle (1575–1629), with his cousin Mme Acarie, was responsible for bringing the Discalced Carmelites to France. Although Bérulle was initially a devoted supporter of Ana's and had encouraged her to take the black veil, they disagreed bitterly over the issue of monastic jurisdiction.

10. This document is not a *vida*, properly speaking, but a brief account of mystical favors. It bears the heading "Relación sobre sus penas y los favores de Dios: Mayo de 1607" ("Account of Her Suffering and Divine Favors: May 1607").

11. Ana's nephew, Toribio Manzanares, had accompanied his aunt to Paris. In 1607, he was an unordained student of theology (*Obras* 1: 139n1). Urkiza's assertion that Ana wrote to "dar cuenta de su alma y vida mística a su prelado o confesor" (1: 280; introd. to *Autobiografía A*) ("to give an account of her soul and mystical life to her prelate or confessor") must be questioned in the light of the letter to her nephew cited above.

12. For an overview of this vexed terminology, see Burke. In early modern Spain, a neat distinction between the beliefs of the elites and popular groups is untenable. As Bilinkoff notes, "The humble and wealthy alike turned to a variety of hermits, prophets, mystics, and faith healers for help and comfort in their daily lives" ("Religion" 309).

13. Ana was, in fact, chastized by her confessor for praying to Teresa before she had been officially canonized. (See 1: 309; *Autobiografia A*.)

14. These and other miracles are related both in Ana's testimony for the beatification proceedings and throughout her autobiographies. On Ana's role in propagating Teresa's postmortem miracles and visions, see Eire 447–50, 481–87.

15. Though Christian doctrine held that women and men were spiritual equals in their capacity to achieve salvation, in Counter-Reformation Europe women were nonetheless prohibited from preaching, explicating Scripture, or appearing to teach doctrine. Influential theologians such as Melchor Cano even objected to women's practice of mental prayer. On the Counter-Reformation distrust of female sprituality, see Weber, *Teresa*, ch. 1. On Teresa's Christian feminism, see Slade, ch. 2; and Ahlgren, ch. 4.

16. Marina Warner has raised these issues in reference to the myth of the Virgin Mary, "who is theologically and doctrinally defined as wholly unique and yet set up as the model of Christian virtue" (334).

17. For the distinction between these two types of argument within the context of secular Renaissance feminism, see Jordan, introd. and ch. 1.

18. The implications of the autobiography—that the tears were a sign of apostolic fervor, to say nothing of the critique of bad preachers—are omitted, as Gracián endorses Ana's devotion to the Passion. The emphasis on the Passion may also have been Gracián's way of dissociating Ana from one of the features of the alumbrado heresy—their alleged lack of Christocentric piety. See *Obras* 1: 216–77; "Diálogos sobre su espíritu" ("Dialogues on Her Spiritual Life").

19. Although Teresa originally drafted new constitutions for her reform between 1562 and 1567, the version that the nuns sought to preserve was

one that had been approved by the first provincial chapter at Alcalá de Henares in 1581. For a more extensive discussion of the resistance to Doria's reforms, see Moriones; Smett 113–25; and Weber, "Administration."

20. See Ana's letter 2: 121 and "Defensa de la herencia teresiana" ("Defense of the Teresian Legacy") 1: 387–97. Ana did, however, support the nuns' freedom to choose confessors from among the Discalced friars.
21. See also the illuminating discussion on this topic by María Milagros Sánchez Díaz.
22. On the significance of the New Testament women as authorizing figures for Teresa and her followers, see Slade 57–64 and Weber, "Margins."
23. On Teresa's physiological views on pseudoecstatic states, see Weber, "Santa Teresa." On the prioress's role in discernment, see Weber, "Administration."
24. Here Ana switches unaccountably to the feminine plural. The most plausible explanation is that more than one nun was involved in this case of religious enthusiasm but that Ana began by thinking of one nun in particular.
25. Arenal and Schlau observe that a "notable feature of [Ana's] *Vidas* is the dignity accorded to peasants and servants" (33). Ana's own racial origins are unclear. Urkiza describes her parents as "cristianos viejos" or "Old Christians" without Jewish blood (1: 56*). However, Manero Sorolla maintains that she was a descendant of converted Jews (131).
26. Ana de Jesús and María de San José were removed from office and severely punished in the aftermath of the nuns' rebellion.
27. For discussions on the influence of teleological narratives on feminist history, see Ezell; Scott. I paraphrase Janet Todd, who warns against the tendency in feminist historiography to "avoid listening to a past that might be annoying through its resolute refusal to anticipate us" (46).

Works Cited

Ahlgren, Gillian T. W. *Teresa of Avila and the Politics of Sanctity.* Ithaca: Cornell UP, 1996.

Ana de San Bartolomé. *Obras completas de la beata Ana de San Bartolomé.* Ed. Julián Urkiza. 2 vols. Rome: Teresianum, 1981, 1985. [Vol. 1 includes historical accounts of the Carmelite reform, autobiographical texts, doctrinal writings, and poetry. Vol. 2 includes the letters.]

Arenal, Electa, and Stacey Schlau, eds. *Untold Sisters: Hispanic Nuns in Their Own Works.* Trans. Amanda Powell. Albuquerque: U of New Mexico P, 1989.

Bilinkoff, Jodi. "Popular Religion in Spain." *Oxford Encyclopedia* 309–10.

———. "Woman with a Mission: Teresa of Avila and the Apostolic Mode." *Modelli di santità e modelli di comportamento.* Ed. Giulia Barone et al. Turin: Rosenberg, 1994. 295–305.

Burke, Peter. "Popular Religion: An Overview." *Oxford Encyclopedia* 295–99.

Eire, Carlos M. N. *From Madrid to Purgatory: The Art and Craft of Dying in Sixteenth-Century Spain.* Cambridge: Cambridge UP, 1995.

Ezell, Margaret J. M. *Writing Women's Literary History.* Baltimore: Johns Hopkins UP, 1993.

Gilbert, Sandra M., and Susan Gubar. *The Madwoman in the Attic: The Woman Writer and the Nineteenth-Century Literary Imagination.* New Haven: Yale UP, 1979.

Jordan, Constance. *Renaissance Feminism: Literary Texts and Political Models.* Ithaca: Cornell UP, 1990.

Manero Sorolla, María Pilar. "Cartas de Ana de San Bartolomé a Monseñor Pierre de Bérulle." *Criticón* 51 (1991): 125–40.

Menéndez Pidal, Ramón. "El estilo de Santa Teresa." *La lengua de Cristóbal Colón y otros estudios sobre el siglo XVI.* 4th ed. Madrid: Espasa Calpe, 1958. 119–42.

Moriones de la Visitación, Ildefonso. *Ana de Jesús y la herencia teresiana.* Rome: Teresianum, 1968.

Myers, Kathleen A. " 'The Addressee Determines the Discourse': The Role of the Confessor in the Spiritual Autobiography of Madre María de San Joseph (1656–1719)." *Bulletin of Hispanic Studies* 69 (1992): 39–47.

Oxford Encyclopedia of the Reformation. Ed. Hans J. Hillerbrand. Vol. 3. New York: Oxford UP, 1996.

Poutrin, Isabelle. *Le voile et la plume: Autobiographie et sainteté féminine dans l'Espagne moderne.* Madrid: Velázquez, 1995.

Sánchez Díaz, María Milagros. "Las recreaciones en el Carmelo: Ana de San Bartolomé (Análisis de una 'Conferencia espiritual')." *Estado actual de los estudios sobre el Siglo de Oro.* Ed. Manuel García Martín et al. 2 vols. Salamanca: Universidad de Salamanca, 1993. 2: 931–39.

Scott, Joan Wallach. *Only Paradoxes to Offer: French Feminists and the Rights of Man.* Cambridge: Harvard UP, 1996.

Slade, Carole. *St. Teresa of Avila: Author of a Heroic Life.* Berkeley: U of California P, 1995.

Smett, Joachim. *The Post Tridentine Period, 1550–1600.* Darien: Carmelite Spiritual Center, 1976. Vol. 2 of *The Carmelites: A History of the Brothers of Our Lady of Carmel.*

Swanson, R. N. *Religion and Devotion in Europe, c. 1215–c. 1515.* Cambridge: Cambridge UP, 1995.

Teresa de Jesús. *Libro de la vida.* Ed. Otger Steggink. Madrid: Castalia, 1986.

Todd, Janet. *Feminist Literary History: A Defense.* Oxford: Polity, 1988.

Urkiza, Julián. Introducción general. Ana de San Bartolomé 1: 53*–205*.

Velasco, Sherry. *Demons, Nausea, and Resistance in the Autobiography of Isabel de Jesús, 1611–1682.* Albuquerque: U of New Mexico P, 1996.

Warner, Marina. *Alone of All Her Sex: The Myth and the Cult of the Virgin Mary.* New York: Vintage, 1983.

Weber, Alison. "On the Margins of Ecstasy: María de San José as (Auto)biographer." *Journal of the Institute of Romances Studies* 4 (1996): 251–68.

———. "Santa Teresa, Demonologist." *Culture and Control in Counter-Reformation Spain.* Ed. Anne J. Cruz and Mary Elizabeth Perry. Minneapolis: U of Minnesota P, 1992. 171–95.

———. "Spiritual Administration: Gender and Discernment in the Carmelite Reform." *Sixteenth Century Journal* 31 (2000): 127–50.

———. *Teresa of Avila and the Rhetoric of Femininity.* Princeton: Princeton UP, 1990.

Juana and Her Sisters: Female Sexuality and Spirituality in Early Modern Spain and the New World

Anne J. Cruz

Sor Juana Inés de la Cruz's life (1648–95) is generally lauded as an exemplary model of feminine subversion at a time when women, oppressed by a patriarchal social system, disposed of minimal personal options. Certainly, her strategy of entering the convent to liberate both mind and body from the social constraints imposed on most women in the early modern period allowed her an escape from the traditional role of wife and mother, as well as from that of women religious dedicated to daily prayer (Arenal; Arenal and Schlau). Yet Sor Juana's experiences were neither unique nor solitary: as Georgina Sabat-Rivers reminds us, Sor Juana maintained close ties with a number of women throughout her life, among whom we may count her female relatives, her friends and noble contacts, and, in particular, the three *virreinas* ("wives of the viceroys") who mentored her at court ("Mujeres" 4–5).

Through their support of and pride in Sor Juana's intellectual and artistic accomplishments, these women nevertheless projected onto the nun their own frustrated desire for emancipation since, unlike Sor

Juana, their activities were restricted to so-called feminine skills—sewing, weaving, knitting, cooking, and cleaning—that Mexican author Margo Glantz labels "labores de mano" ("handiworks"). Glantz finds that these crafts, which were meant to protect women from the moral risk of otherwise indolent hands, function similarly to the typical conventual activities of writing and of spiritual exercises.[1] Although these pursuits were, in the main, carefully directed, exploited, and in the case of writing, "deciphered" by the patriarchal hierarchy whose control over women extended from paternal authority at home to that of confessors in the convent, their practice nevertheless contributed to female empowerment and individuation. Thus, while Sor Juana richly deserves our admiration for her remarkable intellectual powers, her moral strength, and her personal courage, we should remember that she descends from and belongs to a long tradition of strong women, both in Spain and in the New World, whose creativity—indeed, whose very lives—gives witness to female resistance.

If Sor Juana succeeded even partially in eluding the rigorous social constraints of her time, it was because she could avail herself of the example and support, whether potential or articulated, of diverse female role models, from her medieval Spanish "mothers" to her contemporary baroque "sisters" in the New World. The religious and political upheavals that marked the epistemic split separating these two periods produced oppositional discourses, both misogynist and laudatory, that informed historical perceptions of the gender roles of religious women. Michel Foucault has proposed the seventeenth century as the moment when sexuality became repressed, bound to language, and subjugated in a discourse that in turn defined and delimited sexual practices (17). In Spain, however, because of the supposed threat of miscegenation posed by the country's ethnic and religious minorities, sexual control was enacted a century earlier. The religious ferment of the early sixteenth century in part explains women's contested agency in the arenas of sexual and spiritual heterodoxy against this subjugation.

Spain's political restructuring under the Catholic monarchs permitted the development of heterodox religiosity that also brought about a flowering of religious women, beatas, and visionaries. As the *devotio moderna* spread throughout southern Europe, Thomas à Kempis's popular *Imitation of Christ,* with a circulation in Spain of over 700 manuscript copies, responded to the decline of Scholasticism (Sáinz Rodríguez 119). Northern European spirituality was distinguished by an asceticism that isolated practitioners from ecclesiastical control, an autonomy later persecuted as one of the manifestations of heresy. At the time, however, and even though the Inquisition questioned the orthodox nature of their religious practices, female pietists achieved a level of power that encompassed ecclesiastical and political spheres. The visions of the Toledan beata María de Ajofrín, whose revelation of several priests' immoral behavior forcefully attacked clerical corruption, were accepted and promulgated by a frightened church hierarchy that feared future denunciations. On learning of her visions and stigmata, Toledo's Cardinal Pedro González de Mendoza, known for his religious laxity and political aspirations, quickly came to her defense. The beata's role in excoriating the religious leader, as well as her part against the Toledan Judaizers, demonstrates the power brandished by religious women when backed by church officials (Surtz, *Women* 84).

In effect, government and ecclesiastical authorities alike maintained a close watch on the potentially disruptive activities of religious women. Before Carlos V's arrival in Spain, Cardinal Francisco Jiménez de Cisneros, Queen Isabella's confessor, supported and disseminated the novel heterodox doctrines of many prophetesses and visionaries, all the while sustaining the queen's efforts to consolidate religious doctrine in the peninsula. Cisneros sought her approval to abolish the scandalous behavior that often erupted in convents by encouraging the nuns to return to their original rules. Although the cardinal intended to inculcate religious orthodoxy among women by doctrinal instruction, he was also instrumental in promoting religious women whose revelations and ecstasies marginalized them according to traditional church views.

Carlos V's arrival in Spain could not have been more propitious for the cardinal's aims. The event brought to the peninsula new and disparate religious influences from northern Europe, deflecting the Mediterranean's strongly Roman-Christian bias toward Burgundian mysticism and the Erasmian reform movement. According to Marcel Bataillon, this evangelical wave was spearheaded mainly by women (83). Some of their heterodox practices were sanctioned by the church and society; in Avila, five widows founded religious houses, named themselves abbesses, and willed benefices to their heirs (Bilinkoff, *Avila* 40–49). Other women became members of the alumbrados, the only heretical sect considered authentically Castilian and known for its controversial belief in sexual union as a means of reaching religious ecstasy (Burgos 34). The Inquisition would soon come to dread the numerous radical sects springing up throughout the country. At the time, however, Cisneros's advocacy of the mystical asceticism practiced by the Franciscans, though later condemned by the Council of Trent, promoted a liberal climate that allowed visionaries to prophesy outside the convent.

Although the Inquisition would eventually censure women's participation in the various religious movements, the extraordinary number of female visionaries during the period responded as much to the political as to the spiritual aspirations of the male circles of power. By becoming the women's protectors, religious and lay leaders simultaneously endeavored to legitimate their own power before the people and to communicate with the Godhead in a more direct manner through female visions and mystical experiences (Bilinkoff, *Avila* 15; Surtz, *Guitar of God* 2). Although medieval misogyny stressed that, given their mental deficiency and lack of religious education, women were singularly vulnerable to heterodox thoughts, by the early modern period, women's innocence and virtue were considered to endow them with the *docta ignorantia* attributed to mystics by medieval theology (Sánchez Lora 185). The period's religious ambivalence and inconsistency, which tolerated such heresies as crypto-Judaism, messianism, and Illuminism, also justified the protection of numerous beatas and religious women by religious and secular dignitaries such as Cardinal Cisneros and the emperor. Cisneros in particular supported and patronized several religious women, including the Benedictine nun Madre Marta; María de Toledo, "la Pobre"; Madre Juana de la Cruz; and Sor María de Santo Domingo, known by her epithet, "la beata de Piedrahita."

The mysticism of religious women was not the sole reason they attracted large numbers of followers, however. Women's sexuality not merely complemented their spirituality but indeed formed an integral part of their spiritual allure. Although feminine sexual power was at times viewed negatively, as in the case of Francisca Hernández (1519), blamed for beguiling a "mundillo" ("small world") of religious and ecclesiastics (Bataillon 177), female sexuality was regarded positively when sublimated and put to religious purposes, as in the case of Sor María de Santo Domingo (Bilinkoff, "Prophetess"). The ambivalent mix of sexuality and spirituality wielded by female religious in the early sixteenth century allows us to apprehend Glantz's analogy between women's convent writings and handiworks such as sewing, weaving, and cooking. To these typically feminine talents, I would add yet another, one we might call sexual dynamism.

It is not coincidental, after all, that these innocent household tasks are frequently employed euphemistically to denote sexual activity, or that sewing items such as needles, pincushions, thread, and buttonholes often serve as metaphors for genitalia. Golden Age literature abounds with examples: in *La lozana andaluza* ("Portrait of Lozana, the Beautiful Andalusian"), for instance, the young girl coyly announces her libidinal readiness by professing to ask her aunt for sewing supplies: "Señora tía yo aquí traigo el alfilelero, mas ni tengo aguja ni alfiler, que dedal no faltaría para apretar" (Delicado 180) ("Lady aunt, I have here my pincushion, but without needle or pin, and a thimble's not lacking with which to squeeze them").[2] Although considerably more decorous, the writings of female religious nonetheless do not fail to draw attention to the fears and anxieties stirred by women's sexuality and the methods of sublimation and demonization employed by both church and state for its control and repression. Nevertheless, religious women—in particular, prophetesses and women visionaries—often came into contact with male strangers and men outside their family circle. The encounters offered them the opportunity to, in Bataillon's words, "hacer sentir su atractivo" (179) ("display their appeal"). Yet male followers were seduced not only by women's physical attractions but by the prophesies and visions they articulated orally through accounts and sermons. Indeed, these women enjoyed extraordinary freedom of expression: some taught religious doctrine, like María de Cazalla, who read translations of the Epistles at the home of friends in Pastrana. Others followed Francisca Hernández in interpreting Holy Scripture and preaching the tenets of Illuminism (Nieto 295).

It is, then, ultimately through the use of language that religious women's sexuality is conflated and confused with their spirituality, as their visions are depicted and recounted to an avid public. Although presumed to be narrated through the voice of either Christ or the Holy Ghost, the scenes, while iconographically orthodox, often convey a forceful sensuality. One of Madre Juana de la Cruz's sermons from her "Book of Consolation," for example, describes God the Father playing with the Virgin's breasts: "Sube acá fija mía muy amada, e dame tus tetas, que fermosa heres e acabada sobre todas las fijas de Sión e de Gerusalén. [. . .] Dadme vuestras tetas, que quiero jugar con ellas" ("Climb up here, my beloved daughter, and give me your breasts, for you are lovely and more perfect than all the daughters of Zion and Jerusalem. [. . .] Give me your breasts, for I wish to play with them" [cited and translated in Surtz, *Women* 107–08]). Ronald Surtz clarifies that the sermon's eroticism, which partakes of the same sensuality as the Song of Songs, was perceived neither as offensive nor immoral, since the body of the Virgin was never meant to elicit carnal desire. Traditional Christian iconography establishes a connection between the Virgin's milk and the blood of Christ, devising the double intercession "whereby Christ shows his wounds to the Father, while the Blessed Virgin exhorts her son to intercede for sinners, showing him the breast with which she nursed him" (Surtz, *Women* 112). The commingling of purity and sexuality prohibited in earthly women is allowed the Virgin given her uniqueness and incommensurability (116).

Surtz argues that the latent eroticism connoted by the Virgin's naked breasts nonetheless transforms her innocence into a religious sensuality all the more threatening because of its ambiguity. In contrast to women's seduction that condemns men to sin, the virgin's eroticism is redemptive. Yet ironically, the Virgin's sensual image aligns her with Eve. She is only able to free herself from her role as "divine seductress" by the role's worthy purpose in the service of mankind's salvation (Surtz, *Women* 118). I would argue, however, that it is the women visionaries' same combination of sexuality and innocence, along with their freedom of expression, that entices both the secular nobility and ecclesiastics.

María de Cazalla, the sister of Juan de Cazalla (Cisneros's secretary and later bishop of Avila), was often invited to preach in the palaces of the nobility in Guadalajara (Bataillon 178–79). Like Francisca Hernández, she attracted a large male following, and Bataillon is careful to note that she did so without risking her honor (211). Another visionary, the beata Sor María de Santo Domingo, became famous for her ecstasies, during which she would remain many hours with her arms extended. Despite her lack of education, she was presumed to possess great intellectual powers; she would often refer to herself as Christ's companion and wife. Yet what also called the public's attention to Sor María was her abundantly long hair and her sensual movements while dancing. Her loose lifestyle, including sharing her home with her visitors and openly kissing them, occasioned four trials by her superiors. She was saved from opprobrium thanks to the protection of King Ferdinand and Cisneros, who often consulted her on their political projects. The decision by another patron, the duke of Alba, to erect a convent for her in Aldeanueva must be understood both as a means of publicizing the noble's generosity and of securing spiritual and dynastic benefits for his lineage (Bilinkoff, "Prophetess").[3]

In the 1520s, as we have seen, the female religious associated with the Illuminist sect, such as María de Cazalla and Francisca Hernández as well as Isabel de la Cruz and the duquesa del Infantado (coauthor of a book with Bishop Cazalla), all openly read and commented on Castilian translations of the Epistles and the Gospels (Bataillon 210–11). When the Inquisition actively began to prosecute practitioners of heterodoxies in 1533, it apparently managed to halt María de Cazalla's Illuminist proselytizing (Ortega Costa 587). By the 1540s, the Inquisition had prohibited translations of the New Testament, since its tribunals viewed the dissemination of the Bible in the vernacular as tantamount to spreading heresy (Bataillon 554). That this custom was difficult to suppress, however, is evinced by the duquesa de Soma's request, in 1543, for special permission from Cardinal and Inquisitor

General Juan Tavera to read from and keep an Italian Bible in her library (551).

The year 1559 marks the closure of Spain's liberal stance toward manifestations of diverse spiritual practices, as the Inquisition held numerous *autos de fe* in Valladolid and Seville and gained jurisdiction to prosecute ecclesiastic dignitaries. Further, the publication of its Index of forbidden books mirrored the antifeminist position maintained by the Council of Trent. Melchor Cano's theological treatise *La censura de Melchor Cano al* Catechismo *de Carranza* ("Melchor Cano's Censorship of Carranza's *Catechism*"), which denounced the tolerant anti-inquisitional position of the Toledan Archbishop Bartolomé Carranza and pitted intellectual dogmatism against an affective mysticism, contained a strong attack against women (Fremaux-Crouzet 140). By condemning mental prayer and biblical translations, Cano's treatise uncovers its misogynist belief in women's assumed intellectual inferiority: "Por tanto assi como es temeridad [. . .] assi es peligro confiar a mugeres y gente indocta la leccion de la divina escriptura" (540) ("It is both dangerous and reckless to confide the lessons of Holy Scripture to women and the unlettered"). The cases against "false" beatas and nuns, such as the notorious Magdalena de la Cruz, whom the Inquisition accused of demonic possession and processed in 1546, prove that the visions and prophesies so solicited and well received a few decades earlier were now perceived as scandalous and requiring inquisitional scrutiny (Imirizaldu 7).

In mid-century, sexuality and religion again commingle ambiguously, only this time with dire results for women religious. Following medieval misogynist thought, the Inquisition correlated heterodox religious practices with female sexual excess and attributed woman's so-called lack of reasoning to her legacy from Eve. It is important to note that women's confinement in the home or in the convent was encouraged not solely to control their sexuality but also to protect men from possible relapses into heterodoxy (Sánchez Lora 51). The perceived attraction of sexuality over spirituality fostered constant vigilance by inquisitors. Moreover, the need to control eroticism was internalized by women religious, who combined often extremist practices of spiritual exercises and corporal discipline.

The move from relatively unfettered religious practices to cloistered orthodoxy limited convent activities to such innocuous recreations as singing, putting on plays, and composing and reciting poetry. Examples of these activities are the poetry by Sor María de San José and the theater of Sor Marcela de San Félix, Lope de Vega's daughter (Manero Sorolla; Arenal and Sabat-Rivers). Santa Teresa finds that her nuns may no longer enjoy such books as Francisco de Osuna's *Tercer abecedario espiritual* ("Third Spiritual Alphabet") and Juan de Avila's *Audi, Filia* ("Take Heed, Daughter"), which she had been accustomed to reading as a child. In her *Constitutions*, therefore, she instructs the cloistered nuns to keep busy by dedicating themselves to the feminine and humble handiworks of sewing, embroidering, and writing (Rossi 96; Manero Sorolla 188n8). In *Way of Perfection*, however, she tries to instruct the Carmelite sisters in mental prayer to protect them from the accusations of their devotees and confessors, who feared mental prayer's mystical propensities.[4]

Yet Teresa, whose canonization celebrated her so-called virility, never fails to keep in mind the feminine attractions of her monastic community (Weber 17–18). Alert to the young women's vulnerability, she is quick to restrict male ecclesiastics' entrance to and presence in the Carmelite convents: "Nunca haya vicario, que tenga mano de entrar y salir, ni confesor que tenga esta libertad: sino que éstos sean para celar el recogimiento y honestidad de la casa, y aprovechamiento exterior e interior" (*Way of Perfection*, cited in Rossi 107) ("No vicar should enter and leave freely, nor should any confessor have the same liberty; he should instead serve to safeguard the seclusion and decency of the convent and its external and internal improvement"). Santa Teresa recognized the sexual threat of masculine presence, even that of older priests, as she comments to her confessor, Jerónimo Gracián, that her nuns "todas son mozas y créame padre mío, que lo más siguro es que no traten con frailes" (cited in Rossi 184) ("are all young, and believe me, father, it is safest that they not deal with friars").

Increasingly, the struggle between flesh and spirit was displaced in the convents through discourse, as women religious were required by confessors to disclose in writing their lives and visions. Foucault has noted that in the seventeenth century, all forms of sexual expression, including the description of such expression, were censored and expurgated by social institutions (16–18). At the same time, however, this restrictive economy allowed for discursive methods with which to examine the "insinuations of the flesh" (19) in all its aspects, correlations, and effects. In Spain, conventual discourses displaced the direct expression of female sensuality while formulating a new corpus of women's writing that would then be observed and scrutinized.

Recent feminist scholarship confirms the proliferation of religious women's writings at this time, both in Spain and the New World. If seventeenth-century religious women wrote so much, Isabelle Poutrin asserts, it was because male religious demanded it:

> La producción autobiográfica era, en la mayoría de los casos, una manifestación de los proyectos hagiográficos elaborados por los partidarios de una u otra "santa mujer," sea para promover su propia orden como lugar eficaz de santificación personal y colectiva, sea para expresar los intereses de un grupo familiar o de una localidad. (279)

> Autobiographical production was, in the majority of cases, evidence of the hagiographical projects designed by [male] supporters of one "holy woman" or another either to promote their own order as an effective place for individual and collective sanctification or to symbolize the interests of a family or location.

The mounting control over religious women's writings contrasts with the freedom of verbal and bodily expression manifested by earlier mystics and visionaries, even when mediated by male ecclesiastics. These autobiographical writings, however, were never passively produced but incorporated various stratagems that defended their authors from male power and what might otherwise be construed as a form of intellectual voyeurism. Thus Teresa, whose writings served as scriptural models to other female religious, chooses a "rhetoric of femininity" as a strategy to shield herself from accusations of intellectual dishonesty (Weber; Poutrin 277–78).

New Spain's repressive symbolic economy also controlled sexuality by means of discourses reformulating its practice. Female religious followed male-authored spiritual exercises that supervised their physical and mental activities through devotional readings and penitential acts such as fasts and discipline (Lavrin; Sabat-Rivers, "Ejercicios"). The moderation required by Ignatian *Spiritual Exercises* was replaced with self-imposed penances that made excessive use of hairshirts, whips, and near-starvation (Lavrin 170–71). Confession is also transmuted into a visual penitential discourse through which the body expresses its desire by means of the same act that erases and exorcises it. According to Colonial historian Asunción Lavrin, women's writing undergoes parallel regulation: "En el siglo diecisiete la escritura femenina conventual fue podada, escondida, subvertida, plagiada y olvidada" (156) ("In the seventeenth century, convent writing was pruned, hidden, subverted, plagiarized, and forgotten"). Foucault's thesis that sexuality is displaced and institutionalized by public discourses underscores the similarity between the control of feminine corporeality and of female-authored texts.

Like her contemporary sisters, Sor Juana Inés de la Cruz participated fully in penitential practices. In the last two years of her life, she submitted to a discipline that preoccupied her confessor, who, when asked about the nun's health, responded that "es menester mortificarla, para que no se mortifique mucho, yéndole a la mano en sus penitencias, porque no pierda la salud y se inhabilite; porque Juana Inés no corre en la virtud, sino que vuela" (cited in Lavrin 176n10) ("it is necessary to discipline her so she does not discipline herself too much and to limit her penitences so she does not ruin her health and cause herself harm; because Juana Inés does not walk but flies in virtue"). It is important to note, however, that the conflicts faced by Sor Juana and her sisters no longer developed—as they did for her medieval visionary mothers—from the complex ambiguity between religious heterodoxy and sexuality. Instead, both the religious body and its body of discourse are not only increasingly controlled but, as Lavrin comments, "penetrados, inspeccionados y juzgados por el confesor, quien manejaba tanto la creación como la destrucción de la evidencia en su tarea de promover observancia y espiritualidad" (173) ("penetrated, inspected, and passed judgment on by her confessor, who controlled both the power to create and destroy evidence in his duty to promote religious observance and spirituality").

Sor Juana's failed efforts to maintain her intellectual independence, in an atmosphere in which conventual privacy was consistently breached by the male ecclesiastical hierarchy, highlight even more the power wielded by discourse over sexuality. Most women religious anteceding Sor Juana were not known for their literary production; rather, their heterodox religious practices were confused and conflated with their sexuality. Sor Juana's struggle, however, was not between sexuality and spirituality but between her sexuality and her intellect. Indeed, the nun's entire corpus of writing underscores and defends women's intellectual capabilities. She maintained the battle for intellectual freedom throughout her life; the Mexican historian Elías Trabulse has documented her continued intellectual activity, rejecting the opinion held by most historians that she renounced her library willingly.[5]

Sor Juana's rebellious stance proves her strong connections to other women. Her satirical collection of enigmas (*Enigmas ofrecidos a la Casa del Placer*), written in 1693 and sent to an admiring group of aristocratic Portuguese nuns at their request, was, in effect, a spirited defense of her literary enterprise (Trabulse 147). The moving epithet with which she famously signed her avowal of faith, "Yo, la peor de todas" ("I, the worst of all"), was in fact a formulaic expression also utilized by other religious, both male and female (Lavrin 174). Moreover, the signed profession of faith continued to be utilized in the convents in the same document form, with blank spaces where the names of Sor Juana's "daughters" would be filled in at the beginning and at the end of the document.[6]

In conclusion, the male-controlled systems of power in the sixteenth century silenced the voices of beatas and visionaries, inveighing against their ominous sexuality and supplanting it with the discourses of the confessional, corporal discipline, and their own written disclosures at the behest of their confessors. Previously correlated to such domestic handiworks as sewing, weaving, embroidering, and writing, female sexuality was transmuted into the signs of physical self-violence and institutionalized through disciplinary discourses. In Sor Juana's resistance to the final renunciation of her will, she also writes, in her own blood, the last chapter in the lives of those religious women whose sexuality both affirmed and condemned the ambiguous and abiding power of their spirituality.

Notes

1. The application of these domestic tasks as a means of control was already recognized as early as the thirteenth century. Saint Dominic stipulated in his constitutions for the San Sisto convent in Rome that the nuns should dedicate themselves to manual labor when not praying or listening to sermons (Surtz, *Women* 3).
2. Unless otherwise noted, all translations are my own.
3. The reports of María de Santo Domingo's scandalous behavior must be weighed against the political struggles to reform the order. The Dominican hierarchy, which wished to isolate and displace those monastics advocating reform, considered the beata a perturbing and disruptive force (Surtz, *Women* 86).
4. Sáinz Rodríguez's view that mental prayer eradicates quietism and false mysticism (27) is contested by Sánchez Lora, who contrasts the Ignatian composition of place with San Juan de la Cruz's quietism and cites San Juan: "Everything the imagination can imagine and the reason receive and comprehend is not nor can ever be a means to union with God" (214–15).
5. According to Trabulse, Sor Juana continued as the convent's accountant, invested money under her own name, and willed her belongings to her niece.
6. I have found a copy of a 1763 document, based on that of Sor Juana, still used by the Convento Real de Jesús María, and signed by one of their nuns. The document is titled *Protesta de la Fee y renovación de los votos religiosos que hizo y dejo escripta con su sangre la M. Juana Ines de la Cruz, Monja Professa de S. Geronimo de Mexico. Reimpressa A Expensas de la M. Maria Josepha de San Ignacio, Religiosa Professa de el Convento Real de Jesus Maria, por los Herederos de la Viuda de D. Joseph de Nogal. Año de 1763.*

Works Cited

Arenal, Electa. "The Convent as Catalyst for Autonomy." *Women in Hispanic Literature: Icons and Fallen Idols.* Ed. Beth Miller. Berkeley: U of California P, 1982. 147–83.

Arenal, Electa, and Georgina Sabat-Rivers, eds. *Sor Marcela de San Félix, hija de Lope de Vega: Obra completa.* Barcelona: PPU, 1988.

Arenal, Electa, and Stacey Schlau, eds. *Untold Sisters: Hispanic Nuns in Their Own Works.* Albuquerque: U of New Mexico P, 1989.

Bataillon, Marcel. *Erasmo y España: Estudios sobre la historia espiritual del siglo XVI.* Trans. Antonio Alatorre. Mexico City: Fondo de Cultura Económica, 1983.

Bilinkoff, Jodi. *The Avila of Saint Teresa: Religious Reform in a Sixteenth-Century City.* Ithaca: Cornell UP, 1989.

———. "A Spanish Prophetess and Her Patrons: The Case of María de Santo Domingo." *Sixteenth Century Journal* 23 (1992): 21–34.

Burgos, Jesús Alonso. *El luteranismo en Castilla durante el siglo XVI.* San Lorenzo de El Escorial: Swan Avantos and Hakeldama, 1983.

Cano, Melchor. *La censura al* Catechismo *de Carranza: Documentos inéditos del proceso de Carranza: Archivo documental español.* Ed. J. I. Tellechea Idígoras. Madrid: Real Academia de la Historia, 1981.

Charnon-Deutsch, Lou, ed. *Estudios sobre escritoras hispánicas en honor de Georgina Sabat-Rivers.* Madrid: Castalia, 1993.

Delicado, Francisco. *La lozana andaluza.* Ed. Bruno Damiani. Madrid: Clásicos Castalia, 1969.

Foucault, Michel. *The History of Sexuality: Volume I: An Introduction.* New York: Vintage, 1980.

Fremaux-Crouzet, Annie. "L'antifeminisme comme theologie du pouvoir chez Melchor Cano." *Hommage à Louise Bertrand (1921–1979).* Paris: Belles Lettres, 1983. 139–85.

Glantz, Margo. "Labores de manos: ¿Hagiografía o autobiografía?" Poot-Herrera 21–33.

Imirizaldu, Jesús. *Monjas y beatas embaucadoras.* Madrid: Editora Nacional, 1977.

Lavrin, Asunción. "Espiritualidad en el claustro novohispano del siglo XVII." *Colonial Latin American Review* 4 (1995): 155–79.

Manero Sorolla, María Pilar. "La poesía de María de San José (Salazar)." Charnon–Deutsch 187–222.

Maravall, José Antonio. "La oposición político-religiosa a mediados del siglo XVI." *La oposición política bajo los Austrias.* Barcelona: Ariel, 1972. 55–92.

Nieto, José C. "The Heretical Alumbrados Dexados: Isabel de la Cruz and Pedro Ruiz de Alcaraz." *Revue de littérature comparée* 52 (1978): 293–313.

Ortega Costa, Milagros. *Proceso de la Inquisición contra María de Cazalla.* Madrid: Fundación Universitaria Española, 1978.

Poot-Herrera, Sara, ed. *"Y diversa de mí misma entre vuestras plumas ando." Homenaje Internacional a Sor Juana Inés de la Cruz.* Mexico City: Colegio de México, 1995.

Poutrin, Isabelle. "Juana Rodríguez, una autora mística olvidada (Burgos, siglo XVII)." Charnon-Deutsch 268–84.

Rossi, Rosa. *Teresa de Avila: Biografía de una escritora.* Barcelona: Icaria, 1984.

Sabat-Rivers, Georgina. "Ejercicios de la Encarnación: Sobre la imagen de María y la decisión final de Sor Juana." *Literatura mexicana* 1 (1990): 349–71.

———. "Mujeres nobles del entorno de Sor Juana." Poot-Herrera 1–19.

Sáinz Rodríguez, Pedro. *Introducción a la historia de la literatura mística en España.* Madrid: Espasa-Calpe, 1984.

Sánchez Lora, José L. *Mujeres, conventos y formas de la religiosidad barroca.* Madrid: Fundación Universitaria Española, 1988.

Surtz, Ronald E. *The Guitar of God: Gender, Power, and Authority in the Visionary World of Mother Juana de la Cruz, 1481–1534.* Philadelphia: U of Pennsylvania P, 1990.

———. *Writing Women in Late Medieval and Early Modern Spain: The Mothers of Saint Teresa of Avila.* Philadelphia: U of Pennsylvania P, 1995.

Trabulse, Elías. "El silencio final de Sor Juana." *Sor Juana y Vieira: 300 años después.* Ed. Koldobika Josu Bijuesca et al. Anejo de la revista *Tinta,* 1998. Santa Barbara: Center for Portuguese Studies, 1998. 143–55.

Weber, Alison Parks. *Teresa of Avila and the Rhetoric of Femininity.* Princeton: Princeton UP, 1990.

"No Doubt It Will Amaze You": María de Zayas's Early Modern Feminism

Lisa Vollendorf

In her two-volume framed novella collection, María de Zayas y Sotomayor (1590–?) communicates an acute awareness of the difficulties faced by women in seventeenth-century Spain. Zayas's collection, entitled *Novelas amorosas y ejemplares* (*Enchantments of Love*) (1637) and *Desengaños amorosos* (*Disenchantments of Love*) (1647), employs a variety of strategies for criticizing women's secondary status in society. The preface to the *Novelas amorosas* anticipates this pro-woman agenda by offering a defense of women's intellectual equality with these opening lines:

> Quién duda, lector mío, que te causará admiración que una mujer tenga despejo, no sólo para escribir un libro, sino para darle a la estampa, que es el crisol donde se averigua la pureza de los ingenios; porque hasta que los escritos se rozan en las letras de plomo, no tienen valor cierto [. . .]. (21)
>
> Oh my reader, no doubt it will amaze you that a woman has the nerve, not only to write a book but actually to publish it, for

> publication is the crucible in which the purity of genius is tested; until writing is set in letters of lead, it has no real value.
>
> (*Enchantments* 1)[1]

Laying claim to intellectual and artistic production, Zayas shrugs off the fools ("algunos necios") who disparage women's intellect (21). She also plays on chivalric codes, reeling in the readers of this female-authored text with reminders of their obligation to treat women with respect. Clearly, these introductory pages are designed to impress the reader with the author's rhetorical sophistication. At the same time, Zayas uses this rhetoric, just as she uses the texts that follow, to convince the Spanish reading public of women's integrity and value.

What is most intriguing about Zayas's texts is not, as she puts it, that "a woman has the nerve, not only to write a book but actually to publish it," but that a Spanish woman living in the seventeenth century wrote fiction that is guided by a complex, unapologetic feminist point of view. The feminism that informs these texts must be understood in terms of the early modern period. Unlike what we in the early twenty-first century take to be a fully developed feminist consciousness, Zayas exhibits a specifically early modern sensibility. While she protests the treatment of women in society, she does not call for a complete reconceptualization of the patriarchal social structure. However, Zayas advocates women's access to education and arms, promotes women's intellectual equality, and criticizes misogyny. Her female characters denounce men for treating women badly, and her texts denounce society for failing to protect and nurture women.

With a message based on protest and social reform, Zayas's texts advocate better treatment of women—including improved access to the judicial and educational systems—in the existing society. The texts do not present or endorse an alternative social organization. Rather, Zayas points out the many ways that the culture denies women the basic rights accorded to men and suggests significant change at both the behavioral and structural levels. A well-known statement by Laura, protagonist of "La fuerza del amor" ("The Power of Love"), encapsulates one strain of Zayas's feminist message. Addressing the "vain legislators of the world" who refuse women access to education and arms, Laura accuses men of purposefully debilitating women: "vais enflaqueciendo nuestras fuerzas con los temores de la honra, y el entendimiento con el recato de la vergüenza, dándonos por espadas ruecas, y por libros almohadillas" (*Novelas* 241–42) ("you weaken our strength with fears about honor and our minds with exaggerated emphasis on modesty and shame. For a sword, you give us the distaff, instead of books, a sewing cushion" [175]). In this and other comments, Zayas's characters blame women's powerlessness on behavioral codes that constrain women and, more generally, on women's exclusion from full participation in social (e.g., legal and educational) processes. It is with the understanding that Zayas articulates feminist ideas without striving for a full-scale reorganization of all patriarchal social structures that she can be understood as a feminist.[2]

Given this feminist didacticism, the modern reader may be surprised by the popularity of Zayas's fiction: with over ten editions in Spain and a similar number of translations and adaptations in other western European countries in the seventeenth century alone, Zayas's novella collection was a best-seller by any standard.[3] The tantalizing combination of sex, violence, and pro-woman politics has made these novellas both popular and controversial, as the collection's publishing history shows. Despite being regularly edited and reissued for over two hundred years, the collection suffered a major setback in the 1850s. At that crucial moment of canon formation, the novellas were deemed vulgar, lewd, and so inappropriate that they were not reprinted in their entirety until one hundred years later.[4] Yet the proliferation of scholarly articles on Zayas and her recent inclusion in university curricula reveal a belated recognition of this important figure in Spain's feminist history.

Very little is known about María de Zayas. A member of the nobility, she was born in 1590, but the year of her death has never been confirmed. She seems to disappear from the historical record after the publication of the *Desengaños amorosos* in 1647. Zayas's unusual status as an educated, creative, intellectual woman who did not live in a convent continually draws critics and readers to speculate on her personal history. Since the protagonist of her collection enters the convent after suffering her own "disenchantment in love," many critics have made comparisons between the fictional character and the author herself.

Some have said that Zayas must have become disillusioned—either with love or with the literary scene—and entered a convent. This is pure conjecture, however. Based on the multiple editions of her works and on laudatory poems written by prominent authors of the period, we can infer that she enjoyed tremendous success in the public book market as well as in private literary circles. All told, this is little information for a figure of such import.[5]

The impulse to explain Zayas's life attests to her unique status as a popular woman writer in a time when most women had no education whatsoever. Moreover, it is also a testament to the allure of Zayas's fiction that scholars continue to engage in vigorous polemics over the formal, thematic, and ideological elements of her publications. In the 1980s and 1990s, most scholarship addressed the feminism of the texts, as scholars debated the meaning of Zayas's political messages. The vigor of the debate can be seen in a quick review of varying opinions about the author's work. Susan Griswold sees Zayas's feminism as purely rhetorical posturing (100), for example, while Susan Paun de García explains the focus on deception and violence in the *Desengaños amorosos* as tied to the author's soured relationship with her peers (49). Many critics credit Zayas with high levels of literary sophistication that reinforce her feminist didacticism (see Boyer; El Saffar; Williamsen), while Marina Brownlee asserts that Zayas's "literary project is ultimately problematic (unresolved) in terms of gender" ("Subjectivity" 164).[6]

Since readers acknowledge the feminist discourse present throughout the novella collection, the most pressing question in its simplest manifestation still seems to be, Is she or isn't she a feminist? More precisely, to what extent do this author's texts cogently represent pro-woman ideologies and suggestions for social reform? One aspect of the texts that frustrates those of us in search of a satisfying answer to this question is the representation of violence (and violated female bodies) in both volumes. I suggest that this use of violence holds the key to a more thorough understanding of Zayas's feminism. In looking to her representations of violence in conjunction with the overt didacticism of the texts, we can decipher Zayas's innovative, body-based feminism out of the most striking aspects—acerbic cultural criticism and graphic depictions of violence—that appear in her fiction.

An overview of the two volumes that constitute this novella collection highlights Zayas's concern with women's issues and provides a framework for thinking about Zayas's own version of early modern feminism. The *Novelas amorosas* is a series of ten novellas called *maravillas* ("enchantments"), presumably to distinguish them from the myriad other novellas written in the period. These tales are told by male and female characters who attend a soiree convened to entertain the protagonist of the frame tale, Lisis, who is recovering from a severe fever. Although these claim to be tales about the lighter side of love and desire—about the "enchantments of love"—there is ample evidence of problems between men and women. In the frame tale, Lisis's suitor leaves her for another woman, and in the tales themselves, several women are abused both physically and emotionally by men.

In "El prevenido, engañado" ("Forewarned but Not Forearmed"), the threat that women's sexuality and intelligence pose to men emerges in a scene involving violence and sex. The male protagonist, Fadrique, finds his lover, Violante, in flagrante delicto with a young man. Fadrique freezes with fear when the man points a shoe at him as if it were a gun. Violante then laughs uncontrollably at the absurd situation. The twice-insulted hero reacts with violence:

> Desto más ofendido el granadino que de lo demás, no pudo la pasión dexar de darle atrevimiento, y llegándose a Violante la dió de bofetadas, que la bañó en sangre, y ella perdida de enojo le dixo que se fuese con Dios, que llamaría a su cuñado, y le haría que le costase caro. (*Novelas* 203)
>
> The gentleman from Granada felt more humiliated by her laughter than by anything else. His rage exploded; he rushed over to Doña Violante and struck her in the face, bathing it in blood. Furious, she told him to get out, she'd call her brother-in-law, she'd make Don Fadrique pay dearly. (143)

Rather than stop this abuse when Violante threatens to call for help, Fadrique continues to take out his anger on her, "asiéndola de los cabellos y trayéndola a mal traer, tanto, que la obligó a dar gritos" (203) ("grabbing her by the hair and beating her until she was forced to scream" [143]).[7] The emotional and physical dynamics of violence are laid out in this and other scenes in which men abuse women. Through these descriptions we see that Zayas's male characters find their motivations and justifications for violence in their own hostile, proprietary attitudes toward women.[8]

Other characters suffer violence in the *Novelas amorosas*: Laura in "La fuerza del amor" is beaten by her husband; Hipólita in "Al fin se paga todo" ("Just Deserts") is raped by her brother-in-law; and two women avenge themselves by killing the men who wronged them. While the *Novelas amorosas* has considerably less violence than its companion volume, the mix of sex, violence, and aggression in some of its tales typifies the representations of gender relations in the *Desengaños amorosos*. As in the *Desengaños*, some men in the *Novelas* are depicted as dangerous in their relationships with women. Such characterizations and scenes in the midst of the "amorous tales" plant the seeds for the critiques of men and society that are the driving force of the second volume.

Published ten years after the *Novelas amorosas*, the *Desengaños amorosos* has a decidedly different focus from its predecessor. The second volume is tied to the first through the continuation of the frame tale and the focus on gender relations. These ten tales—now called "disenchantments"—air women's concerns and insert women into the dominant discourses of literature and social politics. Only women are allowed to narrate in this volume, and at Lisis's mandate, they must tell so-called true tales of men's deceptive treatment of women. The primary narrator and some of the characters tell us that the *Desengaños amorosos* has the stated purpose of intervening in masculinist traditions. This intention finds its most direct expression at the beginning of the volume, when the principal narrator indicates that Lisis's motivation in having her female guests give voice to these tales is

> volver por la fama de las mujeres (tan postrada y abatida por su mal juicio, que apenas hay quien hable bien de ellas). Y como son los hombres los que presiden en todo, jamás cuentan los malos pagos que dan, sino los que les dan. (118)

> to defend women's good name (so denigrated and defamed by men's bad opinion that there is scarcely anyone who speaks well

> of them). Because men preside over everything, they never tell about the evil deeds they do, they only tell about the ones done to them. (37)

Forming part of a long-standing tradition of the defense of women seen in such diverse writers as Boccaccio, Christine de Pisan, and Moderata Fonte, Zayas denounces men for giving women short shrift. Taking the convention of the defense as a starting place for a more probing critique, the *Desengaños amorosos* does much more than draw attention to the literary traditions that devalue women. Replete with examples of misogyny and injustice, these novellas challenge social institutions and cultural traditions for their denigration and exclusion of women.

The shift in purpose from entertainment in the *Novelas* to education and intervention in the *Desengaños* is accompanied by a shift in content. Female characters narrate numerous representations of violence and criticize men for their unjust treatment of their wives, lovers, daughters, and sisters. The rise in violence in the second volume, where criticism of men's behavior and of women's secondary status comes to the fore, coincides with the sharpened didacticism of the *Desengaños.* Zayas literalizes the repercussions of injustice through relentless representations of its material effects on the body. And the material consequences of violence are lethal: only four out of the ten tales told in the *Desengaños amorosos* feature a female protagonist who survives men's abuses. While the other heroines and many of their sisters perish, the four survivors join the convent in order to escape the perils of alliances with men. All told, nearly three dozen characters fall victim to violence in the entire collection, and most are the women in the *Desengaños.*

Through the repetition of wife murder in the *Desengaños* Zayas articulates a criticism of the factors that motivate men to violence and of the social codes that sanction such acts. In "Mal presagio casar lejos" ("Marriage Abroad, Portent of Doom"), four wives die at the hands of their husbands. Three of the murdered women are sisters, the first of whom, Doña Mayor, is killed by her Portuguese husband. Searching for an excuse to kill Mayor, the husband writes a love letter to his wife and signs it with another man's signature. With this proof of marital infidelity in his wife's hands, the husband stabs her to death. Leonor, the second oldest sister, and her four-year-old child die similarly horrible deaths. Angry at his wife for having innocently praised another man, Leonor's Italian husband enters her room while she is washing her hair:

> entró el marido por una puerta excusada de un retrete, y con sus propios cabellos, que los tenía muy hermosos, le hizo lazo a la garganta, con que la ahogó, y después mató al niño con un veneno, diciendo que no había de heredar su estado hijo dudoso. (339)
>
> her husband came in through the dressing room door and with her own hair, which was very beautiful, he made a noose around her neck and strangled her. Then he poisoned the little boy, saying that he didn't want a child of questionable background to inherit his estate. (244)

As "Mal presagio" progresses, other men act just as violently as the husbands who twist the honor code to justify wife murder. While this novella about the dangers of marrying abroad might be read as xenophobic, it is crucial to note that misogyny—not nationalism—is the only factor that explains the violence throughout the tale. If two Spanish sisters are killed by foreign husbands who fabricate the women's infidelity (and yet another sister dies from injuries sustained during one of these murders), two other women—the youngest sister Blanca and her Flemish sister-in-law Marieta—are killed later on different pretexts. Marieta's husband and father conspire to garrote her to death and then leave her body at the dinner table for all to see. After this spectacle, Blanca correctly foresees her own murder.

Several months later, Blanca finds her husband in bed with his male page. With this discovery, her fate is sealed, for now her husband has an ostensible excuse for desiring her dead. Before her brother can arrive to take her away to safety, Blanca's husband and father-in-law bleed her to death: "[L]a abrieron las venas de entrambos brazos, para que por tan pequeñas heridas saliese el alma, envuelta en sangre, de aquella inocente víctima, sacrificada en el rigor de tan crueles enemigos" (*Desengaños* 363) ("They opened the veins in both arms so that through those tiny wounds the soul of the innocent victim might ooze forth, dripping blood, sacrificed to the cruelty of such harsh enemies" [267]).

Clearly meant to sway the reader's sympathy toward the victims, the language of sacrifice appears in many descriptions of the female characters. The progression in this particular tale from men's fabricated excuses for violence to their undisguised revulsion for women speaks to the large-scale cultural indictment of men and misogyny in Zayas's oeuvre.

The graphic descriptions of women's violated bodies confirm that Zayas is intensely engaged with both the aesthetic and the political impact of her highly didactic texts. Such representations emphasize the repercussions of violence and injustice, showing women suffering material (that is, bodily) consequences of cultural wrongs. One of Zayas's strategies for emphasizing women's victimization is to appropriate rhetorical tropes of feminine beauty. She redeploys the language of love to describe acts of violence against women. In "La fuerza del amor," for example, Laura complains about her adulterous husband. Diego hears her and

> acercándose más a ella y encendido en una infernal cólera, le empezó a maltratar de manos, tanto que las perlas de sus dientes presto tomaron forma de corales, bañados en la sangre que empezó a sacar en las crueles manos. (*Novelas* 238)

> [o]vercome by an infernal rage, he rushed over to her and struck her so violently that the white pearls of her teeth, bathed in the blood shed by his angry hand, looked instead like red coral. (172)

This passage exemplifies Zayas's subversive appropriation of conventional Petrarchisms: violence transforms women's pearl white teeth into the red coral usually reserved for seductive lips or healthy cheeks.

Social commentary communicated through a critique of the lack of integrity of the female body also appears in "Al fin se paga todo." In this tale in the *Novelas amorosas,* the protagonist Hipólita is raped by her brother-in-law. Hipólita subsequently kills the rapist. When she appeals to her ex-lover for help, he undresses her and beats her with his belt. The frame narrator describes Hipólita's wounded body as it is revealed to the man who rescues her in the street: "la hermosa dama mostró a don García lo más honesta y recatadamente que pudo los cardenales de su cuerpo, que todos o los más estaban para verter sangre" (323) ("As modestly and as chastely as she could, the beautiful lady showed Don García horrible bruises all over her body. They looked like they were ready to burst open and gush blood" [237]).

The image of Hipólita's gaping (and beautiful) body is similar to that of the poisoned wife Camila in "La más infame venganza" ("Most Infamous Revenge"). This tale in the *Desengaños amorosos* describes the difficulties faced by another rape victim, Camila. She is poisoned by her husband in retaliation for her bodily corruption. Rather than die immediately, "[Camila] hinchóse toda con tanta monstruosidad, que sus brazos y piernas parecían unas gordísimas columnas, y el vientre se apartaba una gran vara de la cintura" (195) ("her whole body [swelled] monstrously: her arms and her legs looked like huge pillars and her stomach distended at least a rod from her waistline" [108]). The juxtaposition of beauty with violence is again striking in these passages. Like martyrs represented in hagiography, many of Zayas's female characters suffer tremendous physical abuse, yet they often transcend their victimization by maintaining emotional and corporeal integrity.[9]

Through this politicized aesthetic, Zayas expresses a sometimes contradictory and problematic, yet overwhelmingly cogent feminist ideology. While some authors, such as Calderón, Lope, and Cervantes, expose the many ways in which men exploited and controlled women, Zayas stands out as the Spanish writer of the period who most intensely and defiantly explores the issues facing women in society. Unique in Spain, much of Zayas's feminism falls squarely within the boundaries of western European feminism of the period. Like the texts analyzed in Constance Jordan's *Renaissance Feminism*—the most complete book on western European feminist intellectual history to date—Zayas's novellas seek a better place for women in society.[10] In accordance with Jordan's description of early modern feminism, Zayas writes fiction "devoted to securing for women a status equal to that of men" (11). Zayas advocates a guarantee of safety, education, and justice for women, and a guarantee of women's autonomy over their bodies and minds.

Zayas stands out among her male and female peers throughout western Europe for her focus on women's lives through the lens of bodily experience. As we have seen, many of the protests against individual men's treatment of women and against women's exclusion from social justice find their articulation in representations of violated bodies. Among many specific criticisms in the novellas, we find male characters indicted for speaking badly of women (e.g., introduction to the *Desengaños amorosos*), for acting violently toward women (e.g., "Mal presagio casar lejos"), and for denying women the right to self-defense through education and arms (e.g., "La fuerza del amor").

While the descriptions of male violence and female victimization might suggest otherwise, by no means does Zayas limit herself to a one-dimensional portrayal of social ills. The evocation of reader sympathy through violence and through direct appeals for change relies at least partially on a heterogeneity of characterization. Individual subjects with markedly different personalities inhabit the tales, and their actions prevent us from concluding that Zayas depends on an uncomplicated schema in which men are evil and women are good. Occasionally, frame tale characters criticize women and praise men. While many women are portrayed as innocent victims, others get away with love affairs and even murder. Most of the female characters are chaste and virtuous, but some openly and enthusiastically explore their sexual desires. While these diverse characterizations expand the social criticism made patent by repeating complaints about women's lack of access to education, arms, and justice, they broaden the political message by suggesting that problems lie with individuals as well as with society. Through this focus on individual behavior as well as cultural patterns and institutions, the novellas put forth a critique of patriarchal society's treatment of women and of the role of the individual in perpetuating this treatment. In addition to criticizing society, then, the collection also presses readers to reconsider their own attitudes and actions vis-à-vis interpersonal relationships.

The complexities of Zayas's fictional world and her political agenda come through in the final pages of the collection. On the last night of the soiree in the *Desengaños amorosos*, a large number of aristocrats gather to hear one last "disenchantment of love," in which Lisis narrates a tale of savage violence that warns of the dangers of men's control over the female body. This warning will be taken quite literally by Lisis herself, who eschews marriage and enters a convent. Capitalizing on Lisis's role as heroine of the frame tale, this final narrative summarizes many of the previous themes of injustice, power, and violence.

Lisis's novella, "Estragos que causa el vicio" ("The Ravages of Vice"), tells the story of the sexually transgressive Florentina, a woman who has a four-year affair with her brother-in-law. Spurred on by a female servant, Florentina decides to trick her brother-in-law Diego into believing that his wife has taken a lover. The women base their decision on the assumption that Diego, like other men, is so invested in his own honor that he will simply kill his wife rather than live with even the slightest suspicion of her infidelity. According to the women's theory, Diego would marry Florentina if his wife were dead. In addition to the problematic behavior on the part of the women, this scheme relies heavily on the hypocrisies of the honor code: the women expect that this man, himself an adulterer, will not hesitate to punish his wife for committing the same offense as he.

The plan proceeds smoothly. Diego enters the house one night and sees a young page leaving his wife Magdalena's room. Diego's reaction is unanticipated in its violence, however. He becomes so furious that he murders everyone in his house and then commits suicide. After Florentina escapes, a gentleman named Gaspar rescues her on the street. Later, Florentina describes the turn of events that led to the bloodshed. Her description of the ill-fated, innocent Magdalena underscores the perils inherent in a male-dominated honor system:

> En tanto, don Dionís, ya de todo punto ciego con su agravio, entró adonde estaba su inocente esposa, que se había vuelto a quedar dormida con los brazos sobre la cabeza, y llegando a su puro y casto lecho, a sus airados ojos y engañada imaginación sucio, deshonesto y violado con la mancha de su deshonor, le dijo: "Ah, traidora, y cómo descansas en mi ofensa!" Y sacando la daga, la dio tantas puñaladas, cuantas su indignada cólera le pedía. Sin que pudiese ni aun formar un '¡ay!,' desamparó aquella alma santa el más hermoso y honesto cuerpo que conoció el reino de Portugal. (*Desengaños* 496)

> Meanwhile, Don Dionís, by now totally blinded with the affront to his honor, entered his innocent wife's room. She had gone back to sleep with her arms raised over her head. He approached her pure, chaste bed with angry eyes, his deceived imagination seeing it soiled, dishonored, and violated by the stain of his dishonor. He said: "Oh traitor, look how you rest knowing you have offended me!" Drawing his dagger, he stabbed her as many times as his blind rage required. She couldn't even utter 'alas!' before her saintly soul abandoned the most beautiful and chaste body the kingdom of Portugal has ever seen. (392)

Fatally misreading his wife's body, Diego assumes that Magdalena has fallen into a deep, postcoital sleep, and takes her innocent slumber as an added offense to his honor.

Yet Florentina immediately rereads the female body for us, emphasizing the saintliness of the soul and the innocent woman's chastity and beauty. Her narrative intervention highlights the disparity between masculine and feminine views of the female body and implicitly indicts men's unchecked control over women. Even the structure of the tale underscores these fundamental messages: through its repeated accounts of violence and its results, the pointedly sympathetic reading of Magdalena's fate, and the descriptions of Florentina's own wounds and recovery, it is difficult to miss the criticism of the hypocrisies and dangers to which the honor code subjects women.[11]

Like many other novellas in the collection, this final tale obviates an unproblematical reading of Zayas's representation of gender relations. In contrast to the virtuous depiction of Magdalena and of the male rescuer Gaspar, the other main characters' behavior seems utterly debased. Most notably, the glaring defects of the female protagonist complicate the question of responsibility and blame. Florentina, presented as the heroine of the tale, has had an extended affair with her loving sister's husband. Moreover, Florentina agrees to a plan devised by her woman servant that will bring about her sister's death. But, while facing possible death from her stab wounds, Florentina is pardoned by confessors and judicial authorities alike. Even Lisis reads over Florentina's complicity in the events that led to the violence: she blames the servant for betraying the innocent sister Magdalena, for whom "no le sirvió el ser honesta y virtuosa para librarse de la traición de una infame sierva" (*Desengaños* 508) ("it did no good to be chaste and virtuous to free herself from the treachery of an infamous maid" [402–03]).[12] While releasing Florentina from her complicity, Lisis assigns blame to the servant and overlooks Diego's responsibility for what the text portrays as irrational rage.

Lisis's misreading parallels the absolution of Florentina by church and judicial authorities. After Florentina's name is cleared from the moral and criminal records, the texts suggest that we look elsewhere for the culprit. Indeed, the graphic descriptions of Diego's anger and the representation of Magdalena as a sacrificial lamb once again focus our attention on the dynamics of violence. Both structurally and thematically, "Estragos que causa el vicio" makes clear that the larger issue at stake is women's powerlessness.

Lisis responds to this fundamental lesson of the collection with a litany against men, calling for women to protect themselves and for men to change their ways. She also issues her own surprise announcement, one that defies the genre's convention of ending the framed novella with a marriage: she refuses to wed her fiancé. Instead, Lisis makes of herself an example by declaring that she will enter a convent with her friends. Like other women writers—such as Christine de Pisan, Hélisenne de Crenne, Moderata Fonte, and Margaret Cavendish—Zayas depicts women's friendship and an all-female environment as antidotes to male-dominated society.[13] Lisis urges men to change their ways and she urges other women to follow her to safety so they will not meet the same fate as the raped, tortured, and dead women whose stories have been told throughout the collection.

Writing over three centuries ago, Zayas focused on many of the issues that continue to be of concern to women today. Using the female body as a vehicle for her didacticism, Zayas's texts are based on a politicized aesthetic meant to urge readers to enact both individual and social reform. Zayas argues for women's access to education, arms, and justice by aestheticizing the material consequences of women's powerlessness.

The texts lay claim to women's inclusion in the institutions that protected the aristocratic male subject in seventeenth-century Spain. By intertwining political and corporeal messages, Zayas's feminism demonstrates that the integrity of the entire body politic depends on women's incorporation into the social processes that protect and nurture men. Four centuries later, we are well served to remember these calls for inclusion as we continue to struggle for social justice.

Notes

1. Unless otherwise noted, all Zayas translations are taken from H. Patsy Boyer's *The Enchantments of Love* and *The Disenchantments of Love.* Original quotes from Zayas are from Agustín de Amezúa's edition of the *Novelas amorosas y ejemplares* and Alicia Yllera's edition of the *Desengaños amorosos.* All other translations are my own.
2. In *The Creation of a Feminist Consciousness,* Gerda Lerner has emphasized the evolutionary nature of feminism by laying out the basic components of what we now understand to be a full-fledged feminist consciousness: "the awareness of women that they belong to a subordinate group; that they have suffered wrongs as a group; that their condition of subordination is not natural, but is societally determined; that they must join with other women to remedy these wrongs; and finally, that they must and can provide an alternate vision of societal organization in which women as well as men will enjoy autonomy and self-determination" (14). Zayas's texts move toward presenting an "alternate vision of societal organization," but, ultimately, they still remain within the framework of seventeenth-century patriarchal organization. As I argue throughout the essay, Zayas does more than just protest women's mistreatment: she demonstrates the full effects of women's exclusion from the social processes and institutions that protect men. I refer to Zayas's texts as feminist with the understanding that, within her social context and time period, her thinking is in line with the early stages of feminist consciousness.
3. In her introduction to Zayas's *Desengaños amorosos,* Alicia Yllera observes that, despite many claims to Zayas's nearly unsurpassed popularity, the existence of some editions cannot be confirmed. Nonetheless, Zayas was a best-selling author in Spain, and was, after Cervantes, the most popular Spanish novella writer in western Europe (Yllera 64). Yllera's list of known editions, translations, and adaptations of Zayas's prose confirms the intense, prolonged interest in Zayas throughout the continent (64–93).
4. Nineteenth-century critics took many shots at the purportedly vulgar aspects of Zayas's texts. This attitude continued in the twentieth century as well, when, for example, Zayas was called "frankly obscene" in the 1953 *Diccionario de literatura española* (760). The dictionary does note Lena Sylvania's 1922

study on Zayas as a turning point toward recognition of the author's feminism. For an excellent interpretation on the readings of Zayas's texts as obscene, overly detailed, and lewd, see Patricia Grieve.

5. Yllera's introduction provides a publishing history as well as a summary of critical comments on the reception and interpretation of Zayas's life and texts. Poems in Zayas's honor written by Lope de Vega, Alonso de Castillo Solórzano, Ana Caro, and others appear in Amezúa's edition of Zayas's *Novelas amorosas y ejemplares*. Willard King discusses Zayas's participation in the *academias* in *Prosa novelística y academias literarias en el siglo XVII* (59n81).
6. While several studies on Zayas exist (including Foa; Montesa Peydro; Sylvania; and Vasileski), among the most notable are those of Marina S. Brownlee and Margaret Greer, published in 2000. For a treatment of Zayas's feminist politics and aesthetic, see my *Reclaiming the Body: María de Zayas's Early Modern Feminism*. Also see Gwyn Campbell and Judith Whitenack.
7. I have slightly altered Boyer's translation.
8. For another reading of Zayas's use of violence, see my article "Reading the Body Imperiled."
9. Grieve's article "Embroidering with Saintly Threads" draws attention to the importance of hagiography in Zayas's *novelas*.
10. Jordan's analyses and categorizations of feminist texts have been praised for their ambitiousness and criticized for their imprecision. In particular, the discussion of androgyny, the lack of analysis of readership and reception, and the assessment of women's lack of property ownership as a primary hindrance to their autonomy have been criticized for their lack of historical contextualization and nuance (see Ian Maclean). Nonetheless, Jordan's ambitious study certainly represents a solid basis for further consideration of the many manifestations of and departures from feminist discourse (not to be confused with the realities of women's lives) in the Renaissance.
11. William Clamurro has elegantly dealt with the question of structure and repetition in "Madness and Narrative Form."
12. An example of the elitist sentiments present throughout Zayas's collection, the entire quotation is an invective against servants, who are called "animales caseros y enemigos no excusados" (*Desengaños* 508) ("domestic animals and privileged enemies" [403]).
13. Pisan certainly set the stage for a rich tradition of women's writing in which female environments were idealized (see *The Book of the City of Ladies* [1405]). As Jordan tells us, "Like several of her Italian counterparts, Crenne represents conventual life as a refuge from male abuse" (178; see Crenne's *Personal and Invective Letters* [1539]). In *The Worth of Women* (1592, published in 1600), the seventeenth-century Venetian writer Moderata Fonte also creates a fictional community of women in an aristocratic household owned by a woman. Similarly, Margaret Cavendish's *Convent of Pleasure* (1668) portrays the intimacies of makeshift convent life. Cavendish's depictions of women's love and friendship are complicated by a cross-dressed suitor whose male identity is finally revealed.

Works Cited

Boyer, H. Patsy. "Toward a Baroque Reading of 'El verdugo de su esposa.' " Williamsen and Whitenack 52–71.

Brownlee, Marina S. *The Cultural Labyrinth of María de Zayas.* Philadelphia: U of Pennsylvania P, 2000.

———. "Elusive Subjectivity in María de Zayas." *Journal of Interdisciplinary Literary Studies* 6 (1994): 163–83.

Campbell, Gwyn, and Judith Whitenack, eds. *Zayas and Her Sisters I: Essays on Novelas by Seventeenth-Century Spanish Women.* Binghamton: Global, 2001.

Cavendish, Margaret Lucas. *Convent of Pleasure.* London: Maxwell, 1668.

Christine de Pisan. *The Book of the City of Ladies.* Trans. Earl Jeffrey Richards. New York: Persea, 1982.

Clamurro, William. "Madness and Narrative Form in 'Estragos que causa el vicio.' " Williamsen and Whitenack 215–29.

Crenne, Hélisenne de. *A Renaissance Woman: Hélisenne's Personal and Invective Letters.* Trans. and ed. Marianna M. Mustacchi and Paul J. Archambault. Syracuse: Syracuse UP, 1986.

Diccionario de literatura española. 2nd ed. Madrid: Revista de Occidente, 1953.

El Saffar, Ruth. "Ana/Lysis/Zayas: Reflections on Courtship and Literary Women in the *Novelas amorosas y ejemplares.*" Williamsen and Whitenack 192–216.

Foa, Sandra M. *Feminismo y forma narrativa.* Madrid: Albatros, 1979.

Fonte, Moderata. *The Worth of Women.* Ed. and trans. Virginia Cox. Chicago: U of Chicago P, 1997.

Greer, Margaret Rich. *María de Zayas Tells Baroque Tales of Love and the Cruelty of Men.* University Park: Penn State UP, 2000.

Grieve, Patricia. "Embroidering with Saintly Threads: María de Zayas Challenges Cervantes and the Church." *Renaissance Quarterly* 44 (1991): 86–106.

Griswold, Susan. "Topoi and Rhetorical Distance: The 'Feminism' of María de Zayas." *Revista de estudios hispánicos* 14 (1980): 97–116.

Jordan, Constance. *Renaissance Feminism: Literary Texts and Political Models.* Ithaca: Cornell UP, 1990.

King, Willard F. *Prosa novelística y academias literarias en el siglo XVII.* Madrid: Anejos del Boletín de la Real Academia Española X, 1963.

Lerner, Gerda. *The Creation of Feminist Consciousness: From the Middle Ages to 1870.* Oxford: Oxford UP, 1993.

Maclean, Ian. Rev. of *Renaissance Feminism* by Constance Jordan. *Renaissance Quarterly* 47 (1994): 214–16.

Montesa Peydro, Salvador. *Texto y contexto en la narrativa de María de Zayas.* Madrid: Dirección General de la Juventud y Promoción Sociocultural, 1981.

Paun de García, Susan. "Zayas as Writer: Hell Hath No Fury." Williamsen and Whitenack 40–50.

Sylvania, Lena. *Doña María de Zayas y Sotomayor: A Contribution to the Study of Her Works.* New York: Columbia UP, 1922. New York: AMS, 1966.

Vasileski, Irma. *María de Zayas y Sotomayor: Su época y su obra.* New York: Plaza Mayor, 1972.

Vollendorf, Lisa. "Reading the Body Imperiled: Violence against Women in María de Zayas." *Hispania* 78 (1995): 272–82.

———. *Reclaiming the Body: María de Zayas's Early Modern Feminism.* Chapel Hill: U of North Carolina P, 2001.

Williamsen, Amy R. "Engendering Interpretation: Irony as Comic Challenge in María de Zayas." *Romance Languages Annual* 3 (1991): 642–48.

Williamsen, Amy R., and Judith A. Whitenack, eds. *María de Zayas: The Dynamics of Discourse.* Madison: Fairleigh Dickinson UP, 1995.

Yllera, Alicia, ed. Introducción. Zayas, *Desengaños amorosos* 9–99.

Zayas y Sotomayor, María de. *Desengaños amorosos.* 2nd ed. Ed. Alicia Yllera. Madrid: Cátedra, 1993.

———. *The Disenchantments of Love.* Trans. H. Patsy Boyer. Albany: State U of New York P, 1997.

———. *The Enchantments of Love.* Trans. H. Patsy Boyer. Berkeley: U of California P, 1990.

———. *Novelas amorosas y ejemplares.* Ed. Agustín de Amezúa. Madrid: Real Academia Española, 1948.

Eighteenth and Nineteenth Centuries

Playing with Saint Isabel: Drama from the Pen of an Unknown Adolescent

Teresa S. Soufas et al.

An anonymous play entitled *Comedia famosa el ejemplo de virtudes y Santa Isabel Reyna de Ungria* ("Famous Play: The Model of Virtues and Saint Elizabeth, Queen of Hungary"), attributed only to "una dama sevillana a los 14 años de su edad" ("a Sevillian lady of fourteen years of age") and handwritten in eighteenth-century orthography, offers vast possibilities for speculation about its place in that century's production of drama in Spain and the sociocultural position of its unnamed author. As coauthors of this study, we have accepted the female identity of the unknown author.[1] We do so in part because of the intriguingly woman-centered perspective of the drama and in part because there is no obvious reason on which to base a speculation about why a male dramatist would find it necessary to sign his work with the aforementioned rubric.[2]

The beginning of this study is traceable to a notation in the often cited Manuel Serrano y Sanz bibliography of women writers in which the following noteworthy information leaves us with a scant description of two manuscripts, one entitled *El ejemplo de virtudes y Santa Isabel Reyna de Ungría: Compuesta por una dama sevillana a los 14 años de su edad* and the other *La mayor desconfianza y amar Deidad a Deidad. Comedia famosa de una Dama sevillana* ("The Greatest Mistrust and Divinity Loving Divinity. Famous Play by a Young Sevillian Lady"). Serrano y Sanz elaborates: "Estas dos comedias y los sainetes mencionados se hallan en un manuscrito del siglo XVIII; consta de 159 hojas en 4o. Pergamino" (268: 104–05). Against a background of a graduate seminar on early modern Spanish women writers conducted during the spring semester of 1998, our scholarly group decided to take on the project of studying *El ejemplo de virtudes* from the vantage point of its resonance with eighteenth-century theatrical convention and its efficacy as a dramatic filter of cultural issues of that period.

We found a play that conforms to the paradigmatic components of the *comedia de santos* (play about saints) of the seventeenth and eighteenth centuries in Spain but one that redounds with the political implications of its time, when the War of the Spanish Succession and its aftermath did not bring resolution to all the national instabilities that had plagued the Spanish nation for the previous one hundred years. The play dramatizes the life of the thirteenth-century historical figure Saint Elizabeth of Hungary, who rose to political power as the daughter and wife of royal men but who never lost the zeal for good works and self-abnegation. Her sainthood derives from her rejection of secular wealth, her refusal to assume the throne after her husband's death, and her consistent enactment of the virtues in the face of the evil and bad intentions of the people surrounding her.

Grounded in the context of the *comedia de santos*, popular throughout the early modern period in Spain and particularly in the early decades of the eighteenth century, *El ejemplo de virtudes* is typical of the genre through its depiction of selected events in the life of the titular character with some dramatic emphasis given to secular love interests and comic gracioso figures. The Spanish moralists' energetic resistance to the popular *comedia de santos* since the seventeenth century finally culminated in the banning of this dramatic form by the middle of the eighteenth century. The stricture seems not to have been in effect at the time of this play's composition or its staging, if any, thus lending further support to our assumption of a composition date early in that century.

The anonymous author's choice of focusing on Saint Elizabeth is not without precedent. Indeed, the dramatist's stated home city of Seville was the site of exhibition for Bartolomé Esteban Murillo's *Santa Isabel de Hungría cura a los tinosos* ("Saint Elizabeth Cures the Afflicted") in the Charity Hospital (see Perry 25). In addition, Juan de Matos Fragoso's play *El job de las mujeres* ("The Job of Women") of the late seventeenth century, another play written according to the conventions of the *comedia de santos*, was among the most frequently restaged titles during the eighteenth century (see Vallejo González 17). Although it strays significantly from the historical record of Elizabeth's life, Matos Fragoso's piece does portray the protagonist as a chaste and charitable figure whose virtues eventually receive recognition by those who were her antagonists.

We have considered the anonymous eighteenth-century dramatist's portrayal of the historical Elizabeth of Hungary against a background of dramatized political pressures. *El ejemplo de virtudes*'s political components resonate with struggles that parallel the tensions of dynastic succession, the national disappointment over the replacement of weak Hapsburg monarchs by the equally ineffectual first Bourbon king, and the problematic social space of woman in early modern European culture. Our critical approach coincides with Josep Lluis Sirena's model of a religious play set in a distant time period that nevertheless, by a variety of means, allows the playwright to "tender un puente desde la circunstancia histórica concreta de cada obra hacia el presente de autor y público" (68) ("to extend a bridge from the concrete historical circumstance of each work to the present time of the author and audience"). Elements of unrest in the thirteenth-century Saint Elizabeth story become a vehicle for a multilayered commentary on the early eighteenth-century Spanish sociopolitical situation. The distance of time and subject allows the playwright a certain fluidity in assignment of roles and outcomes that serve as a buffer for their correspondence with her contemporary society.

As the new century dawned, the Spanish nation was divided over the issue of monarchical claim to the throne, and the War of the Spanish Succession legitimated the French Bourbon prince Philip as the Spanish king Felipe V. Named by Carlos II as his successor in a last will and testament of 1700, Philip endeavored to transplant, as W. N. Hargreaves-Mawdsley asserts, "French ideas of statecraft to Spain" (1). Useful to the new monarch in this undertaking, for example, was the Council of Castile, which became an "instrument of Bourbon autocracy [. . .] built up and strengthened throughout the eighteenth century as an antidote to regionalism" (1). But the shift toward absolutism brought changes that, John Lynch asserts, "undermined the old social order" (9). He continues:

> While status, precedence, and privilege certainly endured, the traditional society of estates in which nobles fought, churchmen prayed, and commoners paid taxes gave way in the course of the eighteenth century to a society of classes in which wealth rather than function determined social position and divided grandee from *hidalgo*, prelate from priest, proprietor from peasant, merchant from artisan. As the monarchy itself moved towards greater absolutism, so it spoke more clearly to the emerging classes, marginalizing the aristocracy, controlling the Church, and defining policy affecting merchants and manufacturers. (9)

The traditions and habits of the past clashed with the forces new to Spain and inspired in some instances an impetus to reaffirm the values of the past. Our anonymous eighteenth-century *comedia de santos* is a vehicle for such reaffirmation.

Philip V's reign likewise brought forth issues of female succession to the throne with his effort to solidify his bond to Spain and to validate his dynasty. Hargreaves-Mawdsley explains that the king imposed the Salic law to exclude women from the throne as long as there was a male heir. This measure was based on a strategy that extended to the prohibition that those members "of the royal family born abroad could lose their rights of succession. The object of this was to preclude all danger of a foreign dynasty appearing in Spain, as if Felipe's own were not a foreign one!" (1–2). Others who comment on this reinstitution of the Salic law read the more conservative version of its impact, focusing on an effort to exclude women altogether from the dynastic succession, but also noting the same intention to prevent foreign relatives from claiming legitimacy on the Spanish throne:

> Felipe V as of May, 1713, decreed the applicability in Spain of the Salic Law, the French tradition that women cannot rule in their own right. Intended to ensure that no Hapsburg would ever sneak onto the Spanish throne through marriage, past or future, to a Spanish princess, the new statute confirmed by Cortes also had the effect of denying the possibility of a queen regnant in Spain, a principle contrary to Castilian practice in the past. (Bergamini 46)

Thus Spain is not only the site of dynastic struggles but also the focus of numerous contradictory forces summoned to legitimate the ascent of the Bourbon dynasty to the Spanish throne. Louis XIV of France, Philip's grandfather, continued to be very involved from a distance in the reign of the first Spanish Bourbon king. Lynch explains how for a number of years Louis governed Spain through agents such as the Princess des Ursins and Michel-Jean Amelot, the marquis de Gournay (46–52).

The presence of the Bourbon king in Spain did not entirely resolve the power vacuum of the reign of Carlos II, and the many historians who have studied Philip note that his mental and emotional fragility was soon apparent, as was his dependence on the will and guidance of his grandfather and on the women closest to him. Lynch notes first that Philip's Spanish subjects became "disappointed in their new king, who seemed to be little improvement on Charles II and had the disadvantage of being French" (67). He was, by several accounts, "driven by two compulsions, sex and religion" and "spent his nights, and much of his days, in constant transit between his wife and his confessor, torn between desire and guilt, a comic figure easily subject to conjugal blackmail" (Lynch 67). An eighteenth-century observer reported that Philip was "the slave of his wife" (Saint-Simon, qtd. in Bergamini 67), and on the basis of this and other historical accounts, Lynch describes Philip as a "slave of his first wife, he was a child in the hands of his second" (68).

The recurring mental instability that had plagued Philip from the beginning of his reign came to a serious crisis in 1717, when what was described as a series of symptoms of madness became very pronounced. The king isolated himself and was able to resume his duties only after the passage of considerable time, but he did so without energy or direction. According to Lynch, "by 1721 Saint-Simon found him, at the age of thirty-eight, an unexpectedly aged man, with a vacuous expression, shrunken body, pronounced stoop and bow legs, his life confined to an immutable court routine of indescribable tedium, his political decisions taken for him by the queen" (69). The king's instability and infirmities prompted the queen and the royal advisers to move the court to Andalusia, and from 1728 to 1733 it remained predominately at the alcazar in Seville. Philip's mental feebleness was "characterized again by religious mania, profound melancholy, prolonged silence, and violent behaviour" such that the nation was "virtually without a government, for the king refused to see ministers or sign documents" (Lynch 71). Once his condition improved and the court moved back to Castile, Philip was still vulnerable to erratic behavior and symptoms of derangement.[3]

Also of significance in Philip's reign is his aborted abdication of the throne in favor of his son Louis in 1724, a move taken purportedly on the grounds of religious piety and the king's desire to devote the remainder of his life to secluded contemplation and prayer. His son was not well suited to the role of monarch either, and after Louis's death from smallpox in the late summer of that same year, the issue of succession again became problematic. Philip's second son, Ferdinand, was next in line, but he was only eleven years of age and factional divisions split support between him and his father through a renunciation of the latter's abdication. Philip resumed the throne in September 1724.

The legitimacy of a foreign monarch's ascent to the throne, the challenge to a female ruler's legitimacy, and the monarch's own reluctance to continue to reign are elements that dominate the historical reports both about Saint Elizabeth of Hungary and about the national situation surrounding the introduction of the Bourbon dynasty to Spain. These coinciding elements provide a means of expression to the author of *El ejemplo de virtudes y Santa Isabel Reyna de Ungria* for exploring the national crisis around her and for exposing the fragility of numerous alternative resolutions to the political difficulties then current. The historical accounts about the devout Elizabeth describe the resistance of the groom's family to her marriage to Louis of Thuringia, the heir to the throne left vacant upon his father's death and presided over by his mother Sophia. The historical studies report that the thirteenth-century royal family disapproved of the match in part because of their resentment toward Elizabeth's zeal for charitable works. In particular, her future mother-in-law, according to one report, "tried to prevent the wedding out of jealousy and constantly mocked Elizabeth for her charity and humility. She said that she behaved 'like a tired old mule,' when she prostrated herself before the crucifix, and that she was totally unfitted to be Queen" (Coulson 156). The marriage did take place, however, and signaled a happy union for the couple. Three children were born to them, and the pious Louis seems to have supported his wife's devotion to good works. She persisted in wearing garments of coarse cloth, eating sparsely, and practicing remarkable acts of charity. When Louis left to take part in the Crusades, only to die of the plague en route, Elizabeth suffered the wrath of her husband's already alienated family who "accused her of squandering the royal purse on the vagrants of the land" (156).

Although Elizabeth had a son who could rightfully claim the crown, her brother-in-law Henry usurped the throne with the full support of his mother. Banished from the court, Elizabeth and her children suffered severe conditions, as the historical reports make clear:

> Fue acusada de pródiga y disipadora y arrojada del palacio con sus hijos, con severas penas para cuantos la favoreciesen de cualquier modo. Durante tres años hubo de vivir en una choza y mendigar el sustento para ella y para sus hijos. (Sáinz de Robles 600)
>
> She was accused of being wasteful and of being a spendthrift and she was thrown out of the palace with her children, with severe punishment promised to anyone who might help her in any way. For three years she had to live in a hut and beg for food for herself and for her children.

Eventually returned to her status as queen, owing to the intervention of her husband's returning friends and supporters among the Crusaders, Elizabeth renounced her claims to the throne in favor of her son and spent the remaining four years of her life offering charity to the needy and dedicating prayerful service to God. Four years after her death in 1231, Pope Gregory IX canonized her as Saint Elizabeth of Hungary.

El ejemplo de virtudes dramatizes Elizabeth's life beginning at the point of her impending marriage to Louis and ending with her return to court after the enforced exile. The play follows in general the main points of the historical accounts, something typical in the hagiographic plays of Spanish theater. In recognizing this we do not, however, mean to stop at the seemingly pedantic assumption of the mimetic equivalence of the drama and the historical realities of Elizabeth's life or the simple reflection of the historical moment of the text's composition. Rather we prefer to invoke the more interesting and problematic approach that new historicist readings of literary texts suggest about the relation between how a story is told or represented and the context of its representation. In her essay on Calderón's *autos sacramentales* (one-act religious plays), Margaret Greer contends that

> [w]ithin new historicist theory, equal in importance to the question of the relation of literary texts to power structures is its converse: the nature and mode of operation of the power of literary creation. New historicists generally reject both a doctrinaire marxism that would reduce aesthetic objects to superstructural reflections of the material base, and an idealist vision of literature as existing in an aesthetic order apart from material interests. Rather they see literary texts as both social product and socially productive. (46)

So too, as Robert Lauer claims, new historical practice seeks

> to detect in the text gaps and contradictions which in effect turn the text on its instability [. . .] hence exposing its internal conflicts (which have been repressed, silenced, or sublimated) and its "false" or utopian (escapist) solution [and thus] the text is a decentering product of verbal and social practices which questions and destabilizes itself and its milieu. (16)

Such a theoretical perspective provides a way to critique the network of contradictory forces that inform the dramatized world of *El ejemplo de virtudes* in which at the depicted Thuringian court there is no easily identified locus of power. The instability of that world refuses a definitive interpretation of the implications it suggests. Sofía rules but only until her son Luis assumes his royal title. Although she is clearly recognized as an important political presence, Sofía derives her defined authority more as mother of royal sons than as royal personage in her own right. There is no moment when she acts on issues of state autonomously, for she works primarily toward the goals that her sons have validated. Sofía, moreover, is consistently portrayed as dissatisfied over much that happens, particularly when Isabel is triumphant in some endeavor. The author of *El ejemplo de virtudes* develops the tensions inherent in the historical story of Saint Elizabeth that reflect national concerns for monarchical legitimacy, gender-specific role assignment, and the struggle over conflicting reliance on divine and secular authority.

The conflicting forces presented make clear that, with the exception of Isabel herself, there is a lack of admirable characters in the play. When given the opportunity to assume the royal position she is entitled to, however, the pious woman refuses. Satisfaction of the implied best solution is never fulfilled. As the play opens, Sofía expresses her disapproval over the proposed marriage of her son Luis and Isabel of Hungary even though the young woman is generally lauded by all other characters as virtuous and saintly. An early conversation between Luis and the Hungarian count Gualtero introduces elements that threaten to destabilize the court and the citizenry of Thuringia and that lay the groundwork for presentation of this dramatist's understanding of the conflicting situation in which Isabel must try to satisfy competing demands upon her. The absence of declared commitment on Luis's part has left doubts about the potential marriage with Isabel. Gualtero acknowledges both the resistance mounted by Sofía and her son's purported inability to overcome that force: "Bien conozco es la Duquesa / en contra de su belleza / mas vuestro amor es señor / tibio o acaso incapaz / pues amarais como es justo / supieras atropellar / rigores de vuestra madre" (*Ejemplo* fol. 2v) ("I know well that the duchess does not approve of her beauty, but your love, Sir, is lukewarm or perhaps inadequate, for were you to love her as is just you would know how to overcome your mother's harshness"). The gossip of the court focuses on these issues, and, as the count explains, "toda la corte murmura / y aun se llega ya a pensar / que vuelve su Alteza a Ungria" (fol. 2r) ("the whole court gossips and it is even thought that Her Highness is going to return to Hungary"). Such a result would motivate Isabel's father, King Andrés of Hungary, to attack: "sus Escuadras / lo Taringia inundaran" (fol. 2r) ("his squadrons would inundate Thuringia").

Gualtero exhorts Luis to declare himself: "Esto rendido os suplico / me llegueis a declarar" (fol. 3r) ("humbly I beseech you finally to declare yourself to me"). Inspired by Gualtero's words, Luis does affirm that he is "de la Infanta amante fino" ("refined lover of the princess") and vows that "la haré mi Esposa, la haré / mi dueña, aunque a pesar / sea de mi injusta Madre / en nada he de reparar / todo lo atropella Amor" (fol. 3v) ("I will make her my wife, I will make her my lady, although it be against my unfair mother's wishes; I will stop at nothing; love overcomes all"). In subsequent conversations staged among the palace servants, the audience learns that the wedding has been planned despite insurmountable obstacles and that elaborate festivities are to take place that very night in celebration of the union of Luis and Isabel. The maid Insistrudis attributes all to God's will: "Qué confusiones son éstas? / nada conozco ni alcanzo / mas el Poderoso es causa / y en esto anda su Mano" (fol. 5v) ("What confusions are these? I neither know nor perceive anything, but the All Powerful is the cause and his hand is in this").

The first appearance on stage for Isabel is during the masked ball held to celebrate her wedding. She, too, acknowledges God's designs in what is taking place as she comments privately: "O inmenso Dueño y Señor, / porque das premios tan altos, / a la más vil criattura, / sólo a ti Señor alabo" (fol. 6r) ("Oh great Lord and Saviour, because you give such high rewards to the most vile creature, I praise only you Lord"). Sofía in contrast registers her inner thoughts about her dissatisfaction over the marriage that she was unable to stop: "Aquesto es forsoso cielos! / Cómo mi soberbia ajo! / Admitiendo por Señora / a Isabel, Astro inhumano" (fol. 7r) ("Heavens, this is inescapable! How I crush my pride, admitting Isabel as lady, oh inhuman star!"). The dynamic reiterated here is that of the secular or political will in service to the divine one, a struggle that the playwright is careful to negotiate within a positive register for her protagonist but likewise within a complicated network of dramatized issues that center on gender, relation to authority, and a cultural struggle over adherence to traditional values or rejection of them. Not only is Isabel renowned as someone "de hermosura, gracia y garbo / de virtud y de discreción" (fol. 9) ("of beauty, grace and elegance, virtue, and discretion") as well as being "la divina Isabel / cuya virtud y belleza / es asombro de los Astros / y es en todo singular" (fol. 2) ("the divine Elizabeth whose virtue and beauty is the wonder of the heavens and is in all unique"), but she will fulfill before the play ends all roles deemed appropriate for honorable females in Spanish society of the seventeenth and eighteenth centuries: virgin, wife, mother, and widow dedicated to perpetual chastity and devotion to God. What the play makes clear is that in this confluence of forces the woman's adherence to the highest standards of society's notion of female propriety does not protect her from mistreatment and severe difficulties as a consequence of the shortcomings of those around her. The political world is not in order, and the evidence of this disorder centers on the contradictions that Isabel must suffer and that she herself motivates.

As Daniel Whitaker asserts in his studies of eighteenth-century Spanish women intellectuals and writers, even women of prominence in the last half of the century, such as Josefa Amar y Borbón (who wrote works with titles like *Discurso en defensa del talento de las mujeres y su aptitud para el gobierno* ["A Discourse in Defense of the Intelligence of Women and of Their Aptitude for Government"] and *Discurso sobre la educación física y moral de las mujeres* ["A Discourse on the Physical and Moral Education of Women"]), proposed reforms, for example, "for the abysmal state of women's education, often left in the hands of incompetent instructors in convents" ("Voice" 34). But they stop short of proposing a definitive solution for remedying the inequalities and injustices women suffer because of the social and political system that blocked their full participation as citizens. Whitaker writes:

> As progressive as the ideas of Doña Josefa were, she encourages women to work for reform within society as it exists. Women cannot advance alone but must seek the company of enlightened men

> to work with them. In her major published work, *Discurso sobre la educación* (*Discourse about Education*), much emphasis is placed on the traditional role of the woman in the home in matters of childbirth, family diseases, and proper dress, and a chapter is dedicated to "obediencia y respeto a los padres" ("obedience and respect for one's parents"). ("Voice" 34)

Also commenting on Amar y Borbón's position on women's rights and obligations as presented in her texts, Eva Rudat explains that "anything beyond the woman's traditional place in the home is still unattainable" (404).[4] Eighteenth-century female writers and thinkers, like the author of *El ejemplo de las virtudes*, reveal the gendered limitations by which their culture controlled women's exercise of authority and assured that their only sphere of influence was domestic and enclosed.

When the men in society, through whom social and political authority is exercised, abuse their cultural privilege and responsibility, then women often suffer without recourse to any source of justice. Whitaker argues that in the late eighteenth-century rape tragedies *Amnon, Blanca de Rossi,* and *Florinda,* by María Rosa Gálvez,

> the flawed patriarchal societies depicted in [these plays] parallel another notable but constant blemish: the flawed character of the masculine protagonists themselves. Indeed, throughout the theater of Gálvez, males disrupt the harmony of their world through an inability to control a negative personal trait, such as ambition [. . .], avarice [. . .], or jealousy. [. . .] In the three plays that deal with rape, [the male principals] fail to dominate their lust. Invariably, in both her comedies and her tragedies, Gálvez's female characters suffer at the hands of these imperfect males and only infrequently manage to correct their behavior. ("Clarissa" 247)

Similar patterns obtain in *El ejemplo de las virtudes* by Gálvez's anonymous eighteenth-century predecessor.

The chaos of the secular realm is evident in the exchanges among the play's participants during the masquerade at the wedding festivities, when Enrique reveals his jealousy over his brother's good fortune in his ascent to the throne and in his marriage to the beautiful Isabel. The courtier Federico expresses his own jealousy over the loss of any further opportunity to court and win Isabel, whom he claims to love. Inés also reflects her brother Enrique's pique in her envy over Isabel's great personal and political fortune in a loving marriage and new royal position. All these feelings emerge as the celebrants move about the stage trying to communicate with each other without success because of the disguises that hide true identities and add to the confusion. Charity and good will are conspicuously absent until Isabel steps forward to save Federico from imprisonment in the tower, a penalty that Sofía is about to impose on him for causing consternation for Inés when he mistakes that young woman (secretly in love with him) for Isabel (whom he secretly loves).

This scene is placed early in the drama and functions as a microcosm of the rest of the play. The rivalries and resentments that motivate many of the principal characters throughout the ensuing acts are performed in the course of the festivities as they dance and reveal their innermost thoughts of jealousy, desire, greed, resentment, and anger in private declarations. What the playwright depicts is a potentially volatile situation in which Isabel functions both as peacemaker and catalyst for the negative emotions of the other characters. She is the center of everyone's attention—the political resentment of Enrique, the unrequited love of Federico, the disapproval of Sofía, and the envy of Inés.

Act 1 ends with the departure of Luis for the Crusades, and act 2 begins with Sofía's sad announcement to Isabel that he has died in the undertaking. In addition to the sorrow Isabel expresses, she vows "perpetua castidad" ("perpetual chastity") and moves into widowhood still abhorred by her husband's family and desired anew by Federico. An abusive male network takes control of the court and Isabel's life. With the support of Sofía—she does not want Isabel's son, her own grandson, on the throne because of their foreign, Hungarian blood ("sangre enemigo" [fol. 41] ["enemy blood"])—Enrique ejects his sister-in-law and her children from the palace and their rightful political stations. Then Enrique enlists Federico's help, promising, "si favoreces mi intento / haré que seas Señor / de la mitad de mi Esttado" ("if you help me with my plan, I will make you lord of half of my estate"), and adding, "te doy ya la permision / de elegir lo que gustases" (fol. 45) ("I give you permission to choose what pleases you"). Federico responds with a declaration of his only wish, a condition that Enrique is happy to oblige and that objectifies Isabel further as the component of exchange for political gain between men: "Yo no quiero posesiones / ni riquezas apettezco / tan solamentte a Isabel / es la dicha que prettendo / es la fortuna a que aspiro / y la grandeza que aprecio" (fol. 47) ("I do not want possessions nor do I yearn for wealth; I only want Elizabeth; she is the happiness that I seek; she is the fortune to which I aspire and the greatness that I admire").

Act 3 begins with Isabel's profession of humility and belief that her current suffering as an exile from the palace will earn her eternal rewards. In company with her attendants Flora and Insistrudis, she is dressed in rags and complains only that her children have to suffer the same deprivation. Barred from assisting her, the citizenry offers no sustenance. She is punished for her goodness in part because she is now without Luis, the sympathetic husband who could protect her politically. No one, including and especially the servants who suffer with her, praises her religious dedication. She is even alienated from herself in that she accepts blame for everything that has happened: "en todo soy yo culpada" (fol. 58) ("I am guilty of everything"). When representatives from her native land, in company with the archbishop of Bamberg, come to restore her rights, she is firm in her resolution to maintain her vow of perpetual chastity and refuses to entertain the archbishop's proposition that she return with him to the Thuringian court to become Federico's wife.

The play, whether staged or not, provides a dramatic presentation of crisis in a political context and, not unlike the works of Golden Age women dramatists, a portrayal of the lack of social space for a woman despite her efforts to live up to the standards her society determines as appropriate for her sex.[5] The playwright manipulates the elements of her dramatization in interesting and politically sensitive ways. The foreign royal is a woman and thus doubly removed from the throne by eighteenth-century tenets in Spain. This character, however, is the only one worthy of admiration in the play. Praiseworthy for her goodness and dedication to her religious convictions as well as for her humility and kindness to others, Isabel is nevertheless an outsider. She is given no credence, and her foreign blood is equivalent to her piety on the list of qualities that her in-laws and their supporters reject. Thus the dramatist avoids a depiction that challenges the legitimacy of royal figures purely on the basis of their nonnative identity, but she chooses a subject matter that reveals the extent to which those who resist the traditional values are flawed. The challenge is not one that suggests either a positive or a negative political focus on the house of the Bourbon monarchs but rather one that proposes conflicting questions and an almost inexhaustible array of alternatives. The drama remains true to the historical accounts of Saint Elizabeth in that Isabel is not allowed the political space to fulfill the social role that her birth and marriage determine for her. Perhaps most important is that Isabel herself rejects the role of queen of Thuringia because she prefers to follow the reclusive, charitable life that separates her from the secular realm. The historical Elizabeth provides an authentic model for this character and some of her literary ancestors, such as María de Zayas's numerous female protagonists who enter a convent or religious life to escape the ills and injustices of a variety of misfortunes at the hands of men in secular life. The play about Isabel reiterates and promotes the model.

God's will is likewise an issue, but the principal coherence in its depiction is that it is always counter to what the secular will determines as desirable. It is God who receives credit for the arrangement of Isabel's marriage to Luis; but it is also God who inspires the widowed Isabel to pledge herself to good works and perpetual chastity; and her devotion to him is what motivates her to reject the secular title and position she could reclaim—all elements resisted or criticized by the secular court. The protection of a historical account exempts the playwright from potential charges of insulting Philip V and his family, for she follows the known facts of Elizabeth's life in most details. But it is clear that although she portrays the rejection of a woman successor to the royal position, she closes her play with an affirmation that peace is restored when the foreigner does not take her place as monarch. The depiction suggests the invalidation of the French king's reign in Spain as it simultaneously validates him as male monarch and his imposition of the Salic law. With no mention in the play's dialogue of Isabel's son as eventual heir to the throne, Enrique is celebrated as the new ruler of Thuringia. Unlike Philip V, with his dependence on the support, direction, and even rule by proxy of his wives, the male royals in this play do not rely on or even recognize the wishes of the women who could serve the same function in their lives (i.e., Sofía and Isabel). Nevertheless, as the playwright demonstrates, chaos and misrule result either way.

The potential solutions to the dramatized sociopolitical impasse include Isabel's acceptance of the authoritative title and a subsequent reign that is founded on kindness and good works as much as it is on the rights of succession. Also possible is her abdication in favor of another male pretender. The playwright does not rewrite history, and the latter path of action ensues. The male monarch is recognized at the expense of moral balance, but the story presented focuses on a female royal who refuses her title. The abuse of the cultural system is critiqued, not the system itself. Isabel enacts her own exclusion from the seat of authority, but her last lines in the play articulate the delicate equilibrium finally imposed. Sofía registers her ongoing rejection of Isabel's religious, charitable activities (what she terms "toscas inttenciones" ["crude plans"] that "siempre han sido bastardas" [fol. 65r] ["always have been base"]), and Enrique objects that the court does not find appropriate her coarse dress and ascetic demeanor: "que no es gusstto dela cortte, / el miraros humillada, / en un rusttico sayal" (fol. 64v–65r) ("for it does not please the court to see you humbled in coarse clothing"). He notes as well that it does not please him either: "Y si tampoco es mi gustto" (fol. 65r) ("nor does it please me"). And Isabel's last words in the dramatic action reiterate the underlying tension through her appeal to God to protect her from Enrique's renewed treachery and improprieties:

Ay Dios mio, pues que a vos
Ya toda estoy dedicada,
haced pues que no revivan
sus pasiones ya dexadas. (fol. 65v–66r)

Oh, my God, since I am
totally dedicated to you,
don't let his now extinguished
passions become revived.

This suggestion of further chaos and abuse with which the play closes resonates with the historical moment of the early eighteenth century in Spain. It is implied that, in this story at least, a woman promises a sounder reign than her male counterparts. Implied as well is that the occupant of a throne is not a stable fixture of society or necessarily the correct choice to fulfill the responsibilities of royal office. Foreign pretenders are not permanently enthroned in the dramatized tale, but the native sons are themselves the source of the usurpations and the political difficulties portrayed. From a woman-centered perspective, the only happiness achieved by the female principals is based on the most traditional standards of secular marriage, motherhood, or religious service—stations in life that each one seeks and finally embraces as the play ends.

By creating her drama from a well-known story of a saintly woman's remarkable virtue and humility, the fourteen-year-old playwright also captures the political intrigue and instability that surrounded her protagonist and that she and her eighteenth-century Spanish compatriots were familiar with. Without more knowledge about who she was or the circumstances of her life, we are left with only the evidence that she was sufficiently educated to be able to compose a dramatic piece. What her fascination might have been at the age of fourteen with the Hungarian queen-saint who entered public life as her husband's consort, also at the age of fourteen, is something about which we can only speculate. Mirroring the historical Elizabeth's rejection of fame and position, the playwright cloaks herself in anonymity and leaves us with a text that questions the legitimacy of powerful positions and those who occupy them.

Notes

1. As part of the examination of women authors in early modern Spain, the class members of a graduate seminar taught by Teresa Soufas during the spring semester of 1998 contributed to the research and writing of this essay. The coauthors are Dixon Abreu, Laura Barbas, Isabel Crespo, Angeles Farmer, Daniela Flesler, Shani Moser, Roberto Ortiz, Marcie Rinka, Christina Sisk, Teresa Soufas, Paulina Vaca, Juping Wang, and Nancy Whitlock.
2. Such is the speculation about the otherwise unidentified author Ariadne of Restoration England about whose only published play Paddy Lyons and Fidelis Morgan assert: "there is no evidence that any male author of the 1690s thought it worth his while to present himself as a female playwright" (x).

3. Throughout the 1730s in particular the king adopted a reversed schedule in which he took his supper at 5:00 a.m., went to bed at 8:00 a.m., rose at midday, went to mass at 1:00 p.m., received visitors during the afternoon, passed the evening hours in amusements, and transacted business around 2:00 a.m. Thus Lynch comments that "the king inverted the normal order of things and turned night into day" (72).
4. For further discussion see Whitaker ("Voice" 34–35) and the studies by Constance Sullivan.
5. See Teresa Scott Soufas's study of the works of the five Golden Age women dramatists Angela de Azevedo, Ana Caro, Leonor de la Cueva y Silva, Feliciana Enríquez de Guzmán, and María de Zayas; see also Constance Jordan's book.

Works Cited

Bergamini, John D. *The Spanish Bourbons: The History of a Tenacious Dynasty*. New York: Putnam, 1974.

Coulson, John, ed. *The Saints: A Concise Biographical Dictionary*. New York: Hawthorn, 1958.

El ejemplo de virtudes y Santa Isabel Reyna de Ungria: Compuesta por una dama sevillana a los 14 años de su edad. Ms. 17430. Biblioteca Nacional, Madrid.

Greer, Margaret Rich. "Constituting Community: A New Historical Perspective on the *Autos* of Calderón." Madrigal 41–67.

Hargreaves-Mawdsley, W. N. *Eighteenth-Century Spain, 1700–1788: A Political, Diplomatic, and Institutional History*. Totowa: Rowman, 1979.

Jordan, Constance. *Renaissance Feminism: Literary Texts and Political Models.* Ithaca: Cornell UP, 1990.

Lauer, A. Robert. "The Recovery of the Repressed: A Neo-historical Reading of *Fuenteovejuna.*" Madrigal 15–28.

Levine, Linda Gould, Ellen Engelson Marson, and Gloria Feiman Waldman, eds. *Spanish Women Writers: A Bio-Bibliographical Source Book.* Westport: Greenwood, 1993.

Lynch, John. *Bourbon Spain, 1700–1808*. Oxford: Blackwell, 1989.

Lyons, Paddy, and Fidelis Morgan, eds. *Female Playwrights of the Restoration: Five Comedies.* London: Orion, 1995.

Madrigal, José A., ed. *New Historicism and the Comedia: Poetics, Politics, and Praxis.* Boulder: Soc. of Spanish and Spanish-American Studies, 1997.

Perry, Mary Elizabeth. *Gender and Disorder in Early Modern Seville.* Princeton: Princeton UP, 1990.

Rudat, Eva M. Kahiluoto. "The View from Spain: Rococo Finesse and *Esprit* versus Plebeian Manners." *French Women and the Age of Enlightenment.* Ed. Samia I. Spencer. Bloomington: Indiana UP, 1984. 395–406.

Sáinz de Robles, Federico Carlos. *Ensayo de un diccionario de jumeres célebres.* Madrid: Aguilar, 1959.

Serrano y Sanz, Manuel. *Apuntes para una biblioteca de escritoras españolas desde el año 1401 al 1833*. Madrid: Biblioteca Nacional, 1903–05.

Sirena, Josep Lluis. "Los santos en sus comedias: Hacia una tipología de los protagonistas del teatro hagiográfico." *Comedias y comediantes: Estudios sobre el teatro clásico español*. Ed. Manuel V. Diago and Teresa Ferrer. Valencia: Universitat de Valencia, 1991. 55–76.

Soufas, Teresa Scott. *Dramas of Distinction: A Study of Plays by Golden Age Women*. Lexington: UP of Kentucky, 1997.

Sullivan, Constance. "Josefa Amar y Borbón." Levine, Marson, and Waldman 32–43.

———. "Josefa Amar y Borbón and the Royal Aragonese Economic Society (with Documents)." *Dieciocho* 15 (1992): 95–148.

Vallejo González, Irene. *Introducción a la comedia de santos en el siglo XVIII*. Santiago de Chile: Universidad Internacional, 1993.

Whitaker, Daniel. "Clarissa's Sisters: The Consequences of Rape in Three Neoclassic Tragedies of María Rosa Gálvez." *Letras Peninsulares* (1992): 239–51.

———. "A New Voice: The Rise of the Enlightened Woman in Eighteenth-Century Spain." *Continental, Latin-American, and Francophone Women Writers: Selected Papers from the Wichita State University Conference on Foreign Literature*. Ed. Eunice Myers and Ginette Adamson. Vol. 2. Lanham: UP of America, 1990. 31–40. 3 vols.

Constructing Her Own Tradition: Ideological Selectivity in Josefa Amar y Borbón's Representation of Female Models

Constance A. Sullivan

The Spanish Enlightenment produced a woman thinker and writer whose essays approximate, albeit from a different class position, those of her better-known contemporary Mary Wollstonecraft. Josefa Amar y Borbón (1749–1833) began her brief publishing career with two translations from the Italian, a multivolume defense of Spanish literature and—for the Royal Aragonese Economic Society—an erudite treatise on new agricultural techniques. As the first woman member of one of Spain's Economic Societies, Amar boldly intervened in the heated 1786 debate on whether the Madrid Economic Society should admit women, producing a feminist essay arguing for women's membership. Her major work, a book on the education of women, was published in Madrid in 1790.[1]

Amar y Borbón stands out among her female peers in late-eighteenth-century Spain for a number of reasons. She alone was a scholar of recognized erudition. She argued against traditional and new misogynies, and she alone dared to publish essays that challenged the male establishment by using its own intellectual and rhetorical weapons. Having read more deeply and broadly than most Spanish women of her privileged socioeconomic class, Amar had a sharper and more historically contextualized awareness of her condition as a woman subordinated in a world structured to reward men. She knew that gender difference was culturally prescribed and culturally specific. Her knowledge of other cultures and other times brought with it awareness of the existence of women who were respected for their feminine virtues—however their times and places defined them—and for their intelligence, their learning, and the uses to which they put their talents.

Gender roles had experienced a transition or crisis in the European Renaissance that produced a debate on women complete with catalogs of exceptional or famous women. Similarly, when the European Enlightenment brought another significant change in gender prescriptions, it, too, produced many more catalogs of famous women. Those catalogs, whether they pleaded women's equality or women's superiority to men, tended to list women known for anything of note. They included fictional women—literary characters and mythological figures—and historical women who achieved some level of renown for their erudition, heroism, or governing of a nation. Such catalogs were alphabetic grab bags in which one could find an example of practically every human trait. In their diverse and sometimes contradictory representations of women, the texts echoed the late Enlightenment's gender crisis about women's true nature and appropriate social roles.

Given her constant concern for improving the status of women, Amar y Borbón carefully read many such catalogs of famous women, of her own period and from earlier times. It is my contention that in her writings, Amar rejected those catalogs' lack of selectivity and from them culled a number of ancient, classical, Renaissance, and Enlightenment women who served her ideological purposes as a feminist in a society poised between structures and values of the Old Regime and those of the rising bourgeois age. Her two longest original essays, written in 1786 and 1790, contain numerous references to women who exemplify human characteristics and social roles that Amar y Borbón found to be positive for asserting women's dignity in general and for validating what she herself represented in the Spanish society of her time: an intelligent, well-educated, studious wife and mother who did research and wrote on topics of interest to her and then actually made her work available to the larger public.[2]

For ideological reasons Amar excluded many women writers whom we might have expected her to include. The women she picked were meant to mold or construct a carefully chosen community or tradition of historical and contemporary women who excelled in an activity that their society and time may have viewed as appropriate only for men. The rhetorical strength of Amar's use of a specific type of woman as model for the construction of a female tradition of talents well employed is that she permits no negative examples to enter her scheme. I will examine this selectivity, looking at which women made it into Amar's approved list and which women she left out, with the goal of seeing how Amar positioned herself in the Spanish society of the late eighteenth century by aligning herself implicitly with very carefully selected model women of the past and present. The differences in the use of a female-modeling strategy in her fiery 1786 feminist essay, "Discurso en defensa del talento de las mujeres, y de su aptitud para el gobierno, y otros cargos en que se emplean los hombres" ("A Discourse in Defense of the Intelligence of Women and of Their Aptitude for Government and Other Positions Occupied by Men"), and in her more serene and scholarly 1790 book, *Discurso sobre la educación física y moral de las mujeres* ("A Discourse on the Physical and Moral Education of Women"), correspond to the specific occasion and purpose of the two works and to the writer's refinement (in her book) of an ideological project that proposes intellectual work as a necessary and valuable part of the married woman's constructive contribution to society and to herself.[3] The social and gender ideology in Amar's strongly and self-consciously feminist work is an ideology that drew lines between famous women who were acceptable models for female emulation and those who were not.

Amar's selectivity in offering female models seems to challenge today's feminist thinking, which looks for and values all signs of women's participation in culture while also attempting to explain this participation through historical contextualization. If María de Zayas y Sotomayor can be considered the first secular feminist among Spanish women writers, and her novellas were still being reprinted and widely read in the late seventeenth and eighteenth centuries, why did Amar y Borbón, Spain's second secular feminist and the most erudite female intellectual of Spain's Enlightenment, refuse to mention her as a model of women's creative potential? Why did Amar omit reference to Teresa de Jesús, Sor María de Agreda, or Sor Juana Inés de la Cruz, whose works were also available to eighteenth-century readers in Spain? Why did Amar not see fit to allude to any of the few Spanish women writers of her own time? She omits, for example, the translator Catalina de Caso, who had published in 1755 her version of Charles Rollin's *Traité des études* ("Treatise on a Course of Study"), which Amar recommends in the original French, or in a more recent excerpted translation, in her curriculum for women; and the sixth countess of Montijo, who published a translation of Letourneux's *Instructions chrétiennes sur le sacrement du mariage* ("Christian Instructions on the Sacrament of Marriage") in 1774 (Demerson 247–59). Moreover, why did she express such enthusiasm for Mme de Genlis, a French writer of pedagogical novels to whose works a footnote by María Victoria López-Cordón tells us Amar subscribed (Amar y Borbón, *Educación* 266), while she silenced any reference to French *salonnières* of the seventeenth and eighteenth centuries like Mme de Chatelet or Mme d'Epinay? When Amar justified women's extensive learning by citing Pope Benedict XIV's flattery of Mme du Bocage, why did she limit her reference to Bocage's travel accounts and not mention that the French writer had written a number of plays? What caused Amar not to blink an eye at the cross-dressed figure known as the chevalier d'Eon, who was still alive and thought to be a woman when Amar was writing? What was there about Luisa de Padilla, Luisa Sigea, and Oliva Sabuco that drew their names into her work? And what is the discriminating factor when Amar puts forth as celebrated models of female leaders Isabella I of Spain, England's Elizabeth I and Queen Anne, and Russia's Catherine the Great, but not the learned Queen Christina of Sweden? More than reflecting just space and time limitations, the presence and the absence of certain famous women in Amar's work points to something else behind her rhetorical strategy.

There is a perceptible pattern in the author's decisions to underline or silence certain women's lives and achievements in accord with the arguments and proposals her essays make. By looking at the many female figures to whom Amar refers, and the women writers she cites, we can see the outline of an ideological project in her writings that shapes an ideal female model by refining and focusing the catalogs of illustrious women that proliferated in Europe from the Renaissance through the eighteenth and nineteenth centuries. A related issue to the questions surrounding the inclusion or exclusion of certain female models in Amar's essays is why she never once mentions by name any Spanish woman of her time. To my mind we perceive in that specific silence Amar y Borbón's exquisite social discretion and good taste, which rise from several considerations: a recognition of her society's bias against noblewomen's writing for publication, Amar's own social status, and her concern not to alienate her potential readership.

I begin with Amar's discretion vis-à-vis her female contemporaries in Spain. We know that major aristocratic women like the countess of Montijo and the countess-duchess of Benavente were intelligent and well educated (Demerson; Yebes), but Paula de Demerson noted (253) that the former was extremely reluctant to reveal her name on her 1774 translation of Letourneux's book on marriage, and the latter—like other noblewomen who were named members of Madrid's Junta de Damas in the last decade of the eighteenth century—published only the required "letter of appreciation" for that nomination. A female-repressive culture had made it seem that writing for publication, especially by married women, was an expression of a woman's vanity and pride, and indeed, women who published their works in eighteenth-century Spain became targets for criticism and satire.[4] Aristocratic women, whose role included sustaining the dignity of their rank and name, avoided putting their own writing in a public spotlight that might draw such derision. It is difficult to discern whether Amar's avoidance of nonaristocratic Catalina de Caso's translation of Rollin is intellectual snobbery (as I take her frequent insistence on using original texts to be), whether it represents Amar's disapproval of the caliber of Caso's translation, or whether the silence is a social discretion of some sort. In any event, had Amar mentioned as models some women of her time but not others, she would offend those left out and perhaps those she included as well. Beyond these considerations, reference to the talents of aristocratic women might be read as an attempt by Amar to curry favor with those above her station, while reference to actresses, music hall performers, or wealthy women of the merchant classes might mean losing the acquiescence of the snobbish aristocracy, who might sniff at being lumped together with those who were beneath them in rank and status if not always in wealth and reputation.

Amar's delicacy in avoiding these problems has a great deal to do with the reading audience she addressed, most particularly in her book on women's education, *Discurso sobre la educación física y moral de las mujeres.* With the possible exception of the prologue, which seems geared to the men who might approve the publication of her text, the book speaks to privileged women of both the traditional nobility and the emerging middle class of wealthy merchants and the monarchy's extensive bureaucracy. Amar reveals a further sensitivity to women's varied circumstances within the classes she addresses: she is explicit in commenting that social status and the money one needed to sustain its outward appearance in an appropriate lifestyle did not always go hand in hand.

Such careful attention to the varying sensitivities of Spain's shifting class signifiers, from status by birth to status by money, education, and lifestyle, may have a connection with Amar's own social position. She was born into Aragon's untitled lower nobility, the *infanzones,* Aragon's equivalent of the Castilian hidalgos. Because her father and grandfather were doctors of medicine and both her husband and son were lawyers and judges, today's scholars label Amar as belonging to Spain's eighteenth-century "burguesía de profesiones liberales" (professional middle class). We still tend to ascribe social class status to a woman on the basis of the class situation of the men in her family, but that practice minimizes an Old Regime mentality that recognized a woman's own status by her birth or lineage. A clue to Amar's social position is that all her brothers chose the traditional occupations of the nobility—the army or the church. Further, the Amar y Borbón family's marriage strategy revealed its intention to enhance its *infanzón* status by having at least the eldest son and heir marry into the titled aristocracy. Josefa was thus of good class by birth (especially on her mother's side) and of the bureaucratic or administrative professional middle class by association with her father and her husband.[5] Although that dual class ascription placed her among Zaragoza's tiny elite, Amar and her husband were neither titled nor anywhere near as wealthy as such local luminaries as Ramón de Pignatelli, the count of Torresecas, the marquises of Lazán and Ayerbe, or the duke and duchess of Villahermosa. Amar's social circle in her home town was strongly aristocratic but also included the professional elites—particularly of the audiencia, the university, and the church—and the wealthy merchant class. It was this mixed, privileged audience that she addressed so adroitly in her book. That gesture of inclusive address of women of two classes anticipated the nineteenth century's practice of middle-class emulation of aristocratic lifestyle as an element in establishing its own identity and preeminence.

Cataloging as Rhetorical Device

Essayistic use of a rhetoric that argued in part from example or the evidence of history was anything but innovative by the 1780s when Amar wrote. She used such a time-honored rhetoric, however, because of its logical efficacy: if a rule has not just one but many exceptions drawn from historical record or experience, that rule does not stand the scrutiny of logic. Amar's feminist essay of 1786 supported the admission of women to Madrid's Economic Society, one of Spain's new paragovernmental public spaces. In that essay Amar named women whose lives and accomplishments contradicted gender stereotypes of her time, and at one point—as she would do later in the prologue to her book, albeit with different citations—she even listed other lists of famous women. There were many to choose from, and Amar's selectivity and the social and gender ideology that it supports become clear when one compares the catalogs of illustrious women she cites with the individual women whose lives she holds up as examples or models of women's intelligence, capabilities, and achievements.

The precision, depth, and breadth of Amar y Borbón's scholarship causes admiration. My research has found that if she cites a work in her text or in a footnote, she has read it, unless she indicates that she only saw a reference to an interesting text in another book. Thus when Amar rather impatiently rushes through a list of books that defend women's dignity and intelligence, what we read is both a bit of intellectual arrogance and signs of Amar's search for published evidence that supports her feminist argument. In her citations of other lists—such as Damião de Froes Perim's *Theatro heroino, abecedario histórico e catálogo das mulheres illustres* ("Theater of Heroines, or Alphabetized Historical Catalog of Famous Women"), Riballier's *L'éducation physique et morale des femmes* ("The Physical and Moral Education of Women"), or Nifo's *El amigo de las mujeres* ("The Friend of Women") (his translated adaptation of Mirabeau's *L'ami des femmes*)—Amar implicitly makes all the celebrated women mentioned by those authors part of her text. This reference to previous catalogs incorporates female saints, martyrs, heroes, rape victims, goddesses, fictional characters, pious nuns and mystics, queens, titled aristocrats of famed prudence, adventurers, women of famous learning, and women writers. Nevertheless, many women's names do not reach the textual surface of Amar's essays. For her own texts, at the explicit naming and discussing level, Amar y Borbón selected carefully; according to her own thinking about women in the world, she eliminated the negative and accentuated the positive examples.

Who's Not There?

Amar might discuss Eve's greater intellectual curiosity in the Garden of Eden as proof of women's intelligence through their desire to learn, but had Eve been a saint, martyr, mystic, the Virgin Mary, or simply a nun, she would have been edited out of the 1786 essay. Amar shared the Spanish Enlightenment's secularizing reformist mentality that viewed nuns and monks as useless to the state and to the common good. They were economically and socially unproductive.[6] The author's social and gender ideology is promarriage, since for her and her Enlightenment contemporaries in Old Regime Spain, marriage was the foundation of the state or nation in a structural as well as a symbolic sense. She believed that most women should marry for the greater good of the stability of society as a whole as well as for women's own freedom to move about in the world and their greatest chance at happiness. Amar was unsympathetic to any mysticisms: even the famous Joan of Arc is absent from Amar's list of famous women warriors for that reason and perhaps because Joan burned at the Inquisition's stake. To name just three of the many women religious and saints whose names appear in many catalogs of famous women to which Amar refers, Santa Teresa de Jesús, Sor María de Agreda, and Sor Juana Inés de la Cruz are absent from Amar's specific examples because they were nuns or mystics. She knew that these three had been active writers; her husband's library contained Sor María de Agreda's *Mystica ciudad de Dios* ("Mystic City of God") and a complete set of Benito Jerónimo Feijoo's writings in which his 1726 "Defensa de las mugeres" ("A Defense of Women") discussed the writings of Sor Juana Inés and Teresa de Jesús. Feijoo's essay on women, in fact, contains a long catalog or list of women, which was excised from his "Defensa de las mujeres" in every edition from 1800 to 1997. In it, Feijoo had presented a number of cases in which women showed courage by committing suicide or by killing their rapist or abductor. Amar silences such cases, perhaps because the images of violence done to women are negative and involve the mortal sin of suicide, or because they have to do with a cultural stereotype that portrays women as objects of sexual desire.

Also silenced in Amar's writings is the existence of any woman whose sexual chastity was suspect, even if such a woman had been known for her learning and writing. Thus we see Amar allude admiringly to Isabella I of Spain, Elizabeth I of England, and Catherine the Great of Russia as successful heads of state and, in Catherine's case, as a writer, whereas she ignores the existence of the sexually problematic Christina of Sweden and the questionably virtuous French women who hosted famous salons and corresponded with men of Europe's Enlightenment Republic of Letters.

Probably because of Amar's insistent avoidance of the topic of women's sexuality, indeed her belief that women by nature were too susceptible to their passions, she omits reference to most women novelists. In the case of Mme du Bocage, she omits reference to dramatic works by a female author whose existence and travel books Amar otherwise found useful to her purposes. Mónica Bolufer and Catherine Jaffe have analyzed men's fears that women's literacy might lead to intellectual autonomy and written expression and how eighteenth-century Spanish representations of women reading attempted to control and redirect any such autonomy. Like many prescriptive male reformers of the Enlightenment, Amar recommended that women not read novels or plays and that they not attend the theater, for in all such works they would find themselves transported into worlds of fantasy, love, and intrigue that encouraged women's passions by showing adulterous love, female misery in marriage, and other personal and social disasters. Any potential cause of female resistance to or rebellion against the institution of marriage, which was so important a part of Amar's social ideology, had to be avoided. It is not surprising, then, that María de Zayas fails to appear among the other talented, accomplished women whom the author mentions by name, just as it does not surprise that the French women writers of the 1770s discussed in the duke of Almodóvar's pseudonymously published (as Francisco María de Silva) *Década epistolar sobre el estado de las letras en Francia* ("Ten Letters on the State of Literature in France") remain below the textual surface of Amar's evocations of eminent and exemplary women.

Who Makes the Cut?

I see an appreciable difference between Amar's fiery, quickly written feminist essay of 1786 and her lengthier and carefully wrought *Discurso sobre la educación física y moral de las mujeres.* In her defense of women's capacities as a sex, Amar pits one sex against the other, as did her antagonist in the Madrid Economic Society debate, forgetting the class, marital, and maternal standards with which her 1790 book on women's education would posit a gendered ideal figure. The examples of admirable women that the writer offers in the 1786 essay correspond to her will to prove that women can show certain positive character traits equally with men. In her essay's examples that show women's bravery, prudence, ability to keep secrets, diplomacy, discretion, and leadership capacity, Amar echoes Feijoo's rhetoric. The procedure was to argue rationally against the cultural assertion that women are never capable of this or that and then add historical examples that contradict such an assertion.

Of course, in her defense of women's intelligence Amar responds to more than traditional cultural gender concepts or biases. She is also responding to specific arguments against women's participation in the new public sphere of activities that Spain's Economic Societies represented in the late eighteenth century, namely, antifemale arguments made by Francisco Cabarrús, a prominent member of the Madrid Economic Society, who was to become the head of Spain's Bank of San Carlos. In this targeted response, Amar argues some examples of historical women who were not highly educated, married, or of privileged class. These include famous heroines in battle from the time of Carlos V, such as one woman who received from the king a lifetime pension in reward for her soldiery and the biblical Judith, who daringly crossed enemy lines to slay Holofernes in defense of her country. An unmarried woman could enter Amar's 1786 list of model women if she was renowned for her learning like Juliana Morrell (whose story Amar drew from the original seventeenth-century edition of Nicolás Antonio's catalog of Spanish writers). A single or married woman who actually taught at a university (for example, the Italian Cayetana Agnesi at the University of Bologna) would draw Amar's attention and reveal her indirect endorsement of allowing qualified women to teach in universities.

The amazing French chevalier d'Eon, whose eighteenth-century contemporaries did not know was really a man cross-dressed as a woman who cross-dressed as a man, was extensively described in Amar's 1786 essay as an example of how a woman could do everything in the public world that men did: be a diplomat, spy, military officer, or writer and traveler, all in the service of her country. By insisting on this kind of multitalented female figure, Amar was going far beyond Feijoo's discussion of women's roles and capabilities, just as she went beyond Juan Bautista Cubié's 1768 *Las mugeres vindicadas de las calumnias de los hombres* ("Women Vindicated from the Calumnies of Men"), which was, as Sally-Ann Kitts noted, a reworking and at times a near-verbatim plagiarism of Feijoo's "Defensa de las mugeres" (263). In 1726, Feijoo did not give much thought to the idea of women in governing positions, but Cubié devoted his last chapter to negating women's ability to govern at all. Scholars seem to have missed the uniqueness in Spain's Enlightenment feminist discourse of Amar's advocacy of women in public leadership, because Feijoo's list of female examples was dropped from editions of his feminist essay for more than two hundred years and few scholars have read Cubié on the issue. Amar was more radical than either of her eighteenth-century Spanish forebears in arguing that women could be effective in any public activity that men undertook, even if those women had not been born with royal blood.

Amar's book on education draws a clear model for other women of her time and the mixed socioeconomic classes she addresses. In my reading of her work and her life, this model replicates what the author herself aspired to be: an extensively educated married woman of the privileged classes, chaste, and well organized in her daily life so that she could combine her domestic duties with required (and desired) social activities and diligent study. This paradigmatic figure would necessarily attract public admiration and renown for combining "women's work" with intellectual work. Such a model woman would bear the various travails of marriage through strength of character and the acquired skill of conversing in polite society on serious subjects. In Amar's imagined utopia of domestic and social happiness, a diligent woman's solitary reading and study would be compensated with respect, admiration, and desire for her company—from her husband, her sons, and members of polite and even intellectual and scholarly society. This model woman would be the opposite of the empty-headed, fashion-crazed female satirized by eighteenth-century society. She would contradict the Renaissance gender construction that limited extensive learning and erudition to unmarried women. For Amar, a woman did not lose her intelligence when she married or when she had household and child-rearing duties. This centering on married women's lives and capabilities is an innovative aspect of Amar's thinking, and the combined emphasis on married women and extensive learning (even publishing) would be lost in the nineteenth century's construction of the ideal woman.

The strong positive models Amar puts forward in her book are all intelligent, educated women. They may include an Italian scholar who taught at the University of Bologna; the highly educated Mme du Bocage, who inspired the enlightened Pope Benedict XIV to gallant flattery; or the sixteenth-century Juliana Morrell, who won praise for her public examinations at the University of Toulouse. But it is the dignified and respected married woman, mother, intellect, and patriot who wins Amar's true endorsement: Saint Jerome's mother, a pious, chaste, maternal woman and a reader of Latin; certain classical matrons, especially Eurydice, who combined marriage and motherhood with learning and patriotism; the Renaissance personage Luisa Sigea, who shone for her erudition; Oliva Sabuco, whom Amar proudly cited as a medical authority whose book advanced scientific knowledge; Luisa de Padilla, an early seventeenth-century countess of Aranda, whose published book *Nobleza virtuosa* ("Virtuous Nobility") was cast as advice to her son and daughter. Amar quotes and footnotes these female authorities and others, like Mme de Lambert, whenever she can. Clearly, she had searched for them and valued their work. She thereby brought to her female readers examples of constructive things they could accomplish if they willed it.

My reading of Amar's book finds two contemporary or nearly contemporary female examples who fulfill the writer's ideal vision: Sophia Brenner and Mme de Genlis. These two European upper-class married women with children perfectly performed all the gender-based expectations for women of their century. Moreover, they were highly educated teachers and writers. In Amar's portrayal of Brenner one senses the author's enthusiasm at finding an incarnation of her ideal:

> No ha degenerado en estos últimos tiempos el talento ni la aplicación de algunas mujeres. En este mismo siglo ha sido famosa Sofía Isabel Weber, mujer de Elías Brenner, hombre docto, empleado en el Archivo Real de Suecia. Nació en 1659 en Estocolmo, y desde luego se hizo célebre por su vasta erudición y talento poético. Tuvo

> quince hijos, a los cuales dio excelente educación, y cultivó las letras sin faltar a las obligaciones que prescribe el gobierno doméstico. Mantenía correspondencia con varios literatos, y era tan grande la fama de su literatura, que se acuñaron monedas para perpetuar su memoria. Una de ellas representaba en el anverso su efigie, y en el reverso un laurel con esta inscripción: *Crescit cultura.* Y otra, en que se veían las figuras de ella y de su marido con este epígrafe: *Conjuge vir felix, felix erat illa marito.* Murió en 1730.
>
> (*Educación* 69–70)

> Neither the talent nor the diligent study of some women has deteriorated in recent times. In our own century there has been the famous Sophia Isabel Weber, wife of Elias Brenner, a learned man with a position in Sweden's Royal Archive. She was born in 1659 in Stockholm and soon became well known for her vast erudition and poetic talent. She had fifteen children, to whom she gave an excellent education, and she cultivated her own learning without slighting the duties and responsibilities of running her household. She corresponded with a number of men of letters, and so great was her literary fame that coins were minted to perpetuate her memory. One coin had her profile on its face while its other side carried a laurel wreath with this inscription: *Crescit cultura.* Another coin had engraved on it the faces of this woman and her husband with the epigraph *Conjuge vir felix, felix erat illa marito.* She died in 1730.

Amar's contemporary, the countess of Genlis (Stéphanie-Félicité Ducrest de Saint Aubin), appears in the writer's annotated bibliography of recommended readings on education, in the last chapter of her book. A member by birth of the French aristocracy and married to a count, Genlis was well educated, well traveled, a wife and mother, governess to royal children, and already the author of a number of published pedagogical novels, tales, and plays in prose by the time Amar wrote her book. Amar states that the "escritos de esta señora [. . .] merecen [. . .] el aprecio de todos los inteligentes" (*Educación* 266) ("this lady's writings deserve the high regard of all knowledgeable people"). Genlis's books of the 1770s and 1780s were pedagogical novels. *Adèle et Théodore, ou Lettres sur l'éducation* (1782) is an epistolary novel about the correct way to raise a son and daughter of good birth and about a young prince's training to inherit the crown of his country. The novel is totally coherent with Amar's feminist ideology, and it is no wonder that Amar appreciated this French woman's writings. Genlis appended to the novel a detailed, year-by-year curriculum for her character Adèle, in case her readers had been too caught up in the tale itself to recall the intricate, subtle pedagogy implemented by Adèle's mother. In the novel, this maternal figure earns the right to direct her daughter's education (her son's is considered her husband's responsibility); her husband grants her that permission on the basis of the woman's proven discretion, learning, and chaste forbearance of his infidelity to her. Thus we have another instance of Amar's ultimate model, not simply in the protagonist of this narrative, but in Genlis herself as a contemporary author and teacher concerned with improving women's minds as well as providing them with the required social graces and domestic management skills.[7]

The feminist gestures made by Amar y Borbón concern herself as a Spanish woman of the eighteenth century, in the sense that she obviously spent a great deal of her study time searching for other women who had done what she wanted to do and what she thought other women could do. She found imitable figures in narrative histories of the classical age and of other lands and in catalogs of celebrated women of the past and present that ranged from the relatively brief account of the women writers of contemporary France by the duke of Almodóvar to the gigantic grab bags compiled by men of her century and earlier. In her two original essays, Amar left clear signposts for other women that there is a tradition in the world, even a Spanish tradition, of women celebrated for their combination of talents and skills. But in providing such signposts, Amar consciously picked and chose from the large and indiscriminate catalogs female exemplaries who were positive. She chose women whose lives she approved: women who were sexually chaste but yet not nuns, mystics, or saints; married women who ran smooth households and raised healthy children; women whose company was sought after for their extensive learning, their excellent conversation, and their good taste; women who were useful to society. Ultimately, Amar's female models figure a bourgeois ideology of the perfect wife and mother, but with two twists. She directs her modeling effort simultaneously at aristocratic and at middle-class women, a move that potentially shapes the new bourgeois woman through her class's desire to imitate the aristocracy. And by emphasizing extensive book learning for married women, Amar incorporates the Renaissance ideal of the learned unmarried woman into a new ideal of the wife, mother, and scholar.

We have no evidence that any Spanish woman writer of the nineteenth century read their emphatically feminist forebear, Josefa Amar y Borbón. This seems to be true even for the well-educated feminists Concepción Arenal and Emilia Pardo Bazán, each of whom replicated parts of Amar y Borbón's feminist project while believing that in the Spanish eighteenth century only Feijoo had argued for women's equal intelligence and the necessity of women's education. Amar searched far and wide in her readings and culled the ubiquitous catalogs of celebrated women to find and cite dignified, well-educated women writers as models for married women. But in essays, biographies, conduct books, and novels, these and other nineteenth-century Spanish women writers omitted from their representation of women the wife-mother-scholar-writer ideal whose tradition Amar had attempted to construct in the last years of the eighteenth century, just as they omitted Amar y Borbón herself. Happily, new scholarship has begun to recuperate forgotten figures like Amar and to examine closely her contributions to the creation of a feminist tradition in Spain.

Notes

1. An excellent recent study examines Amar's feminist thought in the context of the Spanish and the European Enlightenment: Mónica Bolufer Peruga's *Mujeres e Ilustración* ("Women and Enlightenment").
2. Spanish archives contain a number of manuscript works by eighteenth-century women writers who either did not wish to publish them or were denied that option by government or ecclesiastical censors. I also note here that, in my opinion, the author of the Cádiz periodical of 1763–64, *La pensadora gaditana,* was a man.
3. Amar y Borbón's works do not have published English translations. All translations to English in this essay are my own.
4. It is curious that of the late-eighteenth-century Spanish women writers we know today, all were middle-class and a good number were of foreign extraction: Inés Joyes-Blake, Margarita Hickey, María Gertrudis Hore of the Irish

Rory clan, and María Rosa Gálvez, an orphan raised by a good Spanish family, among others.

5. All information in this essay about Amar y Borbón's personal life and family is drawn from my research for a biography of the author. Also see my articles "Josefa Amar y Borbón (1749–1833)" and "The Quiet Feminism." For more work on women and the Enlightenment, see Bolufer Peruga's "Josefa Amar e Inés Joyes" and Bolufer and Isabel Morant Deusa's "On Women's Reason."
6. From the initial years of Bourbon rule in Spain the monarchy claimed royal prerogative over matters the church had long controlled, even in civil and criminal disputes. By the mid-eighteenth century Spanish economists and governmental figures were arguing that some of Spain's problems were due to the large population of regular clergy (cloistered monks and nuns), who were not productive citizens, and to the clergy's perpetual ownership of extensive landholdings.
7. In *Adèle and Théodore* there is a gripping interpolated Gothic tale, along with other stories of women who ruined their lives, or their daughter's lives, through ignorance, stupidity, greed, lust, and betrayal. Apparently, Amar y Borbón loved a good story, but it had to be edifying.

Works Cited

Agreda, Sor María de Jesús de. *Mystica ciudad de Dios.* 3 vols. Madrid: Imprenta de la Causa, 1725.

Amar y Borbón, Josefa. "Discurso en defensa del talento de las mujeres, y de su aptitud para el gobierno, y otros cargos en que se emplean los hombres." *Memorial literario, instructivo y curioso de la Corte de Madrid* 8.3 (1786): 399–430.

———. *Discurso sobre la educación física y moral de las mujeres.* 1790. Ed. María Victoria López-Cordón. Madrid: Cátedra, 1994.

Antonio, Nicolás. *Bibliotheca Hispana Nova sive Hispanorum Scriptorum qui ab anno MD ad MDCLXXXIV fluorere Notitia.* 2nd ed. 2 vols. Madrid: Ibarra, 1783, 1788.

Bolufer Peruga, Mónica. "*Espectadores* y lectoras: Representaciones e influencia del público femenino en la prensa del siglo XVIII." *Cuadernos de estudios del siglo XVIII* 5 (1995): 23–57.

———. "Josefa Amar e Inés Joyes: Dos perspectivas femeninas sobre el matrimonio en el siglo XVIII." *Historia de la familia: Una nueva perspectiva sobre la sociedad europea.* Murcia: Universidad de Murcia, 1994. 1–24.

———. *Mujeres e Ilustración. La construcción de la feminidad en la España del siglo XVIII.* Valencia: Alfons el Magnànim, 1998.

Bolufer Peruga, Mónica, and Isabel Morant Deusa. "On Women's Reason, Education, and Love: Women and Men of the Enlightenment in Spain and France." *Gender and History* 10.2 (1998): 183–216.

Cabarrús, Francisco. "Discurso [ante socios de la Real Sociedad Económica Matritense de los Amigos del País]." *Memorial literario, instructivo y curioso de la Corte de Madrid* 8.29 (1786): 74–85.

Cubié, Juan Bautista. *Las mugeres vindicadas de las calumnias de los hombres. Con un catalogo de las Españolas, que mas se han distinguido en ciencias, y armas.* Madrid: Pérez de Soto, 1768.

Demerson, Paula de. *María Francisca de Sales Portocarrero, condesa del Montijo: Una figura de la Ilustración.* Madrid: Editora Nacional, 1975.

Feijoo y Montenegro, Fr. Benito Gerónimo. "Defensa de las mugeres." *Theatro crítico universal.* Nueva edición corregida y aumentada. Vol. 1. Madrid: Blas Roman, 1781. 387–473. Barcelona: Icaria, 1997.

Froes Perim, Damião de. *Theatro heroino, abecedario histórico e catálogo das mulheres illustres em armas, letras, acções heroicas, e artes liberaes.* 2 vols. Lisbon, 1736–40.

Genlis, Stéphanie-Félicité de. *Adèle et Théodore, ou Lettres sur l'éducation; Contenant tous les principes relatifs aux trois différens plans d'éducation des princes et des jeunes personnes de l'un et de l'autre sexe.* 2nd ed. Paris: Lambert, 1782.

Jaffe, Catherine. "Suspect Pleasure: Writing the Woman Reader in Eighteenth-Century Spain." *Dieciocho* 22 (1999): 35–59.

Kitts, Sally-Ann. *The Debate on the Nature, Role, and Influence of Woman in Eighteenth-Century Spain.* Lewiston: Mellen, 1995.

Letourneux, Nicolas. *Instrucciones cristianas sobre el sacramento del matrimonio.* Trans. condesa de Montijo. Barcelona, 1774.

———. *Instructions chrétiennes sur le sacrement du mariage et sur les cérémonies avec lesquelles l'église l'administre.* 9th ed. Paris: Mariette, 1727.

Nifo, Francisco Mariano. *El amigo de las mujeres.* Madrid: Ramírez, 1763.

Padilla, Luisa de. *Nobleza virtuosa.* Zaragoza: Lanaja y Quartanet, 1637.

[Riballier]. *L'éducation physique et morale des femmes, avec une notice de celles qui se sont distinguées dans les différentes carrières des sciences et des beaux-arts, ou par des talens et des actions mémorables.* Brussels: Estienne, 1779.

Rollin, Charles. *Modo de enseñar y estudiar las bellas letras, para ilustrar el entendimiento y rectificar el corazon.* Trans. María Cathalina de Caso. 4 vols. Madrid, 1755.

———. *Traité des études, ou la Manière d'enseigner et d'étudier les belles-lettres par rapport à l'esprit et au coeur.* Paris: Estienne, 1726.

Sabuco, Oliva. *Nueva filosofía de la naturaleza del hombre.* Madrid: Madrigal, 1587.

Silva, Francisco María de [duque de Almodóvar]. *Década epistolar sobre el estado de las letras en Francia.* Madrid: Sancha, 1781.

Sullivan, Constance A. "Josefa Amar y Borbón (1749–1833)." *Spanish Women Writers: A Bio-Bibliographical Source Book.* Ed. Linda Gould Levine, Ellen Engelson Marson, and Gloria Feiman Waldman. Westport: Greenwood, 1993. 32–43.

———. "The Quiet Feminism of Josefa Amar y Borbón's Book on the Education of Women." *Indiana Journal of Hispanic Literatures* 2.1 (1993): 49–73.

Yebes, condesa de. *La condesa-duquesa de Benavente: Una vida en unas cartas.* Madrid: Espasa-Calpe, 1955.

Becoming "Angelic": María Pilar Sinués and the Woman Question

María Cristina Urruela

> [L]a mujer es el Atlante sobre cuyos flacos hombros descansa el edificio de la familia; un sólo paso en falso, y el edificio se derriba y se convierte en ruinas [. . .].
>
> —Angela Grassi, *El copo de nieve* ("The Snowflake")

> A woman is the Atlantis upon whose slender shoulders rests the edifice of the family; one false step, and the edifice collapses into ruins.

In the 1990s scholars began to look more carefully at the Spanish "literatas" ("literary ladies") who wrote between 1850 and 1890 and whose work belongs to the sentimental-moralist tradition sanctioned but not validated by the male literary establishment of nineteenth-century Spain.[1] The writers Angela Grassi, Concepción Gimeno de Flaquer, Faustina Sáez de Melgar, Joaquina Balmaseda, and María Pilar Sinués formed a sisterhood among Romantic women poets similar to that described by Susan Kirkpatrick (*Románticas*). They were recognized figures in the feminine press, enjoyed the patronage of Isabella II, won numerous literary awards, prefaced each other's works, and wrote words of praise and encouragement for one another.

Sinués (1835?–1893), the first Spanish woman known to have supported herself exclusively through her writing, was one of the most prolific and successful writers of this group. She published extensively during her lifetime—at least twenty-eight novels, seventeen biographies of eminent women (a recuperative effort whose subjects included Joan of Arc; Mary, Queen of Scots; Santa Teresa of Avila; and Diane de Poitiers, as well as the lesser-known Catalina Gabrielli, María Josefina Tascher de la Pagerie, and Luisa Maximiliana de Stolberg);[2] two books of poetry; two textbooks for girls, which were adopted in the academies for young women; and several translations of popular French women writers. Her novels boasted several editions, and she continued to be very popular within and outside Spain well into the twentieth century. She was widely read in Latin America, where the prescribed social role for women and its inherent contradictions have varied little in the hundred years since she penned her novels. Until 1908, editions of her books were still printed in Lima, Buenos Aires, and Mexico.

For postmodern readers, Sinués's fiction is at times difficult to approach because of her florid prose, convoluted plots, and her insistence on separate spheres for men and women. Sinués's "earnest interventions"—a term coined by Robyn Warhol (115) to describe the frequent interventions of women authors through their narrators in Victorian texts—add to the distance between postmodern and nineteenth-century styles and taste.[3] Nonetheless, Sinués is a key figure in the development of the struggle for feminine autonomy in nineteenth-century Spain, and she actively participated in the debate over the so-called woman question—the debate over women's position in society that involved supporters and opponents of women's advancement during this period of accelerating socioeconomic and political change.[4] To date, most critics who have examined Sinués's work still perceive her as second-rate, "an author as productive as she was mediocre" (Pérez 12–13). She is generally thought of as a promoter of the ideology dominated by the feminine figure of the angel of the house, as Spain's sentimental writer par excellence, and as antiemancipationist.[5] Certainly her fiction offers plenty of examples that suggest her acceptance of the status quo. This attitude is exemplified in the prologue to *Un libro para las damas* ("A Book for the Ladies"), where she states, "yo no soy de las que abogan por la emancipación de la mujer, ni aún entro en el número de las personas que la creen posible" (8) ("I am not among those who advocate the emancipation of women, nor am I even among those who think it possible"). Yet throughout her career Sinués wrote explicitly for women and consistently sought access to a broader education for them at a time when most Spanish women could neither read nor write and when, by law, those who did write needed the permission of a husband, father, or brother to publish (see Enders and Radcliff; Davies; Jover).

As Mary Nash and others have amply illustrated, woman's subordinate status was formalized in the Código Civil (Civil Code) of 1889.[6] It is therefore not surprising that Sinués should mirror dominant cultural attitudes in her fiction long before they were institutionalized. She began to write in an era still influenced by Romantic ideology, when women were unlikely to gain the intellectual autonomy some women writers were advocating. Later, when the realist tradition prevailed, the general perception in Spain was that women could not write realist novels, because they lacked experience. Even the outspoken Pardo Bazán, a generation later, was careful in her fiction "not to expose herself to harsh moralistic criticism," as Joyce Tolliver discusses in "Knowledge, Desire" (909). As evidenced by the example of Concepción Arenal—an early feminist who was open in her criticism of the establishment and who was not only unpopular but also considered cold, dry, and "varonil" ("masculine")—it would have been very difficult for Sinués to gain the support of the male establishment by overtly challenging the widespread derision of women and their capabilities.[7]

Nonetheless, time and again Sinués presented herself explicitly as a woman writer in favor of educating women and furthering their role as productive members of society.[8] Her fiction is very conflicted and nuanced in its treatment of women; overall she creates a strong sense of female strength in settings dominated by women. Her writing needs to be analyzed vis-à-vis her role as an advocate for reform in women's socialization and professional advancement. The cultural influence of the gender ideology she preached is lampooned today in Hispanic women's literature as wide-ranging as that of Isabel Allende and Carmen Martín Gaite.[9]

Sinués's profile as a professional writer also stands in contradiction to the angel-of-the-house feminine ideal seen in her fiction. She was financially independent, childless, and separated from her husband. Yet in spite of her productivity and her popularity as a writer, in her literary life she tried to emphasize a lack of differentiation between herself as a writer and her public persona by striving always to be perceived as a lady in both. A telling anecdote about Sinués that illustrates this point is that she was always found dutifully sewing when visitors arrived; yet, according to Julio Nombela, her contemporary and, like her, a writer of serialized novels, she sewed the same piece all her life.[10] Thus there appears to be a tension in her life just as there is in her fiction. This tension opens areas for interested readers to examine the many ambiguities that recur in her texts, areas that include women's desire, the need for intellectual compatibility in marriage, the benefits of female companionship, and the strength and independence women derive from one another.

Many of the issues confronting women that Sinués addressed in her fiction go against the norms of femininity, even though the discourse she used was almost always couched in terms of dedication to the family and children. The question of marriage and autonomy, for example, is a recurring thematic concern. I have chosen to analyze the novella *La sortija* ("The Ring"), one of the works making up the trilogy *Páginas del corazón* ("Pages from the Heart"), because its themes, characterizations, plot turns, and tensions are representative of several other novels that Sinués published between 1857 and 1875. The intricate plot can be summarized as follows: Lucila, the young protagonist, lives very unhappily with her father and stepmother, Juanita, who is only a few years older than she is. Though her father is financially responsible for her, neither he nor his wife have anything to say to her that is not in the form of an order or a criticism. She is thus constantly made to feel as if she is a burden to them. Lucila is repeatedly reproached for not being mindful enough of her attire, her manners, or her family's needs and desires. She has few friends and takes refuge in reading. She tries to leave her father's house, appealing first to her brother for help and later to women friends, but no one is able—or willing—to do anything for her. The man who wishes to marry her, curiously, has never even met her; he claims to have fallen in love with her beauty upon seeing her miniature portrait. With little to distract her, unable to study or work or leave her father's home, Lucila gradually becomes despondent. She is eventually saved by two women neighbors who understand her (Mrs. Castro—whose very ill daughter Marta, Lucila's age, is traveling in Italy with her aunt in the hope of recovering—and her stepdaughter, Adela). By the end of the novel Lucila has undergone a transformation—however unconvincing—and has changed from a recalcitrant, unangelic young woman into one who is docile, thrifty, and demure. Now that she is recreated, she is ready to begin a home of her own with her prospective husband, Enrique, whom she still has not met.[11] In contrast to the angel-of-the-house ideal, which rests on a notion of woman's submissiveness and abnegation, the attainment of that ideal in this novel is represented as an arduous, untidy process.

How does this change take place and why is the heroine's transformation untidy and problematic, unlike the neat discursive trope of the angel of the house? In this process of becoming angelic, portraits and letters play a key role. For the purpose of this essay, the most significant letter is from Lucila to her brother Fernando, in which she appeals for his help and for asylum in his house. He replies that it would not be proper for a woman, in particular a lady, to abandon her parents' home, no matter what the circumstances; his advice is that Lucila ignore her feelings, endure, and learn to please her stepmother and her father, reinforcing her subordinate status in the private sphere. He also writes that his best friend, Enrique, has passionately exclaimed "¡es una criatura divina!" (325) ("she is a divine creature!") upon seeing Lucila's miniature portrait.[12] Fernando believes marriage to Enrique is the most likely solution to her unhappiness:

> Ahora bien, hermana mía, yo creo que tu belleza ha hecho una profunda impresión en mi amigo, y que le interesa mucho tu desgraciada situación; quizá te llegue a amar algún día; quizá pida tu mano y seas dichosa con él [. . .]; si tú eres prudente y sufrida Enrique te amará sin duda. (326)

> And so, dear sister, I think that your beauty has made a profound impression on my friend and that he is very interested in your un-

> fortunate situation. Perhaps he will come to love you some day; perhaps he will ask for your hand in marriage, and you will be happy with him [. . .]; if you are prudent and long-suffering, Enrique will no doubt come to love you.

He thus tells Lucila to strive to be the divine creature—the objectified, passive woman portrayed in the portrait. This advice is unconvincing not only to the reader but also to the protagonist, who ignores it, leaves her father's house, and appeals for asylum at the house of women friends. There, to her chagrin, she is given the same advice: return home, learn to be patient, and suffer in silence; in short, live up to the ideal of the domestic angel so cogently analyzed by Bridget Aldaraca in *El ángel del hogar* ("The Angel of the House"). When Lucila's efforts at autonomy are met with exhortations of passivity from women as well as from men and when her inability to become an obedient, "good daughter" or her desire for change is met with indifference by those closest to her, she becomes withdrawn and refuses to leave her room. Her unwillingness to conform and her consistent questioning of her prescribed role set her apart from the sentimental values ostensively being delivered. Through Lucila, Sinués presents a range of female responses to the diminished economic and social expectations for women, and they are not tidy and unproblematic. Though Lucila is described as "exigente y caprichosa" ("demanding and capricious"), the narrator offsets the criticism by voicing Lucila's inner thoughts, in which she questions why her life is or must be one of patience and suffering: "'¿Por qué no seré yo buena? ... Pero qué es ser buena, ¡Dios mío!,' añadía después con dolor. '¿Qué es ser buena, ni para qué debo serlo si nadie, nadie me lo ha de agradecer?'" (328) ("'Why am I not good? . . . but what is being good, dear God!,' she painfully added. 'What does it mean to be good? And why should I be good if no one, no one is going to show me gratitude for it?'"). Lucila has gone from being the child "cuya voluntad era la ley para toda la casa" ("whose will was the law of the house") during her mother's lifetime to virtual obliteration under the care of her father and brother. Again, the narrator criticizes Lucila for her "unfeminine" actions and reactions, such as her poor personal appearance and her bad housekeeping habits. The following description of Lucila's bedroom is striking in its representation of the domestic disorder that suggests Lucila's own unease with the feminine role assigned to her:

> Sobre una cómoda se veían algunos libros encuadernados á la rústica y cuyas hojas parecían querer salirse para volar por la estancia; entre estos pliegos, peines sin limpiar, un bote de pomada destapado, que había perdido su perfume, algunos cepillos y multitud de horquillas y alfileres esparcidos [. . .]. Por todas partes se veían prendas de vestir, ajadas y arrugadas, calzado, guantes, mil menudencias, útiles en el ejercicio de su uso, pero muy desagradables a la vista. (316)
>
> On top of a dresser one could see a few crudely bound books with pages that seemed to want to escape and fly about the room. Mixed in were dirty combs, an open jar of pomade that had lost its perfume, a few brushes and a multitude of hairpins and hatpins that were scattered here and there. [. . .] Shabby and wrinkled articles of clothing, shoes, gloves, a thousand trifles, very useful in their own right, but most disagreeable to the eye, were everywhere.

The juxtaposition of books whose pages seem to want to "fly about the room" with a multitude of "feminine" objects that are of little use to Lucila acutely reveals the problem of the "real" woman, who is expected to present herself as an angel at all times; the woman who is constantly exhorted to deny her own individuality and autonomy, to revel in her self-abnegation. Excluded from the masculine circle, the world of action and of books, and also from the feminine one, there is literally no room for a woman like Lucila, who is squeezed into a very small space, both in the portrait and in her room. She perceives silence and seclusion as her only recourses: "había llegado a un estado de pasiva indiferencia; las exhortaciones acerca de la conformidad que debía tener con su suerte habían llegado a serle odiosas, y no veía á ninguna de las pocas amigas que antes tenía" (329) ("she had fallen into a state of passive indifference. Exhortations to accept her lot in life had become odious to her, and she no longer visited with any of the few girlfriends she once had"). But the narrator is also very sympathetic to Lucila's plight and makes frequent allusions to her "indiferencia" ("indifference"), "solitud" ("solitude"), and the "sombría desesperación" ("dark desperation") that accompanies her everywhere. Ignored by her father, her stepmother, and society at large, Lucila remains alone in her room for six years. Sinués does not give her predicament a name, but Lucila's total withdrawal singles her out, at the very least, as severely depressed.

In her study *The Female Malady: Women, Madness, and English Culture, 1830–1980,* Elaine Showalter shows how cultural ideas about the proper behavior of women have affected the diagnosis and the treatment of not-so-proper women—women unable or unwilling to conform to society's image of what they should be. In examining several Victorian English texts, Showalter reiterates the point made earlier by Sandra Gilbert and Susan Gubar that the madwomen that haunt texts written by nineteenth-century women are "the authors' double, the representation of the female author's anger against the rigidities of patriarchal tradition" (4). It is tempting to view Lucila in this light—alone, unloved, odd—a literary representation of Sinués and the creative, intelligent woman in general, one whose desires are untamed and not successfully caged.

Lucila's life begins to turn only after she meets Mrs. Castro and Adela. These women, both of whom conform to the angel-of-the-house ideal, assiduously groom her for marriage, literally and figuratively. When Lucila first meets them, her physical appearance is such that, in addition to bordering on the grotesque, it presents clear symptoms of depression:

> Llevaba un traje de seda de color de lila oscuro, cuyos volantes estaban descosidos y llenos de manchas; su cabello, desgreñado, mugriento, lleno de pomada y manchado, estaba recogido sin gracia ninguna; llevaba sobre su feo peinado unos grandes y pretenciosos lazos de cinta azul con largos cabos que la caían sobre los hombros; un cuello de problemática blancura, y unas mangas en tal mal estado como sus guantes, ajados y descosidos por todas partes. (351)

> She wore a silk dress the color of dark lilac; its ruffles were torn and stained all over. Her matted, filthy hair was discolored, full of pomade and indifferently gathered in; tied over that ugly coiffure in large and pretentious bows were a few blue ribbons with ends that drooped to her shoulders. She wore a collar of questionable

> whiteness and sleeves that were in as poor a state as her gloves—shabby and unstitched everywhere.

Combing her tangled hair and urging her to pay some attention to her personal hygiene and to dress neatly, Mrs. Castro and Adela do a makeover on the troubled Lucila. Mrs. Castro also persuades Lucila to befriend her manipulative stepmother rather than resent her. Whereas Lucila was unable to accept the authoritative discourse of feminine abnegation from her father, her brother, and her women friends, she comes to accept it, or at least make peace with it, when it is transmitted through the mother figure. As Tolliver notes of one of Pardo Bazán's protagonists, it could be said that Sinués's Lucila "vacillates between her own internalization of authoritative discourse and the desire for her own voice" ("Accountability" 106). Bakhtin's word of the fathers ("Discourse")—authoritative, unable to internally persuade its intended audience—is expressed in *La sortija* as the "word of the mothers," with opposite results. Although Mrs. Castro is perpetuating a predetermined discourse (as Sinués herself is doing), she is able to bring Lucila to conform—to a degree—to a traditional Catholic society that does not conform to her. Sinués then writes Lucila out of nonconformity, but the author herself does not do as she is prescribing. What becomes evident as the novel progresses is that as sisters, Lucila, Mrs. Castro, Adela, and Juanita to some extent break down a system of feminine dependence—economic and emotional. In their close-knit ring they read and play the piano, providing sympathetic ears for one another. Their work—embedded in the traditionally gender-marked activities of mending, sewing, and transforming old dresses into new ones—saves them from having to ask men for money for their needs. They become, then, mutually dependent on one another in this inner circle, a feminine sphere emblematized in a ring Juanita ultimately gives to Lucila as a token of friendship. Although in the end Lucila conforms to the angel-of-the-house image, the transition is not idealized by Sinués. The tribulations and humiliation Lucila suffers are not minimized, and she often struggles with herself to become other-oriented, to conform with the normal definition of womanhood (see Bieder).

Even as the novel closes with the conventional wedding ceremony, marriage is possible only after the pawning of Lucila's ring. It brings enough money for Lucila and Enrique to live on for a year. The marriage thus begins with a circumscribed economic independence for Lucila. In a sense the ring, with its implicit sororal bond as it passes from one woman's hand to another, represents feminine autonomy, the opposite of what it usually means in a marriage. Marriage as the conventional subjugation of the female protagonist is further undermined by the narrator's repeated use of imagery that seems to underscore the difference between what things appear to be and what they really are, a constant juxtaposition of absence and presence.

Marta, Mrs. Castro's ailing daughter, is Lucila's counterpoint and an unconvincing character who is barely present in the novella. The young women are the same age, and it is a physical resemblance to Marta that first draws Mrs. Castro to Lucila. The absent Marta's "angelic" nature—soft-spoken, demure, self-effacing, suffering—presents the reader with an image of woman that is extremely passive. As the beautiful Marta travels through Italy, she sends her mother a heliotrope in lieu of a letter because the effort of writing physically exhausts her to the point where the tightness in her chest makes her unable to breathe. Mrs. Castro explains to Lucila, "la pobre niña padece del pecho y se creería que va a morir cuando escribe; tal es la angustia que le da" (363–64) ("the poor child has heart trouble, and the act of writing produces such anguish that she feels as if she is going to die"). The absence of a letter or the act of writing is equated with dying, an unequivocally strong indictment that perhaps mirrors the unenviable position of the Spanish woman writer in the nineteenth century, when flowers, the conventional symbols of femininity, displace female textuality and when projections and dislocations prevail.

Moreover, as the novel closes, the reader learns that Enrique has spent all his savings and a year's salary on a larger-than-life-size portrait of Marta on her deathbed. The portrait in question, "un gran cuadro que dos hombres traían en hombros" (406) ("a large painting that two men carried on their shoulders"), is brought into the Castro household and the dead girl's likeness—"un ángel que volvía a su patria" (408) ("an angel returning to its homeland")—is described in detail. Marta is effaced by an image just as Lucila was replaced, displaced, and constrained by the tiny miniature with which Enrique falls in love. This juxtaposition of images—the small "divine" live woman who is all the while resisting her role and the large "angelic" dead and absent woman—punctuates Enrique's and, by extension, society's, attraction to images. Like nineteenth-century Spain, he quite literally has an emotional and economic investment in the image of the domestic angel, an image that is larger than life. The juxtaposition also highlights the conflictive nature of Sinués's writing, which in *La sortija* is most apparent in Lucila's struggles.

Lucila does not necessarily live happily ever after; the novel ends with the marriage, and the reader is not privy to a sequel. The protagonists do, however, enter a new phase when Lucila and not Enrique grounds the couple in economic reality. As in other novels by Sinués, the question of women's autonomy and, specifically, of their autonomy in marriage is presented from different angles in *La sortija*. On the one hand, the outcome is an unequivocal criticism of woman's position in the marriage equation. On the other, the outcome seems to propagate the trope of the angel of the house, so that her fiction makes problematic the ideology it was designed to convey. What Sinués's female protagonists struggle with most is the psychological burden of living up to the image of this domestic angel of the house, especially since the image conflicts with both the values of the economic marketplace and a woman's own self-image. The female characters of this novel prove to themselves and to others that they can be autonomous and that for them marriage is more of a hindrance than an asset. Nevertheless, their feelings of self-worth are seldom validated by those around them, and this lack of support results in an ambivalence that is never resolved. Sinués exposes the deceptiveness of patriarchal attitudes that assume a woman's first duty is to the men of her nuclear family, when in reality cultural norms and constant badgering (not nature and certainly not nurture) prevail. Women's strength is most revered when it is used in the service of bourgeois ideology, but it is sisterhood, built on the acknowledgment of shared pain and the capacity to endure it that enables women to transcend the need for male approval and male protection.[13]

By building on women's most conventional roles of wife, mother, and friend, Sinués consistently highlights the potential of women to influence the direction of their families and, by extension, of the nation. Nina Auerbach observes that "a community of women may suggest less the honor of fellowship than an antisociety" (3), but for Sinués a community of women becomes a literary motif that underscores the value of a feminine society while subtly challenging masculine assumptions. Sinués's society of women is one in which women can transcend male approval, provide for one another, and then return to their men strengthened. Female archetypes are pitted against one another but ultimately resolve their differences when they discover that their strength lies in unity. This unity is forged in no small part through each woman's common struggle to maintain her autonomy and self-worth on the difficult road to becoming "angelic."

Notes

All translations are mine with the exception of note 19, which contains a translation by Margaret Sayers Peden.

1. In fact, Pérez Galdós parodied some *literatas* in their own time (see Andreu).
2. Sinués thus formed a small reference library for her readers in which she provided female role models. Curiously, her own work and that of other sentimental Spanish writers was conspicuously absent from Pardo Bazán's short-lived series Biblioteca de la mujer ("Woman's Library").
3. In her analysis of narrative intervention, Warhol focuses on how the narrator tells the story and on the ensuing dialogue between the author (represented by the narrator) and the virtual or ideal (female) reader (see preface).
4. According to Karen Offen, the "woman question" "was the expression used by many nineteenth-century writers to describe the complex totality of issues raised for women by their subordinate status in the family and society. Unlike the term 'feminism,' the 'woman question' encompasses the arguments both for and against change in women's position relative to men" (648–49).
5. Sinués has been criticized for political conservatism (Andreu), sentimentalism (Aldaraca; Pérez), and antifeminism (Charnon-Deutsch; Diego 149–52; Kirkpatrick, *Antología;* and Frederick). Bonnie Frederick calls her "the Spanish anti-emancipationist" (47).
6. In marriage, for example, this code established that "el marido debe proteger a la mujer, y ésta obedecer al marido" (Nash 160) ("the husband should protect the wife, and she [must] obey the husband"). It also stipulated, among other things, that a woman had to reside where her husband wished,

that the husband was the administrator of the entirety of the couple's assets and represented his wife, that a woman needed her husband's permission to engage in any civil action, and that a married woman was forbidden to own a business (see Nash).

7. For more on Arenal and her reputation, see María Angeles Durán (Arenal 73–82) and the essays by Lou Charnon-Deutsch and Joyce Tolliver in this volume.
8. An example of Sinués's many direct defenses of women and their engagement with prevailing attitudes about their sex appears in the prologue of her *Galería de mujeres ilustres, narraciones histórico-biográficas* ("A Gallery of Famous Women: Biographical and Historical Narrations") (1884). She writes, "Ilustrar a la mujer ha sido el anhelo que siempre ha guiado mi pluma; si, además de esto, consigo entretenerla agradablemente [. . . ,] ¿quién se ha cuidado hasta ahora de instruirla deleitándola? [. . .] Venid, pues, bellas y encantadoras jóvenes, esposas que estáis aún en la primavera de la vida, madres ancianas y respetables; venid todas las nobles criaturas que pertenecéis a la clase media, que tenéis privaciones sin cuento, por la falta de medios y por la excelencia y delicadeza de vuestros instintos; venid a mi galería de preladas, de guerreras, de poetisas, de santas, de artistas, de reinas, de admirables madres, de heroícas esposas y de ejemplares hijas; busque cada una de ellas la heroína a quien ame o por quien se interese; busque cada una el modelo que le convenga, la virtud que admire, la cualidad que prefiera: todo lo encontraréis en ella: belleza, talento, gracias, heroísmo, sabiduría, santidad, grandeza, virtud y ternura" (7–8) ("My pen has always been guided by the strong desire to educate woman; if, in addition to this, I am able to pleasantly entertain her [. . . ,] who else has taken the time until now to educate her while pleasing her? [. . .] Come then, beautiful and charming young women, wives still in the prime of life, elderly and respected mothers; come, all noble creatures who belong to the middle class, who suffer endless deprivation for lack of funds and because of the goodness and delicacy of your instincts; come to my gallery of prelates, warriors, poets, saints, artists, queens, admirable mothers, heroic wives and exemplary daughters; may each of you look for the heroine you love or admire; look for the model that suits you, the virtue that you admire, the quality that you prefer: you will find it all in the gallery: beauty, talent, gracias, heroism, knowledge, sanctity, virtue, and tenderness [. . .]").
9. In Allende's *Afrodita: Cuentos, recetas y otros afrodisíacos (Aphrodite: A Memoir of the Senses)*, for example, the principles that guided the author to adolescence are not unlike those preached by Sinués a century earlier: "Cuatro principios fundamentales, grabados a fuego desde la más tierna infancia, sostuvieron mi formación de señorita: siéntese con las piernas juntas, camine derecha, no opine y coma como la gente" (64) ("Four fundamental principles, burned into my psyche from earliest childhood, were the underpinnings of my formation as a young lady: sit with your knees together, stand up straight, don't offer your opinion, and eat like a lady" [62]).
10. See Catherine Jagoe. Alda Blanco, quotes Nombela as follows: "Recuerdo que María del Pilar Sinués [. . .] no podía sufrir las chanzonetas de que las

literatas eran blanco lo mismo en España que en los demás países, y cuando iban a visitarla señoras se presentaba a ellas con una labor en la mano, para dar a entender que la había sorprendido dedicada a tareas femeniles. Es seguro que aquel trabajo, solo comenzado, la duró toda la vida" (371) ("I remember that Maria Pilar Sinués couldn't suffer the jokes targeted at literary women in Spain and in other countries, and when ladies came to visit her she greeted them sewing in hand to let them believe that they had found her dedicated to feminine tasks. For sure that piece of work, only begun, lasted her all her life"). The quote from Nombela ends, "y también es seguro que quedó sin terminar cuando la sorprendió la muerte en medio de la más completa y triste soledad" ("And it is also certain that it remained unfinished when death surprised her in the saddest and utmost solitude"). In Nombela's ambivalence and condescension—and in Sinués's possible sense of feminine failure coupled with her insistence, at least in her public persona, that women first and foremost be wives and mothers—we are reminded of the anxiety of authorship that Gilbert and Gubar attributed to nineteenth-century women writers. As Kirkpatrick notes, the needle was still the most important symbol of feminine activity in nineteenth-century culture (*Antología* 11–12).

11. It is relevant to note that Sinués's failed marriage to the playwright José Marco was by proxy.
12. Following Tolliver's analysis of the importance of the gaze, Enrique's words could signal "love at first sight," but they could also express "the male's desire to confirm his own subjectivity, at the expense of converting the woman into object" ("'Sor Aparición'" 399). Moreover, the portrait is an object, and a miniature at that.
13. Again, Sinués's insistence on women's community and solidarity is complex, as evidenced by her assertions that seem to support women's dependence on men: "creo que la mujer necesita la constante protección de un padre, un esposo, un hermano, un hijo; pero también creo que [la mujer] es el apoyo moral, la consolación y la dicha de todos los que la aman; creo que la esfera de acción de la mujer es tan extensa como la del hombre, pero completamente diferente" (prólogo, *Un libro para las damas* 7–8) ("I believe a woman needs the constant protection of a father, a husband, a brother, a son; but I also believe that she is the moral support, the consolation, and the joy of all who love her; I believe that a woman's sphere of duty is as large as a man's but completely different").

Works Cited

Aldaraca, Bridget. *El ángel del hogar: Galdós and the Ideology of Domesticity in Spain.* Ed. María A. Salgado. North Carolina Studies in the Romance Langs. and Lits. 239. Chapel Hill: U of North Carolina P, 1991.

Allende, Isabel. *Afrodita: Cuentos, recetas y otros afrodisíacos.* Barcelona: Plaza y Janés, 1998.

———. *Aphrodite: A Memoir of the Senses.* Trans. Margaret Sayers Peden. New York: Harper, 1998.

Andreu, Alicia. "Maternal Discourse in *La cruz del olivar* by Faustina Sáez de Melgar." *Revista canadiense de estudios hispánicos* 19 (1995): 229–40.

Arenal, Concepción. *El pensamiento igualitario.* Ed. María Angeles Durán. Madrid: Castalia, 1993.

Auerbach, Nina. *Communities of Women: An Idea in Fiction.* Cambridge: Harvard UP, 1978.

Bakhtin, M. M. "Discourse in the Novel." *The Dialogic Imagination: Four Essays by M. M. Bakhtin.* Ed. Michael Holquist. Austin: U of Texas P, 1981. 259–422.

Bieder, Maryellen. "Feminine Discourse / Feminist Discourse: Concepción Gimeno de Flaquer." *Romance Quarterly* 37 (1990): 459–77.

Blanco, Alda. "Domesticity, Education, and the Woman Writer: Spain 1850–1880." *Cultural and Historical Groundings for Hispanic and Luso-Brazilian Feminist Literary Criticism.* Ed. Hernán Vidal. Minneapolis: Inst. for the Study of Ideologies and Lit., 1989. 371–94.

Charnon-Deutsch, Lou. *Narratives of Desire: Nineteenth-Century Spanish Fiction by Women.* University Park: Penn State UP, 1994.

Davies, Catherine. *Spanish Women's Writing, 1849–1996.* London: Athlone, 1998.

Diego, Estrella de. *La mujer y la pintura del XIX español: Cuatrocientas olvidadas y algunas más.* Madrid: Cátedra, 1987.

Enders, Victoria Lorée, and Pamela Beth Radcliff, eds. *Constructing Spanish Womanhood: Female Identity in Modern Spain.* Albany: State U of New York P, 1998.

Frederick, Bonnie. *Wily Modesty: Argentine Women Writers, 1860–1910.* Tempe: Arizona State UP, 1998.

Gilbert, Sandra, and Susan Gubar. *The Madwoman in the Attic: The Woman Writer and the Nineteenth-Century Literary Imagination.* New Haven: Yale UP, 1979.

Jagoe, Catherine. "María del Pilar Sinués de Marco." *Spanish Women Writers: A Bio-Bibliographical Source Book.* Ed. Linda Gould Levine, Ellen Engleson Marson, and Gloria Feiman Waldman. Westport: Greenwood, 1993. 473–83.

Jover, José María. *Política, diplomacia y humanismo popular en la España del siglo XIX.* Madrid: Turner, 1976.

Kirkpatrick, Susan. *Antología poética de escritoras del siglo XIX.* Madrid: Castalia, Instituto de la Mujer, 1992.

———. *Las Románticas: Women Writers and Subjectivity in Spain, 1835–1850.* Berkeley: U of California P, 1989.

Nash, Mary. *Mujer, familia y trabajo en España (1875–1936).* Barcelona: Anthropos, 1983.

Offen, Karen. "Depopulation, Nationalism, and Feminism in Fin-de-Siècle France." *American Historical Review* 89 (1984): 648–76.

Pérez, Janet. *Contemporary Women Writers of Spain.* Boston: Twayne, 1988.

Showalter, Elaine. *The Female Malady: Women, Madness, and English Culture, 1830–1980.* New York: Penguin, 1985.

Sinués, María del Pilar. *Galería de mujeres ilustres, narraciones histórico-biográficas.* Madrid: Suárez, 1884.

———. *Un libro para las damas, estudios acerca de la educación de la mujer.* Madrid: Suárez, 1876.

———. *La sortija. Páginas del corazón.* Madrid: Alvarez, 1887. 287–415.

Tolliver, Joyce. "Knowledge, Desire, and Syntactic Empathy in Pardo Bazán's *La novia fiel.*" *Hispania* 72 (1989): 909–18.

———. "Narrative Accountability and Ambivalence: Feminine Desire in *Insolación.*" *Revista de estudios hispánicos* 23 (1989): 103–18.

———. "'Sor Aparición' and the Gaze: Pardo Bazán's Gendered Reply to the Romantic Don Juan." *Hispania* 77 (1994): 394–405.

Warhol, Robyn. *Gendered Interventions: Narrative Discourse in the Victorian Novel.* New Brunswick: Rutgers UP, 1989.

Rosalía de Castro: Cultural Isolation in a Colonial Context

Catherine Davies

It is extremely ironic that the poet Rosalía de Castro (1837–85) should figure in most literary histories as one of Spain's two most important nineteenth-century poets, second only to her Andalusian contemporary Gustavo Adolfo Bécquer (1836–70). She was Galician, wrote most of her poetry in that tongue, and is credited with the founding of modern Galician literature. When she did publish poetry in Spanish, she was criticized. In 1887 Manuel Tamayo y Baus, director of the National Library and secretary to the Spanish Royal Academy, stated that her Spanish poems were extravagant and full of errors (Blanco Aguinaga 136). Yet the establishment was not keen to see her write in Galician either. The statesman and essayist Juan Valera believed that poets such as Castro should compose in Spanish and refrain from attempting to create a "nuevo idioma literario" from a "dialecto vulgar" (896) ("a new literary language" from a "common dialect"). From the point of view of Madrid, Castro was an outsider, living in the almost inaccessible northwest corner of Spain, writing in what was then considered a dialect only fit for peasants. For making this literary choice and for speaking out on behalf of the Galician poor—particularly the women—she was virtually ostracized by polite society during her lifetime. Conversely, after her death, she was revered by Galicians in Spain and abroad and transformed into a Galician national icon. Castro was thus caught up in one of the most acrimonious political conflicts of modern Spain, a conflict not resolved until after the death of Franco: the struggle between a centralized Spanish government, based in Madrid, and the demands for local, autonomous government in the peripheral regions or nations. That a woman, writing in this political context, from such geographical, linguistic, and ideological margins, should today be recognized in both Galicia and Spain as a major poet is testimony to both the aesthetic quality and the ethical impact of her work.

Castro made few literary contacts. From the age of thirty-four (1871) until her early death, she lived with her children in La Coruña and, later, during the 1880s, virtually isolated in the Galician countryside. At the time, she did not frequent literary *tertulias* ("soirees") and did not enter into correspondence with literary luminaries. Her motive for publishing was to make ends meet: her husband, Manuel Murguía, had been relieved of his post as archivist when the monarchy was restored in 1875.[1] During the Restoration, Castro was far removed from the public eye. This had not always been the case, however. In the 1860s, while living in Madrid, Castro and Murguía had been friendly with G. A. Bécquer, Julio Nombela, and Ventura Ruiz Aguilera. Benito Pérez Galdós even mentioned them briefly in 1868 (Shoemaker 526–28). She and her husband were associated with the progressive Left, supported the revolutions of 1854 and 1868, and worked toward the promotion of a distinctive Galician cultural identity. Once she was married to Murguía (1858), who (like most Galician progressives) did not speak the Galician language, Castro assumed a unique position in the developing nationalist movement. Not only had she spoken Galician since birth (she was brought up among peasants), but she was also educated and could write poetry.[2] She put her literary talents to political ends through her husband's circle of friends, but she first made her presence known to them in her feminist writings. The woman's perspective she adopted in her later work proved crucial for the engendering of Galician cultural nationalism.

The most prestigious woman author with whom Castro first came into contact was Cecilia Böhl de Faber (Fernán Caballero) (1796–1877). Castro dedicated her first important book, *Cantares gallegos* (1863) ("Galician Songs") to Fernán Caballero, "Por ser mujer y autora de unas novelas hacia las cuales siento la más profunda simpatía" (*Poesías* 13) ("because you are a woman and the author of novels that I greatly admire").[3] She also acknowledged Fernán Caballero's positive portrayal of Galicia and her efforts to avoid "los vulgares preocupaciones con que se pretende manchar mi país" (13) ("the rude comments intended to tarnish my country"). She later sent Fernán Caballero a copy of her second novel, *El caballero de las botas azules* (1867) ("The Blue-Booted Knight") (Carballo Calero 101–02). In view of Fernán Caballero's age at the time (over seventy), her traditionalist Catholic ideology, and her naive idealization of rural life, this was not a contact that could flourish into friendship.[4] From a feminist point of view, Castro was influenced predominantly by the Saint-Simonists and George Sand (whose novels Fernán Caballero disliked) (Montesinos 19–20), as she demonstrated in her overtly feminist writings (the prologue to *La hija del mar* [1856] ["The Daughter of the Sea"]; "Lieders" [1858] ["Songs"]; and "Las literatas" [1866] ["Literary Women"]).[5]

According to Murguía, the woman writer who most affected Castro's literary reputation (and possibly her moral sensibility) was Emilia Pardo Bazán (1851–1921). Pardo Bazán was also Galician and, in the 1870s, they lived in the same town (La Coruña). Fourteen years younger than Castro, Pardo Bazán began to make her name locally in the late 1870s when Castro was already an established literary figure. Some of Pardo Bazán's early publications appeared in Alejandro Chao's *La ilustración gallega y asturiana* ("The Galician and Asturian Illustration/Enlightenment"),[6] of which Murguía was chief editor, and in 1880 Pardo Bazán published in her own journal *La revista de Galicia* ("Galician Review") a short poem written to her by Castro (*Obras* 2: 752). In a letter to Teófilo Braga, Pardo Bazán wrote, "que no hay *nacionalidades peninsulares,* ni quiere Dios que se sueñe en haberlas" (902) ("there are no *peninsular nationalities,* and let's hope to God there never will be") (see Varela Jácome; Davies, *Tempo* 326–27, 422–23). During next decade Pardo Bazán and Murguía became bitter enemies: she would not sign a petition proposing a Galician academy to avoid having her signature appear next to his, she refused to contribute to a mausoleum for Castro, and she swore never to mention Castro's name in public while Murguía was alive. Murguía accused Pardo Bazán of consistently slighting his wife during her lifetime and of relegating her to the status of local versifier. Nothing in Pardo Bazán's writings suggests otherwise. This mutual animosity resulted from a deep political divide. Murguía and Castro were the founders of the popular version of Galician cultural nationalism; Pardo Bazán despised the idea of Galician autonomy and the Federal Republican program (as shown in her 1883 novel *La tribuna*).[7] For her the Galician language was an unintelligible dialect (682). Pardo Bazán did not encourage Castro in the least; nor did she recognize the merit of her work.

The centralist-regionalist tension impinged on all aspects of cultural expression in nineteenth-century Spain. Years earlier (1857), in defense of the Catalan poet Josefa Massanés, Carolina Coronado had argued—from a centralist perspective—that the Spanish government should improve the teaching of Castilian in the "provinces." Nevertheless, Coronado did recognize the value of the regional "dialects" in that they facilitated sincere poetic expression, and she also lamented that "provincial" authors were so little known in Madrid on account of writing in another language. She wrote:

> Cada provincia es en España como una diferente nación. Los caminos de algunas de ellas conducen antes al extranjero que a Madrid. El estado de las escuelas en que se enseña castellano está muy lejos de favorecer la cultura de los alumnos, y es por lo tanto una sinrazón el exigir que el poeta hable de diferente modo que habla su pueblo. (qtd. in Rodríguez 215)[8]

> Each Spanish province is like a different nation. The roads of some of them lead out toward foreign lands rather than to Madrid. The state of the schools where Castilian is taught does not favor the

> pupils' education, and therefore it is unjust to demand that the poet should speak in a different language from that of his people.

Curiously, Concepción Arenal (1820–93), another Galician woman who no doubt shared the progressive ideals, though not the nationalism, of Castro and Murguía,[9] was no great friend of Pardo Bazán's either (see Arenal lv). Again, these differences had to do as much with political views as with personalities. After moving from La Coruña to Asturias, Arenal had entered a literary competition in Orense (1876) commemorating the work of Father Feijoo. Whereas Arenal's essay was disqualified outright on account of its radical views, Pardo Bazán's entry was awarded an honorable mention. Yet, as far as we know, Arenal and Castro did not meet or enter into correspondence.

It is also strange that Castro does not mention Gertrudis Gómez de Avellaneda (1814–73) in the long list of famous women inserted in the prologue to *La hija del mar*. With the possible exception of Fernán Caballero, Gómez de Avellaneda was the most prestigious woman writer in Spain in the 1850s and 1860s and certainly the most admired woman poet. She had even lived for a short while in Galicia in 1836, although she did not have a favorable opinion of the region. Gómez de Avellaneda was born and raised in Cuba and on her first trip to Spain was obliged to stay in Galicia with her Spanish stepfather's family. As she wrote in her *Autobiography*, she was appalled at the type of menial work that middle-class Galician women were expected to do (17). She fails to point out, though, that in Cuba such work (washing, sewing, ironing, knitting, cooking) was done by slaves. She much preferred Seville (where she met Fernán Caballero), and it was there, and in Madrid, that she made her name. When she returned to Cuba, for just three years (1860–63), she actively encouraged Cuban women writers (see García de Coronado). Her work might well have influenced Castro. Several passages in Gómez de Avellaneda's 1841 novel *Sab* (144–45) regarding the exploitation of the innocent and the enslavement of women are echoed in Castro's *La hija del mar* and *El caballero de las botas azules* (*Obras* 2: 96, 823), although the analogy on enslavement was common at the time (owing, primarily, to abolitionist and rights discourse). Gómez de Avellaneda's most acerbic criticism of the "bearded" species, however, was published in her article "La mujer" ("Woman") in *El album de lo bueno y lo bello* (1860) ("The Album of the Good and the Beautiful") in Cuba. Her own position with respect to national allegiance was a tricky one. She briefly returned to Cuba with her husband, a Spanish military officer, and their close friends, the new Spanish governor of Cuba, Captain General Francisco Serrano, and his wife, in the period leading up to the first Cuban War of Independence. In Spain she was considered exotically Cuban; in Cuba she was criticized for being pro-Spanish. Gómez de Avellaneda did manage during her brief spell in Havana to create the kind of women's literary circle that was to be so important to aspiring Cuban women writers such as Luisa Pérez de Zambrana, Mercedes Matamoros, Juana Borrero, and Aurelia Castillo, although Castro could not easily participate on grounds of nationality.

From the 1860s on, Castro did not find a place within a peninsular literary network; as mentioned previously, her isolation increased thereafter.[10] Symptomatic is the letter she wrote in 1884 to the Galician emigrant W. A. Insúa, by then established in Cuba, to thank him for organizing, through his Havana newspaper *El eco de Galicia* ("The Galician Echo"), a function to raise funds for her welfare. She knew nothing of the plans or of the article he wrote praising her work. She writes, poignantly, "La sociedad en que vivimos no permitió tampoco que nadie me hablase de un artículo, cosa que siento en el alma" (*Obras* 2: 1015) ("the society in which we live did not permit anyone to mention an article to me, for which I am deeply sorry"). News finally reached her through her friend the mayor of Padrón. As has been amply documented, the only attention paid to Castro in the 1870s and 1880s (following the second edition of *Cantares gallegos*) was that of the Galician diaspora in Cuba and Argentina. *Follas novas* (1880) ("New Leaves"), dedicated by Castro to the Sociedad de Beneficencia in Havana,[11] was published by Alejandro Chao in Havana and Madrid. The book was reviewed favorably in the *Ilustración gallega y asturiana* (1880) by the Republican Emilio Castelar. The paper also published (in 1881) a review letter from Puerto Rico (by Victor G. Cándamo) stating, "Rosalía de Castro [. . .] arrebató su genio a la Avellaneda" (Rodríguez 448) ("Rosalía de Castro has snatched Avellaneda's genius from her"). In 1881, Manuel

Barros, a Galician emigrant (from Padrón) who had left Cuba for Argentina, approached Castro for poems to publish in his Buenos Aires newspaper, *La nación española* ("The Spanish Nation"). The twenty-two poems that appeared there form the basis of Castro's last collection, *En las orillas del Sar* (Madrid, 1884) ("On the Banks of the River Sar"). Just one woman, Antonia Opisso, reviewed the book (favorably), in *La ilustración ibérica* (22 Aug. 1885). Castro was admitted much later into the Spanish literary canon[12] on the basis of her reputation as a popular Galician poet acquired in the former Spanish colonies, among the mostly male Galician diaspora. In complicated and seemingly disparate ways, therefore, the production and reception of her work was shaped almost entirely by national politics.

It is not unlikely that Castro might have acquired a following in Cuba outside the emigrant community, especially in view of the foundations laid by Gómez de Avellaneda. Throughout the nineteenth century Cuba was a Spanish colony or "overseas province." From 1825 it developed into one of the richest colonies in the world thanks to a booming sugar industry run by slave labor that was supplied by the then illegal slave trade (400,000 slaves were imported between 1823 and 1865) (Thomas 109). The ten-year Cuban War of Independence began in the wake of the 1868 Spanish Revolution; the second war (1895–98) finally secured independence. The century was marked by political upheaval, racism, violence, and militarism in Cuba as the colony strained against Spanish tutelage. But politically Cuba was still a part of Spain, and the history of nineteenth-century Spain is inconceivable without it. The relation between Cuba and Madrid was comparable to that between the "provinces"—Catalonia, Galicia, the Basque country—and the center, and the development of Cuban nationalism coextensive with that of Catalonia and Galicia. Autonomy was first mooted in 1837 when Spain deprived the island of parliamentary representation, thus changing its status from "provincia de ultramar" to colony.

The liberal reforms introduced in Spain in 1868 were not applied to Cuba, thus sparking off the war that continued, paradoxically, throughout the Federal Republic (1873–74). The situation was even more complex in that, although Cuba was governed by Madrid and parliamentary representation was reintroduced in 1878, the island's closest economic ties were with Catalonia, a region that did not fully identify with the Spanish state. Yet the Catalan nationalists would not support Cuban autonomy (conceded in 1897), let alone Cuban separatism. Nobody in Spain was in favor of Cuban independence (with the notable exceptions of Francisco Pi y Margall and Pablo Iglesias) since Spain itself was rapidly falling into a dependency relation vis-à-vis the rest of Europe and the United States and had to rely on the overseas capital from Cuba for modernization. Catalan commercial interests were protected by the army of conscripts (working men who could not buy themselves out) raised in the poorer provinces (e.g., Galicia) by the Madrid government and sent to Cuba to usually die either of injury during the wars or of disease. The complex nexus of mutual dependencies substantially blurred the polarization between colony and metropolis. Indeed, the Galician progressives considered Galicia to be a colony of Madrid. For the Spanish, Cuba was a part of Spain and the problem was internal. The Cubans, for their part, had few quarrels with the Spanish people; their enemy was the Spanish state.

Rosalía de Castro's literary connections with Cuba were strong. Unlike many of her acquaintances (including Manuel Curros Enríquez), she had not visited the island and seems to have known little about it. She was fully aware, however, of the impact caused in Galicia by mass immigration to Cuba. Details of this primarily commercial undertaking on the part of unscrupulous entrepreneurs or "ganchos" plying between Galicia and Cuba have been fully documented (Saurín de la Iglesia). Between 1882 and 1894, some 224,000 Spaniards immigrated to Cuba, a good proportion of them young Galician peasants, almost all of them male. They were encouraged to immigrate in order to "whiten" the Cuban population and to take the place of the slaves after abolition (1886) (Thomas 276). After 1886 the Spanish government often paid their passage. Many professionals left Galicia too, and most were men. The negative repercussions of emigration on the Galician environment, society, and culture were a preoccupation in Castro's social poetry. Her message was twofold: Galician laborers should not immigrate to Cuba because there they were treated worse than slaves, while the impact at home entailed the countless sufferings of those left behind (women, children, the old and infirm) and the arrested development of a distinctive Galician cultural identity. There was no future for a Galicia depopulated of young men.

Some of Castro's best-known early poems, in *Cantares gallegos*, are the emotive outpouring of young peasant men about to leave their homeland.

Deixo amigos por estraños,
deixo a veiga polo mar,
deixo, en fin, canto ben quero...
¡Quén pudera no o deixar...!

("Adiós ríos, adiós fontes" [*Poesías* 69–70]
["Goodbye Rivers, Goodbye Streams"])

I leave my friends for strangers,
I leave the meadows for the sea,
I leave everything I love...
Oh that I might not have to leave...!

Other early poems are the laments of those who want to return ("Airiños, aires" [*Poesías* 75] ["Little Breezes, Breezes"]), including soldiers who would write if their girlfriends could read ("Queridiña, dos meus ollos" [*Poesías* 103] ["Love of My Life"]). The theme is especially poignant in the later poems in *Follas novas* ("New Leaves"), where the whole section "As viudas do vivos e as viudas dos mortos" ("The Widows of the Living and the Widows of the Dead") is dedicated to the hardship caused by emigration on the Galician women:

Este vaise y aquel vaise,
e todos, todos se van.
Galicia, sin homes quedas
que te poidan traballar.
Tes, en cambio, orfos e orfas
e campos de soledad,
e nais que non ten fillos
e fillos que non ten pais.
E tes corazóns que sufren
longas ausencias mortás,

viudas de vivos e mortos
que ningén consolará.

("¡Pra a Habana!" [*Poesías* 280] ["To Havana!"])

This one's going, that one's going,
they're all, all leaving now.
Galicia, you're left without menfolk
who can work your land.
You have, instead, girls and boys, orphans,
and desolated fields,
and mothers without sons
and children without fathers.
And heavy hearts suffering
abandoned without hope;
widows of the dead and living
that no one will console.

Castro also attacks the callous men who leave their wives and children, take up with other women in Cuba, and plan not to return to Galicia until they are old ("¿Qué lle digo?" [*Poesías* 299] ["What Shall I Say to Her?"]). In *Follas novas* the emigration issue is presented as a woman's problem, and it is with regard to the welfare of the Galician peasant woman that Castro voices her most feminist concerns. Her knowledge of their hardships, culled from oral testimony "nas súas confianzas" ("their confidences"), reworked as dramatic, emotive poems constitutes "tan sencilla como dolorosa epopeia" ("such a simple and painful epic") finally brought to public attention ("Duas palabras da autora" [*Poesías* 163] ["Two Words from the Author"]). Castro needed no literary contacts in order to write such poetry—this was not the stuff of soirees. Her subjects were the local women themselves, women who

> a emigrazón i o Rei arrebátanlles decontinuo o amante, o irmán, o seu home, sostén da familia de cote numerosa; e así, abandonadas, chorando o seu desamparo, pasan a amarga vida ante as incertidumbres da esperanza, a negrura da soidade i as angustias dunha perene miseria. (*Poesías* 162)

> continually lose to emigration or to the king their lover, brother, husband, the support of their large family; and so, abandoned,

helpless, weeping, they live their bitter lives in the face of uncertain hope, desperate loneliness and the anxieties of endless poverty.

But Castro did need the men in the Galician diaspora to read and publish her work; in many ways, the poems are addressed to them. The emigrants were interested, no doubt, for reasons of nostalgia and collective sentiment at a politically fraught time, but they were presented—like it or not—with a woman's viewpoint of the effects of colonial politics on women. More important, their individual masculine consciences were stung for their selfish ill-treatment of women.

No other Spanish woman poet dared to voice and defy in such a way the sexual exploitation of rural working women, at the level of both the family and the state. Castro voiced this defiance in a three-hundred-page book written in the language spoken by these women. No other poet made public the women's complaints and, in poetry that appealed to the emotions, argued for their cause. As she states in the prologue to *Follas novas, Cantares gallegos* was a book that "pasaba polo mesmo todo atrevemento" ("was extremely daring"); its success convinced her of the need for a second volume: "N'era cousa de chamar as xentes á guerra e desertar da bandeira que eu mesma había levantado" (*Poesías* 163) ("it was not acceptable to call the people to war and then abandon the flag I myself had raised"). These are the spirited words of an author entirely conscious of the political attitude she is striking, words that were quoted (in the Galician original) some years later (1891) by José Martí as he organized the struggle for Cuban independence and South American resistance to United States encroachment (Neira Vilas 171). Little wonder that Castro's poetry impressed the Galician emigrants, especially the illiterate, who learned the lines of the modern *cantares* by heart and often recited them as patriotic hymns.

Some emigrants did eventually come back, but their return was equally destructive for Galician social and cultural cohesion. Castro lampoons the typical returnee in her 1866 social satire "El cadiceño" (*Obras* 2: 477–87) ("The Man from Cádiz"), in which two swaggering young men returning from Havana via Cádiz reveal they have brought little for their family other than old clothes. The Andalusian-Cuban accents they adopt to appear refined renders their Galician speech unintelligible. The author's message is serious:

> Así el cadiceño manda, reina y pervierte de la manera más peligrosa. Enfatuado e ignorante, todo lo mira en torno suyo por encima del hombro, inspirando a los que le oyen el desprecio a su país [. . .]. [S]u ignorancia y el ansia ardiente de hacerse ricos en poco tiempo [. . .] no les permite modificar sus malos instintos. (486–87)

> This way the man from Cádiz orders, dominates and perverts society in a dangerous way. Infatuated and ignorant, he looks down his nose at everything around him, and those who hear him despise their own country [. . .]. Ignorance and a burning desire to get rich quick [. . .] do not permit men such as these to change their bad behavior.

Again, the finger is pointed at the Galician men for their shallowness.

Nevertheless, Castro's view of emigration was one-sided. Although many emigrants were treated atrociously, some did become wealthy (more often Asturians and Catalans than Galicians), and there were even millionaires.[13] Northern Spain prospered thanks to emigrant remittances; the Cubans complained—justifiably—that their wealth was siphoned away by Spain. Also, to judge from the writings of the Galician diaspora, one would imagine the Galician community formed a large part of the Cuban population and played a key role in its collective consciousness. This was not the case, certainly not before Castro died, although the numbers of Spanish immigrants soared during the 1880s (Llordén Miñambres). In numerical terms the Galician diaspora was relatively small (1,130 Galician emigrants contributed to a mausoleum for Castro in 1886) (Neira Vilas 87) and was concentrated in Havana. Paradoxically, given Castro's avowed hatred of Castilian centralism and the Republican ideals embraced by many emigrant professionals, the Galicians were considered in Cuba to be quintessentially Spanish and, indeed, constituted some of the most reactionary sectors of society. Manuel Barros, for example, a Republican and Freemason, was a member of the notorious Spanish Voluntarios, a paramilitary organization that would go to any length to maintain Spanish rule. There is no mention in

Castro's work of the Cuban independence issue or of the abolition of slavery there. She shows no knowledge of the Cuban literary tradition or of the active group of contemporary Cuban women writers.[14] She was not alone, of course; very few Spaniards acknowledged the cultural presence of Cuba at all. Nevertheless, despite numerous articles on her life and work in the emigrant press, including one by the Cuban poet Aurelia del Castillo (*El eco de Galicia* 6, 18 Apr. 1886) and others by Galician women writers Emilia Calé (1886), Sofía Casanova (1897), and Filomena Dato Muruais (1913), the reception of Castro's work in nineteenth-century Cuba hardly extended beyond the Galician diaspora.[15] She was not an important poet for the Cuban women writers of the time. These women (e.g., Luisa Pérez de Zambrana, her sister Julia Pérez y Montes de Oca, Aurelia del Castillo, Mercedes Matamoros, Juana Borrero, and Ursula Céspedes de Escanaverino) were much more preoccupied by the home-rule issue than by the fate of Galician immigrants. And, of course, although their position in Cuba was not quite as marginal as that of Castro's in Spain, their work was not disseminated or encouraged in comparison with that of their male counterparts.

From today's feminist point of view, this lack of communication between women writers caught on the national-colonial divide is regrettable: they were all affected, one way or another, by the political turmoil of their times, shared a distrust of Spanish centralism, and were sympathetic to cultural and political nationalism. It seems to bear out Gisela Kaplan's view (following Virginia Woolf) that "feminism and nationalism are almost always incompatible ideological positions" (3), at least as far as Europe is concerned. As I have shown elsewhere, this statement is debatable in the context of an independent (but neocolonial) Cuba (Davies, *Place*). Cuban women played such an active role in the War of Independence that it was known as the "Women's War" (Smith and Padula 13). In the 1868–78 war Cuban women had suffered in General Weyler's concentration camps, where the civilian population was interned. The exemplary heroine of the time was a black woman named Mariana Grajales, the mother of General Antonio Maceo. Seven of her thirteen children died in the independence wars. *Mambisa* ("independence fighter") par excellence, she exemplified strong-willed, self-sacrificing patriotic motherhood, the fighting spirit and moral virtues of the Cuban motherland. She was a far cry from the Galician national female icon, the *nai chorosa* ("the weeping widow-mother"), wandering abandoned and homeless with her offspring lost across the globe, as depicted in *Cantares gallegos*:

> Probe Galicia, non debes
> chamarte nunca española,
> que España de ti se olvida
> cando eres, ¡ai! tan hermosa [. . .]
> Galicia, ti non tes patria,
> ti vives no mundo soia,
> i a prole fecunda túa
> se espalla en errantes hordas.
>
> ("A gaita gallega" [*Poesías* 128] ["The Galician Bagpipe"])

> Poor Galicia, Spanish
> should never be your name,
> Spain has forgotten you
> though you're beautiful just the same [. . .]
> Galicia, you have no fatherland,
> you live in the world alone,
> and your large and fertile family
> in scattered throngs they roam.

At the time that Castro was bemoaning the loss of Galician manhood to Cuba, a number of Cuban women poets, all sympathetic to Cuban independence, were establishing a literary reputation on the island. Some women had been encouraged by Gómez de Avellaneda: Luisa Pérez de Zambrana (1835–1922) had presented the poet with a crown of laurel in the Havana homage of 1860, and Avellaneda had written the prologue to the second edition of Zambrana's *Poesías* (1860); Julia Pérez y Montes de Oca (1839–75), Luisa's younger sister, published early poems in Avellaneda's *El album cubano de lo bueno y lo bello* in 1860;[16] Aurelia del Castillo (1842–1920)—like Avellaneda, married to a Spanish military officer—published a critical biography of Avellaneda in 1887. Castillo who (for political reasons) spent the years 1875–78 and 1896–98 in Spain, proved to be a vital link in this network of Cuban women writers. She published articles on their work and wrote the prologues of many more (including *Poesías completas* [1892] by Mercedes Matamoros [1851–1906] and *Poesías* [1915] by Nieves Xenes [1859–1915]) (see Yáñez).

Space precludes a detailed study comparing Castro's poetry with that of her Cuban contemporaries. Even at the level of life histories there are intriguing parallels.[17] Suffice it to say that the poems share many characteristics, most ostensibly the women's close identification with their respective homelands and the discursive strategies they employ to establish this identification from a woman's point of view. A constant feature in their poetry is the depiction of rural landscape as a projection of personal feelings or of collective identity. The feminization of landscape is prominent. Symbols and motifs representing the homeland center on family relations (the mother, the sister, the close female friend) and domestic life (the cottage, the daily routine). Localizing strategies, such as lists of toponyms and indigenous plants and animals, are frequent. Similarly, what has been described as the female gaze—picking out the nooks and crannies, the small places and tiny creatures, instead of resting on panoramic, masterful views—is prevalent in the work of all these women poets.

Sadly, the colonial struggle positioned the Cuban and Galician women on opposite sides, though their common foe was the Spanish government in Madrid. Castro's warlike patriotic poems (e.g., "Los robles" [*Poesías* 330–34] ["The Oaks"], first published in *El eco de Galicia,* Havana) are matched by Cuban poems such as Castillo's sonnet "Victoriosa," written to celebrate the 1898 victory over Spain:

¡Muestra tu rostro juvenil, risueño,
Enciende, ¡oh Cuba! de tu pascua el cirio,
Que surge tu bandera como un lirio
Unico en sus colores y diseño [. . .]. (Feijoo, *Sonetos* 138)

Oh Cuba, show your young, happy face
Light the candle of your feast
Let your flag rise like a lily
Unique in its color and design [. . .].

Castro's poems lamenting the immigration of her compatriots to Cuba are matched by Cuban poems in which the female subject either laments leaving Cuba or celebrates her return. Examples include Gómez de Avellaneda's 1836 "Al Partir" ("On Leaving") and her 1859 "La vuelta a la patria" ("Return to the Homeland") (Lazo 19, 86–87), in which she asks the "brisas perfumadas" ("perfumed breezes") to carry her greetings to the island, not to carry her away (as in Castro's "Airiños, aires"), and Pérez de Zambrana's "Adiós a Cuba," written on her departure from Santiago de Cuba to Havana. The final verses of this poem were recited by the Cuban soldiers fighting in the wars of independence:

> ¡Oh Cuba! si en mi pecho se apagara
> tan sagrada ternura y olvidara
> esta historia de amor,
> hasta el don de sentir me negaría
> pues quien no ama la patria ¡Oh Cuba mía!
> no tiene corazón. (Chaple 144–45)

> Oh Cuba, if in my breast such sacred
> tenderness were to fade and I should forget
> this tale of love,
> the very gift of feeling I'd deny,
> for those who don't love the homeland, Cuba of mine,
> have no heart.

Political differences apart, however, Castro's poetry is distinctive from that of the Cuban poets in one major respect regarding the representation of landscape. Given the traditional association between woman and nature (the land, the nation), the depiction of the countryside by women poets is always problematic, yet it is crucially important. A landscape encapsulates the relation between nature and culture. As no gaze is neutral, the scene within the observer's vision represents the relation between the subject and the environment from a specific viewpoint. Landscape poetry is the verbal representation of a form of visual ideology, a means of structuring and giving meaning to surroundings, necessarily involving class and gender relations (Rose). In times of social strife the rural idyll (e.g., the cottage, the garden, the mother) re-creates harmony and stability. Many Cuban poems describe in detail the aesthetic beauty and natural wealth of the lush Cuban countryside; it tends to be viewed by the women poets as sensual, pleasurable, exhilarating. The

Galician poems also depict a rich landscape. But in Castro's poetry the landscape does not represent social harmony; quite the reverse, its beauty is presented as delusive, deceptive, paradoxically cruel. Her landscapes, unlike those of the Cuban poets discussed here, are almost always populated, usually by poor people; the presence of these people negates the myth of natural harmony. In "Cenicientas las aguas" (*Poesías* 343–44; in *Orillas*) ("Ashen the Waters") the dramatic winter scene is crossed by a lone laborer, accompanied by his "helado mastín" ("frozen hound")."En Cornes" (*Poesías* 273–74; in *Follas*) depicts a starving child hiding amid the trees and pretty wild flowers; as the poet states, "Donde hai homes hai pesares" (273) ("where there are people/men there is suffering"). At times the beauty of the countryside is shown to be deceptive in the Cuban poems too. Mercedes Matamoros's sonnet "En un ingenio" ("On a Sugar Plantation") describes the "Opulentos y verdes campos míos, / testigos de los juegos de mi infancia" ("my green and opulent fields, / witness to my childhood games"), now "Negros escombros, tenebrosas ruinas, / luto y desolación" ("black ashes, dark ruins, / mourning and desolation"). But the transformation has been brought on by the liberation wars and the ending of the poem is triumphant: "¿qué importa, si brilló en su llama / ¡Oh, Libertad! tu sacrosanto idea?" (Feijoo, *Sonetos* 147) ("what does this matter, when in [the torch's] flare, the sacred idea of Liberty flamed?").

This construction of collective Cuban optimism may be contrasted to the collective Galician despair. In a moving poem, "La vuelta al bosque" ("Return to the Woods"), reminiscent of Castro's "En las orillas del Sar," Pérez de Zambrana depicts the woods she once enjoyed as now sad and lonely: "Bosque querido / ¡tétricas hojas! ¡lago solitario!" (Feijoo, *Cantos* 191) ("Dear woods / gloomy leaves! solitary lake!"). She feels "desterrada" (190) ("exiled"). Here the transformation has taken place as a result of a personal tragedy, the death of her husband; in Castro's poem the tragedy is personal, too, but the scope of the poem extends to the collectivity, "¡Oh tierra, antes y ahora, siempre fecunda y bella! / Viendo cúan triste brilla nuestra fatal estrella [. . .] siento [. . .] el hambre de justicia" (*Poesías* 317, in *Orillas*) ("Oh my land, now and before, always fertile and beautiful! / Seeing how sadly our star of destiny shines [. . .] I feel [. . .] the thirst for justice").

Related to this representation of landscape is Castro's skillful use of prosopopeia that offers a dialogical, multiple viewpoint rather than the single voice of the lyrical self. In this way her poems give voice to the thoughts, feelings, and words of the working country people—primarily to the women—as individual human beings. Castro comments on the emigration issue, for example, not by discussing it in the abstract but by presenting the worries and experiences of the individual members of a family. In contrast to Gómez de Avellaneda (in the poem "Al partir"), she is unlikely to have referred to the ship's crew as "la chusma" ("the rabble").[18] These differences mark the division between elitist and popular cultural nationalism. While Castro gave voice to the Galician peasant woman, the social and political situation in Cuba made a comparable act difficult for Cuban women writers. There the fields were sugar (or coffee or tobacco) plantations, and the laborers, of course, black slaves.[19]

The greatest irony, of course, is that Castro felt she was an "estranxeira na súa patria" (*Poesías* 195; in *Orillas*) ("a foreigner in her fatherland"). As we have seen, this was not an inaccurate appraisal, whether "patria" stands for Spain and its overseas possessions, Peninsular Spain, or Galicia. She occupied what Gillian Rose terms "paradoxical space," a "space imagined in order to articulate a troubled relation to the hegemonic discourse of masculinism" (159). By virtue of her politically engaged writings, Castro positions herself simultaneously at the center (of Galicia) and the margins (of Spain), experiencing at the same time "inside-ness" and "outside-ness," hence the sense of belonging nowhere. For today's feminist reader, this stance makes her poetry particularly subversive. But in the context of nineteenth-century colonial politics and the resulting social injustice, Castro was not keen to cross international borders:[20]

Vós, pois, os que naceches na orela doutros mares
que vos qentás á llama de vivos lumiares,
e só vivir vos compre baixo un ardente sol,
calá, se n'entendes encantos destos lares,
cal, n'entendendo os vosos, tamén calamos nós.

("¡Calade!" [*Poesías* 249; in *Follas*] ["Silence!"])

You, then, you who were born on the shores of other seas
who warm yourselves at the flame of resplendent beams,
you who can only live beneath the burning sun,
be silent, if you don't understand this land's delights
just as we, not understanding yours, keep quiet.

Notes

1. Other intellectuals who lost their posts with the restoration included Francisco Gíner de los Ríos. On learning this, his friend Concepción Arenal sent him a letter from her son in which he stated he hated Spain and wished he were not Spanish. (See Arenal xli).
2. Castro was urged to write and publish *Cantares gallegos* (1863) in the late 1850s by Murguía, Benito Vicetto, and other progressives. They may have been inspired by the success of the Catalan poet María Josefa Massanés (1811–87), who wrote in Catalan at the time and was crowned queen of the Jocs Florals in Barcelona in 1862. Massanés led a group of Catalan women writers (including her friend Dolors Monserdà [1845–1919]), who gave one another support. There was no such group in Galicia. Castro was a lone figure in this respect.
3. All the quotations of poetry by Castro are from *Poesías*. All translations are my own unless otherwise indicated.
4. It was on the basis of their shared Catholic beliefs (and their residence in Seville) that the two very different women Fernán Caballero and Gertrudis Gómez de Avellaneda became close friends.
5. Other names mentioned in the prologue to *La hija del mar* are Malebranche, Feijoo, Mme Roland, Mme de Staël, Sappho, and Santa Teresa.
6. The *IGA* was increasingly sympathetic to the Republican cause after 1880. Alejandro Chao and his brother Eduardo were close friends of Castro and Murguía's. Alejandro was the godfather of their eldest daughter, Alejandra, and had immigrated to Cuba in 1859.
7. Murguía was secretary of the Santiago Xunta Demócrata Progresista (1868), the type of organization ridiculed by Pardo Bazán in *La tribuna*.
8. The Coronado quotation originally appeared in "Galería de poetisas españolas ilustres," *La discusión* 1 May 1857. See also Kirkpatrick.
9. Arenal published her first article in the progressive newspaper *La Iberia* (1855) at a time when Murguía contributed regularly.
10. The only Galician poet of some standing who could be said to have followed in Castro's footsteps was Francisca Herrero Garrido (1869–1956), for whose first book of poems (1915) Murguía wrote a prologue. Herrero Garrido certainly wrote in Galician, but her Catholic conservatism does not tally with Castro's more radical worldview.
11. The society was precursor to the majestic Galician Centre (today's Teatro García Lorca in Havana) founded in 1880. By 1890 the center had six thousand members.
12. Castro was admitted into the canon thanks to a belated but favorable recep-

tion by Juan Ramón Jiménez and Miguel de Unamuno in the first decades of the twentieth century. (See Davies, "Later Poetry.")

13. Examples of those who made their fortune from slave trading, sugar, or tobacco are Ramón Pelayo de la Torriente, marqués de Valdecillas (Santander); Juan Manuel de Manzanedo, marqués de Manzanedo, duque de Santoña (Santander); Florencio Rodríguez Rodríguez (Gijón, Asturias). (See Fernández.)
14. In fact Castro ridicules the brash Cuban *Criolla* Marcelina la Blonda (possibly modeled on Gómez de Avellaneda?) in *El caballero de las botas azules* (*Obras* 2: 632–33).
15. Castro's wider recognition in Cuba coincides with her acceptance into the Spanish literary canon, that is, from around 1910. The centenary of her birth (1937) was celebrated, among others, by the Cuban-Dominican academic Camila Enríquez Ureña at the women's Lyceum club in Havana. Castro certainly influenced later Cuban women poets, such as Emilia Bernal (who translated much of the Galician poetry into Castilian), Dulce María Loynaz, and Fina García Marruz. For a useful bibliography see Neira Vilas.
16. Julia Pérez y Montes de Oca published her only collection, *Poesías* (1875), in Barcelona, and Aurelia del Castillo her first book of poems (1879) in Cádiz. Among Castillo's numerous works, two collections of prose were published by Alejandro Chao's La Propaganda Literaria, which also published *Follas novas.*
17. Luisa Pérez de Zambrana, born in Oriente, lived in Santiago de Cuba in the 1850s. Her first book of poems, *Poesías* (1856), circulated among the Cuban literati and came to the attention of Ramón Zambrana, doctor, journalist, and newspaper proprietor, who later married her. In 1858 the couple moved to Havana, where she published poems in the press. In 1866 Zambrana died, leaving his wife and five children in a precarious financial position; between 1866 and 1899 all the children died. The bright optimism of Pérez de Zambrana's early work gave way to despairing, melancholic poems that were not collected in a published volume until 1920. She spent her last days almost forgotten, until a homage was organized for her in 1918.
18. "La chusma diligente, / para arrancarme del nativo suelo / las velas iza" (Lazo 19) ("the diligent rabble / to wrench me from my native soil / hoist the sails").
19. In 1861 there were 370,000 slaves in Cuba, 26.5% of the total population. It should be remembered that Avellaneda's antislavery novel, *Sab* (1841), was banned by the authorities in Cuba, and all copies were returned to Spain.
20. One poet who did cross borders, literally and metaphorically, was Lola Rodríguez de Tió (1849?–1924). Puerto Rican by birth, she was forced to leave her homeland because of her separatist ideas. She took refuge in Cuba, where she stayed until her death. One of her most famous poems, "A Cuba" ("To Cuba"), was dedicated on her arrival in 1863. Here she wrote the memorable lines. "Cuba y Puerto Rico son / de un pájaro las dos alas, / reciben flores y balas / sobre el mismo corazón" (Ripoll 189–90) ("Cuba and Puerto Rico / are like the two wings of a bird, / receiving flowers and

bullets / in the same heart"). She is one of the few poets of the time to voice a postcolonial pan-Antillean perspective.

Works Cited

Arenal, Concepción. *Obras completas de Dña Conceptión Arenal.* Ed. Carmen Díaz Castañón. Madrid: Atlas, 1993. Vol 1 of *Biblioteca de autores españoles* 302.

Blanco Aguinaga, Carlos, Julio Rodríguez Puértolas, and Iris Zavala, eds. *Historia social de la literatura española (en lengua castellana).* Vol. 2. Madrid: Castalia, 1979. 3 vols.

Carballo Calero, Ricardo. *Contribución ao estudo das fontes literarias de Rosalía de Castro.* Lugo: Celta, 1959.

Castro, Rosalía de. *Obras completas.* Ed. Victoriano García Martí. 2 vols. Madrid: Aguilar, 1977.

———. *Poesías.* Ed. Ricardo Carballo Calero. Vigo: Patronato, 1973.

Chaple, Sergio. *Estudios de literatura cubana.* Havana: Letras cubanas, 1980.

Davies, Catherine. *A Place in the Sun? Women Writers in Twentieth-Century Cuba.* London: Zed, 1997.

———. *Rosalía de Castro no seu tempo.* Vigo: Galaxia, 1987.

———. "Rosalía de Castro's Later Poetry and Anti-regionalism in Spain." *Modern Language Review* 79 (1984): 609–19.

Feijoo, Samuel, ed. *Cantos a la naturaleza cubana del siglo XIX.* Havana: Universidad Central de las Villas, 1964.

———. *Sonetos en Cuba.* Havana: Universidad Central de las Villas, 1964.

Fernández, Aurelia Matilde. *España y Cuba, 1868–1898: Revolución burguesa y relaciones coloniales.* Havana: Ciencias Sociales, 1988.

García de Coronado, Domitila. *Album poético fotográfico de escritoras y poetisas cubanas escrito en 1868 para la señora Doña Gertrudis Gómez de Avellaneda.* 3rd ed. Havana: El Fígaro, 1926.

Gómez de Avellaneda, Gertrudis. "La mujer." *Biblioteca de autores españoles* 288. *Obras de Doña Gertrudis Gómez de Avellaneda.* Vol. 5. Madrid: Atlas, 1981. 275–84.

———. Sab *and* Autobiography. Trans. Nina M. Scott. Austin: U of Texas P, 1993.

Kaplan, Gisela. "Feminism and Nationalism: The European Case." *Feminist Nationalism.* Ed. Lois A. West. London: Routledge, 1997. 208–43.

Kirkpatrick, Susan. *Las Románticas: Women Writers and Subjectivity in Spain, 1835–1850.* Berkeley: U of California P, 1989.

Lazo, Raimundo. *Gertrudis Gómez de Avellaneda: La mujer y la poesía lírica.* Mexico: Porrúa, 1972.

Llordén Miñambres, Moisés. "Las asociaciones españolas de emigrantes." *Arte, cultura y sociedad en la emigración española a América.* Ed. María Cruz Morales Saro and Llordén Miñambres. Oviedo: Universidad de Oviedo, 1992. 9–55.

Montesinos, José F. *Fernán Caballero: Ensayo de justificación.* Mexico: Colegio de Mexico, 1961.

Neira Vilas, Xosé. *Rosalía de Castro e Cuba.* Vigo: Patronato, 1992.

Pardo Bazán, Emilia. *Obras completas.* Vol 3. Madrid: Aguilar, 1957.

Ripoll, Carlos. *Naturaleza y alma de Cuba: Dos siglos de poesía cubana.* New York: Latin American, 1974.

Rodríguez, Francisco. *Análise sociolóxica da obra de Rosalía de Castro.* Vigo: AS-PG, 1988.

Rose, Gillian. *Feminism and Geography: The Limits of Geographical Knowledge.* Cambridge: Polity, 1993.

Saurín de la Iglesia, María Rosa. *Apuntes y documentos para una historia de Galicia en el siglo XIX.* La Coruña: Diputación Provincial de La Coruña, 1977.

Shoemaker, W. H. *Los artículos de Galdós en* La Nación, *1865–1866, 1868.* Madrid: Insula, 1972.

Smith, L. M., and A. Padula. *Sex and Revolution: Women in Socialist Cuba.* Oxford: Oxford UP, 1996.

Thomas, Hugh. *Cuba: The Pursuit of Freedom.* London: Eyre, 1971.

Valera, Juan. *Obras completas.* Vol. 2. Madrid: Aguilar, 1961.

Varela Jácome, Benito. "Emilia Pardo Bazán, Rosalía de Castro, y Murguía." *Cuadernos de estudios gallegos* 6 (1951): 405–29.

Yáñez, Mirta. "El discurso femenino finisecular en Cuba: Aurelia del Castillo y otras voces en torno al 98." *Spain's 1898 Crisis: Regenerationism, Modernism, Post-colonialism.* Ed. Joseph Harrison and Alan Hoyle. Manchester: Manchester UP, 2000. 252–66.

Concepción Arenal and the Nineteenth-Century Spanish Debates about Women's Sphere and Education

Lou Charnon-Deutsch

Aquí no prejuzgamos la cuestión de la altura a que podrá elevarse la mujer por el pensamiento; llegue hasta donde pueda, que más allá no ha de ir.

—Concepción Arenal, *La mujer de su casa*

Let us not predetermine here the question of the heights to which a woman could aspire through her wits; let her rise as high as she may, beyond that she will not go.

Issues regarding appropriate public and private gender roles were hotly debated in the press during the years that the reformist and feminist Concepción Arenal wrote over four hundred essays and books. Although she assessed women's intellectual capacity and social position, forcefully expressed in the above epigraph, she herself often participated in the ambivalence of a society struggling with the heights to which a virtuous woman should aspire and an evaluation of whatever wit would get her there. Still, in her many tracts on women—*La mujer del porvenir* (1868) ("The Woman of the Future"), *La mujer de su casa* (1881) ("The Stay-at-Home Woman"), *Estado actual de la mujer en España* (1884) ("The Current State of Woman in Spain"), and "La educación de la mujer" (1892) ("Woman's Education")—Arenal strongly challenged the popular notion of separate spheres that during her lifetime represented women's principal impediment to social and political advancement. She distinguished herself from the group of dogmatists and reformists who were her contemporaries, becoming, as Alda Blanco explains, a key figure in the development of a feminist consciousness among middle-class women (448).

One of the earliest to incorporate a discussion of spheres as a rationale for segregating the sexes was Angela Grassi, the doyenne of domestic fiction who construed woman's sphere as both a physical space, the home, and a guarantor of a specific social rank. In her multipart essay "Memorias de una casada" ("Memoirs of a Married Woman") she warned that stepping outside this sphere brought ruin to the family: "Miseria y vanidad: ruina total de la familia, por querer salirse de su esfera" (219) ("Misery and vanity: the total ruin of the family, all for wanting to leave one's sphere").[1] Men dominate through their strength and intelligence, argued Leandro Angel Herrero in "De la mujer" (1) ("On Woman"), while women provide the essential and inexhaustible source of tenderness and love required by men. While a man sacrifices himself for the public good, it is in woman's angelic nature to sacrifice herself within the family that is her private and sublime sphere:

> En una esfera superior, la mujer es una especie de ángel custodio que vela constantemente por la felicidad humana y realizando en su tránsito un eterno sacrificio: madre, es la providencia del hombre niño; esposa o hermana, es una tierna figura que se reviste de hechiceros arreboles para verter suaves rocíos de júbilo sobre nuestro yerto corazón. (2)
>
> Dwelling in a higher sphere, woman is a kind of guardian angel keeping a constant watch over human happiness and performing an eternal sacrifice: as mother she is the providence of the man child; as wife or sister, she is a tender figure who festoons herself with bewitching crimson clouds to shower gentle drops of jubilation upon our hardened hearts.

Herrero's ecstatic tribute to the sublime sacrifices of the domestic angel would be repeated over and over again as the century progressed and the bourgeois ideal of blissful domesticity gripped the popular press. Even liberal women's magazines offered subscribers glowing reports of how Christianity had raised women to what Venustiano Rodríguez

Hubert described as the "grandeza de su destino" (3) ("their lofty destiny") as domestic angels, while they reminded readers of women's former enslavement and argued for improved education so that women might better fulfill their destiny.[2] Eduardo Bustillo preached to his readers that the good wife must know enough to understand the "deberes y compromisos de la vida pública" ("duties and compromises of public life"), follow her beleaguered husband into his study with the sweetest of smiles on her face, and say comfortingly, "Vengo a saber todo lo que pasa; quizá tiene menos gravedad y más fácil remedio de lo que tú supones" (291) ("I'm here to find out what has happened; perhaps it's not so serious and there is an easier solution than you imagine"). A woman should stimulate her husband's pride, recall his past successes, appeal to his nobility, and urge him forward in attaining his career goals. That weighty question of how to make a man happy neatly tied into the bourgeois ideology of separate spheres: if women's principal responsibility was to make men happy, men, in turn, had to provide an appropriately calm and protected space for them to perform this mission. Happiness in both cases depended on men successfully occupying one sphere, women performing their mission in another, and both accepting this separation as natural and good. It was a given that if men were happy, women would also be satisfied because they would have accomplished the greatest mission that had been determined for them by either God or nature.

Conservative women's magazines, such as *La margarita*, *La violeta*, or *La flor de lis*, extolled women's innate virtues and the timeless pleasures of the domestic sphere, attacked liberals for destroying traditional family values, and enlisted women into reactionary causes with the argument that they should be informed about politics if they were to advise their sons and husbands judiciously. Conservatives also argued that women should not engage in public politics, which according to Juan de Luz was "el mayor enemigo de la felicidad doméstica" (162) ("the greatest enemy of domestic happiness") but they have a duty to wage a campaign for Christian values and the monarchy any other way possible (for example, through tears, smiles, or physical beauty), as long as their activities are confined to the domestic sphere. Writers for the more liberal papers, such as *La mujer*, responded by insisting that it wasn't their wish to see women on any revolutionary firing line and attacking the hypocrisy of Carlist and *moderado* ("moderate") papers like *La margarita* for enlisting women into conservative causes. What is important in this debate is that both liberals and conservatives accused each other of enticing women away from what conduct manuals argued was their natural place, the sphere in which they were destined to circulate "por la mano de Dios" ("by the hand of God"), according to Faustina Sáez de Melgar (3).

Even ardent defenders of women's education like Ramón García Sánchez warned women not to stray into the public sphere of politics if they expected to be loved:

> Que avance la humanidad cuanto quiera por la senda de la civilización; ella no debe ambicionar otros derechos que los que hoy posee, si desea conservar la adoración que el hombre la profesa.
>
> El día que se igualará con éste, interviniendo en la cosa pública, sería el último de su felicidad, porque en ella vería el hombre un rival más de su ambición y de su egoísmo.
>
> No; la mujer ha nacido para sentir y amar en la tranquilidad del hogar doméstico.
>
> En el momento en que abandone esta esfera ha perdido la categoría de ángel y arrojado a los azares de la suerte la corona de su virginidad. (7)

> May humanity advance as much as it desires along the path of civilization; she should not strive for more rights than she already possesses if she wishes to conserve the adoration that man professes for her.
>
> The day that she equals man, intervening in public affairs, will spell the end of her happiness, because then man will see her as just another rival of his ambition and egoism.
>
> No, woman was born to feel and love the tranquility of the domestic sphere.
>
> The moment that she abandons that sphere she forfeits the category of angel, casting to the winds of fate her crown of virginity.

Articles on women's education published between the 1840s and the revolution of 1868 stressed the necessity of moral and religious training or, for certain classes, of instruction at the primary level, which at that time consisted of two to three years of schooling on subjects ranging from devotional reading to sewing men's shirts. In the 1880s and 1890s, however, the issue of women's formal schooling began to take center stage in debates about the most appropriate form and place to educate women (Jagoe, Blanco, and Enríquez de Salamanca 127). One of the main arguments for justifying women's education was still that an uneducated woman made a poor moral instructor for young children. But increasingly fathers, brothers, husbands, and even nonfamily members were included among women's ideal pupils, and this widening mission was accompanied by arguments in favor of more formalized instruction at the secondary level. Such a tactic had been employed successfully in other European countries and also in America to encourage secondary education for women and to open the doors of the university to women students if only for the purpose of training teachers of children.[3] In the 1880s several progressive newspapers took up similar arguments in their discussions of Spain's inadequate educational system, which was also a subject of debate in a series of pedagogical congresses that took place in 1882 and 1892.[4] Writing in the progressive women's magazine *Instrucción para la mujer,* J. A. Rebolledo proposed that a woman should receive professional training in order to gain economic independence because then

> Ya no buscará como una *colocación* el casarse con un hombre porque tenga medios de fortuna, sino porque su corazón se lo dicte por creerle digno de ella; [. . .] que sea el hombre el que se considere afortunado al unirse con una mujer en cuya frente resplandezcan tales prendas. (102)

> She will no longer seek a position as a man's wife simply because he has the means to support her, but because her heart dictates that he is worthy of her; [. . .] it will be the man who considers himself fortunate to unite himself with a woman whose brow shines with such glowing achievements.

A series of articles published that same year by Pedro de Alcántara García made it painfully clear how far countries like Sweden, the United States, Germany, England, and France had progressed in relation to

Spain. A woman's most noble mission, he argued, was to educate the human race because "parece nacida la mujer" (4) ("woman seems born") to be the best educator of children. Women's maternal sentiment, patience, and tenderness suited them especially for this mission. Alcántara García emphasized women's emotional suitability as teachers of their own children in an ad hominem argument for their suitability as schoolteachers, and he expressed shock that in primary schools male teachers still predominated. Together with other members of the Asociación para la Enseñanza de la Mujer (Association for the Education of Women), his aim was to formalize feminine education and make it more available to women of all classes. It is irresponsible and illogical for men to speak in glowing terms of maternal education of children, he believed, and leave women unprovided with any qualifications other than their own instincts.

In this case an argument that relegated women to one sphere was turned on its head to demonstrate why women were suited to occupations outside that sphere. Ironically, the tender mother-child scenes that proliferated in the 1880s feminine press might have (as an unintended by-product) lent graphic support to the argument made by a handful of reformists, such as Alcántara García, Gil de Azcárate, Sofía Tartilán, or Arenal, not just that it was dangerous not to educate women but that they should become schoolteachers or even professionals in other service industries because of their special nurturing skills. As Giuliana Di Febo notes, the Krausist program to improve feminine education did not respond entirely to egalitarian goals:

> La ecuación "educación igual a transformación de la sociedad" sigue siendo una prerrogativa masculina. Se defiende el acceso de la mujer a la instrucción, pero dentro de esquemas formativos de tipo tradicional, a fin de garantizar la realización de un *status* social que no rompa el equilibrio del ámbito patriarcal. (53–54)
>
> The equation "education equals the transformation of society" continues to be a masculine prerogative. Woman's access to education is defended, but within traditional formative schemas, to guarantee the continuance of the social status quo that would not disturb the equilibrium of the patriarchy.

During the latter decades of the century there was also a growing polemic regarding women's work outside the home. While Socialist papers in the 1880s and 1890s (e.g., *El Socialista,* which began publication in 1886) called for greater participation and rights for women workers, intellectual leaders of the movement generally did little to challenge the reigning concept of woman as first and foremost suited to the task of motherhood. Luis Araquistáin, like other important figures in the Spanish Socialist Party, held to the tenet of woman's traditional role as mother: "la mujer es madre sobre todo y siempre, y la actividad política al dotarla de una mayor independencia económica, ha de rebustecer ese instinto en lugar de debilitarlo" (qtd. in Scanlon 236) ("woman is ever and above all mother, and any political activity offering her greater economic independence must fortify her instinct instead of debilitating it"). Most liberal papers, meanwhile, argued that if women had to work for a wage, they should for moral reasons do it at home as seamstresses, wet nurses, and servants. In May 1882 G. Vicuña argued that factory work was not only morally unsuitable but also endangered the very stability of the family:

> [O]bliga a la mujer a desatender el cuidado de su casa, distrae al niño del cultivo de su inteligencia, separa al hombre de los goces del hogar, contribuye a relajar los lazos del parentesco, es incentivo constante para la desmoralización y materia dispuesta para las revoluciones. (81)

> [I]t obliges the woman to neglect the care of her home, distracts the child from the cultivation of his intellect, separates man from the pleasures of his home, contributes to the loosening of parental ties, and is a constant incentive for moral laxity and the material for revolutions.

I have included this sampling of quotes from Arenal's contemporaries to compare them with her own writings on women and to highlight how her reasoning either coincided with or differed from the prevailing thought about the social organization of sexual difference. By all accounts Arenal was a resolute, intelligent, and successful public figure, and she richly deserved her reputation as one of the century's most avid feminists. She believed that more professions should be opened to women, yet she shared the prevailing attitude that women should not hold positions of great power or jobs that required great physical endurance. She held this view even though she recognized like her contemporary Emilia Pardo Bazán that rural Galician women were capable of backbreaking physical exertion. Like her friend Alcántara García she spoke approvingly about the fact that American women had more political rights than Spanish women. Yet she believed, as most educated women and men would for the next fifty years, that for the moment Spanish women should not vote and should avoid politics altogether since they lacked "la instrucción, el prestigio, el carácter, la firmeza que necesitarían para servir de dique a la depravación" (*Mujer del porvenir* 121) ("the education, prestige, character, and fortitude necessary to serve as a hedge against depravation"). This someday-but-not-yet attitude, used for years to deny minority populations the vote in countries around the world, characterized even the most ardent apologists for women in Spain, where a type of acknowledged or unacknowledged sexual apartheid existed until recently. A critical assessment of Arenal's positions regarding women in the public and private spheres reveals the knot of contradictions in her thinking that every intelligent Spanish woman would have to negotiate well into the twentieth century, even after the question of women's suffrage and legal rights was settled. As Blanco argues, however, we should not judge Arenal's feminism by her stand on women's suffrage, since to do so would be to mistake present-day definitions of the term, which focus on legal issues, for historical perspectives (452–53).

Like the Krausists who influenced her thinking, Arenal placed great stock in the capacity of education and science to solve the problems of class and sex inequality. In tracts such as "La educación de la mujer" ("Woman's Education") (her contribution to section 5 of the 1892 Pedagogical Congress) and "El pauperismo" ("On Pauperism") (a collection of essays published posthumously), she argued that real social progress could never be achieved unless the problem of women's physical, vocational, and intellectual education was addressed. That Arenal was willing to disguise herself as a man to study law at the University of Madrid (1842–44) showed her earliest commitment to the ideals that her

Krausist friends Fernando de Castro, Gumersindo de Azcárate, and Francisco Giner de los Ríos would later espouse in their campaigns for women's education. The reason Arenal believed women would make good lawyers, doctors, professors, and even priests (*Mujer del porvenir* 116), however, was not their educability but their innate feminine virtues that were honed in the private sphere. Compassion, fairness, spirituality, common sense, honesty, and a well-developed conscience were all attributes that would be as useful to the professions as the specialized knowledge, strength, and genius that were considered men's domain. These feminine virtues, however, would exclude a woman from the professions of greatest power: her compassion would limit her ability to be a good judge, surgeon, or soldier. Her gentle nature would crumble before the militancy of public politics, and in any case the political terrain of the home ought to remain neutral to conserve the integrity of the family. The home should remain, just as proponents of the "domestic angel" ideal maintained, a masculine refuge from the public sphere: "[n]ecesita ser neutral, sagrado, el hogar que custodia la mujer; allí debe estrellarse el oleaje de las pasiones políticas" (*Mujer del porvenir* 121) ("the home should be a neutral, sacred place where the swell of political passions can be dispersed").

Despite Arenal's desire to preserve the private sphere as an environment free of ideology, she was one of the few who questioned the validity of separate spheres. The ideal of the "stay-at-home wife" or "mujer de su casa" was anachronistic and erroneous, she wrote in her 1881 essay by the same name. It caused both women and their families endless grief: for women it was especially debilitating because it devoured their time with trivial, unnecessary pursuits and prevented them from fulfilling any social mission outside the home or from contributing to social progress and the common good of the nation. Instead of a haven, the home was all too often a place of wasted sacrifices, poor hygiene, lax virtue, a "núcleo de egoísmo" (*Casa* 206) ("nucleus of egoism"), and altogether a negative asset to the nation. If women did not become involved in the public good, they would inevitably lure their husbands and children away from activities in the public sphere and thus contribute to a social decline:

> La mujer de su casa, que vive sólo en ella y para ella, no entiende ni le interesa nada de lo que pasa fuera, y juzga imprudencia, absurdo, quijotismo, disparate, tontería, según los casos, el trabajo, los desvelos y los sacrificios que por la obra social están dispuestos a hacer el padre, el esposo o el hijo. (207)
>
> The housewife who lives solely in and for herself neither understands nor takes an interest in anything that happens outside the home, and she accordingly judges as imprudent, absurd, quixotic, disparate, and stupid the work, sleepless nights, and sacrifices that her father, husband, or son are willing to make for the social good.

Arenal understood intuitively that new metaphors were needed to combat the reigning sexual ideology of separate spheres with its extensive symbolic system representing women as guardian angels, pillars, sanctuaries, temples, priestesses, and other metaphors relegating women to the interior spaces of the home and church. She did not abandon the saccharine terminology of the conduct manuals and women's magazines altogether. Rather, she used it to argue for a more extensive public role for women: if by nature woman was a pillar of compassion, patience, affection, and self-sacrifice (*Mujer del porvenir* 141), then she had a duty to practice these same virtues within the walls of hospitals, prisons, and orphanages. Arenal also fashioned a creative set of metaphors, using mostly aquatic images, to describe women's disadvantageous roles and circumstances, and variations of these metaphors would be used effectively by the generation of feminists who followed her. For example, in *Estado actual de la mujer en España* she compared women to a body adrift at sea:

> La opinión pública en España respecto a las mujeres podría compararse a esas poderosas corrientes que, después de haber arrastrado un cuerpo, empujándolo en distintas direcciones y hécholo girar rápidamente, acaban por sumergirle. (39)
>
> In Spain public opinion regarding women could be compared to those powerful currents that after having engulfed a body, dragging it in different directions and whirling it around rapidly, end by drowning it.

Similarly, in *La mujer de su casa,* she imagines women as a ship's engine that in the midst of a tempestuous sea maintained the ship afloat but did not permit it to move forward (201). The ship, in this case, is Spanish society at large, crippled by its suppression and neglect of women's talents. Later in that tract, women are the waves tossed about by the forces of nature and society:

> [A]prisionadas entre obstáculos artificiales, retrocediendo, variando de dirección, chocando con las que venían detrás, formaban conos rugientes y espumosos, y un hervidero de corrientes encontradas de donde no hubiese podido salir la nave más velera. (258)
>
> [C]aught between artificial obstacles, retreating, changing direction, crashing into those behind them, they formed roaring, foamy peaks, a cauldron of conflicting currents from which not even the swiftest ship could escape.

Men see the effects of this feminine turmoil, she complained, yet instead of trying to understand its causes, they depict woman as an enigma (258). Other times, instead of an object or wave tossed about, Arenal's woman is simply absent or silent. Neglected and underutilized, she is like a "labyrinth whose path has been lost" (*Educación de la mujer* 64).

In many of these images, forward movement is a politically progressive, male attribute, while women are associated with things lost, silent, drowning, or immobile:

> La mujer de su casa es un ideal erróneo, hemos dicho; señala el bien donde no está; corresponde a un concepto equivocado de la perfección, que es para todos progreso, y que se pretende sea para ella inmovilidad. (*Casa* 202)
>
> The stay-at-home woman is an erroneous ideal, as we have said; it describes a good where there is none; it corresponds to a mistaken concept of perfection that is progress for everyone but that for her is immobility.

The same dichotomy of progress versus stasis would be exploited by Emilia Pardo Bazán, who a few years later complained bitterly about women's destiny forever being defined in relation to that of her children or her husband:

> Para el español, —insisto en ello—, todo puede y debe transformarse; sólo la mujer ha de mantenerse inmutable y fija como la estrella polar. [. . . E]l español la quiere metida en una campana de cristal que la aísle del mundo exterior por medio de la ignorancia. (*Mujer* 32–33)
>
> For the Spanish man, I want to insist, everything can and should be transformed; only woman must remain immutable and fixed like the polar star. [. . .T]he Spanish man wishes to see her placed in a crystal bell that isolates her from the exterior world by keeping her ignorant.

For Pardo Bazán, worldwide progress for men, while desirable, was widening the gulf that existed between the sexes:

> Suponed a dos personas en un mismo punto; haced que la una avance y que la otra permanezca inmóvil: todo lo que avance la primera, se queda atrás la segunda. Cada nueva conquista del hombre en el terreno de las libertades políticas, ahonda el abismo moral que le separa de la mujer, y hace el papel de ésta más pasivo y enigmático. Libertad de enseñanza, libertad de cultos, derecho de reunión, sufragio, parlamentarismo, sirven para que media sociedad (la masculina) gane fuerzas y actividades a expensas de la otra media femenina. Hoy ninguna mujer de España—empezando por la que ocupa el trono—goza de verdadera influencia política; y en otras cuestiones no menos graves, el pensamiento femenil tiende a ajustarse fielmente a las ideas sugeridas por el viril, el único fuerte. (33)
>
> Imagine two people standing in the same place; make one advance and the other remain immobile: as much as the first advances, the other remains behind. Each new conquest for man in the area of political freedoms deepens the moral abyss that separates him from woman and renders her role more passive and enigmatic. Freedom of education, freedom of religion, the right to assembly, suffrage, and parliamentarism all allow half of society (the masculine half) to acquire strength and activities at the expense of the feminine half. Today no woman in Spain—beginning with the one who occupies the throne—has any real political influence; and in other questions no less grave, feminine thinking tends to adjust itself dutifully to the ideas suggested by the virile half, the only strong one.

An exception to Pardo Bazán's dismal portrait of Spanish women, Arenal exerted considerable political influence among social reformists. She devoted much of her energy not only to visiting prisons and the poor but also to writing manuals urging women to follow her example and avoid spending too much time on home management. Setting an example for women readers, she expanded her list of public social duties over the years: from her early participation in the Vincent de Paul Society (1860), she became active in the Red Cross and was appointed visitor of women's prisons in La Coruña (1863) and later inspector of women's houses of correction (1868). She founded and wrote for the periodical *La voz de la caridad* ("The Voice of Charity"), argued tirelessly for prison reform, participated in the creation of the Institución Libre de Enseñanza (Free School of Instruction), and sat on the board of directors of the Women's Ateneo that organized the first university-level lectures for women. Besides writing various treatises on women and manuals for visiting the poor and the prisons, Arenal also exerted political influence through dozens of articles on legal issues, such as the Australian penal colonies, the Spanish penitentiary system, and universal human rights (see Lacalzada de Mateo).

In addition to juggling her private duties as wife and mother with extensive public responsibilities, Arenal had to face skepticism and hostility to her presence in the public sphere and health problems that plagued her throughout her career. Resistance to her public work developed as soon as her essays began to be published. For example, her *Cartas a los delincuentes* ("Letters to Delinquents") resulted in her being fired from her post as visitor of women's prisons. In 1865 she wrote to complain that she was being banished from the public sphere because she had dared to suggest prison reforms:

> S. M. (Q. D. g.) Ha tenido a bien dejarme cesante, y lo más terrible del caso, lo que me tiene inconsolable es, que no ha quedado satisfecha del celo, lealtad e inteligencia con que he desempeñado mi destino, o por lo menos no me lo dice. [. . . E]l gobierno no quiere moralizar las prisiones, aleja de la esfera oficial a quien procura moralizarlas y contesta al primer libro que con este objeto se escribe dejando cessante al autor. (*Mujer del porvenir* 13)

> You have seen fit to dismiss me, and worst of all, what makes me truly inconsolable, you have expressed dissatisfaction with the dedication, loyalty, and intelligence with which I have performed my duties, or at least you do not tell me differently. [. . . T]he government not only does not wish to see a moral improvement in its prisons, it is banishing from the official sphere the one person who has sought to reform them, and it has answered the first book with this objective by dismissing its author.

Influenced by the writings of Arenal and other Krausist reformists, the bourgeois press slowly began to acknowledge that activities like caring for the sick and needy would necessarily take women outside of the home. The progressive pedagogue Gumersindo de Azcárate, while insisting that woman's natural place was "el seno del hogar" (19) ("the bosom of the hearth"), praised and recommended Arenal's *El visitador del pobre* ("Visitors of the Poor") to his women readers, arguing that in order for women to perform the public duty of caring for the poor, they needed better formal training. Azcárate agreed with Arenal that the poor and sick required more than religious instruction, more even than bandages and food: they needed to be educated in hygiene and principles of economics (20).

Pardo Bazán was also deeply influenced by Arenal's work, as a close reading of the commemorative essay "Concepción Arenal y sus ideas acerca de la mujer" ("Concepción Arenal and Her Ideas on Woman") shows. In this and her other essays in *La mujer española* collection, Pardo Bazán echoed nearly all of Arenal's arguments in favor of a wider sphere of influence for women, except in regard to the priesthood, which Pardo Bazán thought should remain a male bastion. However, not wishing to lag behind her countrywoman's feminist stance, she indirectly challenged Arenal's reservations about appropriate professions, claiming that there was no serious impediment to women performing well in politics or becoming medical doctors like the gynecologist Concepción Aleixandre. She even expressed admiration for the courage and strength of the transvestites Catalina de Erauso (the famous "Monja Alférez" ["Lieutenant Nun"]) and Feliciana Enríquez de Guzmán, who "se disfrazó de hombre para seguir al campamento al galán de quien estaba enamorada" (*Mujer* 131) ("masquerading as a man, followed the man whom she loved to his camp"). Finally, although Pardo Bazán understood and sympathized with Arenal's objection to women's suffrage, she argued that there was no evidence that if given the vote women would abuse it ("Concepción Arenal" 194).

Until recently the feminist legacy of Arenal has been partially obscured not only by the contradictions of her protofeminism but also by the rupture that either silenced or exiled her feminist admirers in 1936. For example, one of her greatest admirers was the parliamentarian Victoria Kent, who was named director general of prisons in 1931. Like Arenal, Kent undertook substantial prison reforms, summarized in María Telo Núñez's *Concepción Arenal y Victoria Kent: Las prisiones: Vida y obra* ("Concepción Arenal and Victoria Kent: The Prisons: Life and Works"). Under Kent's reforms, prisoners were no longer subject to ideological pressure, living conditions were improved, torture and chains prohibited, and education and other rehabilitation projects initiated. But like Arenal, Kent failed to receive the support of male colleagues at critical moments in her project: she was fired from her position in June 1932 by malcontents worried about coddling prisoners and about a general decline in prison discipline resulting from the reforms. Later a paternalistic President Manuel Azaña wrote of her:

> Victoria es generalmente sencilla y agradable y la única de las tres señoras parlamentarias simpática. Pero en su cargo de Directora General ha fracasado. Demasiado humanitaria, no ha tenido por compensación, dotes de mando. (qtd. in Telo Núñez 68)

> Victoria is in general simple and agreeable, the only pleasant one of the three women parliamentarians. But she has failed in her job as General Director of Prisons. She is too humanitarian, and she has failed to compensate for this with leadership skills.

The issue of women's rights is also complicated in the case of Kent and Arenal. Kent clearly believed in equal rights under the law for both sexes, and she publicly stated that since women had fought for the Republic, the Republic should reward them with the same rights that women in other Western nations enjoyed. Yet in 1931 Kent voted against including a clause on women's suffrage in the new Republican Constitution. For some, the reason for her vote was one of party alliance taking precedence over personal conviction: as a member of the Radical Socialist Party, it was assumed that Kent was pressured to vote against the suffrage clause, fearing for the future of the party if she dissented. Her statement is a poignant testimony to the kind of political compromises that women such as Arenal and Kent have had to make throughout Spanish history:

> [E]s significativo que una mujer como yo, [. . .] se levante en la tarde de hoy a decir a la Cámara, sencillamente, que creo que el voto femenino debe aplazarse. Que creo que no es el momento de otorgar el voto a la mujer española. Lo dice una mujer que, en el momento crítico de decirlo, renuncia a un ideal.
>
> (qtd. in Telo Núñez 85)

> [I]t is significant that a woman such as I [. . .] rises this evening before the Chamber to state simply that I believe that the issue of women's suffrage should be postponed. That I do not believe that this is the moment to concede the vote to Spanish women. I say this in full realization that by doing so, I am renouncing an ideal.

Clearly Kent feared that giving women the vote might sway the electorate to the right at a critical moment in Spanish history. But in her dissenting speech she also echoed Arenal's reservation that women had not sufficiently broken out from the infantilizing yoke of the private sphere: where, she wondered, were the thousands of women who should have been in the streets clamoring for the Republic or protesting the war in Morocco? Women have first to liberate their conscience through work and education; only then will they make just claim to the vote: "si las mujeres españolas hubiesen atravesado ya un período universitario y estuvieran liberadas en su conciencia, yo me levantaría hoy frente a toda la Cámara para pedir el voto femenino" (qtd. in Telo Núñez 87) ("if Spanish women had already gone through a university period and liberated their conscience, I would rise today before the entire Chamber and ask for the vote for women").

Kent's speech was followed by a rousing defense of women's suffrage by Clara Campoamor, another great admirer of Arenal, after which the vote passed in favor of unrestricted voting rights for women and men.[5]

Arenal would hardly have approved of the invoking of her name in Campoamor's campaigns for equal rights for women, just as she disapproved of Pardo Bazán's use of her name to argue for women's recognition in the academies.[6] Yet nearly everyone who joined the struggle for women's rights in the twentieth century cited Arenal as the mother of the women's rights movement in Spain. The reason for Arenal's influence among early twentieth-century women reformists, then, has less to do with her convictions on such issues as the vote for women and more to do with her general call for women to demand a better education and assume a greater role in solving social problems. Campoamor sums up Arenal's goals in a fitting inscription for her commemorative statue: "Concepción Arenal amó la ciencia y consoló la desgracia" (Gutiérrez Zuloaga 137) ("Concepción Arenal loved science and consoled the unfortunate"). The kind of love and consolation that Arenal preached transcended the mission of the domestic angel to reach out to society's least fortunate members.

Notes

1. All translations from the Spanish are mine. See also Grassi's 1957 essay "La misión de lá mujer" ("Woman's Mission").
2. Geraldine Scanlon cites J. Olmedilla y Puig's 1882 "Algunas páginas acerca de la importancia social de la mujer" ("A Few Pages about Woman's Social Importance") as an example of the ironic fact that journalists were proclaiming the end of women's enslavement even while the penal codes were being modified "con arreglo a las deprimentes opiniones prevalecientes acerca de la naturaleza de la mujer" (122) ("to adjust to the depressing prevailing opinions about woman's nature"). For one example of the "the end of woman's slavery" fictions, see Eduardo Bustillos's series of articles entitled "La mujer y la familia ante el espíritu del siglo" ("Woman and the Family vis-à-vis the Spirit of the Times") that ran in *El museo universal* from August to September 1868.
3. New and powerful arguments were also launched against women's education. One of the most influential of these was summarized in "Causa de esterilidad de la mujer" ("The Cause of Sterility in Women") in *El mundo femenino* that reports the claim of American and Danish researchers that women who receive formal education are prone to illness and sterility.
4. For a general review of the 1882 Congreso Pedagógico, see E. Bartolmé. See Scanlon for a detailed survey of the development of women's education in Spain and Jagoe, Blanco, and Enríquez de Salamanca (147–217) for key texts and laws.

5. Campoamor was a member of the Radical Republican Party. Margarita Nelken, a member of the Socialist Party, was the third woman deputy elected to Parliament in 1931. However, she was not eligible to vote in this decision because she had not yet been sworn in. For a description of the tumultuous days leading up to the vote, see Paloma Castañeda's *Carmen de Burgos* (120–30). The survey that Burgos took in the *Heraldo de Madrid* in 1906 convinced her at first to argue, as Arenal did, that women were not ready for the vote. Eventually, however, Burgos was swayed by the Portuguese feminists Elzira Dantas and Ana de Castro that the time had come to demand the vote for women. In 1921 she organized the first public demonstration to demand that Parliament take up the issue. Later, as president of the Liga Internacional de Mujeres Ibéricas (The International League of Iberian Women), she continued her fight for unrestricted voting rights that culminated in the 1931 vote.
6. See Adolfo Sotelo Vázquez (15–19) for a summary of this interesting episode in the relationship between Pardo Bazán and Arenal.

Works Cited

Alcántara García, Pedro de. "De la mujer." *Instrucción para la mujer* 1 Mar. 1882: 4–6.

Arenal, Concepción. *Cartas a los delincuentes.* Ed. Fernando García Arenal. Madrid: Rivadeneyra, 1894. Vol. 3 of *Obras completas de Doña Concepción Arenal.* 23 vols.

———. "La educación de la mujer." Armiño 61–95.

———. *Estado actual de la mujer en España.* Armiño 27–58.

———. *La mujer del porvenir.* Ed. Vicente de Santiago Mulas. Madrid: Editorial Castalia (Instituto de la Mujer), 1993.

———. *La mujer de su casa.* Armiño 189–284.

———. *El visitador del pobre. Concepción Arenal: Obras completas.* Ed. Carmen Díaz Castañón. Vol 1. Biblioteca de Autores Españoles 302. Madrid: Atlas, 1993. 3–66.

Armiño, Mauro, ed. *La emancipación de la mujer en España.* Madrid: Júcar, 1974.

Azcárate, Gumersindo de. "La instrucción de la mujer y la educación del hombre." *Instucción para la mujer* 1 Mar 1882: 17–22.

Bartolomé, E. "El congreso pedagógico." *Instrucción para la mujer* 16 June 1882: 118–21; 1 July 1882: 139–41; 16 July 1882: 156–58.

Blanco, Alda. "Teóricas de la conciencia feminista." Jagoe, Blanco, and Enríquez de Salamanca 445–72.

Bustillo, Eduardo. "La mujer y la familia ante el espíritu del siglo." *El mundo universal* 8 Aug. 1868: 230; 15 Aug. 1868: 258; 22 Aug. 1868: 266; 28 Aug. 1868: 274; 5 Sept. 1868: 282; 12 Sept. 1868: 290.

Castañeda, Paloma. *Carmen de Burgos, "Colombine."* Madrid: Horas y Horas, Dirección General de la Mujer, Comunidad de Madrid, 1994.

"Causa de esterilidad de la mujer." *El mundo femenino* 30 Sept. 1886: 8.

Di Febo, Giuliana. "Orígenes del debate feminista en España. La escuela krausista y la Institución Libre de Enseñanza (1870–1890)." *Sistema* 12 (1976): 49–82.

García Sánchez, Ramón. "La mujer." *La mujer* 16 July 1871: 6–7.

Grassi, Angela. "Memorias de una casada." *La educanda* 31 July 1865: 218–20.

———. "La misión de la mujer." Jagoe, Blanco, and Enríquez de Salamanca 55–58.

Gutiérrez Zuloaga, Isabel. "La mujer en España. (Madrid, primer tercio de nuestro siglo)." *Educación y marginación social: Homenaje a Concepción Arenal en su centenario.* Ed. Julio Ruiz Berrio. Madrid: Universidad Complutense, 1994. 129–37.

Herrero, Leandro Angel. "De la mujer." *La violeta* 28 Dec. 1862: 1–3.

Jagoe, Catherine, Alda Blanco, and Cristina Enríquez de Salamanca, eds. *La mujer en los discursos de género: Textos y contextos en el siglo XIX.* Barcelona: Icarian Antrazyt, 1998.

Lacalzada de Mateo, María José. *La otra mitad del género humano: La panorámica vista por Concepción Arenal (1820–1893).* Málaga: Universidad de Málaga, 1994.

Luz, Juan de. "A las lectoras de *La margarita.*" *La margarita* 20 Aug. 1871: 162.

Pardo Bazán, Emilia. "Concepción Arenal y sus ideas acerca de la mujer." Pardo Bazán, *Mujer española* 173–95.

———. *La mujer española y otros artículos feministas.* Ed. Leda Schiavo. Madrid: Editora Nacional, 1976.

Rebolledo, J. A. "La mujer educada." *Instrucción para la mujer* 1 June 1882: 101–03.

Rodríguez Hubert, Venustiano. "La mujer." *La mujer* 30 July 1871: 1–3.

Sáez de Melgar, Faustina. "La mujer política." *La mujer* 8 June 1871: 3–4.

Scanlon, Geraldine. *La polémica feminista en la España contemporánea, 1868–1974.* Trans. Rafael Mazarrasa. Madrid: Akal, 1986.

Sotelo Vázquez, Adolfo. Prologue. *Concepción Arenal.* By María Campo Alange. Barcelona: Círculo de Lectores, 1993. 7–21.

Telo Núñez, María. *Concepción Arenal y Victoria Kent: Las prisiones: Vida y obra.* Madrid: Instituto de la Mujer, 1995.

Vicuña, G. "La gran industria y la industria doméstica." *Instrucción para la mujer* 16 May 1882: 81–82.

"My Distinguished Friend and Colleague Tula": Emilia Pardo Bazán and Literary-Feminist Polemics

Joyce Tolliver

Emilia Pardo Bazán (1851–1921) is not generally known for her solidarity with other women writers.[1] We might see this as one of the many contradictions inherent in the work and public persona of this writer, for we might expect that, as one of Spain's most outspoken and incisive feminist commentators, she would actively support and promote the work of her female peers. And yet, Pardo Bazán considered her peers to be not Spanish women writing within the sentimental-moralist tradition but women whose writing was recognized and validated by the male literary establishment. Her insistence on playing with the big boys, on identifying herself not as a woman writer but simply as a writer, provoked hostility from her contemporaries (and perhaps continues to do so today). Since at the time of Pardo Bazán's most vigorous literary production—the 1880s and 1890s—this criterion of male acceptance excluded most women writers in her country, her models were from previous generations and even from other national traditions. As Mary Lee Bretz has rightly pointed out in reference to Pardo Bazán's essay *La cuestión palpitant* ("The Burning Question"), "the text speaker takes every available opportunity to applaud the valor and value of female precursors, both anonymous and known" (96). Thus Pardo Bazán speaks at length of the key contributions to literary history of Mme de Staël and of George Sand, mentioning Gertrudis Gómez de Avellaneda and Concepción Arenal as her Spanish predecessors, while also paying the obligatory homage to Fernán Caballero.[2] Further, she credits wet nurses and grandmothers for their contributions to the tradition of oral narrative, without which the novel would not have been born (Bretz 96). Pardo Bazán consistently alludes to a female literary history in many of her essays.[3]

Pardo Bazán's essays also reveal an acute consciousness of the role that gender attitudes played in the public reception and perception of the works of women writers and of their public personae. Her many discussions of "the woman question" insistently place this issue in a historical context. This tactic serves not only to demonstrate her erudition but also to depersonalize her antifeminist contemporaries' attacks on her ideas and personality by implicitly placing those attacks in proper historical perspective. Nevertheless, whether Pardo Bazán was successful in focusing her reader's attention on issues rather than on personality is questionable. Well into the twentieth century, critics viewed Pardo Bazán's defense of the intellectual woman largely as a manifestation of her own personal ambition and lack of modesty. In an article that is otherwise an excellent introduction to Pardo Bazán's contributions to feminist polemics, Ronald Hilton comments that

> it would have been well had Doña Emilia contented herself with working for the amelioration of feminine education in Spain. It was perhaps unfortunate that she should have been even more active in her attempts to obtain official recognition for the intellectual achievements of Spanish women and that, being undoubtedly the most prominent Spanish woman of her time, the recipient of this recognition should be inevitably she, and usually she alone. (40)

When Pardo Bazán praises other women writers and intellectuals and suggests that they are worthy of official public recognition, even today she is accused of insincerity, of using the accomplishments of other women to advance her own reputation.[4]

Pardo Bazán's literary and critical work was, of course, strongly criticized by her peers. As she herself argued, her being a woman should certainly not exempt her from her colleagues' reasoned assessment; yet clearly much of the faultfinding leveled against her took the form of *ad feminam* attacks. Many criticisms of Pardo Bazán's work emanating from male contemporaries in fact merely repeated well-worn commonplaces regarding the proper domain of "ladies'" writing—a domain outside of which Pardo Bazán persistently strayed. Leopoldo Alas's review of Pardo Bazán's *Los pazos de Ulloa* (*The House of Ulloa*) serves as a prime example. According to Alas, Spanish ladies were, by definition, incapable of writing good realist novels: "Una señora española que no quiere dejar, no ya de serlo, sino de parecerlo, no puede escribir una novela como *Nana* o *Safo*" (226) ("A Spanish lady who wishes not only to continue to be a lady but to appear to be one cannot write a novel like *Nana* or *Sappho*").[5] Alas thus implicitly accuses Pardo Bazán either of not being a real writer or of not being a lady, even in appearance. Pardo Bazán never responded directly to this charge or to any of the other many hostile remarks Alas directed toward her writings and her public persona. Nevertheless, in the prologue ("Breve noticia") she wrote for an edition of María de Zayas's novellas, published in her Biblioteca de la Mujer (Woman's Library) series, she quotes an eerily similar remark that the literary historian Eustaquio Fernández de Navarrete made years earlier about Zayas and offers a spirited response to it.[6] By placing Alas alongside the earlier Navarrete in his myopic view of "ladies'" ability to produce good novels, Pardo Bazán dismisses the misogynist thinking of both critics and reveals the existence of a masculinist critical tradition, one prevalent in an earlier period and in which her contemporaries still participated. Equally important is the connection she traces between herself and Zayas as novelists who, because they are "ladies," must write under the most restrictive conditions.

The very selection of Zayas's novellas for inclusion in her Biblioteca de la Mujer, along with translations of John Stuart Mill's *The Subjection of Women* and August Bebel's *Women under Socialism,* is intriguing for the recuperative gesture it represents. The parallel implied in Pardo Bazán's prologue between Zayas's work and her own is equally suggestive, for the writings of both authors were condemned by some as pornographic. José María de Pereda, Alas, and Emilio Bobadilla all attacked Pardo Bazán's *Insolación* (*Midsummer Madness*) (1889) as not only frivolous but even licentious. Bobadilla finds the character Asís's afternoon at the fair with Pacheco morally censurable: "la viuda [. . .] resulta una tía, mal que pese a doña Emilia. Una señora, una verdadera señora no va de juerga, y menos con un hombre a quien apenas conoce. Y no hay psicología que valga" (Review 222) ("the widow [. . .] turns out to be a tart, no matter how much Doña Emilia might deny it. A lady, a true lady, does not go running off, much less with a man she barely knows. And psychology has nothing to do with it"). He adds that the ending of the novel is not believable because Pacheco marries Asís after having spent the night with her: "Crea doña Emilia que pocos se casarían si les dejasen probar antes la fruta prohibida. ¡La primera noche! He aquí el secreto de muchos matrimonios al vapor" (224) ("Doña Emilia should realize that few men would marry if they were allowed to taste the forbidden fruit first. The first night! That is the secret of many hastily arranged marriages").

In response to a request from a novice writer for advice from a seasoned member of the literary establishment, Pardo Bazán claims that she never publicly responded to any criticism of her writings:

> Con tanto como he escrito, no escribí un solo artículo encaminado a discutir las críticas de mis obras. [. . .] ¡En estas defensas oficiosas se ve la hilaza de un modo! [. . .] Conque lo dicho, joven [. . . , p]az, firmeza, buen humor [. . .]. Las cicatrices del alma no deben ser de rasguños de pluma.
>
> ("Cartas a un literato novel" ["Letters to an Apprentice Writer"] 25)
>
> With all I have written, I never wrote a single article dedicated to discussing the criticisms of my works. [. . .] In this sort of officious self-defense people really show their true colors! So, as I say, young man [. . . , p]eace, firmness, good humor [. . .]. The scars of the soul should not be caused by swipes of the pen.

While advising her young protegé to take the high road and ignore hurtful criticisms, she also acknowledges that some of the criticism of her work has served as a pretext for personal insult and challenges to her honor—challenges to which she, as a woman, cannot respond:

> Mi sexo es un impedimento (sobre esto habría mucho que hablar, pero no aquí) para que yo pudiese castigar ofensas personales; sin embargo, a falta de la *acción,* cabría en mí el *sentimiento* de furor y de cólera a que la acción responde. Pues el sentimiento me falta, o por lo menos cede ante la idea de que los furores de un individuo [. . .] llevan cierto sello de mezquindad y egoísmo mal entendido, que los hace moralmente feos e indignos de cultivo en el jardín del alma. [. . .] Una vida no más se nos concede en este planeta, ¿y la hemos de emponzoñar con rencores, suspicacias, iras, *turbieces* y venganzas? (32–33)

> My sex is an obstacle (about this one could say a great deal, but this is not the place) that keeps me from punishing personal insults; however, even if no *action* is taken, one might expect to find in me the *emotion* of fury and rage that would motivate the action. Well, I do not have that emotion, or at least it is held in abeyance by the idea that the furies of an individual [. . .] leave a certain trace of pettiness and misguided egotism, which makes them ugly and unworthy of being cultivated in the garden of the soul. [. . .] We are given only one life on this planet; must we poison it with resentment, suspicion, fury, turbulence, and vindictiveness?

Gender expectations thus serve as a frame for Pardo Bazán's response to those who have used erudite criticism of her work as an excuse to insult her personally. Since so many of these insults revolve around her transgression of gender norms, it is entirely appropriate that these norms be brought to the forefront in her response. This tactic allows her to defend herself in the most ladylike manner possible: by relinquishing the right to such a self-defense. She even goes one step further, alleging that those writers (according to her logic, all of them male) who do indulge in "officious self-defense" are petty and indeed morally inferior to her. In this way she very neatly places herself as a model of the still-dominant ideal of the "angel of the house," which would require women to exemplify morality, self-control, and self-sacrifice in a world filled with corruption and egotism. According to this logic, her critics are guilty of the lowest and meanest sort of ungentlemanly conduct:

insulting a lady who cannot defend herself. Ironically, Pardo Bazán's foregrounding of the gender dynamics in her response to personally motivated criticism denaturalizes gender norms: her sex is an "obstacle" to her ability to defend herself. We can perceive, in this very ladylike paragraph, a not very successfully disguised frustration with an imagination of the woman writer that would allow male critics to proffer personal insults but not allow her to respond to them except at the risk of upholding the charge of immorality or *marimachismo*, an unseemly masculinity.[7]

Although certainly Pardo Bazán ignored countless attacks on her work, it is not true that she never responded to any of them. She carried on an extended critical exchange with Pereda ("Pereda") and with Víctor Balaguer and Luis Alfonso ("Coletilla a *La cuestión palpitante*" ["Postscript to *La cuestión palpitante*"]). In both these exchanges, in which the intersection of gender and genre forms a context for Pardo Bazán's discussions of realism and naturalism, the underlying (or sometimes readily apparent) gender biases of her opponents' arguments are brought to the surface and repudiated.

When, in several open letters, the ethnographer Ferdinand Blumentritt took issue with Pardo Bazan's review of a book on the Philippines question, she ignored the repeated goading, apparently making an effort to follow the advice she had given the novice writer. Finally, seven months after the publication of the review, she responded with perceptible annoyance to Blumentritt's charge that she was an "*agent provocateur* del separatismo" ("agent provocateur of separatism") and "sacerdotisa del filibusterismo" ("high priestess of filibusterism") ("Notas literarias" ["Literary Notes"] 88). Again, she brings to the forefront the presence of expectations regarding the appropriate domain of women's writing:

> En cuanto al sr. Blumentritt, ya que él se permite señalarme lo que debe y lo que no debe escribir una mujer, voy a señalarle a mi vez lo que no debe hacer una persona de buena crianza. Cuando una señora corta o termina una conversación; cuando rehusa discutir; cuando se aparta y sigue su camino, los caballeros no porfían, ni insisten, ni machacan, ni se descomponen, ni llenan columnas y más columnas con lucubraciones inconvenientes e indigestas.
>
> (88–89)

> As for Mr. Blumentritt, since he permits himself to tell me what a woman should and should not write, I in turn will tell him what a well-brought-up person should and should not do. When a lady cuts off or ends a conversation, when she refuses to argue, when she steps aside and continues on her way, a gentleman does not plead or insist or nag or become upset, nor does he fill columns and more columns with impertinent and half-baked lucubrations.

Pardo Bazán, then, repeatedly unmasked and foregrounded the role gender played in the critical reception of her work, in terms of notions of what topics and styles were appropriate for women's writing and in terms of feminine behavior in the public sphere. Both these concerns converged in what was perhaps the most prolonged public polemic involving Pardo Bazán, which she herself referred to as "la cuestión académica" ("the academy question").

In 1889, a vacancy occurred in the Royal Spanish Academy, and Pardo Bazán's name was mentioned. The notion that she might be named provoked a heated polemic, to which Pardo Bazán responded in a series of essays and open letters. In February of that same year, the newspaper *El correo* published a series of letters that Gertrudis Gómez de Avellaneda had written thirty years earlier to an unnamed recipient regarding her own attempts to be named to the academy. These letters were reproduced, under the title "Las mujeres en la Academia" ("Women in the Academy"), along with a preface from a sr. Vior, "describing Avellaneda's sorry failure to obtain the coveted seat and prophesying the same unpleasant fate for Pardo Bazán" (Hilton 41). The title of the collection establishes, through the use of the plural, that Avellaneda's private letters might be relevant to the general issue of women entering the academy, and the preface makes an open allusion to Pardo Bazán's own presumed pretensions to the honor. In responding to this face-threatening challenge, Pardo Bazán fully exploits the implication of a parallel between her case and Avellaneda's. She transforms the implied insult—that she herself is as ambitious, and as doomed to failure, as Avellaneda—into the bedrock of her argument, which is that the controversy over her admission to the academy rests on ideological considerations rather than personal ones. The same sexual ideology that kept Avellaneda—and other women before her—out of the academy is operating again in her case, according to Pardo Bazán's logic. This response allows her to turn her readers' attention away from the question of her putative immodesty and toward the misogyny underlying the dispute.

Rather than reply directly to the editor, Pardo Bazán chooses to frame her response—which she loses no time in drafting—in a set of two letters ("La cuestión academica: A Gertrudis") to Avellaneda herself, "en los campos Elíseos" (173) ("in the Elysian fields"). Pardo Bazán makes the rhetorical choice to reply only obliquely to Vior and in the process to turn his own logic against him. Her use of an extended apostrophe to Avellaneda places Vior, and the *Correo*'s male readership, in the position of eavesdroppers rather than addressees; the true dialogue is between Pardo Bazán and her literary foremother. By framing her reply as an affectionately admiring letter to an illustrious woman writer of a previous generation, Pardo Bazán neatly undermines Vior's attempt to shame her by association with Avellaneda, who had caused a certain degree of scandal in her own time, not only because of her pretensions to the academy but also because of her personal life. Instead of denying the validity of the comparison with the earlier writer, Pardo Bazán embraces it and reframes it as a compliment. In addressing herself to Avellaneda, she goes one step further in her appropriation and redefinition of Vior's attempt to humiliate her, for she puts herself in the position of Avellaneda's anonymous interlocutor. Her letter overtly responds to Avellaneda's letters; it is only obliquely that she responds to Vior. Were her open letter to be addressed to Vior, much of the rhetorical force of her argument would be lost, for the adversarial open letter was the standard method for responding to polemics. Her choice of identifying Avellaneda, not Vior, as her interlocutor reinforces her celebration of the comparison between the two while it excludes Vior as a worthy adversary.

The opening, "Mi excelsa compañera Tula" ("My distinguished friend and colleague Tula"), establishes a note of equality and even intimacy with the Romantic writer, one that embraces and celebrates Pardo Bazán's connection with her predecessor. Later in the essay, Pardo Bazán suggests a genealogy of Spanish women's writing that begins with

Santa Teresa of Avila, includes Carolina Coronado and Gómez de Avellaneda, and extends, in the present moment, to herself, thus reinforcing her positioning of "la cuestión académica" within a historical, ideological context rather than a personal one. Nevertheless, Pardo Bazán does address herself at least nominally to the question of feminine immodesty, since this is the underlying charge leveled at her and Avellaneda. Here, too, she subverts the force of the insult, at the same time that she is very careful to differentiate between Tula and herself as individual writers and as public personae.

Pardo Bazán states emphatically that, unlike Avellaneda, she has never actively sought nomination: "No ha salido una palabra de mis labios, ni ha trazado una línea mi pluma en son de ruego tácito o explícto para que se me admita en la tertulia filológico-literaria de la calle de Valverde" (174) ("Not one word has left my lips, not one line has my pen written as a tacit or explicit plea to be admitted to the philological-literary *tertulia* held on Valverde Street"). But, lest her readers conclude that, in differentiating herself from Avellaneda, she is implicitly admitting the impropriety of the earlier writer's ambition, she specifies that her aim is to defend Avellaneda, while also explaining why she herself has not sought out a seat in the academy (175). In fact, the force of Vior's attack lies in his implication that Pardo Bazán is guilty of the same sort of unfeminine ambition as Avellaneda and that this ambition will inevitably only work against her. Were she to simply deny the charge, Pardo Bazán would be granting validity to it, even while insisting on its inapplicability to her own comportment. In a remarkable rhetorical move, she squarely refuses to do this.

Instead, Pardo Bazán insists that Avellaneda had every right to expect to enter the academy and that if she was bitter over not having gained that honor, her bitterness took the form of the disillusionment caused in the good-hearted by "el espectáculo de la injusticia y la pequeñez" (176) ("the spectacle of injustice and narrowmindedness"). In assuming that the members of the academy would be happy to grant her the honor she so clearly deserves, Avellaneda was in fact merely showing her own ingenuous faith in the goodwill of her male peers. Further, Pardo Bazán says that her candidacy was supported by the best academicians, including Angel Saavedra, Ramón de Mesonero Romanos, Mariano Roca de Togores, Manuel José Quintana, and Nicomedes Pastor Díaz (177). In responding to the encouragement of these illustrious members of the literary establishment and in assuming fairness in the other members of the academy, Avellaneda was in fact demonstrating her own modesty and good will (178). Pardo Bazán thus exposes the presupposition of feminine immodesty in Vior's insidious attack on Avellaneda's character and then inverts it entirely. In contrast, she presents her own refusal to seek nomination to the academy as a result of her pride:

> si hoy resucitasen Quintana y Angel Saavedra, o sintiesen como ellos los que siguen su huella literaria, y yo me creyese tan digna como tú de ocasionar reñida lid, no sé Gertrudis, si dominando mis instintos de orgullo en favor de una causa buena, hubiese practicado esas gestiones que en ti apruebo y juzgo señal de modestia y de ánimo benigno. (171–72)
>
> If Quintana and Angel Saavedra were to come back to life or if those who follow the literary path set by them were to feel as they did, and if I considered myself as deserving as you were of causing a hard-fought battle, I don't know, Gertrudis, whether, overcoming my instincts of pride in the name of a good cause, I might have taken those same steps that in you I endorse and consider the sign of modesty and good will.

Pardo Bazán refuted any implication that Avellaneda's rejection by the academy was due to her lack of worth as a writer and intellectual, since Avellaneda was in fact on a par with the best male writers of her day. Only sixteen years after Avellaneda's death, Pardo Bazán asserted that the Cuban writer had already earned her place in Hispanic letters on the basis of the quality of her poetry and plays and her brilliant use of language. She supported her assertion by evoking the authority of Villemain, who considered Avellaneda as equal in talent to José María de Heredia (175), as well as the monumental Alberto Lista, who claimed that she had a gift for "conciliar el genio con el respeto al idioma" (175) ("combining genius with respect for the language"). The mention of

Lista in support of her judgment is significant here, for Lista was one of the most powerful literary figures of Avellaneda's time. He also happened to have been the teacher of José de Espronceda and of his lesser-known friend Patricio de Escosura. Escosura himself is held up in Pardo Bazán's open letter as a prime example of the injustices perpetrated by an academy that would admit clearly mediocre male writers while excluding women of the rank of Avellaneda. As it happens, Escosura was one of the academicians who militated most actively against Avellaneda's entrance into the august body (while, Pardo Bazán comments, calling himself her friend when outside those hallowed walls). Before he would cast a vote for Avellaneda's admission, he said, she must first join the army. A generation later, says Pardo Bazán, Escosura had already fallen into oblivion as a writer: ¿"quién se acordaría [de Escosura] hoy, Gertrudis, a no ser por la memoria de éste, más que varonil, pueril amaño? Tú le salvas del olvido" (176) ("Who would remember [him] today, Gertrudis, were it not for the memory of this childish, rather than manly, trick? You save him from oblivion").

Pardo Bazán thus suggests that Avellaneda was supported in her desire to enter the academy primarily by writers whom literary history has consecrated; she implies that those who most vigorously and memorably opposed her admission did not themselves deserve the country's highest literary honor. Her logic would seem to dictate that the validity of a nomination to the academy might be judged by considering which individual academicians supported it. But in discussing her own nomination, which according to her, only Emilio Castelar supported, she veers away from this consideration of individual evaluations and outlines instead what she sees as a historical trend toward an increasing misogyny in the academy.

Pardo Bazán's own refusal to campaign for entrance to the academy was based overwhelmingly on her consciousness of the academicians' prejudice. The question of whether she considered herself a writer worthy of that honor is irrelevant, according to this logic; she would not fight for entrance, she says, because she had little hope of seeing any woman enter the academy in her lifetime. Adopting a diachronic perspective, she places her own identification as a "serious" female writer alongside Avellaneda's and argues against conventional notions of linear social "progress":

> La época en que España poseyó mayor número de mujeres sabias, acatando en ellas el sagrado derecho a la instrucción y el soberano don del entendimiento, fue la edad de oro de nuestras letras, los siglos 16 y 17. [. . .] El respeto y equidad para la inteligencia femenina empieza a perderse durante nuestra lastimosa decadencia del siglo 18, y ya Feijóo se ve en el caso de escribir su famosa *Defensa de las mujeres.* (177)
>
> The age in which Spain possessed the greatest number of learned women, revering their sacred right to education and their sovereign gift of intelligence, was the golden age of our letters, the sixteenth and seventeenth centuries. [. . .] The respect and equity shown for women's intelligence begins to disappear during the piteous period of our decadence in the eighteenth century, and Feijoo is led then to write his famous *Defense of Women.*

Pardo Bazán notes that even in the period of decline, the academy granted an honorary seat to a woman, Doña Isidra de Guzmán. The respect for women as intellectuals had continued to decline since the eighteenth century, says Pardo Bazán, so Avellaneda's rejection by the academy simply reflected a gradual intensification of prejudice (177). Pardo Bazán places her own historical moment at the extreme end of this process, thus explaining why it is that, in her day, only one member of the academy would support her publicly.

If Castelar had his way, says Pardo Bazán, Avellaneda would certainly have been granted a seat in the academy, and so would "el tierno poeta Carolina Coronado" (179) ("the tender poet Carolina Coronado"). The use of the masculine article and the term "poeta" rather than "poetisa" to describe Coronado is not insignificant here, for Pardo Bazán also describes Avellaneda as "*poeta* de alto vuelo y estro fogoso" ("a *poet* of high artistic standards and ardent inspiration") and "aplaudidísimo *autor* dramático" (173; my emphasis) ("most celebrated dramatic *author*"). Both writers, for Pardo Bazán, are worthy of being honored precisely because their work may be judged by gender-neutral standards. In using the so-called generic masculine to refer to these writers, Pardo Bazán reflects her conviction, expressed eloquently in the "Coletilla a *La cuestión palpitante,*" that the biological sex of writers should not enter into aesthetic judgments of their work. Her defense of the public validation of women's writing ultimately rests on an aesthetic ideal of androgyny, an ideal that was markedly at odds with the prevailing practices of the literary establishment at that time.

But in her own period, in which liberalism and social reform supposedly reigned, if Santa Teresa herself were to appear at the doors of the academy, she would be told,

> Vade retro, señora Cepeda. Mal podríamos, estando usted delante, recrearnos con ciertos chascarrillos un poco picantes y muy salados que a última hora nos cuenta un académico. [. . .] En las tertulias de hombres solos no hay nada más fastidiosito que una señora, y usted, doña Teresa, nos importunaría asaz. (181)
>
> Get thee behind me, Señora Cepeda. With you here, we could scarcely enjoy certain rather spicy, risqué jokes that an academician likes to tell. [. . .] In all-male gatherings there is nothing more annoying than a lady, and you, Doña Teresa, would bother us quite a bit.

Pardo Bazán thus contrasts the impartial consideration of a gender-neutral artist's work—the expected criterion for inclusion in the academy—with the reality of the "Valverde Street *tertulia*" as an organization dedicated primarily to male bonding or a sort of not-too-intellectual men's club. Santa Teresa, rather daringly presented here as the literary foremother of both Avellaneda and Pardo Bazán, is similar to Tula and to Emilia in another way: for her insistent desire to "andar *públicamente embuelta con los omes*" (182) ("go among the men in public places"). This scandalous insistence on appearing in the public (i.e., male) sphere would disqualify "Señora Cepeda" from admission to the academy as well, suggests Pardo Bazán. Four years after the publication of the Tula letters, a remark by Alas demonstrates that Pardo Bazán's satirical barb was well placed, for he complained of her "mania" to "mezclar a hombres y mujeres, de hacerlos andar juntos y codearse en Academias, Ateneos, y Universidades" ("Congreso pedagógico ["Pedagogy Conference"] 176) ("mix together men and women, to make them walk together and rub shoulders in academies, athenaeums, and universities").

Once Pardo Bazán establishes that her predicament is due to historical, cultural, and ideological factors—indeed, that the personal is political—she then squarely faces the question implicit in *El correo*'s publication of Avellaneda's letters: Is she in fact campaigning for admission to the academy? She replies, "[Q]ue sí, que tengo conciencia de mi derecho a no ser excluida de una distinción literaria *como mujer* (no *como autor*), pues sin falsa modestia te afirmo que soy el crítico más severo y duro de mis propias obras") (182) ("Yes, I am aware of my right not to be excluded from a literary distinction *as a woman* [not *as an author*]; for without false modesty I assure you that I am the severest and harshest critic of my own works"). She points out that there is no clause in the statutes of the academy that would exclude women from being appointed to it but confesses her belief that there is very little chance of her, or any other woman, being named during her lifetime. Therefore, purely for the sake of the advancement of women's rights, she states, "[C]reo que estoy en el deber de declararme candidato perpetuo a la Academia. [. . .] Seré siempre candidato archiplatónico, lo cual equivale a candidato eterno" (184) ("I believe I have an obligation to declare myself a perpetual candidate to the academy. [. . .] I will always be a thoroughly platonic candidate, which is equivalent to being an eternal candidate").

The conclusion of this open letter to Avellaneda underlines the insistently historical context in which Pardo Bazán places the question of her being named to the academy, for she vows that while she waits for what will never happen, she will occupy herself by writing a history of Spanish literature that will vindicate Avellaneda's place in literary history.

In March 1891 Pardo Bazán published another essay about the academy polemic, also called "La cuestión académica," in which she expands on the notion that her exclusion from the ranks of the hallowed ones is an ideological issue, an issue that establishes a sisterhood between herself and other women writers of merit. Here she is quite explicit: "Como cuestión puramente personal, no merece la tinta que se gaste en dilucidarla. Mas como cuestión objetiva y de principios vale cuanto vale toda reivindicación del derecho [. . .]." ("La cuestión académica: [al sr. Rafael Altamira]," Schiavo 198) ("As a purely personal question, it is not worth the ink it would take to explain it. But as an objective question and as one of principle, it is as worthwhile as any vindication of rights"). She comments insightfully on the degree to which the personal has overshadowed the ideological in this polemic: since she has a personality that she describes as lacking false modesty, even "militante," she has been perceived as the most arrogant person since Nebuchadnezzar (200). To take the spotlight off herself as an obnoxious public figure and to emphasize the ideological aspect of the academy debate, she suggests that another woman be named to the academy, specifically, Concepción Arenal.

Pardo Bazán recommends Arenal's inclusion not in the Academia de la Lengua but in the Academia de Ciencias Morales y Políticas. Surely no one would accuse this reclusive "anciana señora, reducida a sus libros y a su familia" (203) ("elderly lady, restricted to her books and her family") of the arrogance and blind ambition so routinely attributed to Pardo Bazán. Evoking the image of Arenal as an elderly recluse, removed from active participation in public life, Pardo Bazán once again points toward the aspect of her persona that doubtless contributed most to her vilification by her peers: her public visibility. At the time of Pardo Bazán's involvement in the "academy question," Arenal was in poor health and made few public appearances. After having spent years inspecting prisons and campaigning for penal reform—activities that formed a striking contrast to the domestic feminine ideal still dominant in late nineteenth-century Spain—Arenal lived in relative seclusion. Nevertheless, she certainly had not retired from her intellectual pursuits. It was in this same year, 1891, that Arenal's *Manual del visitador del preso* ("Manual for Prison Inspections") was published, and the following year, she presented "La instrucción del obrero" ("The Education of the Worker") and "La educación de la mujer" ("Woman's Education") both of which she prepared for the second Congreso Hispano-Luso-Norteamericano (Santiago 23). Eliding Arenal's history as a pathbreaking figure in Spanish feminist thought and in the developing science of sociology, Pardo Bazán ironically portrays her as a slightly pathetic figure, one whose infirmity and age render her inoffensive. By presenting the private image of Arenal as a contrast to her all-too-public image, she subtly reinforces her implicit argument that much of the objection to Pardo Bazán's own entrance into the academy rests on a conviction that women should be neither seen nor heard outside the home. Clearly, Arenal would have been a much more obvious choice for a nomination to the academy during her professional prime had she been a man. As a woman, she was only considered a potential candidate for this honor after she retired from public visibility and was therefore no longer threatening.

Just after Arenal's death in 1893, the Ateneo de Madrid organized a series of three lectures in Arenal's honor. One dealt with her ideas about penal reform, the second with her social ideas in general, and the third with her literary production. Glaringly absent was any mention of Arenal's feminist writings. In an attempt to begin to correct an egregious oversight, Pardo Bazán published an essay in her *Nuevo teatro crítico* ("New Critical Theater") called "Concepción Arenal y sus ideas acerca de la mujer" ("Concepción Arenal and Her Ideas about Women"). She censures what she sees as a general tendency to

> prescindir de las ideas emancipistas que la ilustre señora había llegado a formarse; a no nombrarlas, a esconderlas como un delito [. . .] y el empeño pueril de retratarla consagrada a las que en los padrones y cédulas de vecindad se llaman por antonomasia *labores de su sexo.* (Schiavo 174–75)
>
> ignore the emancipationist ideas that the illustrious lady had formulated; to not mention them, to hide them as if they constituted a crime [. . .] and [to insist] on portraying her as dedicated to what are referred to in census registers and identity cards as *women's tasks.*

The tendency to portray the mature Arenal as a simple housewife is particularly ironic, suggests Pardo Bazán, in that it transforms her into the same feminine type that Arenal herself criticized as an "erroneous ideal" (175). Pardo Bazán thus reverses her earlier silencing of Arenal's feminist contributions, replacing the image of the reclusive homebody with an image of the vigorous feminist social reformer. Not only does she correct the selective blindness of those who just acknowledge Arenal's work on penal reform, she also suggests that her feminist work has a far greater transcendence. Pardo Bazán's logic anticipates the dictum that women's issues are by definition social issues because "women are half of humanity":

> La mujer es más de medio género humano; nadie ignora que nacen y se conservan más hembras que varones; con sólo recordar este sencillo e incontestable dato estadístico, se entiende que cuanto afecte al destino general de la mujer reviste importancia superior a la de otras cuestiones. (174)
>
> Women make up more than half of the human race; everyone knows that more women than men are born and survive; if we just remember this simple, indisputable statistical fact, it becomes clear that whatever affects the general fate of women must be of greater significance than other questions.

Using as a pretext the fact that, like Benito Jerónimo Feijoo, Arenal was born in Galicia, Pardo Bazán traces an explicit connection between these two thinkers and, by extension, establishes a link between them and herself. She mentions that she and Arenal submitted essays on Feijoo to the 1876 Juegos Florales of Orense.[8] As she does in several essays, she mentions Feijoo's "Defensa de las mujeres" and lauds Arenal's contribution to critical studies of this important work. She affirms that, just as Arenal was moved by a sense of gratitude to Feijoo to write her essay on his feminist ideas, she herself has been motivated by gratitude to her foremother in writing her essay on women. Pardo Bazán thus presents her essay as a duplication of Arenal's gesture, recovering a foundational contribution to feminist thought. It is worth noting that, in tracing the tradition of feminist essays, Pardo Bazán looks back originally to a male figure, in keeping with her insistence on the androgynous nature of the intellect and of art.

Pardo Bazán's summary of Arenal's *La mujer del porvenir* ("The Woman of the Future"), written in 1861 and published in 1868, and *La mujer de su casa* ("The Woman of the House"), the critique of the *ángel del hogar* ("angel of the house") ideal that followed it almost thirty years later, is presented as a sort of dialogue between Arenal's thinking and Pardo Bazán's feminist ideas. As she did in "La cuestión académica: A Gertrudis" and in many other essays, Pardo Bazán historicizes and denaturalizes both her feminist critique and her position as a female, and feminist, writer. In this, I suggest, she anticipates the revolutionary notion expressed a generation later by another foundational figure in the history of women's literature. Pardo Bazán would, I believe, agree with Virginia Woolf's assertion that "we think back through our mothers if we are women" (79). Throughout Spain's history, Pardo Bazán repeatedly suggests, women writers preceding her have been subjected to the same misogyny in the guise of intellectual criticism. In her essays, Pardo Bazán foregrounds and historicizes this critical double standard, at the same time that she places her own figure in its rightful place at the end of a long line of women. Speaking alternately as "respectful daughter" (Bieder, "Literary Women" 24) and as intimate friend and colleague, Pardo Bazán renders the homage due to Santa Teresa, to Zayas, to Coronado, to Avellaneda, and to Arenal. In this, she anticipates Woolf's exhortion that "all women together [. . .] let flowers fall upon the tomb of Aphra Behn" (69).

I do not suggest that we lay flowers on Pardo Bazán's tomb or even on Santa Teresa's. I suspect this quintessentially romantic gesture would be one Pardo Bazán herself would consider hopelessly *cursi,* both kitsch and sentimental. Nevertheless, it is time that we recognize Emilia Pardo Bazán for her perceptive and unremitting analysis of the role of gender in the critical reception of literature. She deserves credit, as well, for her crucial contributions to the formation of a genealogy of Spanish women's writing. One might say that both these contributions are continued, almost a century later, in the volume you now hold in your hands.

Notes

1. Maryellen Bieder has documented the rather chilly relations between Pardo Bazán and her female contemporaries ("Literary Women").
2. One woman writer whose literary success Pardo Bazán largely ignores is Rosalía de Castro. In keeping with a critical tradition that emphasizes Pardo Bazán's personality and personal life when assessing her work, her silence

on Castro has been explained as personal animosity and even envy, either toward Castro herself or toward her husband, Manuel de Murguía. Catherine Davies comments insightfully on this relationship in her essay in this volume and in *Spanish Women's Writing* (65–66).

3. Pardo Bazán's essay production has received far too little critical attention. Of note, however, are the studies by Bieder ("Women"), Bretz, Adna Rosa Rodríguez, and Geraldine Scanlon. In part, this critical neglect reflects a dearth of scholarly analysis of the essay as a genre. Along with the four above-mentioned studies, the anthology edited by Kathleen M. Glenn and Mercedes Mazquiarán de Rodriguez represents an important step toward remedying this oversight.
4. Bieder, for instance, claims that Pardo Bazán's "ostensible deference and humility constitute an act of appropriation, most evident in her use of Avellaneda [. . .] to put forth her own claim to a chair in the Real Academia Española" ("Literary Women" 24).
5. All translations are my own. Of the hundreds of essays Pardo Bazán wrote, to my knowledge the only essays available in English are her monograph *La revolución y la novela en Rusia,* translated by Fanny Hale Gardiner as *Russia, Its People and Its Literature,* and "La mujer española," which first appeared in English as "The Women of Spain" in the *Fortnightly Review.* For a comprehensive list of works by Pardo Bazán translated into English, see Tolliver (Introduction xxvii–ix).
6. See my *Cigar Smoke and Violet Water* (23–26) for a more detailed account of Alas's review and Pardo Bazán's oblique response to it in her "Breve noticia sobre doña María de Zayas."
7. Alas, Pereda, Bobadilla, Manuel Gutiérrez Nájera, and others all questioned Pardo Bazán's femininity in print. For a more detailed discussion of these charges of *marimachismo,* see Tolliver (*Cigar Smoke* 20–26).
8. Pardo Bazán discreetly passes over the well-known significance of this regional and literary competition for her own literary career, for it was she, and not the older and better known Arenal, who came away with the prize.

Works Cited

Alas, Leopoldo ["Clarín"]. "Congreso pedagógico." *Palique.* Madrid: Suárez, 1893. 175–80.

———. Review of *Los pazos de Ulloa,* by Emilia Pardo Bazán. *Nueva campaña.* Madrid: Fe, 1887. 215–37.

Bieder, Maryellen. "Emilia Pardo Bazán and Literary Women: Women Reading Women's Writing in Late Nineteenth-Century Spain." *Revista Hispánica Moderna* 46 (1993): 19–33.

———. "Women, Literature and Society: The Essays of Emilia Pardo Bazán." Glenn and Mazquiarán de Rodríguez 25–54.

Bobadilla, Emilio. "Pedanterías de doña Emilia." *Triquitraques.* Madrid: Fernando Fe, 1892. 133–39.

———. Review of *Insolación,* by Emilia Pardo Bazán. *Triquitraques.* Madrid: Fernando Fe, 1892. 215–25.

Bretz, Mary Lee. *Voices, Silences and Echoes: A Theory of the Essay and the Critical Reception of Naturalism in Spain.* London: Tamesis, 1992.

Davies, Catherine. *Spanish Women's Writing, 1849–1996.* London: Athlone, 1998.

Fernández de Navarrete, Eustaquio. "Bosquejo histórico sobre la novela española." *Novelistas posteriores a Cervantes.* Ed. Cayetano Rosell. Madrid: Rivadeneyra, 1851.

Glenn, Kathleen M., and Mercedes Mazquiarán de Rodríguez, eds. *Spanish Women Writers and the Essay: Gender, Politics, and the Self.* Columbia: U of Missouri P, 1998.

Gutiérrez Nájera, Manuel. "La señorita matemática." *Escritos inéditos de sabor satírico: Plato del día.* Ed. Boyd G. Carter and Mary Eileen Carter. Columbia: U of Missouri P, 1972. 228–29.

Hilton, Ronald. "Pardo Bazán and Literary Polemics about Feminism." *Romantic Review* 44 (1953): 40–46.

Pardo Bazán, Emilia. "Breve noticia sobre doña María de Zayas y Sotomayor." *Novelas de doña María de Zayas.* Biblioteca de la mujer 3. Madrid: Avrial, 1892. 5–16.

———. "Cartas a un literato novel." Pt. 2. *Nuevo teatro critico* 15 (1892): 18–35.

———. "Coletilla a *La cuestión palpitante.*" Pardo Bazán, *Polémicas* 105–44. Rpt. in Pardo Bazán, *Obras completas* 3: 648–60.

———. "Concepción Arenal y sus ideas acerca de la mujer." *Nuevo teatro crítico* 26 (1893): 269–304. Rpt. in Schiavo 173–95.

———. "La cuestión académica: A Gertrudis Gómez de Avellaneda (en los Campos Elíseos)." *La España moderna* 26–27 (1889): 173–84.

———. "La cuestión académica (al sr. Rafael Altamira, secretario del Museo Pedagógico)." *Nuevo teatro crítico* 1 (1891): 61–73. Rpt. in Schiavo 197–204.

———. "La mujer española." *La España moderna* 2.7 (1890): 101–13. Rpt. in Schiavo 25–70.

———. "Notas literarias." *Nuevo teatro crítico* 10 (1891): 82–94.

———. *Obras completas.* Ed. Harry L. Kirby. 3 vols. Madrid: Aguilar, 1973.

———. "Pereda." Pardo Bazán, *Polémicas* 5–104. Rpt. in *Obras completas* 3: 1002–27.

———. *Polémicas y estudios literarios.* Madrid: Avrial, 1891.

———. *La revolución y la novela en Rusia.* Pardo Bazán, *Obras completas* 3: 760–880.

———. *Russia, Its People and Its Literature.* Trans. Fanny Hale Gardiner. Chicago: McClurg, 1901.

———. "The Women of Spain." *Fortnightly Review* 1 June 1889: 879–904.

Rodríguez, Adna Rosa. *La cuestión feminista en los ensayos de Emilia Pardo Bazán.* La Coruña: Castro, 1991.

Santiago Mulas, Vicente de. Introducción. *La mujer del porvenir.* By Concepción Arenal. Madrid: Castalia, 1993. 7–44.

Scanlon, Geraldine. "Gender and Journalism: Pardo Bazán's *Nuevo teatro crítico.*" *Culture and Gender in Nineteenth-Century Spain.* Ed. Lou Charnon-Deutsch and Jo Labanyi. Oxford: Clarendon, 1995. 230–49.

Schiavo, Leda, ed. *"La mujer española" y otros artículos feministas.* By Emilia Pardo Bazán. Madrid: Nacional, 1976.

Tolliver, Joyce. *Cigar Smoke and Violet Water: Gendered Discourse in the Stories of Emilia Pardo Bazán.* Lewisburg: Bucknell UP, 1998.

———. Introduction. *"Torn Lace" and Other Stories.* By Emilia Pardo Bazán. Trans. María Cristina Urruela. New York: MLA, 1996. ix–xxxiv.

Woolf, Virginia. *A Room of One's Own.* 1929. New York: Harcourt, 1957.

Twentieth Century

Carmen de Burgos: Modern Spanish Woman

Maryellen Bieder

Carmen de Burgos [. . .] es la liberal, la romántica, la que compromete su pluma y su vida cuantas veces es menester por tomar una actitud generosa y rebelde, tan rebelde y tan generosa a veces que aparentemente parece ir contra la rebeldía.

—Ramón Gómez de la Serna

Carmen de Burgos [. . .] is the liberal woman, the romantic woman, the woman who commits her pen and her life as often as is necessary by adopting a generous and rebellious attitude, at times so rebellious and so generous that it visibly seems to negate her rebellion.

A remarkable woman in her private, public, and professional life, Carmen de Burgos (1867–1932) was one of Spain's few early-twentieth-century career women. A prolific writer—"indefatigable" one critic notes with a tinge of disparagement—she reached a wide reading public, especially among Spain's lower middle class (Nora 49). She studied to become a school teacher in an era when few Spanish women received much formal education and even fewer had any professional training. She learned the newspaper trade and launched herself as a reporter for a Madrid newspaper. As an author, writing under the popular sobriquet "Colombine," she penned novellas, novels, short stories, translations, essays, biographies, interviews, travel books, and that staple moneymaker, self-help manuals for women (see Starcevic; Núñez Rey; Castañeda).

Burgos, limned a critic in 1968, was "la perfecta *vulgarizadora,* con todas las limitaciones e inconsistencia final que ello comporta" (Nora 49–50) ("the perfect *popularizer,* with all the limitations and ultimate insubstantiality this term implies").[1] Nevertheless, in her day she enjoyed privileged access to Madrid's exclusively male avant-garde literary circles, through her longtime male companion, Ramón Gómez de la Serna.[2] In his clever sketch entitled "Colombine," published in his own literary magazine at the start of their relationship, he lightly disparages her work while ostensibly praising the gendered nature of her writing in which "interviene la madre, la amante, la hermana, la hija, y la oficianta" (3) ("the mother, the lover, the sister, the daughter, and the female officiant all participate"). The recovery and rereading of women authors in the last two decades has radically revised these dismissive attitudes. Recent studies of Burgos recognize in her a "defensora de la mujer" (Starcevic) ("defender of women"), "una escritora comprometida" (Martínez Garrido) ("a socially committed writer"), and "a feminist *avant la lettre*" (Ugarte, "Burgos").

Spanish feminism at the turn of the century was tenuous and freighted with contradictions. Writers, both female and male, deployed the feminist label in very different ways. Spain maintained a keen awareness of the developments for women taking place in other cultures over the preceding decades, especially when such phenomena could be portrayed as dangerous excesses or humorously trivialized as absurd exaggerations. Critics of women's rights invoked the word *feminism* to characterize almost any proposed change in or challenge to the rigidly traditional roles for women. In her indispensable study of the "feminist polemic" in Spain, Geraldine Scanlon associates Spain's failure to produce a significant feminist movement with its largely inflexible class structure and its protection of class interests. International feminism, she observes, is essentially a middle-class movement, while the weakness of the petite bourgeoisie in the wake of Spain's 1868 revolution and its lack of a group dynamic made it politically and socially ineffective (11).

The historian Mary Nash, in her closely argued analysis of Spanish feminism, demonstrates the need to recognize the plural "feminisms" that developed in Spain, that is, "la formación de las plurales estrategias de resistencia y de cambio social de las mujeres" (157) ("the creation of plural strategies for resistence and social change for women"). In a culture that grounded gender construction in difference, not equality, feminism cannot be equated with the discourse of equality and the right to vote, the two underlying tenets of feminism in England and the United States. At the end of the nineteenth century and in the first decades of the twentieth century, "la construcción socio-cultural de género demarcó el ámbito de actuación y la función social de la mujer" (161) ("the sociocultural construction of gender marked out women's sphere of action and their social function"). Thus, for example, the most visible and outspoken woman in nineteenth-century Spain, Emilia Pardo Bazán, wrote passionately about educational opportunities for women and the need to respect women as individuals in their own right, instead of linking her name to specific social and political reforms. Although Pardo Bazán was undoubtedly one of Spain's few supporters of feminist ideals, she rarely championed feminism in any overt way until her later years. Writing in 1902, the normal school teacher Concepción Saiz bluntly characterized Spain as unprepared for the agenda of international feminism: "¡Hablar de feminismo en España, donde todavía no saben leer ni escribir tres millones y medio de hombres y dos millones y medio de mujeres! ¡Feminismo aquí, donde la instrucción y la educación se hallan en mantillas y apenas presentida su compenetración!" (249–50) ("How can one speak of feminism in Spain when 3.5 million men and 2.5 million women still can't read or write! Feminism here, where teaching and education still wear their mantillas and where their effect can scarcely be felt!"). Burgos took a more optimistic view, declaring a few years later that "la mayoría de las españolas, especialmente las de la clase media, son hoy ilustradas y de conciencia libre que si no se manifiesta con más energía es por falta de medios para desenvolverse" ("Femeninas" 1) ("most Spanish women, especially those from the middle class, are now educated and think for themselves, and if they do not demonstrate this more forcefully, it is because of the lack of opportunities for them to do so"). While this characterization may be overly generous toward the urban middle class of Madrid, where Burgos transformed herself into a successful career woman, it most certainly applies to her.

Nash draws an important distinction between the few women who led the fight for reform and the many Spanish women who supported the status quo (155–56). In a country that did not legislate universal male suffrage until 1890, female suffrage was not of central concern to most women, and even those who upheld the right for women such as themselves to vote did not necessarily support the vote for all women. The existing voting rights for all men provoked some educated women to argue that women were at least as well prepared as chimney sweeps to make intelligent electoral choices (Gimeno, *Eva* 7; Burgos, *Misión social* 21). Indeed, Nash affirms that until the 1930s "la legitimización social de los derechos individuales no representaba un factor clave de la tradición liberal y democrática en España" (159) ("the social legitimization of individual rights was not a key factor in the liberal democratic tradition in Spain").

Feminism in Spain, as Nash conceptualizes it, is "un proceso social de renegociación de los términos del contrato social de género, es decir, de modificación y de reajuste de las bases de dominación de género establecidas en la sociedad" (158) ("a social process of renegotiating the terms of gender's social contract, that is, of modifying and readjusting the bases for defining gender as established within society"). Since in early-twentieth-century Spain the discourse of domesticity still functioned as the basis for the construction of women's cultural identity, any women's movement was necessarily premised on a recognition of gender difference, rather than on gender equality (161). Burgos similarly points to the inhibiting nature of gender differentiation: "Aquí la fiebre feminista no reviste un carácter agudo precisamente porque la mujer recibe el culto caballeresco y la protección del hombre, que en contadas excepciones no pueden eclipsar" ("Femeninas" 1) ("Here feminist fever has not taken a firm hold precisely because women are recipients of gentlemanly attentions and male protection, from which with few exceptions they cannot extricate themselves"). Nevertheless, Burgos denounces as myth the idea that men are the enemy of women and takes pains to argue that it is not men but the weight of custom and convention that bars women's access to careers and cultural institutions.

Not until Spain's transition in 1931 from a monarchy to the Second

Republic did it enact such political reforms as universal suffrage, which for the first time gave women the right to vote, civil marriage, and divorce. During the first three decades of the century, Burgos played a significant role in informing public opinion on such issues and in giving voice to women's dependent status and limited choices. She did this as a journalist, a fiction writer, and a public figure. Along with the art critic and author Margarita Nelken and the lawyer and Republican legislator Clara Campoamor, Burgos agitated forcefully for social and legal reform in the 1920s (Scanlon 139). All three women were central in shifting the terms of the debate over the place of women in Spanish society from gender difference to gender equality, including the right to vote and to receive equal protection under the law. Burgos's social evolution and engagement continued to her death in 1932.

Arriving in Madrid in 1901, Carmen de Burgos, as Michael Ugarte envisions her, was "a single mother fleeing the gender restrictions of her small Andalusian town [. . .] as well as the scandal she had aroused by separating from her husband" ("Generational Fallacy" 268). Accompanied by her sister and her daughter, she launched a new life and plural careers at age thirty-four (she acknowledged twenty-four years, at most) in the cultural and literary capital of Spain. The death of her husband in 1906 eliminated the ambiguity of her social position and the impropriety of her public activities. What makes Burgos a woman of a new generation is her status as a professional in three simultaneous careers: teacher, newspaperwoman, and author. After training to be a teacher and obtaining a position by competitive examination, she eventually maneuvered her way into a post in Madrid's Normal School for Women. She used her knowledge of newspapers—her father-in-law owned a newspaper, where she had learned the work of typesetter and copywriter—to become one of the first women in Spain to be hired as a journalist. During the previous century, women had written for women's magazines and even had edited such publications. Burgos took pride in being the first woman named to the position of *redactora* ("writer") for a Madrid newspaper, with her own regular column on women's affairs. Her first editor suggested the pseudonym "Colombine"; the feminine white flower and commedia dell'arte stylization accompanied her name for the remainder of her life. Burgos never used her pen name to disguise her identity, as some Spanish women of earlier generations had done; instead it served to supplement her name with traditional female icons that more easily engaged her less sophisticated readers. Although it did not limit her tone or choice of topics, it perhaps nonetheless offset, to some degree, her frequent departures from conventional women's subjects. Deploring the tendency of newspapers to offer only sensational accounts of women's behavior, she identified the corrective role newspaperwomen can play by portraying the Spanish woman as she is: "no con artículos feministas sino justificándola frente a la inverosimilitud" (*Influencias recíprocas* 20) ("not with feminist articles but by defending her against improbable accusations").

As a journalist, Burgos made contact with the few Spanish women who were prominent cultural figures, among them two writers from an older generation who represented different strands of feminist discourse, Emilia Pardo Bazán and Concepción Gimeno de Flaquer. Despite the generational difference, Burgos had much in common with these women in her early years in Madrid. All three authors had settled in the capital as a base from which to write and to support themselves through publication. Even the wellborn Pardo Bazán, who, like Burgos, lived separated from her husband, boasted proudly that she earned her living from her writing, despite her inherited wealth. As a career journalist, however, Burgos was both more circumspect in her writing and more publicly involved in feminist causes than either Pardo Bazán or Gimeno. Burgos and Pardo Bazán became "los primeros socios femeninos" ("the first women members"—it is worth noting that Burgos uses the masculine plural)—of the Atheneum, the capital's progressive scientific, literary, and artistic center for male intellectuals (*La mujer en España* 37). They also served together on a jury that selected candidates for teaching positions, a function previously exercised exclusively by men (see Burgos, "Doña Emilia").

Soon after Burgos's arrival in Madrid, she singled out Gimeno as a "campeón decidido del progreso de la mujer española" (*La mujer en España* 37) ("a firm champion of progress for Spanish women"). In her review of Gimeno's 1903 lecture at the Atheneum, "El problema feminista" ("The Feminist Problem"), Burgos declared, "Pocos actos tan importantes registra en sus anales la historia del feminismo español" ("Lecturas" 1) ("The history of Spanish feminism records few events of such import"). The attention Burgos devoted to the presence on the dais of Princess Eulalia suggests that any public discussion of feminism was best cloaked in social respectability, even as the Atheneum venue granted it intellectual authority. This seeming incompatibility between the subject of Gimeno's lecture and its social character exemplifies the author's brand of "feminismo moderado" ("moderate feminism"). In Gimeno's words, "el credo de los feministas moderados es conservar a la mujer muy femenina, porque masculinizada perdería la influencia que ejerce sobre el hombre, precisamente por su feminilidad" ("El problema feminista" 13) ("the credo of the moderate feminists is to keep women very feminine, because once masculinized they would lose the influence they currently exercise over men precisely because of their femininity"). Although she espoused education, moral and intellectual participation in public life, and economic and legal rights for women, Gimeno carefully distanced herself from the more radical dimensions of international feminism that, in her view, threatened to do violence to the social fabric (Bieder, "Feminine Discourse" 466). In consonance with the gender difference that Nash identifies at the core of Spanish feminism, Gimeno wanted women to retain their feminine difference while attaining financial, intellectual, and legal parity with men.

With her growing cultural and social sophistication, Burgos came to identify less with Gimeno's attempts to unite feminine virtues with feminist reforms and more with Pardo Bazán's modeling of intellectual and literary engagement and her negotiation of gender conventions to create a space for personal and artistic freedom. In a 1921 obituary of Pardo Bazán, Burgos praised her as "la primera mujer que libra a la literatura femenina de ese aire, piadoso o fútil, con que las escritoras marcaban su sexo en los escritos" ("Doña Emilia") ("the first Spanish woman to free women's literature from that pious or trivial tone with which women writers imprinted their writings"). Acknowledging that Pardo Bazán avoided identifying herself as a feminist, Burgos asserted that by her example she nevertheless did more for Spanish women "que todas las predicaciones y campañas feministas" ("than all the feminist preaching and campaigns"). While at times Burgos mirrored Gimeno's interweaving of feminist and feminine rhetoric, at other times she reflected Pardo Bazán's more forthright stances and her enactment of a feminist agenda in her own life.

Like many writers of the earlier generation, Burgos took pains to downplay her difference from other women and emphasize her normative femininity. In an early autobiography, whimsically dialoguing with her readers, she queried, "No se adivina que soy escritora ¿verdad?" ("Auto-biografía" 45) ("You wouldn't guess I'm a writer, would you?"). Although the sketch appeared in a literary magazine, she stressed her role as mother and her attention to "las labores propias del sexo" (45) ("the tasks appropriate to my sex"), a phrase she highlighted. Her companion and fellow author Ramón Gómez de la Serna depicted the room where she worked as maternal space:

> Este salón es como una extensión de su regazo y él ampara y acoge con un afecto más allá del bien y del mal, de las juntas de señoras, de los patronatos y del cariño que simboliza la matrona de bronce de la Equitativa. (3)
>
> This large room is like an extension of her lap and it protects and welcomes with an affection that goes beyond good and evil, beyond women's organizations, charitable organizations, and the loving care symbolized by the bronze matron on the Equitable Insurance building.

Rafael Cansinos-Asséns remembered Burgos as an expert multitasker, juggling the activities of cook and mother while working on a translation and simultaneously dictating to her secretary the final copy of an interview for the evening edition of the newspaper (189).

Burgos made her dramatic break with the circumspection of earlier Spanish women through her use of the print medium. By launching surveys on attitudes toward such controversial issues as divorce and women's suffrage, she created a public debate in the press. The polemic linked her name with these hot-button issues without her necessarily having to stake out her own position. In 1903 she announced the formation of a Club of Unhappily Married Couples to draw up a proposal for a divorce law; this pretext gave rise to the publication of a spate of letters on divorce in her column in the *Diario universal.* Until the Second Spanish Republic enacted a divorce law in 1932, the word *divorce* in Spain meant a form of legal separation that freed the woman from her marital obligations and permitted her to recover the remains of any wealth she took into the marriage (Scanlon 136–37). In her response to Burgos's divorce query, Gimeno flatly announced, "La mujer española no es partidaria del divorcio" (Burgos, *Divorcio* 44) ("Spanish women are not in favor of divorce"). Somewhat coyly, Gimeno professed not to know whether women's opposition to divorce came from their satisfaction with their husbands or whether they had such a poor opinion of men that they lived in terror of men being handed such an easy way to satisfy their "inconstantes pasiones" (44) ("inconstant passions"). At the other extreme, Pardo Bazán discreetly responded that she had no opinion at all about divorce, a stand similar to the one the writer Miguel de Unamuno took. Pardo Bazán's rationale was characteristic of her self-presentation: "Necesito dedicarme a estudiar esa cuestión, y no dispongo de tiempo" (71) ("I need to undertake a study of the question, and I lack the time for it"). Despite such responses, Burgos concluded that Spanish women supported divorce, since hundreds more women voted for divorce than against it (*La mujer en España* 42). Burgos's own attention-grabbing contribution to her divorce series was a discussion of Pope Pius's proposed reform of convent life that she headlined, "El divorcio de las monjas" (*Divorcio* 14–16) ("The Nuns' Divorce"). If nuns' vows are no longer unbreakable, if nuns can change their minds, she asked, why not married women?

In 1906 Burgos undertook an opinion poll on the vote for women in which she asked whether all or only some women should have voting rights and whether women should be eligible to hold office if granted the vote ("Voto" [19 Oct.] 1). Deliberately veiling her own stance, she playfully ended with a call for women and men to cast their votes in her survey: "Señoras y señores: ¡A votar!" ("Ladies and gentlemen: Let the voting begin!"). When the debate closed one month later, the paper had received 4,562 responses, of which 3,640 opposed enfranchising women. Only 815 votes supported universal women's suffrage, and only 39 recommended letting women hold elected office. Burgos observed bitterly that among the Spanish people "es aún mayor el peso de los atavismos que la fuerza del progreso" ("Voto" [25 Nov.] 2) ("the weight of atavistic thinking is greater than the force of progress"). She perceived that before Spanish women could hope to have the right to vote, they must first forge a culture of their own; avail themselves of their civil rights; and gain greater freedom, respect, and the conditions for an independent life.

Burgos's championing of women's right to vote was, like much of her thinking, uneven and tailored to the audience she was addressing. Earlier in 1906, in a lecture to fellow journalists in Rome, Burgos spoke against women's suffrage as equivalent to "poner un arma peligrosa en manos de un niño. Claro que no por ser mujer, sino por ser ignorante" (*La mujer en España* 46) ("putting a dangerous weapon in the hands of a child. Not, of course, because she is a woman but because she is uneducated"). While Burgos recognized that the same argument applied to men, she reasoned that the situation would only get worse if women voted (47). Consonant with the position frequently taken by other educated women in Spain, including Pardo Bazán (but not Gimeno), her remark was well received by her audience.

By 1913 Burgos had made significant advances in her teaching and newspaper careers, marking out a path that was distinctively her own. In addition to her position in Madrid's Normal School for Women, she was, in her own words, a reporter for a leading newspaper, the *Heraldo de Madrid*; a contributor to a hundred newspapers; and the editor of the *Revista crítica* ("Critical Review"), which she had founded ("Autobiografía" xi). Despite these achievements, she attached greatest importance to her creative writing. Her considerable success in breaking into the male world of publishing echoes in her declaration, made about this time in a lecture to a provincial audience: "El feminismo es una tontería como doctrina, pero existe de hecho como necesidad" (*Influencias recíprocas* 21) ("Feminism is nonsense as a doctrine, but it exists in fact because it is a necessity"). As she frequently does in her public statements, she takes both sides of the issue, opposing feminism but recognizing its fundamental role in enacting social change. Nearly a decade later, in 1922, with her literary success and social position well established, Burgos declared unequivocally to an interviewer, "Yo soy feminista: presido la Cruzada de mujeres españolas, y fui de las que fueron a las Cortes a pedir los derechos electorales para la mujer" (González Fiol 115) ("I am a feminist: I chair the Spanish women's Crusade, and I was one of the women who went to Parliament to petition for voting rights for women"). In a more humorous vein, she declared that trolleys and feminism are women's true enemies, because "en ellos nos disputamos el sitio" ("Mujeres" 40) ("in both we fight to make a place for ourselves").

In her last years, Burgos became a member of the Radical Socialist Party, joined the Masonic Order along with her sister and daughter, and became grand master of the Masonic lodge she herself founded. The traditional account of Burgos's death at a political forum places the final words "¡Viva la República!" ("Long live the Republic!") on her lips (Castañeda 156–58). Unconventional to the end, in a Catholic country with a newly elected Republican government, she chose burial in a civil cemetery. Burgos lived a life plotted with as much drama, imagination, and resolve as any of her novels.

The scant appreciation accorded Burgos's fiction by literary critics before the 1970s derives in part from the author's reliance on the realist mode and on everyday language in an era of literary modernism and vanguard experimentation. In addition, Burgos published much of her fiction in the popular, mass-market novella format. Whereas her male contemporaries, the authors of the Generation of '98, essayed innovative forms and new modes of expression to convey their preoccupation with Spain and the future of humankind, Burgos unabashedly employed the familiar conventions inherited from nineteenth-century fiction (Johnson, "Generation" 3–4). The male writers saw themselves as an intellectual elite melding philosophical questions into fictional form, while Burgos conceived of her narratives as entertainment for a mass audience and a forum for social concerns. Despite her personal ties to members of the younger generation of male writers, the literary vanguard, her fiction displays little of their linguistic and formal play. As Alison Booth reminds us, "Fictions that, in current feminist readings, yield powerful revisions of social codes often have been built on foundations of traditional story or discourse" (11). Burgos's novels, short stories, and many novellas weave together multiple threads of contemporary social, feminist, economic, sentimental, and even biological discourse. She frequently foregrounds a woman protagonist confronted by adverse social, monetary, and personal conditions or at a defining moment in her relations with men. Novels by women, as Roberta Johnson rightly observes, "continue to center on economic issues" in the early years of the twentieth century ("Generation" 4). Women's quest for autonomy, authority, or financial freedom thus displaces the more abstract concerns of male authors.

The desire for economic independence defines the working-class women in Burgos's novel *La rampa* ("The Ramp"). The new phenomenon being worked out in her fiction is the possibility of jobs that would make women financially independent and self-sustaining. Earlier women authors who imagined economic solutions for their protagonists found them in solitary endeavors, such as seamstress, copyist, translator, or flower maker. Burgos's working women, however, run the gamut from seamstress in a shop to nurse, writer, actress, or clerk in the new department stores. In her novellas she depicts the monetary and emotional concerns of the ever-precarious middle classes. Even a social satire like *Los huesos del abuelo* ("Grandfather's Bones") explores an underlying economic reality in tracing a middle-class family's use of an illustrious ancestor's name to generate both desired status and needed income. Judith Kirkpatrick reads *Los huesos* as a feminist parable in which the granddaughter chooses to align herself with the male cult of authorship, rather than "recognize the strengths and possibilities of her own female voice" (398). Social classes converge in the decadent artistic world of *El veneno del arte* ("Artistic Poison"). The male protagonist is an aristocrat; the leading female character, a former actress whose successful career still maintains her in style, while aspiring artists of questionable talent live on the edge of starvation.

The female body is the site of struggle in the marriage plots of Burgos's more overtly feminist fictions. She dramatizes gender polarization by exploring the problematic nature of women's status in sexual relationships, both within and outside marriage. Social expectations, legal codes, and especially marital obligations come into conflict with a woman's desire for self-definition and self-preservation. In marriage women either lose control of their bodies or circumvent gender proscriptions to bring their bodies under their control. The penal code ties a wife to an abusive marriage in *El artículo 438* ("Article 438"), which derives its title from the law allowing a husband to kill a wife caught with her lover in flagrante delicto. The same law exacts no punishment for the husband. Divorce law gives a wife a legal separation from her corrupt and immoral husband in *El hombre negro* ("The Man in Black"), but it cannot give her a new life. In *La malcasada* ("The Unhappily Married Woman"), legal separation is almost impossible to obtain and socially anathema; once obtained, it is subsequently revoked, requiring a woman to return to a man she detests. The wife kills her husband with her scissors rather than "verse obligada a cumplir aquella *obligación*" (262) ("see herself forced to fulfill that *obligation*"). Such acts of sacrificial violence offer both protagonist and reader a cathartic release from the violence implicit in hierarchical structures of power. Burgos's fiction displaces "bourgeois respectability," as Johnson notes, by questioning its underlying institutions ("Gender" 172). Burgos describes marriage as ongoing physical consummation, something that most nineteenth-century novels—and novels by her male contemporaries—tend to address only covertly, if at all. She unravels the romance plot of unconsummated desire and replaces it with the drudgery and oppression of cohabitation. Marriage in her fiction is a physical and, by extension, a mental and emotional reality for women. Even the globe-trotting feminist explorer-politician in *La entrometida* ("The Busybody") ultimately makes choices about the disposition of her body. She can either reinvent herself through language, as a writer, or recast her body as a cocotte (Bieder, "Self-Reflexive Fiction").

To counter the weight of prevailing gender construction, Burgos's fiction often takes as its point of departure the dominant cultural paradigm: woman as daughter, wife, and mother, shaped by the example of her own mother. To open up a space for gender redefinition, especially for lower-middle-class working women, Burgos makes her protagonists motherless, orphans, or, if married, childless. This allows them to tread their own moral, economic, and social path without a model to follow, thus creating the work's dramatic tension. Novels and the example of other women also exercise an influence on the choices a character makes, as does, disastrously, her own romantic idealism. The woman who violates gender norms, even under legal protection, tends to find herself isolated and alone. The woman who rejects her husband in *El hombre negro* ends up friendless, exploited even by the sympathetic lawyer who gained her freedom for her. But the hardworking seamstress who splurges on a holiday by the sea with her boyfriend and discovers terminal boredom in *La Flor de la Playa* ("Paradise Beach") comes to no harm from her adventure; she merely avoids a disastrous marriage. The seamstress in *La prueba* ("The Test") who misses the train and spends the night with her boyfriend comes to her senses and is set to marry him at the end. In Burgos's melding of discourses, the couple's holiday on a Portuguese beach affords a tantalizing travelogue within the titillating framework of an illicit relationship played out in public space in a foreign land. The reader vicariously enjoys the trip, while the exotic locale shows up the dreariness of the disillusioned characters' relationship.

In other narratives Burgos probes gender construction. She parodies men who impose the male code of behavior on their girlfriends, only to discover they have shot themselves in the foot because of their closed-mindedness. In a male parody of the fickle woman, *¡Todos menos ese!* ("Anyone but Him!"), the male protagonist dismisses his girlfriend because he feels diminished when he sees her with his friend, as if she could not distinguish between them. A broader satire of male desire underlies *El anhelo* ("Desire"), in which an older man engaged to a much younger woman wears himself out preparing for the wedding and has a stroke before the day arrives. A novel set in Paris, *La mujer fantástica* ("The Amazing Woman"), subverts the myth of the Parisian woman and highlights the artificiality of male desire. By placing the action of the story abroad, Burgos can scandalize her readers with forbidden subjects—abortion, interracial relationships, lesbianism, even electrolysis—without running the risk of alienating them. But Burgos also makes the prostitute a defective woman, unable to fulfill her natural function of motherhood, and finally traps her in her need to control perceptions of her body. The prostitute narcissistically finds in a much younger woman the mirror of her lost youth (233). Parody, satire, and voyeurism are essentially conservative modes with implicit normative values that offset the seeming modernity and daring of the subject matter.

In her 1927 book *La mujer moderna y sus derechos* ("The Modern Woman and Her Rights"), Burgos attempts to coalesce the multiple facets of her thinking about women into a series of fully articulated arguments. Although the volume reproduces sections from her previous works, it marks a departure from her earlier formulations of women's place in Spanish society (Martínez Garrido 32). Since Burgos has no audience in front of her in *La mujer moderna,* she is more forthright in her assertions and denunciations. She openly identifies herself with feminism, understood as "la causa de la liberación femenina, de acuerdo con su naturaleza" (10) ("the cause of woman's liberation, in accord with her nature"), but in a way that still acknowledges gender difference. Contending that the social upheavals following World War I attenuated hostility to international feminism, she nevertheless enumerates the forces that continue to oppose it. In recognition of the fear that radical social agendas still arouse, she rejects any association between feminism and "un deseo de inversión de sexos o de funciones, y mucho menos la aspiración a la igualdad, que hace imposible la naturaleza" (9) ("a desire to invert the sexes or their functions and much less the aspiration for equality, which nature itself makes impossible").

Burgos's concern lies with redressing the subordination of women in Spanish society, a sexual hierarchy that, she affirms, has no basis in nature. At the same time, however, she accepts the different social roles of men and women: "ambos sexos tienen un papel claro y bien definido" (24) ("both sexes have a clear and well-defined role"). Rather than equals, they are "sexos complementarios" (26) ("complementary sexes"), with distinct forms and unique roles, who share a social mission. Nevertheless, she rejects the traditional exaltation of women as mothers, considering the idealization of motherhood a form of slavery that denies any value or function to women without children. She posits instead that feminism strengthens the bonds of love and family: "Ser *feminista* es ser mujer respetada, consciente, con personalidad, con responsabilidad, con derechos, que no se oponen al amor, al hogar y a la maternidad" (21) ("To be a *feminist* is to be a respected, self-aware woman, with personality, with responsibilities, with rights that are not in opposition to love, home, and motherhood"). She contends that historically feminism arises in response to a changing family structure that no longer protects women, thus compelling them to enter the workforce to support themselves. She therefore champions women's right to education, to work, and to equal protection under the law. And she takes it for granted that women's liberation will ultimately resolve the contentious issues of marriage and divorce (188).

Departing from her earlier rejection of biological determinism—the thesis prevalent in the nineteenth century that linked women's inferiority to physical characteristics—Burgos came to admire the renowned endocrinologist Gregorio Marañón, who pioneered in Spain the theory of universal, organic *intersexualidad* ("bisexuality"). Paul Julian Smith cogently defines Marañón's "dream and nightmare of bisexuality" as "the incorporation of one sex into the other" (26) and notes that as a result his gender stereotypes are "perversely unstable" (29). Thus, for example, Marañón held that great women, "a los ojos del fisiólogo, son seres alejados del centro de la feminilidad" (qtd. in Burgos, *Mujer moderna* 28) ("from the physiologist's point of view, are beings far removed from the core of femaleness"). In adopting the idea of "la primitiva bisexualidad de los seres" (26) ("the primitive bisexuality of all beings"), Burgos seems to endorse a form of biological determinism. Her last novel, *Quiero vivir mi vida* ("I Want to Live My Own Life"), for which Marañón wrote a laudatory prologue, puts these ideas into play. The novel plots the trajectory of an intersexed woman with two antagonistic natures, which is like having within her a twin of the opposite sex (80). Not attracted to motherhood—Marañón contended that women derived sexual pleasure only from motherhood—the protagonist laments, "¡Si yo fuese hombre!" (34) ("If only I were a man!"). Living one's own life thus represents a refusal to eliminate the "other" and enact one's dominant gender.

Marañón's metaphorical advice is to "'[k]ill the phantom of the other sex which each of you bears within; be men, be women'" (qtd. in Smith 30). Burgos's novel reverses this metaphor when the protagonist kills her husband with the cry, "¡Al fin le he robado su alma de hombre!" (249) ("At last I have robbed him of his man's soul!"). Here, a woman's body is, more than in any other of Burgos's narratives, her enemy.

The contradictions and ambivalence that characterize Burgos's plotting of women and gender issues infuse all her writings and reflect the unresolved tensions in early-twentieth-century Spanish society. Even in novels with a clearly feminist core, one recent critic has identified antithetical readings, one regenerative and the other a more conservative paternalist reading grounded in female masochism (Martínez Garrido 33). In part this dichotomy is an intentional rhetorical device. Since both her fiction and her lectures seek the acceptance of a wide public, Burgos accommodates—while nevertheless confronting—the prejudices of her audience. She tends to frame her social agenda in the comfortable rhetoric of womanhood, establishing at the outset her commonality with her listeners and then returning after each bold call for action to the ground of hearth and home. Her lectures and essays thus alternate between a bold defense of feminist positions in favor of women's self-determination and conventional backpedaling designed to shore up the support of straying members of her listening and reading public (see also Ugarte, "Carmen de Burgos"). Hers is a balancing act, both revolutionary and reactionary, forward-thinking and comfortably familiar. *Feminism* is clearly still a problematic term in the early decades of the twentieth century, and while for most of that time Burgos avoided declaring herself a feminist in public forums, her espousal of legal, political, economic, and social parity for women constituted one of Spain's more radical feminisms. She also joined the fight to eliminate the death penalty, end wars, and allow women to be named guardians of their own minor children (*Influencias recíprocas* 19). By living her feminist agenda in ways that no earlier Spanish women authors had—in her private choices, her professional careers, her public life, and her political activism—Carmen de Burgos came closer than other women writers of her generation to embodying the modern woman.

Notes

1. All translations from Spanish are my own.
2. For a counterpoint to Burgos's marginal but palpable access to male literary culture, see the memoirs of Carmen Baroja, sister of the Generation of '98 author Pío Baroja. She laments the isolation and frustration of women with literary aspirations and no access to education or Madrid's cultural institutions.

Works Cited

Baroja y Nessi, Carmen. *Recuerdos de una mujer de la generación del 98.* Ed. Amparo Hurtado. Barcelona: Tusquets, 1998.

Bieder, Maryellen. "Feminine Discourse / Feminist Discourse: Concepción Gimeno de Flaquer." *Romance Quarterly* 37 (1990): 459–77.

———. "Self-Reflexive Fiction and the Discourses of Gender in Carmen de Burgos." *Self-Conscious Art: A Tribute to John W. Kronik.* Ed. Susan L. Fischer. Lewisburg: Bucknell UP, 1996. 73–89.

Booth, Alison. Introduction. *Famous Last Words: Changes in Gender and Narrative Closure.* Ed. Booth. Charlottesville: UP of Virginia, 1993. 1–32.

Burgos, Carmen de. *Al balcón.* Valencia: Sempere, 1913.

———. *El anhelo. La novela semanal* 3.106 (21 July 1923): 1–59.

———. *El artículo 438. La novela semanal* 1.15 (1 Oct. 1921): 1–60.

———. "Autobiografía." Burgos, *Al balcón* vii–xiv.

———. "Auto-biografía." *Prometeo* Aug. 1909: 40–46.

———. *El divorcio en España.* Madrid: Romero, 1904.

———. "Doña Emilia íntima." *El heraldo de Madrid* 18 May 1921: 1.

———. *La entrometida. La novela corta.* 16 July 1921: n. pag.

———. "Femeninas: En defensa de las damas (feminismo inglés)." *El heraldo de Madrid* 19 Dec. 1906: 1.

———. *La Flor de la Playa.* 1920. La Flor de la Playa *y otras novelas cortas.* Ed. Concepción Núñez Rey. Madrid: Castalia / Instituto de la Mujer, 1989. 309–63.

———. *El hombre negro. La novela corta* 8 July 1916: n. pag.

———. *Los huesos del abuelo. Los contemporáneos* 7 Dec. 1922: n. pag.

———. *Influencias recíprocas entre la mujer y la literatura.* Logroño: Rioja, 1912.

———. "Lecturas para la mujer: De feminismo." *El diario universal* 27 May 1903: 1.

———. *La malcasada.* Valencia: Sempere, 1923.

———. *Misión social de la mujer.* Bilbao: Sociedad "El Sitio," 1911.

———. *La mujer en España.* Valencia: Sempere, 1906.

———. *La mujer fantástica.* Valencia: Sempere, 1924.

———. *La mujer moderna y sus derechos.* Valencia: Sempere, 1927.

———. "Las mujeres y la literatura." Burgos, *Al balcón* 40–45.

———. *La prueba. La novela femenina* 15 Feb. 1914: n. pag.

———. *Quiero vivir mi vida.* Madrid: Biblioteca Nueva, 1931.

———. *La rampa.* Madrid: Renacimiento, 1917.
———. *¡Todos menos ese! La novela corta* 30 Mar. 1918: n. pag.
———. *El veneno del arte. Los contemporáneos* 28 Jan. 1910: n. pag.
———. "El voto de las mujeres: Pidiendo opiniones." *El heraldo de Madrid* 19 Oct. 1906: 1.
———. "El voto de las mujeres." *El heraldo de Madrid* 25 Nov. 1906: 2.
Cansinos-Asséns, Rafael. *La novela de un literato: Hombres, ideas, efemérides, anécdotas.* Ed. Rafael M. Cansinos. Vol. 1 (1882–1914). Madrid: Alianza, 1982.
Castañeda, Paloma. *Carmen de Burgos "Colombine."* Madrid: Horas y Horas, 1994.
Gimeno de Flaquer, Concepción. *Una Eva moderna. El cuento semanal* 26 Nov. 1909: n.pag.
———. "El problema feminista." Madrid. 1903.
Gómez de la Serna, Ramón. "Colombine." *Prometeo* July 1909: 1–3.
González Fiol, E. "(Colombine)." *La esfera* 1922. Rpt. in *Puñal de claveles por Carmen de Burgos* Colombine. Ed. Miguel Naveros. Almería: Cajal, 1991. 109–16.
Johnson, Roberta. "Gender and Nation in Spanish Fiction between the Wars (1898–1936)." *Revista canadiense de estudios hispánicos* 21 (1996): 167–79.
———. "The Other Generation of '98." The Lady Vanishes: Spanish Women Writers (1900–1930). MMLA convention. Hyatt Regency Hotel, Minneapolis. 5 Nov. 1993.
Kirkpatrick, Judith. "Skeletons in the Closet: Carmen de Burgos Confronts the Literary Patriarchy." *Letras peninsulares* 8 (1995–96): 389–400.
Martínez Garrido, Elisa. "Amor y feminidad en las escritoras de principios de siglo." *Carmen de Burgos: Aproximación a la obra de una escritora comprometida.* Ed. Miguel Navarros and Ramón Navarrete-Galiano. Almería: Instituto de Estudios Almerienses, 1996. 13–38.
Nash, Mary. "Experiencia y aprendizaje: La formación histórica de los feminismos en España." *Historia social* 20 (1994): 151–72.
Nora, Eugenio de. *La novela española contemporánea (1927–1939).* 2nd ed. Madrid: Gredos, 1968.
Núñez Rey, Concepción. "Carmen de Burgos, *Colombine* (1867–1932): Biografía y obra literaria." Diss. Universidad Complutense de Madrid, 1992.
Saiz y Otero, Concepción. "El feminismo en España." *La escuela moderna* 13 (1897): 248–60, 321–34.
Scanlon, Geraldine. *La polémica feminista en la España contemporánea: 1868–1974.* 2nd ed. Madrid: Akal, 1986.
Smith, Paul Julian. *The Theatre of García Lorca: Text, Performance, Psychoanalysis.* Cambridge: Cambridge UP, 1998.
Starcevic, Elizabeth. *Carmen de Burgos: Defensora de la mujer.* Almería: Cajal, 1976.
Ugarte, Michael. "Carmen de Burgos ('Colombine'): Feminist *Avant la Lettre.*" *Spanish Women Writers and the Essay: Gender, Politics, and the Self.* Ed. Kathleen M. Glenn and Mercedes Mazquiarán de Rodríguez. Columbia: U of Missouri P, 1998. 55–74.
———. "The Generational Fallacy and Spanish Women Writing in Madrid at the Turn of the Century." *Siglo XX / 20th Century* 12 (1994): 261–76.

The Tapestry of a Feminist Life: María Teresa León (1903–88)

Nancy Vosburg

¡Mujeres de España! Creo que se movían por Madrid sin mucha conexión, sin formar un frente de batalla, salvo algunos lances feminísticos [sic], casi siempre tomados a broma por los imprudentes.

—María Teresa León,
Memoria de la melancolía

Women of Spain! I believe they moved around Madrid without much connection, without forming a battlefront, except for a few feministic [sic] skirmishes almost always taken as a joke by uninformed people.

María Teresa León's commitment to the Republican cause often overshadows her feminist concerns, just as her writings are frequently obscured by those of the men of the Generation of '27. Since her death, she has primarily been remembered, when acknowledged at all, as the wife and lifelong companion of Rafael Alberti, with whom she shared thirty-eight years of exile. Her loyalty to Alberti and her self-chosen role as the "cola" ("tail") to his brilliant "cometa" ("comet") (*Memoria* 114) tend to cast León as a somewhat traditional Spanish woman. Yet the young León was anything but traditional, as her peers and acquaintances were quick to point out. Santiago Ontañón, for example, the theatrical designer of the Art and Propaganda Theater that León directed during the Civil War, remarked that while Alberti and León were united in the political struggle, León was the real leader (Rodrigo 101). He would later declare that León and La Pasionaria (Dolores Ibárruri) were the two most important women of the Civil War period (Ontañón 60). Antonina Rodrigo recalls León as combative, valiant, energetic, audacious, admirable, and one of the most dedicated and popular women of the war years (110). While León never publicly identified herself as a feminist, there is a decided feminist dimension to her life activities that can be traced not only through her biography but through her bibliography as well. León's own "feministic skirmishes," as she called them (see epigraph), can be seen in her earliest short stories, written when she was a teenager, and culminate with her 1970 autobiography, *Memoria de la melancolía* ("Memoirs of Melancholy").

Like many Spanish women, León experienced the Second Republic and the Spanish Civil War as an exciting, exhilarating time that enabled her to develop her potential and defy traditional gender restrictions in ways never before permitted by Spanish society.[1] León dedicated her life to the belief that through collective freedom women would become free as well. In support of that belief, she became a defender of working-class women, a transgressor of social taboos, and a protagonist of many of the activities carried out by leftist intellectual organizations such as the Revolutionary Writers and Artists, the Alliance of Antifascist Intellectuals, the Art and Propaganda Theater, the traveling Guerrillas del Teatro (Theater Guerrilla Band), and the Committee for the Defense and Protection of the National Artistic Treasure.

While the interpretative frameworks for northern European and North American feminism have tended to constrict the definition of feminism to individual political rights and equality with men, several recent works on the history of feminism in Spain have provided alternative conceptualizations that are vital for understanding León's feminist consciousness (see Durán; C. Blanco; Nash). The historian Mary Nash's work on women in the Spanish Civil War, for example, underscores the social rather than political orientation of Spanish feminism in the years leading up to the Civil War. Nash attributes the focus on social and civil rights to Spain's inefficient and corrupt political structures in the nineteenth and early twentieth centuries, on the one hand, and to the predominance of the ideology of domesticity, on the other (35–36). As Nash explains:

> [Spanish] mainstream feminist thought was based on gender difference and the projection of women's social role as wife and mother to the public arena. Although it did not come to question women's gender definition as a mother, it represented, to some extent, a questioning of one of the basic parameters of the ideology of domesticity, that is, women's restriction to the private sphere. This questioning of the separation of public and private and the redefinition of women's spaces within the confines of both were eventually to facilitate the legitimacy of a more public, individual, and egalitarian discourse in the formulation of Spanish feminism. (35)

As the Second Republic ushered in new civil legislation that was in harmony with the liberal feminist current, women's presence in both social and political activity increased (C. Blanco 59). It was precisely at the birth of the Republic that the twenty-eight-year-old León shed both her bourgeois past and her difficult first marriage and committed herself intellectually and politically to the revolutionary ideology that would define her legacy in Spanish literary and feminist history.

The daughter of a well-to-do military officer, León's early privileged social milieu was decisive in her intellectual development, even as those privileges would eventually lead her to challenge the puritan female stereotypes, the bourgeois norms of propriety, and the hypocrisies of her socioeconomic class. In *Memoria,* León recalls some of her relatives, like her old unnamed uncle in Aragón who allowed her free access to all the books deemed "scandalous" by the Catholic Church, such as the novels of Dumas, Hugo, and Diderot (59–60). She also recalls the hours spent playing with her cousin Jimena at the home of another uncle, Ramón Menéndez Pidal, and his wife, María Goyri, one of the first women in Spain to earn a PhD. After being expelled from the Catholic school in Leganitos (Madrid) because "se empeñaba en hacer el bachillerato, porque lloraba a destiempo, porque leía libros prohibidos" (*Memoria* 58) ("she was determined to complete her bachelor's degree, because she cried at inopportune moments, because she read prohibited books"), her studies were conducted under the tutelage of her famous aunt and uncle (Mangini 222). Recalling the hours spent at their home, León writes:

> En aquella casa aprendí los primeros romances españoles. A veces sacábamos un viejo gramófono de cilindro. Allí escuchábamos las canciones recogidas por María Goyri y Ramón Menéndez Pidal, durante su viaje de novios, siguiendo la ruta del Cid hacia su destierro. Por primera vez oí la voz del pueblo. Por primera vez tomé en cuenta a los inteligentes y a los sabios. (*Memoria* 65)
>
> In that house I learned my first Spanish ballads. Sometimes we pulled out an old cylinder gramophone and listened to the ballads that María Goyri and Ramón Menéndez Pidal had gathered on their honeymoon as they followed El Cid's route into exile. For the first time I heard the voice of the people. For the first time I gave consideration to those who were intelligent and wise.

Both María Goyri and her daughter Jimena, who studied at the Institución Libre de Enseñanza (Free School of Instruction), were important role models for the young María Teresa. Above all, we sense León's awakening to gender politics upon hearing her grandmother Amalia Goyri's narration of the humiliation suffered by her daughter when she appeared at the university: she was locked in an office until class time and escorted to her classroom by a male professor, who then sat by her side as she listened to lectures (*Memoria* 23).

Declaring herself always maladjusted to the prescribed norms and the cult of domesticity befitting her social condition (*Memoria* 11), León's narration of her early childhood and youth hints at a series of sexual transgressions and evokes other social and intellectual awakenings that enabled her to develop early what she calls "un principio de crítica" (25) ("principles of criticism"). Besides her encounters with Benito Pérez Galdós, on walks in Madrid, and Américo Castro, who taught María Teresa and Jimena how to play tennis, León recalls female literary figures from her childhood:

> Dentro de mi juventud se han quedado algunos nombres de mujer: María de Maeztu, María Goyri, María Martínez Sierra, María Baeza,

> Zenobia Camprubí [. . .] y hasta una delgadísima pavesa inteligente, sentada en su salón: Doña Blanca de los Ríos. Y otra veterana de la novelística: Concha Espina. Y más a lo lejos, casi fundida en los primeros recuerdos, el ancho rostro de vivaces ojillos arrugados de la condesa de Pardo Bazán [. . .]. (310)
>
> The names of a few women remain associated with my youth: María de Maeztu, María Goyri, María Martínez Sierra, María Baeza, Zenobia Camprubí [. . .] and even a very thin, intelligent, decked-out woman, seated in her salon: Doña Blanca de los Ríos. And another veteran of the novel: Concha Espina. And further away, almost fused with my first memories, the wide face and lively, wrinkled little eyes of the countess Pardo Bazán.

On the occasion of León's first communion, Pardo Bazán gave her one of her novels (*El tesoro de Gastón*) with an inscription urging her to pursue "el camino de las letras" (*Memoria* 24) ("a career in literature"). The mature León notes that while the famous novelist loved to challenge men, "no los venció. Jamás pudo entrar en la Academia de la Lengua Española" (24) ("she didn't conquer them. She never managed to become a member of the Academy of the Spanish Language").

León evokes in her autobiography the limitations of her Catholic education, her guilt-laden awakening to her own sexuality, her father's adultery, her family's class-based snobbery, and her early intuitions of upper-class hypocrisy. Her references to her early youth are distinguished by a shift from first- to third-person narration—"she," "the blond child," "the young girl"—which serves to underscore the mature Leon's self-estrangement from her childhood experiences. As Alda Blanco has noted:

> la narradora se sirve de la tercera persona no solamente para narrar aquellos fragmentos de vida en los cuales se sintió vivir dentro de una imagen culturalmente determinada para la mujer, sino para resaltar que esa identidad, a diferencia de la de su presente autobiográfico, le fue impuesta. (46)
>
> the narrator uses the third person not only to narrate those fragments of her life in which she felt that she was living an image culturally determined for women but also to underscore that this identity, in contrast to her current self-image, was imposed on her.

Despite León's "vacillation between self-revelation and concealment" (Bauer 259) and her refusal to identify textually with the young, bourgeois María Teresa, it is clear that her encounters with some of the significant intellectual figures of the early twentieth century were decisive influences in her life.

León embarked on her career in letters, as Pardo Bazán had urged her, at the age of fourteen or fifteen when she began submitting articles to the *Diario de Burgos* under the pseudonym of Isabel Inghirami (a fictional heroine created by Gabriele D'Annunzio). Among her published articles was a defense of a young unwed servant who had drowned her newborn baby:

> Isabel Inghirami salió en defensa de la pobre criatura jovencísima que había creído posible entregar su culpa a las ranas del arroyo. Dijo Isabel Inghirami lo que pensaba de la sociedad que permite la ignorancia y la desesperación que llevan al crimen. Defendió a la muchacha, afrontó los prejuicios que ataban tan fuerte las correas sobre las infelices indefensas. El hombre, claro es, había huido. (*Memoria* 71)
>
> Isabel Inghirami defended the poor young creature who had believed that she could pass on her guilt to the frogs in the stream. Isabel Inghirami said what she thought about a society that allows the kind of ignorance and desperation that lead to such crimes. She defended the young girl, and challenged the prejudices that so constricted wretched, defenseless women. The man, of course, had fled.

León's solidarity with working-class women was to be a defining mark of her political and cultural activity throughout her life.

León's writing career was briefly interrupted by her marriage, at age sixteen, to Gonzalo de Sebastián, and the birth of her first son shortly thereafter. A second son was born in 1925, and while her husband apparently accompanied her during some of her cultural activities—conferences, summer seminars, a trip to Argentina where her articles appeared in *La Nación* and *Diario español*—their marriage, marked by his infidelity, ended in 1928. León's references to her first marriage are minimal yet revealing; she alludes to her failed marriage, her betrayed youth, and her feeling that her soul had been "scratched by the fingernails that some men use to deal with women" (*Memoria* 30–31). In a further signal of her estrangement from this period in her life, both her husband and her sons remain nameless in her memoir.

Perhaps more revealing of her disillusionment at the time of her separation from her husband and sons is her second published collection of short stories, *La bella de mal amor* (1930) ("The Beauty of Bad Love").[2] The six stories, as the title suggests, have as a common theme the frustrated love and adverse destiny of six women. Of particular interest is the title story, which resonates with León's references to her own first marriage in *Memoria de la melancolía*, published forty years later.[3] The first-person narrator of "La bella de mal amor" listens as tío Ugenio recites the "Romance de la Malmaridada," a ballad of marital betrayal, and adapts the ballad to her own life story. In this and other stories in the collection, León deplores the situation of women who are subjected to codes of behavior that deny them free choice in their amorous relationships or who become victims of family or social pressures.

When León met Alberti shortly after separating from her husband, she found a new personal freedom that would cement her rupture with her bourgeois Catholic past. Although León was still legally married, Alberti recalls in his 1959 book of memoirs, *La arboleda perdida* ("The Lost Grove"), their joint renunciation of the petty norms of propriety that controlled her early life:

> Con María Teresa me pasaba las horas trabajando en algunos poemas o ayudándola a corregir un libro de cuentos que preparaba. Una noche—lo habíamos decidido—no volví más a casa. Definitivamente, tanto ella como yo empezaríamos una nueva vida, libre de prejuicios, sin importarnos el qué dirán, aquel temido qué dirán de la España gazmoña que odiábamos. (305–06)

> I spent my time with María Teresa working on poems or helping her correct a book of short stories that she was writing. One night—we had already decided—I didn't return home. Definitively, she and I would begin a new life, free of prejudice, without worrying about judgmental gossip, that feared gossip of the prudish Spain that we both hated.

León's relationship with Alberti and the advent of the Second Republic in 1931 transformed her life, both privately and publicly. The new Republican legislation enabled her to finally obtain a legal divorce from her husband and marry Alberti. Already sympathetic to Communist ideals, León and Alberti traveled through Europe and the Soviet Union, where they became familiar with the revolutionary literary aesthetics of writers such as Piscator and Maksim Gorky and with S. M. Eisenstein's revolutionary cinema (*Memoria* 106). León's writings changed considerably during the Republic. While her first three collections of short stories (*Cuentos para soñar* ["Stories for Dreaming"], *La bella del mal amor,* and *Rosa-fría, patinadora de la luna* ["Cold-Rose, Moonskater"]) are linked stylistically to the poetics of the Generation of '27, León's deep commitment to Communist Party doctrine and revolutionary writing resulted in her own experiments with social realist literature, which she hoped would be more effective in denouncing the injustice and social oppression that had been a theme in her earlier works. Her writing acquired a more tendentious ideological thrust, starting with her 1933 drama *Huelga en el puerto* ("Strike in the Port") and continuing with the 1937 *Cuentos de la España actual* ("Stories of Present-Day Spain"). While these works contribute to forming class consciousness, as both Janet Pérez and Carolyn L. Galerstein note, they also reflect what Gregorio Torres Nebrera has described as "las tendencias de reivindicación feminista de los años veinte y treinta, ya sea en el contexto del movimiento anarquista—Teresa Claramunt y Federica Montseny—o en el del socialista—Margarita Nelken y María Cambrils" (373) ("the feminist tendencies of the 1920s and 1930s, whether within the context of the anarchist movement—Teresa Claramunt and Federica Montseny—or within that of the socialist movement—Margarita Nelken and María Cambrils"). Yet once again we must keep in mind the parameters within which these tendencies were configured to understand Torres Nebrera's statement.

Of the three classifications of Spanish feminism identified by Carmen de Burgos in 1927—Christian, revolutionary, and independent—León's words and works clearly situate her in the stream of revolutionary feminism, which looked to socialism as the means to achieving women's emancipation.[4] Like La Pasionaria, León was fully committed to the Communist Party ideology, believing that women's oppression was a function of class and economics rather than one of gender (Mangini 54). The great anarchist Federica Montseny had similarly linked women's freedom to that of men (57). Although there were a few minority organizations in the years leading up to the Second Republic that were more clearly suffragist and feminist in their demands, the predominant revolutionary feminist thought conflated women's freedom with the emancipation of the working class and the modernization of the State.[5] Like the mainstream feminists of the period (see Nash 35), revolutionary feminists like León did not directly challenge women's subordinate status to men.

León's feminist impulse, intimately tied to the class struggle, finds its expression in her 1937 *Cuentos de la España actual,* particularly in the lead story, "Liberación de octubre" ("October Liberation"). The story deals with the frustrated lives of a working-class couple who, during the October 1934 revolution in Asturias, are forced into a new awareness. While Ramón is reluctant and fearful of joining the revolt, his wife, Rosa, "se precipitó en la revolución. Adivinaba que libertad quiere decir liberarse de la angustia del jornal miserable, de la espera de la muerte con los brazos cruzados, día a día" (*Estrella* 32) ("[Rosa] plunged into the revolution. She intuited that freedom means escaping from the anguish of miserable wages, from waiting for death with one's arms crossed, day after day").

While León's protagonist takes up arms in the revolutionary struggle, recognizing that collective freedom would bring about her own, León herself chose the pen and the podium as combat weapons:

> Muchas veces he tenido que subir a hablar a una tribuna, o a un balcón o a una silla o a cualquier sitio, porque los tiempos españoles de aquellos años nos hicieron tomar una posición clara en nuestra conciencia política. Me preocupaba encontrar las palabras justas, pero pronto comprendí que lo que necesitaban era el amor, el contacto de la comprensión de su problema, hablarles de sus derechos a la tierra, a la vida, a la palabra. (*Memoria* 47)

> On many occasions I had to climb up onto a platform, a balcony, a chair, or wherever, to speak, because the realities of those years in Spain made us take a clear political position. Finding the right words worried me, but then I understood that what they [the listeners] needed was love, an understanding of their problems, and for me to speak about their rights to land, to life, and to speech.

Like thousands of ordinary Spanish women, León was stirred to an immediate participation in antifascist resistance and revolutionary endeavors. As Nash has documented, the turbulent years of the Second Republic and the Civil War brought new roles to women and expectations for a range of political, cultural, and social activities previously denied them (58–59). León's feverish pursuits on the intellectual front, particularly her articles in ideological journals and her work in the theater, aimed at the dissemination of the Marxist dialectic among the proletariat and placed her in the forefront of the cultural activists of her time.

During the war years, León's role expanded even more. As Madrid fell under siege, León took her Guerrillas del Teatro to the battlefronts to animate and encourage the Republican troops: "María Teresa, embutida en su mono de miliciana y su simbólica pistola al cinto, recorrió los frentes recitando, declamando, dirigiendo teatro, dando mítines [. . .]" (Rodrigo 110) ("María Teresa, wrapped up in her militia overalls with a symbolic pistol at her waist, traveled along the battlefronts reciting, declaiming, directing plays, holding meetings [. . .]"). León also became the protagonist of one of the most important art preservation efforts of the twentieth century, evacuating paintings and other artistic treasures from Toledo, El Escorial, and the Prado Museum in Madrid.

One of her final roles (literally) of the war years was the allegorical figure of Spain in Alberti's play, *Cantat de los héroes y de la fraternidad de los pueblos* ("Song of the Heroes and of the Fraternity of Nations"), that the Guerrillas del Teatro performed for the departing International Brigades:

> Un día vestí el traje de luces de las campesinas, arreglé sobre mi cabeza las trenzas como la Dama de Elche lo hiciera siglos antes y traté de que mi emoción no me traicionase al decir:

Yo soy España.
Sobre mi verde traje de trigo y sol han puesto
largo crespón injusto de horrores y de sangre.
Aquí tenéis en dos mi cuerpo dividido:
un lado, preso; el otro, libre al honor y el aire. (*Memoria* 42)

One day I put on a peasant dress, I arranged my hair the way the Dama de Elche had centuries earlier, and I tried not to let my emotions betray me as I recited:

I am Spain.
Over my green suit of wheat and sun they have placed
a long and unjust crape of horrors and blood.
Here you have my body split in two:
One side, a prisoner; the other, free to honor and to the air.

At the time, the words seemed to have a special significance for León, for they spoke not only to the divisions produced by the war but also to her own experience of having forged an identity different from that of her bourgeois upbringing. León would remain loyal to that "other" Spain, "libre al honor y el aire," the rest of her life, most of which was spent in exile.

On 6 March 1939, shortly after the fall of Barcelona, León and Alberti fled Spain. Seeking refuge first in Paris, less than two years later they were forced to flee France when the Vichy government began arresting and turning over Spanish political refugees to the Franco regime. Their years of exile in Argentina and Rome, however, did not quash their tremendous cultural and political activity. Especially during her years in Argentina (1940–63), León was active in film, television, and radio, and she published a number of literary works. *Contra viento y marea* (1941) ("Against All Odds"), *Morirás lejos* (1942) ("You Will Die Far Away"), and *Juego limpio* (1959) ("Fair Play") are testimonials of events that León witnessed or participated in during the Civil War. While there is still a strong ideological dimension in these works, León devotes more attention to character development and the portrayal of psychological motivations. Also during this period León published three other works that merit special attention in that they reveal peculiar facets of her feminist dimension: *Las peregrinaciones de Teresa* (1950) ("Teresa's Travels"), *Nuestro hogar de cada día* (1958) ("Our Everyday Home"), and *Doña Jimena Díaz de Vivar, gran señora de todos los deberes* (1960) ("Doña Jimena Díaz de Vivar, the Great Lady of All Duties").

Las peregrinaciones de Teresa, a collection of nine short stories, is, as Pérez has noted, "one of León's most interesting works for the feminist critic" in its "profound exploration of feminine psychology, passions, and resignation" (48). The nine distinct protagonists, each named Teresa, together project a universal vision of the feminine condition. They emphasize women's quotidian burdens and the religious education, superstitions, and norms of propriety that control their existence and frustrate their desires. Each story captures a moment of awakening or consciousness-raising on the part of Teresa. While the awakening allows some of the Teresas to carry out successful rebellions, for others it is not enough to enable them to overcome their oppressive situations.

Nuestro hogar de cada día is a curious book that has escaped notation in León bibliographies.[6] The book's format suggests an imitation of the convent rule, intentionally subverted through the author's worldliness and erudition. Targeted at the "timonel de la casa" ("helmsman of the house"), *Nuestro hogar* is a strange concoction of household hints (ranging from hygiene and etiquette to how to set a bridge table), international recipes, historical and cultural information, and literature. The latter category includes poems of mostly twentieth-century Spanish and Hispano-American poets, literary quotations, recommended reading (some eighty-four different works suggested, only ten by women), and short biographies of over sixty real and fictional figures from the classical period to the present. Of the seventeen poems, only five are by women—Alfonsina Storni, Silvia Ocampo, Gabriela Mistral, Sor Juana, and Elizabeth Barrett Browning—none of whom is Spanish. It is in the biographical category that León gives special attention to women (only six biographies deal exclusively with men), particularly to the women behind such famous artists as Rembrandt, Schiller, Hugo, Schumann, Wagner, Liszt, Durero, and Tchaikovsky. This focus on the woman behind the man might be seen as reaffirming the value of León's own role vis-à-vis Alberti.

We also find in *Nuestro hogar* brief histories of the book, the short story, bookbinding, and lullabyes; explanations of the origins of coffee, eye makeup, casserole dishes, and cloth. León includes reflections on topics like women's position in the social and political life of the twentieth century, the Argentine legend of "la Umita," Santiago Ramón y Cajal's theory on the brain, prehistoric flirting, planetary influences, and how to organize a bookshelf. Directed at the bourgeois housewife, this "breviary" underscores, as in so many of León's novels and short stories, both women's daily burdens and their often unrecognized achievements. Her references reveal a universal mentality that eschews national and ethnic boundaries. As a manual of helpful household hints, *Nuestro hogar* seems to reaffirm women's role in the domestic sphere. Yet the book also makes visible a number of strong historical and literary female role models, and through the juxtaposition of the quotidian with the erudite, it celebrates the diverse aspects of women's culture and ingenuity in both private and public realms.

It was León's sense of shared experience with so many other exiled women that induced her to write the fictional biography, *Doña Jimena Díaz de Vivar,* about the wife of Spain's medieval epic hero El Cid. In *Memoria,* León pays homage to the thousands of "mujeres de mi casta" (257) ("women of my caste") who, like Doña Jimena, followed their husbands into exile after months or years of waiting:

> En esta dispersión española le ha tocado a la mujer un papel histórico y lo ha recitado bien y ha cumplido como cumplió doña Jimena, modesta y triste. Algún día se contarán o cantarán las pequeñas historias, las anécdotas menudas, esas que quedan en las cartas escritas, a veces, por otra mano, porque no todas las mujeres españolas saben escribir [. . .]. Y se contará la pequeña epopeya diaria, el heroísmo minúsculo de los labios apretados de frío, del hambre, de los trabajos casi increíbles. (257)

> In this Spanish diaspora, women have been given a historic role and they have played it well, just as Doña Jimena, modest and sad, played hers. Some day the small stories, the minute anecdotes will be told or sung, those stories that remain only in letters written at times by another hand, because not all Spanish women can write [. . .]. And the small, daily epic, the minuscule heroism of lips

> pressed together from the cold, from hunger, from incredible feats, will be told.

León's Doña Jimena, after suffering "una suma de obediencias, de soledades, de deberes cumplidos, de silencios" (*Doña Jimena* 195) ("an accumulation of obediences, of solitudes, of fulfilled duties, of silences"), becomes a "new woman" (197) when she assumes her final duty of governing and defending Valencia after the death of her husband. León's protagonist has remarkable emotional and spiritual depth. It is almost as if León breathed into Doña Jimena her own ideals, anxieties, and "deberes"—to the Republican cause, to her husband, to their daughter Aitana (b. 1941), and to their many friends who remained loyal and supported them throughout their years of exile.

Yet it is León's monumental *Memoria de la melancolía* that, in my opinion, stands as her most important feminist legacy. Anna Caballé has noted that autobiographical writing assumes "un ejercicio de autoestima y valoración de la propia subjetividad que muy difícilmente hallaremos en manos de la mujer en etapas anteriores a su emancipación real" (111) ("an exercise of self-esteem and self-worth that we rarely find in women before their real emancipation"). In one sense, León's autobiography has much in common with the features of postmodern self-representational writing that have been discussed by Janice Morgan: "fragmentation, discontinuity, duality, and above all, a pervasive textual self-consciousness." But as Morgan has also pointed out, these features "have in fact frequently been present in women's autobiographies" and play a key role in the elaboration of an alternate, "feminine" poetics (7).

For Sidonie Smith, the so-called postmodern features deployed by women writers throughout history correspond to an identity constructed through alterity, one that is based on complex, interwoven patterns of exchange that result in pervasive self-awareness of women's multiple roles and identities. Smith has also noted that in classical autobiography written by men, memory is often consciously used to construct a linear narrative that reaffirms the coherence and orderly progression of the life lived while excluding all that is unruly, irrational, and contradictory (19). In contrast, memory is neither controlled nor controlling in Leon's text; her memories break upon her randomly, provoked by sights, smells, sounds, and emotions. In the resulting narrative, leaps from one time period to another and from one theme to another—past and present, outside and inside, emotion and reason, other and self—become co-extensive, not disjoined by a hierarchy that subordinates one term to the other. León's text thus actively resists traditionalist autobiographical and historiographical pretenses of objectivity, temporal and spatial coherence, and hierarchical positioning.

With memory acting not as a plotting device but as an umbilical cord connecting León to the lives of others, the web of relationships, rather than events, becomes the focus of her story. The book abounds with anecdotes of her encounters, friendships, and collaborations with well-known literary and political figures, both national and international. Thus *Memoria de la melancolía* expresses an understanding of individual and collective history as a deeply intertwined web of subjective attachments. Jessica Benjamin, who has delineated the distinctions between the intersubjective and phallic modes, theorizes that the former has its counterpart in spatial rather than symbolic representation (95). If this is true, we might also expect to find a different spatial arrangement in a textual self-representation that employs the intersubjective mode, one that re-creates a continuum of "inner space," which for Benjamin includes the space between the "I" and the "you."

Benjamin's theory provides an alternative means of conceptualizing León's fragmented, discontinuous narrative. Besides the temporal jumps and "I"-"she" shifts in León's narration, the text is spatially fragmented by blank spaces. These blank spaces, while perhaps signaling the feminine poetic disjunction between a woman's multiple roles and identities or the postmodern disappearance of self in textuality's shadowy hall of mirrors, can also be seen as an integral part of a seamless fabric. The narrative fragments, oddly juxtaposed and shifting in time, place, and perspective are nevertheless connected by the invisible thread represented by the blank space. This thread enjoins the reader (you) to supply the unvoiced, perhaps because unvoiceable, connections between the disorderly discursive segments. The blank space becomes a discourse of resistance: resistance to logical coherency, resistance to rational chronology, resistance to language's illusory referential power to name and to fix reality, resistance to the absolutism of a single-voiced perspective.

León's repetitive references in *Memoria* to weaving, sewing, threading, basting, braiding, tying, knotting, and joining reproduce linguistically both the process and the object of creation. Just as images on a tapestry flow into each other and are knotted together on the reverse side of the fabric, inextricably joined and invisible to the casual observer, so León's text intertwines visions and voices of the past with dreams of the future. Like a tapestry, her autobiography presents a complex nonlinear history that captures, more than anything, the dynamic bonds and transitory emotions underlying the facts, the deeds, and the events. Alda Blanco has noted that León's autobiography "intenta establecer una continuidad histórica entre los exiliados y el presente" ("tries to establish a historic continuity between the exiles and the present"), on the one hand, while recuperating "las voces perdidas de la mujer en el horizonte cultural español" (45) ("the lost voices of women on the Spanish cultural horizon") on the other. As León weaves her textual tapestry, she emphasizes again and again the "pequeñas historias" ("the small stories") of an extraordinary cast of characters, both famous and ordinary, that spans generations, socioeconomic classes, and national borders.

León's words and works are testimonials to her political commitment and her vision for a more just society. Along with such figures as Burgos, Montseny, Margarita Nelken, Clara Campoamor, and Victoria Kent, León played an important role as a feminist activist, most overtly on the cultural front. Her political and cultural activism, evoked by many of her contemporaries and recorded by León herself primarily in *Juego limpio* and *Memoria de la melancolía,* helps us to understand the possibilities and the parameters of liberal Spanish feminism in the dynamic years leading up to the Spanish Civil War. While León did not outrightly reject the ideology of domesticity, that is, women's gendered role as wife and mother, she did widen its boundaries by rejecting, through her political activism and her literary voice, women's restriction to the private sphere. Central to her socialist vision of a more just society is the recognition that the traditional constraints imposed on women have prohibited them from being full participants in the social order. In her many decades of writing, León articulated the social and economic oppression of women, suggesting, but never openly acknowledging, its gender-based dimension. But by emphasizing women's "small epics" in her works and women's achievements "against all odds," María Teresa León contributed *her*story to the cultural and political history of mid-twentieth-century Spain.

Notes

The epigraph of this essay is from *Memoria* 311. All translations from Spanish in this essay are my own.

1. In the chapter entitled "The Battle Lost," in *Defying Male Civilization,* Mary Nash recounts the myriad opportunities that became available to women during the Second Republic and the Civil War (see 177–82). León often refers to this time period in her autobiography as "the most luminous days of my life" (*Memoria* 28).
2. *Cuentos para soñar,* a collection of children's stories, was León's first book, with a prologue written by María Goyri.
3. The similarities between what León reveals about herself in *Memoria* and the details of the narrator's story in "La bella"—marriage at a very young age; temporary residence in another city (León and Gonzalo resided temporarily in Barcelona); her realization, after suffering her husband's infidelity, that she had fallen in love with a man with a "cerebro de artista" (31) ("brain of an artist")—suggest a more autobiographical context to the story than had been noted previously and may fill in the evasions of León's autobiographical text.
4. See Nash's discussion of Carmen de Burgos's feminist thought and activities (40).
5. Among the organizations that demanded the political enfranchisement of women were the Asociación Nacional de Mujeres Españolas (National Association of Spanish Women), the Liga Internacional de Mujeres Ibéricas e Hispanoamericanas (International League of Iberian and Hispano-American Women), and the Cruzada de Mujeres Españolas (Spanish Women's Crusade) (Nash 40).
6. I am grateful to Marisa Mediavilla Herreros, founder and director of the Biblioteca de Mujeres in Madrid, for bringing this book to my attention and lending it to me for a few weeks to study.

Works Cited

Alberti, Rafael. *La arboleda perdida.* Buenos Aires: Fabril, 1959.

Bauer, Beth Wietelmann. "María Teresa León." *Spanish Women Writers: A Bio-Bibliographical Source Book.* Ed. Linda G. Levine, Ellen E. Marson, and Gloria F. Waldman. Westport: Greenwood, 1993. 253–63.

Benjamin, Jessica. "A Desire of One's Own: Psychoanalytic Feminism and Intersubjective Space." *Feminist Studies / Critical Studies.* Ed. Teresa de Lauretis. Bloomington: Indiana UP, 1986. 78–101.

Blanco, Alda. "Las voces perdidas: Silencio y recuerdo en *Memoria de la melancolía* de María Teresa León." *Anthropos* 125 (1991): 45–48.

Blanco, Carmen. *El contradiscurso de las mujeres: Historia del proceso feminista.* Vigo: Nigra, 1995.

Caballé, Anna. "Memorias y autobiografías escritas por mujeres (siglos XIX y XX)." *Breve historia feminista de la literatura española (en lengua castellana).* Coord. Iris M. Zavala. Vol. 5. Barcelona: Anthropos, 1998. 111–37.

Durán, María Angeles, ed. *Mujeres y hombres: La formación del pensamiento igualitario.* Madrid: Castalia, 1993.

Galerstein, Carolyn L. "The Spanish Civil War: The View of Women Novelists." *Letras femeninas* 10.2 (1984): 12–18.

León, María Teresa. *La bella del mal amor: Cuentos castellanos.* Burgos: S. Rodríguez, 1930.

———. *Contra viento y marea.* Buenos Aires: Espasa-Calpe, 1941.

———. *Cuentos de la España actual.* México: Dialéctica, 1937.

———. *Cuentos para soñar.* Burgos: S. Rodriguez, 1928.

———. *Doña Jimena Díaz de Vivar, gran señora de todos los deberes.* Buenos Aires: Losada, 1960.

———. *Una estrella roja.* Madrid: Espasa-Calpe, 1979. Rpt. of *Cuentos de la España actual.* 1937.

———. *Huelga en el puerto. Octubre* 3 (1933): 21–24.

———. *Juego limpio.* Buenos Aires: Goyanarte, 1959.

———. *Memoria de la melancolía.* Buenos Aires: Losada, 1970.

———. *Morirás lejos.* Buenos Aires: Americalee, 1942.

———. *Nuestro hogar de cada día: Breviario para la mujer de su casa.* Buenos Aires: Fabril, 1958.

———. *Las peregrinaciones de Teresa.* Buenos Aires: Botella al Mar, 1950.

———. *Rosa-fría, patinadora de la luna.* Madrid: Espasa-Calpe, 1934.

Mangini, Shirley. *Recuerdos de la resistencia: La voz de las mujeres de la guerra civil española.* Barcelona: Península, 1997.

Morgan, Janice. "Subject to Subject / Voice to Voice." *Redefining Autobiography in Twentieth-Century Women's Fiction: An Essay Collection.* Ed. Morgan and Colette T. Hall. New York: Garland, 1981.

Nash, Mary. *Defying Male Civilization: Women in the Spanish Civil War.* Denver: Arden, 1995.

Ontañón, Santiago. "María Teresa León." *María Teresa León.* Ed. Junta de Castilla y León. Valladolid: Sever-Cuesta, 1987.

Pérez, Janet. *Contemporary Women Writers of Spain.* Boston: Twayne, 1988.

Rodrigo, Antonina. *Mujeres para la historia: La España silenciada del siglo XX.* Madrid: Compañía Literaria, 1996.

Smith, Sidonie. *A Poetics of Women's Autobiography.* Bloomington: Indiana UP, 1987.

Torres Nebrera, Gregorio. "La obra literaria de María Teresa León (cuentos y teatro)." *Anuario de estudios filológicos* 7 (1984): 361–84.

Margarita Nelken: Feminist and Political Praxis during the Spanish Civil War

Josebe Martínez-Gutiérrez
Translated by H. Patsy Boyer

I have been researching the work of Spanish women intellectuals exiled after the Civil War (1936–39) in an effort to incorporate new material into the peninsular literary canon. Although it is common knowledge that large numbers of Spanish intellectuals went into exile during the Franco regime, studies of the exiles' work have focused almost exclusively on men.[1] In a move to restore the voices of women exiles to history, I have concentrated on Margarita Nelken (1896–1968), a writer, art critic, and socialist parliamentary representative during Spain's Second Republic (1931–39). To give an overview of Nelken's importance in twentieth-century feminist activism both in Spain and abroad, I trace the evolution of her ideas and her work using information collected in Spain, the United States, and Mexico.

The Second Republic

As a liberal regime, Spain's Second Republic brought about a feminization of discourse by allowing women to enter the public arena and by promoting their access to economic and social independence, as well as to the political apparatus. The Civil War increased women's participation in public life: it diminished the boundaries between public space and domestic privacy and, by necessity, involved women in political and military organizations at the front and in the factory. The war made women's collaboration essential on the home front and often required their participation on the front lines in battle. In general, women did support work (providing supplies and clothing, working in hospitals) or filled jobs previously held by men who had entered into combat.

The various political parties and labor unions had different strategies for the incorporation of women; the Communist Party placed women in the rearguard, and Nelken claimed to support this role in her propaganda, even though she was active on the front. There was no clearly defined feminist position in the Spanish Civil War as there had been, for example, in the case of American or British women in World War I. In the latter, there were clear, though divergent, positions: pacifist opposition by some feminist movements (e.g., among Socialists) and support for women's participation in the war effort by feminist groups that believed women would be given first-class citizenship by taking part in wartime activities. By contrast, in the Spanish Civil War women adopted their position on the conflict in accordance with the ideology of their party; they went to war in support of their political organizations, not as members of a feminist movement. For many, this was a war against a fascist insurgency on their own soil, a war in defense of the civil and constitutional rights—including women's rights—that were being implemented at the time of the insurrection.

Women's incorporation into public life, which had developed slowly in the early decades of the century, increased rapidly during the war, only to be suffocated on the Peninsula in 1939 and later to be reshaped among exiles. Since exile resulted in both a diaspora and the loss of the homeland, there were consequences—some affecting all exiles, others affecting women in particular—that produced a significant step backward for the generation of women who left Spain. Women suffered setbacks in all areas in which they had made prior advances, but most especially in their involvement in public life: politics, culture, ideological issues, and the arts. The characteristics of Spanish exile that caused these setbacks included a precarious economic situation, the need among exiles to adapt to a new environment, and exclusive concentration on anti-Franco politics. These factors aggravated other conditions that traditionally have hindered women's writing: a lack of interest in a woman's voice and the belief that women writers are amateurs (i.e., not professional).[2]

The lives and the writing of women intellectuals who were already sophisticated thinkers at the time of the war, including Isabel de Palencia (b. 1878), Nelken, and Victoria Kent (b. 1898), underwent a radical change in the topics, themes, and styles they explored during this period. The Spain they had come from, the Spain of the early twentieth century, was largely agrarian and Catholic, economically and culturally less developed and more conservative than most European countries. During the reign of Alfonso XIII, along with an underdeveloped economy, there was a certain liberalism that gave rise to new urban social movements and ideas. However, the female population was far removed from the influence of British and American suffragists and from French feminists. As Nelken saw it, Spanish women remained unaware of their rights and were silent, submissive, and essentially antifeminist. The intellectuals who went into exile, however, were part of the cultural elite, primarily in the capital, where women's participation in art and politics and their advocacy for the right to vote were an integral part of the climate. The works of these intellectuals reflected a broad spectrum of ideological and social concerns. Art, a woman's identity, social criticism, political analysis, and the theater are recurring subjects in the writing of Nelken and Palencia in this period. It was a time of broad perspectives and significant cultural growth. The advent of the war restricted these varied topics and narrowed them down to one: the fight for the ideals of the Second Republic. Exile prolonged this generation of women's dedication to politics.

Margarita Nelken's Early Life

Born in Madrid in 1896 to German Jews who were clock makers for the Royal Palace, Nelken received a meticulous education in arts and letters, conducted in a number of languages. At a young age she devoted herself to painting, but she later gave up art because of eye problems and redirected her energies to art criticism. She published her first article as a critic in the London-based journal *Studio* when she was fifteen. This signaled her entry into the world of the press and writing, where she would eventually move beyond art criticism to publish articles and books on women, feminism, literature, and, in particular, politics.

To illustrate the evolution of Nelken's thinking, I focus on three time periods that reflect her main areas of interest: feminism (1920–31), political praxis (1931–39), and her return to art criticism (1940–68).

Margarita Nelken and the Feminist Debate (1920–31)

Nelken's concept of women rests on the questioning of a woman's natural character, which she considered to be both socially and biologically determined. As she explains in *La condición social de la mujer en España* ("The Social Condition of Women in Spain"):

> Cierto es que no es posible decir de antemano cuáles son las condiciones *naturales* de un ser revestido casi en absoluto de prejuicios y reglas de conducta arbitrarios; lo impuesto es siempre postizo, pero la imposición metódica durante siglos y siglos, tradiciones y tradiciones, llega, en ciertos casos, no sólo a presentarse con apariencia de realidad, sino también a tomar apariencia de *segunda naturaleza* y entonces, claro está que la *distinción* es punto menos que imposible. (43)[3]

> Indeed, it is not possible to say beforehand what the *natural* condition of a being almost entirely surrounded by prejudice and arbitrary rules of conduct is; what is imposed is always false, but the methodical imposition for century after century, in tradition after tradition, begins at times not only to look like reality but to appear to be *second nature,* and therefore the *distinction* between the two is almost impossible.

Nelken's innovation consists primarily of debating the controversial topic of the "natural origin" of a woman's social attributes. This is the driving mechanism of her thought, which often oscillates between the poles of a binary, constituted by the social construction of a woman and her biological makeup. Nelken seeks to unmask the social interests that underlie certain supposedly natural functions of women. Despite her concerns for these issues, however, biology, and especially maternity, played major roles in her thinking.

Immersed in a discursive universe that asserted that a woman's nature was the element that defined her social role, Nelken gave credence to the most advanced medical positions (often more innovative than the religious or the moral positions) in an effort to reconcile an emancipatory agenda with determinism. She believed social attributes that appeared to be second nature were, in reality, imposed constructs. But maternity, as a natural function in women, was viewed as almost a biological mission by Nelken. Within the medical and social environment surrounding women, perhaps the concept most strongly espoused by Nelken, and much in vogue at that time, was hygiene. Adapting the concept studied by such scientists as Gregorio Marañón and Santiago Ramón y Cajal, Nelken revised the idea of hygiene substantially, applying it to the health of the more liberated bourgeois woman and to the needs of the worker.

The hygiene of living conditions that Nelken embraced involved sanitation and health and the dignification of all work as a necessary component of social justice and human productivity; the hygiene of place and person connected a woman's human nature with her role as a social being. In the final analysis, hygiene presupposed mental and economic health, that is, a healthy body and mind in a healthy economy. This well-being could be achieved in two ways: through access to cultural activities and through economic independence, both of which boil down to education. An education would provide women with knowledge about themselves and of the world, would train each woman to perform a job that could support her, and would allow her to be economically independent. Nelken considered the economic dependence that subjugated women to be unhealthy, something that stunted their proper development. According to Nelken, good hygiene is a relation between the natural and the social, between biology and culture. Education is the key to a developmental process that provides women with the ideal opportunity to overcome dependence and isolation.

> Aquí [en España] resulta ridículo para muchos el trabajo de una mujer; pero a todo el mundo le parece natural la posición de una mujer dependiendo por completo del trabajo, no ya de un padre o de un marido, sino de un hermano, de un tío o de cualquier deudo masculino. [. . .] De ahí también la desconsideración de un marido que sabe muy bien que, *pase lo que pase*, su mujer habrá de aguantar todas las humillaciones y todas las afrentas, ya que apartándose de su esposo no podría ni comer. (*Condición* 52)
>
> Here [in Spain] many find a woman's work absurd; but everybody thinks it is natural for a woman to be entirely dependent on the work not only of her father or husband but of her brother, uncle, or some other male relative. [. . .] This situation also leads to the inconsiderate behavior of a husband who knows full well that, *no matter what*, his wife will have to bear every humiliation and affront, because if she leaves him, she won't even be able to eat.

As this passage hints, Nelken was an open supporter of divorce. She campaigned for its passage, trying to educate people about its benefits for women. She began with the premise that Spanish women were convinced, a priori, that establishing divorce would only harm women. Nelken asserted the opposite of this attitude by arguing that divorce would function as a healing mechanism, ensuring a woman's safety, because the married woman was, above all, sexually submissive. Accordingly, Nelken considered education and economic independence as indispensable to any solution:

> Uno de los mayores temores que abriga la mujer española respecto al divorcio, es el que su implantación podría ser utilizada impunemente por cuantos maridos quisieran, por mero donjuanismo, "deshacerse" de su mujer. [. . .] Pero, y esto es lo verdaderamente importante en la implantación del divorcio en España, lo que verdaderamente ha de tenerse en cuenta en la perpetración de sus leyes, el divorcio es principalmente arma defensiva y protectora para la mujer. (*Condición* 91)
>
> One of the greatest fears the Spanish woman harbors about divorce is that its implementation could be used with impunity by any

> husband who wanted, out of sheer Don Juanism, to get rid of his wife. [. . .] But, and this is the most important aspect of establishing divorce in Spain, what must be taken into account in the formulation of these laws is that divorce is primarily a protective and defensive weapon for women.

That Nelken led the first women's strike in Madrid (in the tobacco factories) attests to her interest in the condition of the working woman. As she stated in *La condición social de la mujer en España,* Nelken believed that one of the principal goals of feminism should be the organization of women's work:

> España, que es tal vez el país donde la emancipación económica de la mujer ha encontrado menos trabas sociales, ello sin duda porque el feminismo español se ha desarrollado tardíamente, cual reflejo de los de otros países, y principalmente al calor de las contingencias económicas de la posguerra, España es también, paradójicamente, el país en donde el trabajo de la mujer obrera se verifica en peores condiciones. (46)
>
> Spain is perhaps the country where the economic liberation of women has encountered fewest social impediments, owing to the fact that Spanish feminism was late in developing, as an echo of feminism in other countries, and mainly in the light of the economic situation of the post–World War era; Spain is, paradoxically, the country where working women suffer the harshest conditions.

Another aspect of women's work that Nelken vigorously addressed was the need to eliminate the unfair competition of the religious orders. She was concerned with the importance of taking control of convent labor and other religious functions both in centers of production and in institutions. Finally, she wanted to put a stop to the dominant system in Spanish social work of giving charity in exchange for "sumisión a conciencia" or "conscientious submission," a practice that required recipients of charity to embrace Catholic teachings and ideology.

Yet another pressing issue facing women during the first few decades of the twentieth century was the debate over women's suffrage. Before the establishment of the Second Republic, Nelken opposed the granting of this right to women. In *La mujer ante las Cortes Constituyentes* ("Woman before the Constitutional Assemblies"), Nelken writes:

> No hay una sola mujer española, católica practicante, es decir, una sola mujer que se confiese, que no haya sido interrogada por su confesor acerca de sus ideas políticas y acerca de la inclinación que ha de darles y que ha de procurar dar a las de cuantos la rodean. (20)

> There is not a single Spanish woman who is a practicing Catholic, that is, a woman who goes to confession, who has not been asked by her confessor about her political ideas, about which side she favors, and about how she ought to influence those around her.

It was Nelken's feminism that prevented her from supporting a woman's right to vote because she saw the vote as quantitative and not qualitative. Nelken believed that, except for intellectuals and working women in the capital, most Spanish women would vote the way their husbands, fathers, or confessors told them to. As seen in the large scope of her activism, Nelken's advocacy for women's causes took into account the multiple factors affecting women's economic, social, and personal independence.

Political Praxis (1931–39)

Nelken was a Socialist member of all three Republican legislatures (1931–39) and an active participant in Spanish politics at key moments. In one of her most crucial campaigns, she supported the 1931 peasant uprising in Castilblanco (in Badajoz, the province that elected her as its representative) by requesting the removal of the government delegate for being repressive and antidemocratic. Nelken's support for the peasant movement was criticized by the government, which accused her of inciting the uprising and the violence that culminated in the death of two civil guards.

In February 1936, Nelken's *Por qué hicimos la revolución* ("Why We Made the Revolution") was published. In it she reflects on the Badajoz and Asturias revolts and reconstructs the events:

> Una única vez los trabajadores, ametrallados por la Guardia Civil durante una manifestación pacífica, habían tenido el coraje de contestar [. . .]. La manifestación señalaba la terminación de una huelga de cuarenta y ocho horas, decretada en toda la provincia para hacer comprender al Gobierno que la presencia del gobernador "republicano" de aquel entonces no podía resistirse más. Era una huelga decretada como último recurso, no sabiendo ya a qué medio apelar [. . .]. (63)
>
> Only once had workers, machine-gunned by the Civil Guard during a peaceful demonstration, had the courage to respond [. . .]. The demonstration marked the end of a forty-eight-hour strike decreed throughout the province to make the government understand that the presence of the "Republican" governor at that time could no longer be tolerated. It was a strike decreed as a last resort, the people not knowing any other means of appeal [. . .].

Another of Nelken's controversial positions was her advocacy of the Asturias rebellion of 1934, in which she supported the miners who revolted against the conservative and repressive governments of Alejandro Lerroux and Gil Robles. Sanctioning the uprising cost her parliamentary immunity and resulted in a year's exile in the USSR. In *Por qué hicimos la revolución*, she equated the Asturias revolt with the 1917 Russian Revolution:

> He aquí seguramente la fuerza absoluta de la conminación revolucionaria que había de borrar momentáneamente las consignas particulares a cada partido. Una sóla orden: la insurrección. Una sóla bandera: la bandera roja. Una sóla consigna: la lucha por la dictadura del proletariado. Un sólo título: el de revolucionario, que anula o, mejor dicho, que integra todos los distintivos de los partidos. (77)
>
> Here we have the absolute force of the revolutionary threat that was to momentarily erase the watchwords particular to each party. One single order: insurrection. One single flag: the red flag. One single cause: the struggle for the dictatorship of the proletariat. One single name: that of revolutionary, which annuls or, more accurately, integrates all the distinctions among the parties.

Finally, Nelken's most emblematic political intervention: her active participation in the Spanish Civil War (1936–39). When she returned from exile in the USSR, she was reelected as a representative by the Frente Popular (Popular Front) on 16 February 1936. As part of the Republican government, she would be a central figure in defending the nation against the Franco uprising of 18 July. The defense of Madrid can be seen as epitomizing the struggle of the Spanish people during the Civil War. On 7 November, Nelken assumed executive power, ascending to the leadership in Madrid, while the government itself had moved to Valencia. To the cry of "No entrarán" ("They will not get in"), Nelken led the city's resistance over the airwaves, in the streets, and at the seat of the acting government.

As described in the following excerpt, the importance of the Communist Party during the siege in Madrid cannot be overstated. It was because of the party's aggressive response to the events of 1936 that Nelken defected from the ranks of the Socialists to join the Communist Party. Referring to Franco's forces, she explained:

> Lo que les detuvo fue el pueblo. Fue Madrid, sus hombres, sus mujeres, y hasta sus chiquillos. [. . .] El llamamiento [que Nelken había hecho desde la radio] había sido oído en todo Madrid: "Lo mejor que puedes hacer es que te vean," dijo un camarada. Decidimos recorrer todos los centros obreros. En todos idéntico fervor, e idéntica ira contra los que habían traicionado la confianza puesta en ellos [i.e., el gobierno y los dirigentes de varios partidos]. [. . .] El Partido Comunista, el único que quedaba en pie y ENTERO, era ya, para todos, el alma de la defensa de Madrid. ("Defensa" 14)
>
> What stopped them was the people. It was Madrid, her men, her women, and even her children. [. . .] The call [which Nelken had made over the radio] had been heard all over Madrid: "The best thing you can do is be visible," said a comrade. We decided to visit all the workers' centers. Everywhere the same fervor, the same anger against those who had betrayed the confidence placed in them [i.e., the government and the leaders of various parties]. [. . .] The Communist Party, the only one still standing and UNFRAGMENTED, became for everyone the heart of the defense of Madrid.

Nelken took pride in her political activities, not merely as an elected official but as a woman and an intellectual. She tirelessly struggled for a wide range of objectives through various organizations and mediums. She belonged to the Agrupación de Mujeres Antifascistas (Group of Women against Fascism) and to the Asociación Internacional de Intelectuales Antifascistas (International Association of Intellectuals against Fascism). Through these two organizations, she enjoyed a position within the intellectual and political vanguard all during the war. An example of this organizational affiliation was her attendance at the 1937 II Congreso Internacional de Escritores Antifascistas (Second International Conference of Writers against Fascism). She also appeared on the battlefront beside leaders like Enrique Lister, Vicente Rojo, and Valentín González Campesino and as a war correspondent for *Crónica, Estampa,* and *Mundo Obrero.* Indeed, *Mundo Obrero* was the paper that publicly announced Nelken's affiliation with the Communist Party, in December 1936. Nelken was not the only quasi-moderate-leftist militant who, to support the war effort more effectively, joined the Communist Party, a party with a concrete strategy and iron discipline.[4] The "mujer pública número uno" ("public woman number one"), as Spanish workers and peasants called her, fought in the war following the directives of the Communist Party, and she went into exile under its banner.

Exile: Intellectual Loyalty and the Return to Art Criticism (1940–68)

The Spaniards in exile gathered under the auspices of their respective political parties, which, through a number of organizations, channeled aid to the Spanish Republicans. In 1942, Nelken was expelled from the Communist Party for opposing its proposed Unión Nacional (National Union), which would support the Communist Party's alliances with national parties if and when they abandoned Spanish fascism. Nelken did not consider this a viable strategy, viewing it as a betrayal of the Republican cause. Expulsion cost Nelken the social and economic veto power wielded by the party, in addition to its network of influence. Forced to discover another means of subsistence outside the world of politics, she devoted herself to art criticism.

Nelken's break from the Communist Party in no way signified a diminution of the allegiance and admiration she felt for the Soviet system (her son, Santiago de Paul, continued to fight in the ranks of the Red Army). Her loyalty and devotion to the USSR was clearly outlined in *Las torres del Kremlin* ("The Towers of the Kremlin"), a book she wrote in 1943, a year after her expulsion. Nelken paid homage to Stalin and to the Soviet system, while simultaneously analyzing the contemporary European climate and the rise of Nazism and the Allied politics of World War II. As a testimonial to loyalty to a cause, the book shares this viewpoint with Nelken's *Primer frente* ("First Front"). Published in 1944, this is a poetic work dedicated to the Red Army and its struggle for world liberation. The connection to Nelken's own life is palpable, since her son fought and died in the defense of the Russian front at Mitrofanovka.

In Mexico, the Spanish Communist Party openly rejected Nelken, directing negative propaganda against her that was too widespread to be ignored. She was denied access to publication, to cultural organizations, to involvement in political activity in any way linked to the Communist Party. Nelken sought assistance from the Mexican presidents Manuel Avila Camacho and Miguel Alemán, who subsidized many of her projects and made her publications possible. This patronage put her in a delicate and ambiguous situation. She was a woman ideologically linked to the Communist Party, while dependent for economic support on presidents committed to policies that forwarded the development of Mexican capitalism.

Another negative repercussion of Nelken's separation from the Communist Party was the distance it created between Nelken and the muralists Diego Rivera and David Alfaro Siqueiros, both members of the Mexican Communist Party. Her subsequent distance from muralism, Mexico's most significant movement in painting, prevented her from contributing her talent to this vibrant dimension of Mexican culture. In response to this ostracism, she began to write with great authority on a series of trends: the vanguard, expressionism, cubism, futurism, and abstract geometrism. Her writings on these forms opened the way for and promoted figures who today stand at the forefront of Mexican art: José Luis Cuevas, Carlos Mérida, Ignacio Asúnsolo, Lucinda Urrusti, Feliciano Béjar, to name a few. Nelken's monographs and her numerous articles that continued to be published in *Hoy, Presente, Tribuna Israelita,* and *Excelsior* until two weeks before her death, in March 1968, described and shaped Mexican artistic production in the second half of the twentieth century.

Nelken in Retrospect

When Nelken was elected as a deputy in 1932, her groundbreaking example inspired many women who saw in her an achiever in the world of labor and politics. She was also a model for many women who, for the first time, perceived themselves as capable of making decisions at the highest levels. Her role as a politician set an important example: it showed that women could be elevated to the status of men and that women had a place as equal citizens who could participate in the governing of the nation.

Nelken was elected not only because she was an outstanding member of her party but also because she represented the social and professional aspirations of many women in Spain. She was emblematic of the national spirit of the times, of the consciousness that created the Second Republic. The defeat of her ideas was due to the inability of the economic and political elite to accept the desires and rights of the working class and other social groups anxious to participate in the national project.

Franco's uprising in July 1936 destroyed the progressive work that Nelken and a host of other women were performing in Spain. After the war, her exile drastically changed her social and economic status. But exile did not change her political beliefs or her understanding of the professional and economic potential of women in the public arena. Her work as a writer and art critic provided food for her family. Her interventions as a politician gave hope to men and women who lived abroad in exile and to those who lived in silence in Spain. Through her, many found the strength to fight for social justice. In 1975, after Franco's death, a publishing house in Madrid printed a second edition of *La condición social de la mujer en España.* This second printing is a reflection of the continuing importance of Nelken's work today. For feminist scholars in a new millennium, Margarita Nelken's legacy summarizes in a clear and dramatic fashion many of the economic, social, and political struggles of women in the twentieth century.

Notes

1. Margarita Nelken's works, like those of most women writers in exile, are characterized by being scattered and forgotten (see the collections or bibliographies of Julián del Amo and Charmion Shelby, *Obra impresa de los intelectuales españoles en América, 1936–45* ["Printed Works by Spanish Intellectuals in America, 1936–45], and Joaquina Rodríguez, *La novela del exilio español* ["The Novel of the Spanish Exile"], or the Ateneo Español de México's *Bibliografía literaria del exilio* ["Bibliography of Exile Literature"]). As sources of narrative written in exile, these works discuss only Luisa Carnés and Cecilia G. de Guilarte as women writers resident in Mexico, when, in fact, the number was much greater. For more on Nelken, see my *Margarita Nelken.*
2. The conditions holding back women writers apply to the generation who went into exile and not to the women writers born in exile. For example, the so-called Hispanomexican generation were only partially affected by displacement since they did not have to adapt to a new environment. While I stress the obstacles to women's intellectual productivity in exile, I must point out that they are in no way comparable to the intellectual oppression of women in Spain, which reflected ideological submission. For more on Spanish exile literature in general, see Michael Ugarte.
3. All quotes from *La condición social de la mujer en España* are taken from the 1975 edition.
4. According to data by the party secretary general José Díaz, from the 40,000 members the Communist Party had before the war, the number rose to 249,000, even though support throughout the nation was much higher during the war (Bolloten 229).

Major Publications of Margarita Nelken

La condición social de la mujer en España.†

"La defensa de Madrid."†

Las escritoras españolas. Barcelona: Labor, 1931.

El expresionismo en la plástica mexicana. México: Mexicanas, 1951.

Los judíos en la cultura hispánica. México: Tribuna Israelita, 1954.

Maternología y puericultura. Valencia: Generación Consciente, 1926.

La mujer ante las Cortes Constituyentes.†

Por qué hicimos la revolución.†

Primer frente.†

† See Works Cited

"¿Retratos?" (Unpublished). Madrid: Archivo Pablo Iglesias.
Las torres del Kremlin.†
La trampa del arenal. Madrid: Sucesores de Hernando, 1923.
Tres tipos de Vírgenes: Angélico, Rafael, y Alonso Cano. Mexico: Secretaría de Educación Pública, 1942.

Works Cited

Amo, Julián del, and Charmion Shelby. *Obra impresa de los intelectuales españoles en América, 1936–1945.* Stanford: Stanford UP, 1951.
Ateneo Español de México. *Bibliografía literaria del exilio.* Mexico: Ateneo, 1979.
Bolloten, Burnett. *La Guerra Civil española: Revolución y contrarrevolución.* Madrid: Alianza, 1989.
Martínez-Gutiérrez, Josebe. *Margarita Nelken.* Madrid: Ediciones del Orto, 1997.
Nelken, Margarita. *La condición social de la mujer en España.* Madrid: Rivadeneira, 1919. Madrid: CVS, 1975.
———. "La defensa de Madrid." *España Popular* [México] 9 Nov. 1940: 7+.
———. *La mujer ante las Cortes Constituyentes.* Madrid: Castro, 1931.
———. *Por qué hicimos la revolución.* Barcelona: Sociales Internacionales, 1936.
———. *Primer frente.* Pub. Nelken. Mexico, 1944.
———. *Las torres del Kremlin.* Mexico: Industrial Distribuidora, 1943.
Rodríguez, Joaquina, ed. *La novela del exilio español.* Mexico: UAM, 1986.
Ugarte, Michael. *Shifting Ground: Spanish Civil War Exile Literature.* Durham: Duke UP, 1989.

† See Works Cited

Feminism and Anarchism: Remembering the Role of Mujeres Libres in the Spanish Civil War

María Asunción Gómez

Translated by Patricia Santoro

Wars, particularly civil wars, have understandably served as catalysts for the appearance and expansion of feminist movements and for the transformation in social roles that women are expected to fulfill.[1] Although the Spanish Civil War (1936–39) unleashed radical social changes that might have affected the fate of many Spanish women, the victory of the reactionary wing virtually eliminated any hope for the continuation of radicalism. Ideas about women's roles that emerged during this crucial period were defined, in general terms, by the ideology of the two opposing sides. Contrary to the apparent ideological homogeneity among the women of the right wing who were associated with the Sección Femenina (Women's Sector of the Falange), within leftist groups the problem of women's emancipation was subject to debate. This debate involved a division between those who felt that women should postpone their demands until the war was won and those who believed the revolution to be meaningless as long as social inequality between the sexes continued to exist.

The controversy about women's issues manifested itself at various levels and in different ways within the leftist groups. One of the largest and most radical of these groups was the Asociación de Mujeres Libres (Association of Free Women). Its members undertook a twofold revolution and attempted to emancipate themselves not only as workers but also as women. In retrospect, it may appear strange that anarchist women of the Civil War period have received scant attention from official history and have been almost totally disregarded by the world of the arts.[2] Oddly enough, the utopian nature of this subject, while appropriate for a literary or cinematographic work, did not for many years bear fruit, either in Spain—because of the obvious restrictions of the Francoist dictatorship (1939–75)—or in exile.[3]

It was not until 1988 that Sara Berenguer (b. 1919) published her autobiographical narrative, *Entre el sol y la tormenta: Treinta y dos meses de guerra* ("Between the Sun and the Storm: Thirty-Two Months of War"). Berenguer was one of the twenty thousand women affiliated with Mujeres Libres who fought for the freedom of working-class women. Despite the importance of the Berenguer autobiography as a testimony to the work of anarchist women in the Spanish Civil War, the work has been almost entirely overlooked by critics. This lack of interest and the book's small distribution are probably due to Berenguer's anonymity and to the stylistic deficiencies of the narration, which the author herself acknowledges by explaining that she only attended school until the age of twelve. Whatever the reason, the public was generally unaware of the existence of Mujeres Libres until the premiere of Vicente Aranda's film *Libertarias* (1996), an adaptation of Antonio Rabinad's novel *La monja libertaria* ("The Libertarian Nun"). *Libertarias*, a tragic and comic work, represents an ambitious project that had been in the planning stages for more than ten years. The director created a film with a distinctly feminist tone as an homage both to a libertarian utopia and to the revolutionary dream of a group of women who struggled to free themselves from the patriarchal and capitalist oppression that had enslaved them on a social and a personal level. This essay explores these two different approaches—in film and autobiography—to rescuing the memory of Mujeres Libres. I discuss how these two works attempt to capture and interpret the objectives and achievements of Mujeres Libres, its ideological coherence, its internal problems and contradictions, and the association's original contribution to the feminist movement.

Film as History: Vicente Aranda's *Libertarias*

The Asociación de Mujeres Libres was born in April 1936, several months before the beginning of the war, and was disbanded in February 1939 on the exodus of its members to various European and American countries.[4] The significance of the organization in the historical development of a feminist consciousness in Spain is crucial since it constitutes the first attempt to alert working-class women to the importance of asserting their rights in both the public and the private spheres. Adding this new component of social class to women's emancipation signified a rupture with the bourgeois feminism that had been prevalent since the end of the nineteenth century in Europe and the United States, where the social structures underlying the subordination of women were not questioned.[5] The primary goal of Mujeres Libres was to promote the emancipation of a particular group of women—members of the industrial and farming proletariat—and the organization's ideology and objectives were closely linked to anarchist ideals. Contrary to the individualism that characterized many of the bourgeois feminist movements, Mujeres Libres, in consonance with libertarian ideology, firmly believed that women developed autonomy through their relationship to the community and their involvement in social tasks. Furthermore, members of Mujeres Libres refused to be labeled *feminists,* since this adjective connoted opposition to men and the substitution of male hierarchies by female hierarchies.

When the association was created, it focused on the triple enslavement that had subjugated working-class women for generations: "esclavitud de ignorancia, esclavitud de mujer y esclavitud de productora" (Nash 73) ("slavery of ignorance, slavery as woman, and slavery as producer"). Members of the association concentrated on the concrete tasks of eradicating illiteracy and directing the cultural and technical training of many proletarian women. Another central concern of Mujeres Libres was the eradication of prostitution, which was considered the most flagrant example of the relation between the economic exploitation and the sexual subordination of women. To this end, they created the Liberatorios de Prostitución, centers that provided economic support, psychological assistance, and education and work training for women who stopped engaging in prostitution.

Mujeres Libres tried to empower working women through education and active participation in the public sector.[6] Contrary to other mass movements, such as socialism and communism, anarchist organizations have always manifested a visceral rejection of institutional hierarchies and the concept of centralization of power. Instead, they promote a self-regulating, collectivist ideology in which the ends never justify the means and in which decisions originate from the base and not from the party's top echelon. In Republican Spain, this theory of direct action was implemented by a total revolution that transformed life during the course of the Civil War, particularly in the regions of Aragon, Catalonia, and Valencia. Factories, services, and landholdings were collectivized and placed under the control of the workers, employees, and peasants, thus belying the purely utopian character that had often been attributed to anarchism. However, libertarian ideology considered this practice unthinkable without the moral and cultural regeneration that would allow each militant to live harmoniously within the community. Social and individual revolution ran hand in hand at the apex of the Spanish anarchist movement. It is not surprising that it was precisely within this antiauthoritarian, regenerative, emancipatory, communal, and revolutionary ideology that the first proletarian Spanish feminist movement would emerge. Despite its identification with anarchist ideals, Mujeres Libres remained autonomous at all times, as did the associations that were part of its federal structure. In fact, the relations between Mujeres Libres and other anarchist organizations were often tense, since the women's organization was relegated to a marginal position within the libertarian movement.[7] This marginality explains its almost total exclusion from history books. Even the most detailed historiographic accounts have relegated to oblivion the active participation of this group of at least twenty thousand anarchist women (see Carr; Jackson; Payne; Preston; and Thomas).

When members of the public attended the premiere of *Libertarias* in 1996, they discovered an aspect of the war that had hardly ever been encountered in history books. *Libertarias* presents a heroic tale that is only loosely based on historical fact. Recounting the story of militia women who are joined by a group of prostitutes and a nun who fled a burning convent, the film glorifies the role of women as fighters and neglects the important educational, activist, and rearguard roles of Mujeres Libres. The predominantly nostalgic vision of anarchism and the strongly melodramatic and sentimental component of the film undermine the political message and distort the historical reality.

Possibly the most paradoxical aspect of *Libertarias* is its attempt to join a fictitious and sometimes unlikely plot with real people, events, and historical documents.[8] It is no coincidence that three of the four Mujeres Libres fighters bear the names of representatives of the organization.[9] In addition, the script includes fragments of documents, newspaper articles, and pamphlets that are incorporated into the fiction in a somewhat anachronistic fashion. The film's attempt to legitimize its historical discourse is apparent from the first images, reconstructed black-and-white archival footage, that serve as a backdrop to the opening credits.

Despite using the names of several of Mujeres Libres' most active militants, the film is not inspired by the life of any one of them. On the contrary, in seeking to validate the work of these anarchist women, the film distorts their historical roles. The spectator who is not familiar with the real role of Mujeres Libres in the war leaves the theater with the false impression that its crucial participation was at the front, when its real contribution was in the rearguard. Apparently, this role did not appear sufficiently heroic to Aranda for the narration that he had in mind.[10] He adds several morbid scenes bordering on the horrific or naturalistic that are characteristic of films of the 1990s.[11] Furthermore, the title *Libertarias* only pertains to the first part of the film, in which we see scenes that help clarify the role that anarchist women were supposed to play in the Spanish Civil War. This role is reflected on three levels: within leftist groups, within the libertarian movement, and within the organization Mujeres Libres itself.

Aranda develops the first level by describing how dissension within leftist groups affected the female militia who fought at the front, a theme that the British director Ken Loach expertly treats in his film on the Spanish Civil War, *Land and Freedom* (1995). As shown by Aranda, the militarization of the popular front army, a shift that was promoted by the Communist Party, forced the women to the rearguard. The leader of the anarchist militias, Buenaventura Durruti, who was ready to sacrifice everything except victory, took forceful and radical measures to demand the retreat of all women from the trenches. An earlier scene in which a group of prostitutes who arrive at a hospital for gynecological tests are seen laughing irreverently and urinating on the floor justifies Durruti's decision. Although the spread of venereal disease at the front is a historical fact, Aranda presents this episode in a grotesque fashion. Making light of this very real and painful problem, the scene is at odds with the feminist tone of the film. The stereotyped and invariably comic representation of the prostitutes in *Libertarias* reflects a contradiction that we see in the supposedly feminist representations of women in several contemporary films (e.g., *¿Qué he hecho yo para merecer esto?* by Pedro Almodóvar).[12]

On the second level, the attitude toward members of the Mujeres Libres on the part of their anarchist comrades ranges from disdain, especially from those in power, to outright admiration from the militiamen who have witnessed their heroism at the front. Although Aranda underscores the latter attitude, historiographic documents confirm that in reality the anarchists regarded the work of Mujeres Libres with suspicion or, at best, paternalism. Despite its absolute identification with libertarian ideology and its important function in drawing women into the libertarian cause, Mujeres Libres never won the support of the CNT (National Confederation of Workers), the FAI (Iberian Anarchist Federation), or the FIJL (Iberian Federation of Libertarian Youth), the only three official anarchist organizations (see Nash 103–06). That anarchist groups disagreed with the tenets of Mujeres Libres is reflected in the response the association gave in several of its reports (see Nash 20–21).

On the third level, *Libertarias* outlines a characteristic of Mujeres Libres that is obvious to the careful reader of the articles published in the association's homonymous magazine: the lack of ideological uniformity and the frequently contradictory positions that their members espoused when faced with a problem. Aranda reflects this dissension in a scene at a meeting of Mujeres Libres when the speaker advocates the withdrawal of the women from the trenches. The speech is based on an anonymous article published in July 1937 in the magazine *Mujeres Libres.* Aranda extracts fragments and incorporates them verbatim into his script: "Es la hora de cambiar el fusil por la máquina industrial y la energía guerrera por la dulzura del alma de mujer" ("It is time to exchange the rifle for the industrial machine, and the energy expended in war for the sweetness of the woman's soul").[13] In response to this speech, which is disturbingly similar to the speeches of the leaders of the right-wing Sección Femenina, Pilar, one of the anarchist women in the film, expresses a point of view to which the rest of the audience shows its agreement by bursting into applause:

> No entendemos por qué la revolución tiene que correr a cargo de la mitad de la población solamente. Somos anarquistas. Somos libertarias. Pero también somos mujeres y queremos hacer nuestra revolución. [. . .] Queremos pegar tiros, para poder exigir nuestra parte a la hora del reparto.
>
> We don't understand why the revolution has to be fought by only half the population. We are anarchists. We are libertarians. But we are also women and we want to create our own revolution. [. . .] We want to shoot so that we can demand our own share when the time comes.

Though this scene is based on a real controversy and though real documents published by Mujeres Libres are used, the contextualization of this meeting in the film is clearly anachronistic, since women are asked to withdraw from the fight when this stage of the Civil War has not even begun. Furthermore, Pilar's speech, which is warmly accepted by the women attending the meeting, does not reflect the majority position of Mujeres Libres with respect to the role that women were asked to fulfill in the war. The participation of women at the front was never considered a decisive element in the attainment of women's liberation. The efforts of the organization were focused on preparing a women's workforce that would fill the positions that the men had left vacant.[14]

Aranda's film reinforces some of the stereotypes of patriarchal ideology even as it attempts to criticize them. In this respect, the filmic representation of the nun (who succumbs to martyrdom) and the prostitute (who defiantly urinates on the clinic floor) as prototypes of women who convert to anarchism reaffirms rather than destroys the myths surrounding these women. In addition, the burning of convents and the anticlerical emphasis reinforce the black legend associated with anarchism. The religious element in the film takes on so much importance that it clouds and dilutes the political message. Although the film's characters belong to Mujeres Libres, Aranda's narration has much in common with the great masculine narratives whose historical re-creations are shaped by heroic deeds and political and military events.

Memory as History: Sara Berenguer's *Entre el sol y la tormenta*

Far from the heroic and epic tone that characterizes *Libertarias*, the work of Berenguer presents another side of the coin as she gives her testimony to the arduous and anonymous contribution of the anarchist women in the Spanish Civil War.[15] Berenguer humbly admits that her role in the revolution "no fue ni singular ni pomposo. Fui algo así como una hormiga que va haciendo camino entre los matorrales" (12) ("was not special or wonderful. I was like an ant who makes its way through the brush").[16]

Berenguer's memoirs, as any attempt to reproduce a remembered past, cannot be strictly referential, and she is aware of this fact. The author does not aspire to historical truth in an absolute sense and reminds us of the unreliability of her memory and of the temporal inaccuracies of her work, factors that she attributes to the emotional implications of the turbulent social and political events of the war. However, as Maroula Joannou explains, the autobiographical "I," regardless of its unreliability, "is not merely a textual construction, but the textual double of a woman in history who has been produced by the material differences in men and women's lives, and has selected, from the totality of her experiences, those which retrospectively appear to her to be the more significant" (32). Berenguer relies on the subjective view of memory and presents the Spanish Civil War as an event mediated by her place in history, both past and present.

Although there is a lapse of more than forty years between the time of the narration and the time period being narrated, the urgency and the passion hidden behind each line of these memoirs reveal, on the one hand, the mark that the war left on the narrator and, on the other, the strength of her repressed desire once again to express herself freely in her own country. With the arrival of democracy in Spain, after the death of Franco in 1975, Berenguer, along with many other exiles, was impelled to refocus her life and reflect on a critical moment both in Spanish history and in the lives of many women who shared her ideals of women's liberation:

> Para la mayoría de las mujeres, sumisas e ignorantes, la revolución fue como un estallido de luz que vino a nosotras y nos abrió un camino, el cual hasta entonces habíamos tenido vedado [. . .]. [P]ara mí fue un tiempo de enriquecimiento, a pesar de las muchas dificultades en que me debatí. (11–13)
>
> For the majority of women, submissive and ignorant, the revolution was like an explosion of light that came to us and opened up a path that had been forbidden to us until that moment [. . .]. [F]or me it was a time of enrichment, in spite of the many difficulties through which I struggled.

By reliving her past, Berenguer accomplished a double objective: she provided a perspective that had been omitted from official historiography, and she re-created a historical moment and ideal that transformed not only her life but also the lives of thousands of Spanish women. The writing of her memoirs therefore serves as a collective testimony and as a personal exorcism. They respond to a desire for historical truth and a need to recuperate a lost identity. It is significant that Berenguer began her memoirs with an ironic allusion to the loss of her paternal last name at the beginning of her exile in France: "A los pocos meses después de haber pasado a Francia en 1939, donde la mujer tiene tanta libertad, pierde su apellido para ir ya siempre por la vida con el del marido. Así, yo me convertí en Sara Guillén, abandonando el de Berenguer de mi padre" (15) ("A few months after having arrived in France in 1939, where a woman has so much freedom, she loses her last name and goes through life forever with the name of her husband. So I became Sara Guillén, leaving behind the Berenguer of my father"). For Berenguer, exile meant not only the physical uprooting from her native land but also the wrenching away of an identity that had been forged during the years of fratricidal fighting.

Berenguer's narration is not strictly chronological. At times, it has a fragmented, illogical flow. In addition, she intersperses various registers and literary conventions, shifting from a poetically inspired paragraph to a historical tale, from intimate experiences to quotes from historical documents, books, and personal letters. As Mary Jacobus suggests, this amalgam of genres is in itself a transgressive act since it indicates a rejection of predominantly masculine literary and historiographic conventions. This phenomenon, which Jacobus defines as "feminist metafiction," constitutes a "transgression between literary boundaries that exposes those boundaries for what they are—the product of phallocentric discourse" (12).

The frequent time shifts that characterize the narration correspond both to natural shifts in memory and to the effects that spatial and temporal distancing, subsequent disillusionment, life in exile, and return to Spain have on Berenguer's writings. The author reflects on these stylistic and structural variances, asking our forgiveness for the possible inaccuracies and lack of chronology in the events that appear in the narration. She explains that the political and emotional turbulence during the war caused her certain difficulties in remembering dates and the exact locations of her activities, all of which were dedicated to the evolution of the working masses and to the emancipation of women. These two objectives of workers' and women's freedom gave meaning to Berenguer's life and determined her participation in the war, the revolution, and her affiliation with Mujeres Libres.

Since Berenguer was only seventeen years old when the conflict began, the war formed the background for her initiation into adulthood through a political and feminist activism that would radically change her vision of the world. With a force that is the domain of youth and with a firm belief in her ideals, Berenguer energetically participated in multiple activities. In the span of a few weeks she worked as a seamstress and a night nurse, a typist and a guard of a munitions dump. Her desire to be useful to the revolution and her restless spirit led her to learn how to pilot a plane and to handle a rifle. After her work in the Catalan Regional Committee of the Building, Wood, and Decoration Industry (a branch of the CNT), she went on to collaborate closely with Mujeres Libres and in 1938 became the association's secretary of propaganda in Barcelona, a post she held until the end of the war.

Berenguer's valuable memoirs afford the reader access to her contribution to the revolution and the contribution of other militant anarchists who belonged to Mujeres Libres. Moreover, the memoirs substantiate the important yet scarcely recognized work of this organization in the Spanish Civil War.[17] Faithful to her anarchist ideology, in these memoirs Berenguer interweaves her individual history with the collective history to which her destiny is closely bound. Her appearance in the public sphere as a revolutionary who fought for the eradication of social injustices is interwoven with her personal development as a self-sacrificing woman in the service of the community. This integration within the collective enterprise finds its rhetorical correlative in the continuous shifting between the use of the first-person singular and the first-person plural. This usage emphasizes the plurality of the "I," a characteristic that, according to Doris Sommer, is common in most women's testimonial narratives, in which narrators find their own identity as an extension of the collectivity (108).

The formation of a female identity and its bond to a collective subjectivity corresponds perfectly to the emphasis on constructing a sense of community that is a characteristic of militant anarchists who aspire to political, economic, and sexual freedom and equality within a communal context. Martha Ackelsberg describes this communitarian ideology as follows: "In place of inequality as a basis of organization, anarchists offer mutualism, reciprocity, and federalism. In place of hierarchy and domination, they propose to empower everyone to achieve his or her full potential, thus obviating the need for social, political, or sexual inequality"

(*Free Women* 21). This tendency toward the abolition of inequality and hierarchies and toward the development of individual potential reappears as a constant throughout Berenguer's memoirs and forms the basis of the process of identity formation and empowerment that the author experienced during her participation in the Spanish Civil War. In the same fashion, the struggle of Mujeres Libres to achieve a nonauthoritarian society was based on the concept of the social nature of freedom. The organization recognized that, in addition to economic exploitation, the subordination of women was a culturally constructed phenomenon.

Since individual freedom of both men and women is a basic premise of anarchism, many activists considered the existence of a specifically women's organization superfluous, and even damaging, to the success of the revolution. Berenguer represents an emblematic stance among anarchist women who, despite their active militancy, either in the rearguard or at the front, rejected the sectarianism that characterized bourgeois feminism and the most radical sectors of Mujeres Libres. The author herself confesses her initial refusal to collaborate with Mujeres Libres, considering that to win the battle for human rights, men and women must work together. A relatively insignificant event changed her mind: she witnessed a group of young men deriding the announcement of an upcoming lecture by Concha Guillén, a delegate to the local federation of Mujeres Libres.

> Me indigné; en el instante que escuché los comentarios despreciativos y sin control de aquellos jóvenes, pasaron mil pensamientos por mi mente. El corazón me bullía, recordé el machismo sin freno. [. . .] Se despertó un resentimiento dormido en mí. La cólera y la rabia alteraron mi pasividad. (115)
>
> I was indignant; the moment I heard the derisive, freewheeling comments of those young men, a thousand thoughts passed through my mind. My heart was racing, I was reminded of unchecked machismo. [. . .] A hitherto dormant resentment awoke in me. Anger and rage altered my passivity.

What released the thoughts that raced through her mind was the memory of the sexual harassment that Berenguer was subject to at the age of thirteen, when she was obliged to work as a helper in a butcher shop. Her memory goes back in time and opens a parenthesis in the narration as she describes this unpleasant incident that marred her adolescence and that, a few years later, would be decisive in raising her awareness of the two-pronged revolution she was to join. Nevertheless, Berenguer's incorporation into the federation of Mujeres Libres was slow. The author herself admits that she participated in several meetings as a spokesperson before obtaining her membership card.

In laying out the precedents for the Asociación of Mujeres Libres, Berenguer describes the cultural and training activities that took place in the Casal de la Dona Treballadora (The Center for Working Women), including literacy campaigns, supplementary elementary education classes, technical and social formation, and talks on contraceptives, child care, maternity, and abortion. Her description encompasses the transcription of slogans, propaganda leaflets, and fragments of other publications produced by Mujeres Libres, as well as a collage of letters, pages from magazines, photographs, and posters that set this text apart from the traditional memoir format but legitimize it as a historical document.[18]

Berenguer also offers the reader her opinion on the role of Mujeres Libres, stressing that to reach its objective of empowering women rather than simply to defy masculine authority, the association worked to contribute to the creation of a new society together with its male comrades. Whereas much of the action of *Libertarias* deals with the challenge to men's power, the vision that Berenguer presents is very different, even after her active militancy in Mujeres Libres.[19] In the same fashion, Aranda's treatment of the issue of sexuality reflects prevailing clichés about free love that had been diffused and misinterpreted from the first decades of the twentieth century and that likened free love to sexual intercourse with different partners, without any commitment. In this respect, when the occasion presents itself, the militia women of *Libertarias* seem to accept casual sexual relationships rather easily. However, this is not what most members of Mujeres Libres understood as free love. For them love could be nothing other than free: "Libre amor o amor a secas. No existe amor esclavo" (Nash 171) ("Free love or just plain love. Enslaved love does not exist").[20] A few members of Mujeres Libres stated that the campaigns for sexual freedom undertaken by some anarchists and anarcho-syndicalists only harmed women.[21] It is with these members' conception of free love that Berenguer seems to identify, as she alludes to the different meaning that the idea of freedom in love (she never uses the term *free love*) has for her and for several of her comrades who propose "sin preámbulos una relación sexual inmediata" (210) ("a sexual relationship right away, with no preliminaries"). Berenguer's rejection of a casual free love, with many partners, is consistent with that adopted by Mujeres Libres and by many anarchists all over the world.[22] These reflections on the issue of free love represent one more instance of Berenguer's gendered perspective. As is common among female autobiographical subjects, "her place within history is produced by difference and reproduces difference" (Joannou 32).

Entre el sol y la tormenta presents an alternative historiographic vision that focuses on a group of women whose active participation in the making of history undermines the culturally constructed notion of feminine passivity. Berenguer's point of view as a woman is indispensable for understanding the crucial role that Mujeres Libres played as the first proletarian feminist movement. Contrary to bourgeois feminism, Mujeres Libres attempted to raise the consciousness of the working woman and to integrate her into a social and individual revolution without precedent in working-class history. In contrast to other types of proletarian women associations, such as the Communist Asociación de Mujeres Antifascistas (Association of Antifascist Women) and the Socialist Unión de Muchachas (United Girls), Mujeres Libres advocated an associative feminism striving for total freedom for women within a global revolutionary process that placed great emphasis on female bonding. The lesson of Mujeres Libres continues, and Berenguer brings her insight to bear on this lesson, intermingling the referential and the denotative aspects of the narration and reformulating historical facts that have remained largely unknown. In this sense, Berenguer's testimony becomes a space of resistance through which we may come to know the other side of history.

Notes

1. The development of a feminist consciousness within the context of war has become an increasingly important area of study. See, for example, the collection of essays edited by Helen Cooper et al.
2. Mary Nash was the first historian who attempted to rescue the important work of this group of women from anonymity. Her 1976 anthology includes some of the most representative writings produced within Mujeres Libres. The articles were originally published between 1936 and 1939 in the magazine *Mujeres Libres* and in other anarchist magazines of that time. Although J. Gutiérrez-Alvarez wrote the only subsequent article to appear in Spain, Martha Ackelsberg contributed several valuable English-language studies on Spanish anarchism.
3. In this sense, we have to take into account that there was no personality that stood out within the association, since Federica Montseny, the most famous woman anarchist of the Civil War, neither agreed to join the group nor recognized the importance of a women's organization.
4. In the transitional stage to democracy (1975–76), another association of feminists was formed that took on the name of Mujeres Libres. Nevertheless, as Martha Ackelsberg observes in her article "*Mujeres Libres*," the friction and recriminations between these two groups have been continuous and have made a mutual working relationship impossible.
5. In their studies on Mujeres Libres, both Nash and Ackelsberg emphasize the social characteristic that distances this group from the bourgeois feminist movements, which have been studied in greater depth than those headed by working-class women.
6. Women's emancipation, which social dynamics of the war had indirectly encouraged, only held meaning for Mujeres Libres within the framework of the social system of libertarian communism, whose goal was to create a society in which a real equality of rights and obligations existed between the sexes (Nash 23).
7. The repeated requests of Mujeres Libres to be considered an arm of the libertarian movement were invariably rejected. The report that the federation of Mujeres Libres presented to the national committees in 1938 defended the important work that the association carried out and criticized the movement's lack of understanding or indifference. This report emphasized one of Mujeres Libres's most important achievements, namely, its twenty thousand women "sustraídas a la penetración marxista" (Nash 104) ("rescued from Marxist penetration").
8. The attempt to fictionalize history unleashed a controversy among the spectators who had lived through the war, and their reactions were published in the letters-to-the-editor section of *La vanguardia.*
9. The actress Laura Maña plays the role of Concha Liaño, one of the leading figures in the documentary *Vivir la utopía,* broadcast in 1997 by Radio Televisión Española. The historical referents for Aura (Blanca Apiláñez) and Floren (Victoria Abril) could be Aurea Cuadrado and Florentina, both active collaborators on the magazine *Mujeres Libres.*

10. The story of *Libertarias* is far removed from the sentiment that directors such as Jaime Chávarri (*Las bicicletas son para el verano* ["Bicycles Are for the Summer"], 1984) and Carlos Saura (*¡Ay, Carmela!*, 1990) achieved in their films on the Spanish Civil War. *Bicicletas* deals with a middle-class family and *Carmela* with a pair of vaudevillian comedians.
11. As an example, I refer to *Nadie hablará de nosotras cuando hayamos muerto* (1995) ("Nobody Will Talk about Us When We're Dead"), directed by Agustín Díaz Yanes. Aranda, like Díaz Yanes, reserves the crudest scenes for Victoria Abril, who carries them out in a realistic fashion.
12. In *Libertarias,* Aranda uses two of the oldest stereotypes in the history of the representation of women in literature and film: the nun and the prostitute. Both characters are portrayed unrealistically; they need only to hear a few indoctrinating words from their "liberators" to embrace the feminist-anarchist ideology and sacrifice their lives at the front.
13. The article entitled "Las mujeres en los primeros días de la lucha" ("Women during the First Days of the War") is included in Nash (91–92).
14. Contrary to the temporary incorporation of women in the workforce in the United States during World War II or on the nationalist side in Spain, Mujeres Libres advocated a permanent change in the division of the workforce along gender lines. See the articles "La mujer, factor indispensable para el triunfo de la guerra y de la Revolución" (Nash 96–97) ("Woman, Determining Factor in the Triumph of the War and the Revolution"), "Cultura" (119–20) ("Culture"), and the announcements of the Casal de la Dona Treballadora (The Center for Working Women) (121).
15. Berenguer's memoirs contribute to a body of autobiographical texts that Shirley Mangini has studied in her extremely valuable work *Memories of Resistance,* but Mangini only dedicates a few paragraphs to Berenguer (88–89). The Spanish version of Mangini's study was recently published in Barcelona with the title *Recuerdos de la resistencia.*
16. Doris Sommer observes that this humble attitude is characteristic of testimonial narratives: "They are written neither for individual growth nor for glory, but are offered through the scribe to a broad public as one part of a general strategy to win political ground. One part of the strategy is simply to record the history of popular struggles. [. . .] Another part of the strategy is to pry open the process of subject in formation, to rehearse it with the reader in a way that invites her to hook into the lateral network of relationships that assumes a community of particular shared objectives rather than interchangeability among its members" (109). Despite her limitations, Berenguer constitutes herself as her own scribe. However, the dual strategy pointed out by Sommer is visible throughout the narration of *Entre el sol y la tormenta.*
17. Although Berenguer acknowledges the work of Lola Iturbe entitled *La mujer en la lucha social,* she is conscious that, despite their efforts, neither woman has been able to rescue from oblivion the altruistic women whose dream of freedom cost them their lives. Most of them have remained anonymous (229).
18. However, Berenguer advises us that this meager information will be supple-

mented by "a group of veteran comrades of '*Mujeres Libres*' who are compiling works for the publication of a book dealing with the important and decisive activities of that time" (204). To date, I have not confirmed publication of this book, which, according to Berenguer, includes the history of her comrades. If it has been published, it has not reached the public at large and does not appear in any of the most important databases.

19. Berenguer's view of the relationship between the sexes is in complete accord with what is presented in the association's publications. See Nash's anthology (109–13, 178–80) for articles that advocate relationships of mutual understanding, compatibility, and reciprocity between men and women.
20. Free love was defined in this manner in a statement signed by Mujeres Libres and published in the magazine *Ruta* in June 1937. Ackelsberg points to the scant importance that members of Mujeres Libres afforded the theme of sexual freedom (137). Contrary to their feminist contemporaries, they considered it a personal matter rather than a political issue.
21. In Berenguer's memoirs, one does not see the degree of radicalism concerning the issue of sexuality that underlies, for example, the works of Lucía Sánchez Saornil.
22. See Martin Henry Blatt's *Free Love and Anarchism* (109–12). Theoretically, the very nature of free love connotes monogamous relationships, but, as Berenguer points out, some men did not understand it in those terms. They constantly encouraged women to make use of what they understood as sexual freedom.

Works Cited

Ackelsberg, Martha A. *Community and Empowerment: Lessons from Mujeres Libres.* Cambridge: Mary Ingraham Bunting Inst., Radcliffe Coll., 1984.

———. *Free Women of Spain: Anarchism and the Struggle for the Emancipation of Women.* Bloomington: Indiana UP, 1991.

———. "*Mujeres Libres*: The Preservation of Memory under the Politics of Repression in Spain." *Memory and Totalitarianism.* Ed. Luisa Passerini. Oxford: Oxford UP, 1992. 125–43.

¡Ay, Carmela! Dir. Carlos Saura. Iberoamericano Films Internatl., 1990.

Berenguer, Sara. *Entre el sol y la tormenta: Treinta y dos meses de guerra (1936–1939).* Barcelona: Seuba, 1988.

Las bicicletas son para el verano. Dir. Jaime Chávarri. Jet Films, 1984.

Blatt, Martin Henry. *Free Love and Anarchism: The Biography of Ezra Heywood.* Urbana: U of Illinois P, 1989.

Carr, Raymond, ed. *The Republic and the Civil War in Spain.* London: Macmillan, 1971.

Cooper, Helen, et al., eds. *Arms and the Woman: War, Gender, and Literary Representation.* Chapel Hill: U of North Carolina P, 1989.

Gutiérrez-Alvarez, J. "El feminismo anarquista de las Mujeres Libres." *Historia y vida* 229.20 (1987): 33–39.

Iturbe, Lola. *La mujer en la lucha social en la guerra civil de España.* Mexico: Mexicanos unidos, 1974.

Jackson, Gabriel. *The Spanish Republic and the Civil War: 1931–1939.* Princeton: Princeton UP, 1965.

Jacobus, Mary. "The Difference of View." *Women Writing and Writing about Women.* Ed. Jacobus. New York: Barnes, 1979. 10–21.

Joannou, Maroula. "'She Who Would Be Politically Free Herself Must Strike the Blow': Suffragette Autobiography and Suffragette Militancy." *The Uses of Autobiography.* Ed. Julia Swindells. London: Taylor, 1995. 31–44.

Land and Freedom. Dir. Ken Loach. Parallax Pictures, 1995.

Libertarias. Dir. Vicente Aranda. Lola Films, 1996.

Mangini, Shirley. *Memories of Resistance: Women's Voices from the Spanish Civil War.* New Haven: Yale UP, 1995.

———. *Recuerdos de la resistencia.* Trans. Teresa Kennedy. Barcelona: Península, 1997.

Nadie hablará de nosotras cuando hayamos muerto. Dir. Agustín Díaz Yanes. Alta Films, 1995.

Nash, Mary. *"Mujeres Libres": España 1936–1939.* Barcelona: Tusquets, 1976.

Payne, Stanley. *The Spanish Revolution.* New York: Norton, 1970.

Preston, Paul, ed. *Revolution and War in Spain: 1931–1939.* London: Methuen, 1984.

Rabinad, Antonio. *La monja libertaria.* Barcelona: Planeta, 1981.

Sommer, Doris. "'Not Just a Personal Story': Women's Testimonios and the Plural Self." *Life/Lines: Theorizing Women's Autobiography.* Ed. Bella Brodzki and Celeste Schenck. Ithaca: Cornell UP, 1988. 102–17.

Thomas, Hugh. *The Spanish Civil War.* New York: Harper, 1961.

Vivir la utopía. RTVE, Madrid. 1997.

Vindicación Feminista and the Feminist Community in Post-Franco Spain

Margaret E. W. Jones

The first issue of *Vindicación feminista* ("Feminist Vindication") appeared in 1976, at the beginning of the turbulent years of the transition to democracy after Franco's death. Although this journal's short-lived span of three years and its relatively limited sales belie its important place in Spanish women's history, it made a significant contribution to the feminist cause. Its pages offered a counterdiscourse to the rhetoric and policies that were a legacy of the Franco regime: its treatment of uncomfortable or forbidden topics broke the silence of historical and cultural taboos. *Vindicación feminista* dealt directly and unapologetically with issues (politics, civil law, working conditions, women's rights) affecting women in post-Franco Spain.

To understand the impact of *Vindicación feminista* and its radical position, it is necessary to consider its mission in the light of the social and political environment in which it emerged. Official policy and social pressure during the Franco years (1939–75) discouraged feminist activities and isolated the dissidents who questioned the status of females. The government reinforced patriarchal and political norms by rewarding women who assumed the prescribed roles of housewife and mother and by disparaging the independent woman. The official attitude toward women in post–Civil War society had roots in the traditional Spanish culture that had supported patriarchal norms and defined woman as a possession or an object rather than as an individual in her own right. After the Spanish Civil War (1936–39), the Fascist government reversed the advances in women's rights gained by the Second Republic and instituted policies that obstructed change in women's situation for the next several decades. Government regulations curbed economic independence for women, determined the conditions under which women could work outside the home, and offered incentives and rewards to encourage them to marry, have a large family, and stay at home. Civil law treated women as minors who passed from father to husband: they could not have their own bank accounts; they could obtain passports only with the approval of their husbands. Birth control was outlawed and adultery was a crime punishable by a prison sentence for the woman.[1] The Spanish legal system legislated morality with a modern equivalent of the Golden Age honor code that mandated a less severe punishment for an unmarried woman who aborted or killed her newborn child in order to "hide her dishonor" (Arango 215). These and other policies effectively deterred feminist activities during much of the Franco period.

The Franco regime exalted the hierarchical family, understood as a microcosm of the national political structure, with a vertical chain of command that gave complete control and authority to the husband, including clear directives that the wife defer to him in all matters.[2] Propaganda extolled "woman's work" as patriotic service. Pilar Primo de Rivera (director of the Sección Femenina of the Falange Party and sister of the party's founder) gave an impassioned speech in which she declared that "la única misión que tienen asignada las mujeres en la tarea de la Patria es el Hogar" (Gallego Méndez 89) ("the only mission to which women are assigned in the work of our fatherland is the home").[3] This institutionalized sexism provided feminists with a clear agenda for reaction and subsequent—although irregular—action through protests and exposés in the press, in meetings and demonstrations, and in the eventual formation of organizations devoted to women's interests.

Franco's society carefully prescribed the course of a young woman's future. It taught a woman that marriage, not independence, was the highest ideal to which she could aspire. It promised her that sexual innocence and religiosity would attract her ideal husband. The dress code for young women reveals more about this attitude than any single regulation; physical restriction seems to have been the overriding principle. The most important article of clothing was a good, strong girdle; tightly pinned hair was a sign of purity (Martín Gaite, *Usos amorosos de la posguerra española* 133 ["Love Customs of the Spanish Postwar Period"]). In short, the middle-class woman of the period was an object whose life choices, sexuality, and civil rights were dictated by a paternalistic code. She was confined—literally and figuratively—by the norms of a patriarchal system.

Spanish society had no rewarding place for a woman who wished to be independent or remain unmarried; it regarded her with suspicion and caricatured her in the press. The approved choices open to a woman were simple: she could choose a domestic or a religious path. These professions—housewife or nun—ensured that she would be supervised and protected for the rest of her life. Both professions also entailed sacrifice and renunciation, the most admired of virtues, embodied in models like the Virgin Mary, Isabel la Católica (Queen Isabella), Santa Teresa, and other female patron saints of the Falangist ideology. Motherhood was recognized as a kind of Christian martyrdom, as seen in this description published in 1957 in *El ciervo* ("The Stag"): "Se llega a la maternidad por el dolor como se llega a la gloria por la renunciación... Maternidad es continuo martirio. [. . .] Sólo es mujer perfecta la que sabe formarse para ser madre" (Martín Gaite, *Usos* 107–08) ("One achieves motherhood through suffering just as one achieves eternal life through renunciation . . . Motherhood is continual martyrdom. [. . .] Only the woman who can train herself for motherhood is a complete woman").

The influential Sección Femenina of the Falange, the Spanish Fascist party, assumed responsibility for preparing young women for their place in the Spain of the future. Mandatory social service (Servicio

Social) entailed classes in cooking, domestic arts, nutrition, and child care, as well as indoctrination ("formación teórica"), which defined the ideal woman as the uncomplaining helpmate. Girls learned to be cheerful, supportive, self-sacrificing wives, waiting for the return of their husbands to a spotless home and a happy family. Carmen Martín Gaite recalls her days of training with the Sección Femenina:

> Todas las arengas que monitores y camaradas nos lanzaban en aquellos locales inhóspitos [. . .] donde cumplí a regañadientes el Servicio Social, cosiendo dobladillos, haciendo gimnasia y jugando al baloncesto, se encaminaban, en definitiva, al mismo objectivo: a que aceptásemos con alegría y orgullo, con una constancia a prueba de desalientos, mediante una conducta sobria que ni la más mínima sombra de maledicencia fuera capaz de enturbiar, nuestra condición de mujeres fuertes, complemento y espejo del varón.
>
> (*El cuarto de atrás* 93–94)

> All the harangues that our instructors and female comrades subjected us to in those inhospitable buildings [. . .] where I grudgingly did my social service, sewing hems, doing gymnastics, and playing basketball, all turned out to have the same aim: to get us to accept, with pride and joy, with a steadfastness that nothing could discourage, our status as strong women, the complement and mirror of the male, as shown in sedate conduct that would never be clouded by the slightest shadow of slander. (*Back Room* 87)

The national role model for women was Isabella the Catholic: this exemplary queen set the standard for wives and mothers, who also were to defend religion and traditional values.[4]

With strong rhetoric and social programs, the Sección Femenina provided a highly visible and cohesive force for women during the Franco period. It actively defined an "ideal" community of women, united through their specific mission. The socialization process devised by the Sección Femenina had long-term effects beyond its immediate impact.[5] Along with the positive reinforcement of feminine values like submissiveness went a negative campaign against any ideas of self-assertion. As Geraldine Scanlon has documented, high on the blacklist was feminism and its encouragement of independence.[6]

Indoctrination began in early childhood. Textbooks for children glorified religious wars, justified persecutions and Catholic missionary zeal in the name of salvation, and called the overthrow of the secular Second Republic a "crusade." Official history discredited any kind of heterodoxy.[7] Falangist propaganda depicted Spain as a lone crusader, struggling to uphold Catholic ideals that were disappearing in an impious and materialistic world. Proudly affirming that Spain was different, the party would invariably point to the family and women as illustrations of the nation's highest values. A representative article of the period reflects this attitude through rhetoric and encoding that simultaneously defend Spain and affirm the traditional woman's place in it. The cadences of Fascist discourse make the point with heavy-handed sarcasm, thanking heaven for Spain's "backwardness" because she upholds time-honored values that are fast disappearing (e.g., the family as a hierarchical society; marriage as a sacrament and not a plaything).[8]

The regime took full advantage of the mass media's increased ability to enculturate the feminine ideal. Radio—and later television—linked the home to a wider network of normalizing discourses that included the image of the socially acceptable "good woman." As Rosa Franquet has written, the popularization of these media allowed the regime to diffuse its ideologies widely:

> Las tendencias discriminatorias están impregnadas en lo más profundo de las estructuras comunicativas radiofónicas y se han ejercido a lo largo de tantas décadas que han conseguido consolidarse como algo "natural" hasta ser interiorizadas por las propias mujeres. (401–02)
>
> Discriminatory practices are very deeply ingrained in the structure of broadcast communications and practiced for so many decades that they have managed to be consolidated as something "natural," to the point that they have been internalized by the women themselves.

Women's publications—the romantic novel (*novela rosa*) and women's magazines—had the same normative effect.[9] Thus official legislation, the Servicio Social, the Sección Femenina, the broadcast and journalistic media, the traditional educational system, and the pervasive influence of the church designed and imposed an ideal community of Spanish women. The community space was the home; its inhabitants, members of the family. For this reason, both home and family became special objects of scrutiny in feminist writing.

The feminist movement had no such unifying institutions, no official community. Urgent needs of postwar survival delayed immediate resumption of the struggle for women's rights. In addition to the blatant antifeminist reactions of the Franco government, deep-rooted tradition stood in the way of feminist activism.[10] As Lidia Falcón said in 1969, "Se han abandonado y olvidado las luchas feministas, las reivindicaciones de igualdad y progreso para la mujer. Bien es verdad, que la española jamás tomó con verdadero entusiasmo la idea de la equiparación con el hombre" (*Mujer y sociedad* 256–57 ["Woman and Society"]) ("The feminist struggle, the restoration of equality and progress for women have been abandoned. It's quite true that the Spanish woman never really enthusiastically accepted the idea of being equal to men"). Nonetheless, a few committed women continued to address gender issues from various perspectives, as a growing bibliography reveals (see Scanlon; Folguera, *Feminismo*).

In efforts to regroup, feminists began by allying themselves with special interest organizations as an attempt to affect the sociocultural and political climate. They found, however, that restrictions of the post–Civil War period made mobilization on any significant level very difficult, if not impossible; so they channeled feminist activity through organizations such as the illegal Socialist or Communist Parties.

The year of Franco's death coincided with increased feminist activity around the world. The International Women's Year, organized by the United Nations in 1975, the celebration of the I Jornadas por la Liberación de la Mujer (First Women's Liberation Days) in Madrid (also 1975) and two important events in 1976—an international Tribunal of Crimes against Women, in Brussels, and the Jornades Catalanes de la Dona (Catalan Women's Days)—encouraged leaders of the feminist movement and provided the impetus for the formation of new women's interest groups. The various organizations shared common goals only in the widest sense;

they often diverged in membership and priorities—some were political, some extremely theoretical, others more practical in their demand for immediate improvement of specific conditions. The range of organizations is vast and includes branches of the traditional political parties; associations representing various regions or cities; women's groups from neighborhood associations; and associations with specific membership such as university women, divorced women, housewives, or Latin American women. Several organizations rejected the standard procedure of having a president conduct the meeting because it reflected the hierarchical structure of the patriarchy. Instead, they tried to replace the usual system with equal participation, which became time-consuming and difficult to manage. The names of a few representative organizations suggest just how disparate their interests were: the Movimiento Democrático de Mujeres (Women's Democratic Movement), the Asociación Nacional de Comunicación Humana y Ecología (National Association of Human Communication and Ecology), the Moviment de Dones (Women's Movement), the Frente de Liberación de la Mujer de Madrid (Women's Liberation Front of Madrid), LAMAR (Lucha Antiautoritaria de Mujeres Antipatriarcales Revolucionarias [Antiauthoritarian Struggle of Antipatriarchal Revolutionary Women]).

Despite the rise of interest in women's rights during this period, the lack of cohesion within the movement suggests difficulties in creating and maintaining a spirit of community. The formation of numerous women's organizations in the 1970s was proof of the rising interest in feminism, but at the same time, there appeared to be little formal communication or agreement among feminists. The feminist writer and journalist Carmen Alcalde alludes to the lack of cooperation among organizations in which she participated by describing them as "watertight compartments" (Levine and Waldman 29). One book on women in Spanish history offers a more cynical account: in a section entitled "La difícil solidaridad entre mujeres" ("The Problem of Solidarity among Women") the authors say that the movement appeared willful, heterogeneous, disconnected, and "muy expuesta, además, a una refutación seudohumorística" (Voltes and Voltes 171) ("besides, quite open to humorous refutation").

This lack of a cohesive, unified voice to express women's needs doubtless reinforced their isolation and resignation. As Scanlon notes, "Las propias mujeres son en parte culpables de que se les sigan asignando trabajos mal pagados y con poca responsabilidad. [. . .] Las escasas ambiciones de las muchachas son en parte un resultado de la persistencia de actitudes tradicionales" (350) ("Women themselves are partly to blame for being assigned work that is poorly paid and involves little responsibility. [. . .] Girls' low level of ambition is in part a result of the survival of traditional attitudes").[11] Even female activists within the leftist political parties were not united in the feminist project. A disillusioned member of the Communist Party wrote, "Muchas [de las camaradas] se hacen profundamente antifeministas; orgullosas de haber sido aceptadas en el círculo político de los hombres, el recuerdo de la opresión femenina les hiere como un obstáculo a su propia conciencia de mujeres 'liberadas' " (Sardá 104) ("Many women comrades have become deeply antifeminist; they are proud of having been accepted into the men's political circle, and memory of women's oppression pains them and is an obstacle to their awareness of themselves as 'liberated women' ").

Amparo Moreno Sardá's article on feminism in Spain adds a generational component to the list of reasons for the lack of community. Sardá traces disagreements that "ponen de manifiesto no ya sólo las diferencias entre los planteamientos de mujeres de la primera y la segunda generación, sino que también anuncian ya la presencia de mujeres que, nacidas en torno a la década de los cincuenta [. . .] se habían tenido que enfrentar a la autoridad y la mentalidad patriarcal [. . .] en un ambiente ya de crisis" (107) ("show not only differences between the approaches of the first and second generations of women but also proclaim the presence of women who were born during the 1950s and had to face authority and a patriarchal mentality [. . .] in an environment that was already in crisis"). The most serious differences concerned the ideological platform that would determine future courses of action. There were two general directions that Spanish feminism took around the 1970s. One group, the "double militancy" feminists, advocated joining the existing struggle to redress social, economic, and political wrongs. They believed that it would be possible to achieve their aims by working within current frameworks, such as workers' organizations and political parties. The second group, the radical feminists, considered women a separate, oppressed class that suffered from exploitation both by capitalism and by men. They proposed organizations separate from men's groups and from existing party networks; they advocated dismantling traditional family structures that fomented the exploitation of women (Levine and Waldman 84).

All this activity set the stage for a phenomenon that was possible only in post-Franco times: the appearance of *Vindicación feminista* in 1976. This monthly journal assumed the task of creating a rallying point for women and had as a clear objective to provide some kind of unification for the feminist sector. The title itself conveys its objective and direction in its homage to Mary Wollstonecraft's 1792 feminist manifesto, *Vindication of the Rights of Women.*

Two individuals were mainly responsible for the journal's genesis and oversight: Lidia Falcón, lawyer, writer, and tireless social activist, and Carmen Alcalde, author and journalist, who perceptively stated that even before it appeared on the streets, *Vindicación feminista* was already in the minds and hearts of every feminist in Spain (Levine and Waldman 38). The all-woman staff had an impressive roster of regular and occasional contributors. In addition to a number of important lawyers, scholars, and journalists, the list includes figures who are well known in today's literary world, such as Ana María Moix, Rosa Montero, and Cristina Peri-Rossi. Before coming on board as contributors to *Vindicación,* many of these women had already been honored with awards for contributions to their fields.

Falcón hoped that *Vindicación feminista* would foment the community spirit that seemed to be lacking among her contemporaries. In her telling of the history of the journal, Falcón continually mentions its potential for opening the lines of communication among feminists: "Era preciso disponer de la revista que fuera el núcleo de unión de todas las mujeres que quisieran compartir el ideal feminista. [. . . E]l inmediato paso que yo tenía que dar [. . .] era fundar un medio de comunicación entre las mujeres españolas" (Falcón, "*Vindicación*" 54) ("It was necessary to make the journal the unifying nucleus for all women who would like to share in the feminist ideal. [. . . T]he immediate step I had to take [. . .] was to establish some means of communication among Spanish women"). Connecting women to their forgotten history was another way to create a sense of alliance: "*Vindicación* redefinió, redescubrió, reivindicó a las grandes figuras de la literatura y del feminismo internacional que habían sido censuradas y ninguneadas por el régimen franquista" (61–62) ("*Vindicación* reestablished, rediscovered, vindicated the great figures of literature and of international feminism who had been censored and belittled by the Franco regime"). The journal put Spanish women in contact with centers of feminist activity by providing lists and addresses of various national and international groups ("uno de los mejores servicios a nuestras lectoras" [60] ["one of the best services for our readers"]). Falcón adamantly refused to make a pact with other organizations. In her opinion, "Las mujeres debían conquistar su libertad y ellas, *todas, unidas,* alcanzarían sin duda la victoria" (64, emphasis mine) ("Women had to win their freedom and *all, united,* would doubtless achieve victory"). Falcón's sense of urgency is apparent in the militant overtones with which she expresses her mission (i.e., women's unification resulting in eventual freedom).

The cover of the first issue of the journal (1 July 1976) offers a startling visual image that is a statement of its purpose: it is a photograph of a Saharan woman in traditional garb, her veil pulled back, aiming a machine gun. The title reads, "Sahara: Las mujeres luchan por su libertad" ("Sahara: Women Fight for Their Freedom"). A reference to a second article bears the title "Tribunal de crímenes contra la mujer" ("Tribunal of Crimes against Woman"). This cover-page allusion to violence against, and retribution by, women is no coincidence. The two headlines encapsulate the principles that will guide the direction of *Vindicación feminista*: to air issues that had been suppressed for years and to redress problems that were beginning to appear in post-Franco Spain. To this end, the editors designed an ambitious program that would provide women with information and resources.

The first full page, in large type, outlines the principles under which the journal would operate:

> *Vindicación* se propone cubrir el vacío de los medios informativos dedicados a la mujer. Tratar con dignidad sus problemas específicos de promoción laboral y profesional, deficiencias de la legislación civil y penal vigentes, todas las dificultades derivadas de una infraestructura inadecuada para la mayor participación de la mujer en el trabajo asalariado. Discutir, a través de una correspondencia y de un dinámico intercambio informativo, entre las lectoras y nosotras, las situaciones más conflictivas en la familia. Informar, y recibir información, sobre, y de, los movimientos de liberación de la mujer en todo el mundo. Analizar los temas de actualidad política y cultural que nos afecten, de una u de otra forma.
>
> Practicaremos el servicio de una información profunda y paciente sin dejar nunca de lado la óptica irónica, sugestiva y creadora, que nos dará el descubrimiento crítico de ese enorme, ignorado, potencial que encierra el ser de la mujer, nunca totalmente asumido, ni reconocido.
>
> Romper la alienación de los acostumbrados tutelajes. Reconocernos, y hacernos reconocer, hacia el poder y la libertad.

> *Vindicación* intends to fill the vacuum of news dedicated to women. To treat with dignity their specific problems concerning work or professional advancement, shortcomings in civil or criminal legislation now in force, all the difficulties that come from an infrastructure that is inadequate for women's maximum participation in work for pay. To discuss, by means of correspondence and a dynamic and informative exchange between readers and ourselves, the most stressful family situations. To report on and receive information about women's liberation movements throughout the world. To analyze current political and cultural topics that affect us in one way or another.
>
> We will carry out the service of thorough and painstaking news reporting, but we will never depart from the ironic, suggestive, and creative point of view, which will allow us a critical discovery of the essence of woman: that vast, little-known potential that is never completely grasped or understood.
>
> To break down the traditional, alienating power structures. To learn about ourselves and have others learn about us, on our way toward empowerment and liberty.

Vindicacion feminista attempts to teach and sensitize by encouraging the reader to think critically. The sometimes heavy-handed use of sarcasm or parody conveys a sense of indignation in the face of inequities, but more direct approaches induce the reader not to accept reality at face value by demonstrating that tradition—based on unchallenged patriarchal convention—may be neither ethical nor legitimate. Articles on social, legal, and political issues look beyond the current event to search out the deep structures responsible for it. *Vindicación* fulfills its cultural objective with reviews of books, movies, theater, and art that emphasize material of interest to women. It corrects the errors of Francoist historiography by reclaiming individuals, publications, and institutions deliberately or inadvertently overlooked. Many issues examine a single problem, such as divorce, prostitution, women's prisons, or pornography. In these cases, the journal approaches the subject from different perspectives: a relatively objective essay supplies historical and factual information; examples from personal experience and interviews provide human interest. This multifaceted approach invites the reader to identify with the women or the problems discussed on personal, anecdotal, and intellectual levels.

The journal widens the readers' awareness by including international news in short reports or researched articles on specific (usually developing) countries. The stories provide brief historical overviews to lay the foundation for the main topics, which often concentrate on repression, the curtailment of civil rights, or torture; the struggle for independence and revolutionary activities to counteract repression; the effects of colonial hegemony or the self-serving and often aggressive intervention of capitalistic powers in underdeveloped countries. Reports on Rhodesia, Uganda, Lebanon, Ethiopia, and China illustrate these cycles.

Whenever possible, the international sections supply information about women, either as part of a political exposé or as a separate report. Articles about South Africa show the effects of authoritarianism on a human level: the relocation of tribes and subsequent disintegration of families and the crushing poverty that forces black women into prostitution (*Vindicación feminista* 1 July 1976). Essays recount the heroic actions of women who assume responsibility in the struggle for freedom or national independence, undergoing hardships, suffering torture, and risking death side by side with their male counterparts. The sheer number of examples—North Africans, Cubans, Chileans, Argentines—corroborates one of the unstated but obvious goals of *Vindicación feminista*: to break down traditional gender assumptions (in this case, the submissive, helpless female) and, specifically, to portray an alternative to the idea of woman as passive helpmate that had been such a powerful role model under Franco. After celebrating the accomplishments of these brave but anonymous women, the articles reveal the negative side of the story: the aftermath of the struggle, with emphasis on the fate of the women who helped make it happen. All too often, according to the reporters, men are willing to accept women's sacrifice to reach an objective; but once they have established the new political framework, men in positions of power ignore the crucial feminist issues, refuse to grant women access to the power structure, and even go so far as to insist that women resume second-class status. A 1976 study on Cuban women claims that despite their active participation in the revolution, women are still relegated to the traditional areas (1 Aug. 1976); a visit to a kibbutz in Israel surprises a writer who notices that women are still in charge of secondary domestic tasks (1 May 1977). These and other examples reveal hypocrisy and opportunism in the politics of patriarchy. They also provide support for the assumptions of radical feminism and its independent agenda.

While international news undoubtedly encourages the reader to be open to other points of view, the selection of subject matter points to a definite local agenda that a Spanish woman could easily apply to her own situation. The evils of oppression, the profiteering from human and natural resources, the courage of those who rebel against unfair treatment, and the insistence on the worth and dignity of all people emphasize a struggle that is played out on material and theoretical levels.

As would be expected, *Vindicación feminista* devotes most of its space to subjects of national interest. In reviews of current events, the writers criticize those responsible for planning and executing the political changeover after Franco's death. They accuse the liberal parties of disregarding promised reforms and neglecting to include women in the planning sessions. One indignant reporter reveals the political opportunism of the liberals in an article that asks, Where are the women? She shows a photograph of an important political press conference in which no women had been invited to participate ("Oposición"). When election time approaches, the political parties do an about-face, shamelessly trying to attract what one writer sarcastically describes as more than half the voting population. Falcón writes a scathing article about the hostility toward radical feminism, noting that the attacks are coming not from the right, as one would expect, but from so-called progressive leaders who had once paid lip service to women's liberation. Every one of these men, she states contemptuously, "ha tenido sojuzgada una o varias mujeres durante su cómoda vida, y hoy teme estremecido que le deje los platos por fregar, los niños sucios y hambrientos, la cocina apagada y la cama vacía" ("Ofensiva") ("has kept one or more women subjugated during his comfortable life and now is quaking at the thought that the women might leave him with unwashed dishes, hungry and dirty children, a dark kitchen, and an empty bed"). These words are an excellent example of the openly confrontational style of this journal. Its radical tone was a call to arms, but at the same time, it made many people, who should have been sympathetic, uncomfortable and consequently hostile to its aims.

The writers insistently return to the fundamental problem of women's place in society. What about women? Where are they? Where do they fit? And why are they absent from prominent roles? Their marginalization is so ingrained that even the population most affected—women—takes it for granted. The writers dissect complicated legal, political, and religious questions, such as gender discrimination or women's right to control their bodies. Time and again, the journal confronts problems of divorce, adultery, birth control, and abortion, issues that also engage the debate concerning the separation of political, religious, and civil rights in Spanish law. Because of the historically symbiotic relationship between the state and the Catholic Church, what might be considered a purely moral or religious issue enters the public sphere as a political or legal question, backed by the criminal code. Adultery is a case in point. According to the reporter, until the decriminalization of adultery in 1977, the penal code allowed a husband to kill his adulterous wife practically without punishment (Beltrán 22). A woman could expect imprisonment of up to six years for adultery, even if she was separated from her husband; the same standards did not apply to men unless they flaunted their behavior so outrageously that it could not be ignored—for example, if the husband brought his mistress into the home. Since this obvious case of legal discrimination had long been a rallying point for Spanish feminists and since this problem had the potential to affect a large population of women, *Vindicación feminista* returns insistently to the subject, introducing it in many forms: in status reports, documents, editorials, letters to the editor, and in examples of women who have suffered because of these laws.

Prostitution comes under similar scrutiny because of discriminatory legal practices. The writers also use the topic to expose the exploitation of poverty and what *Vindicación feminista* calls the double standard of patriarchal Catholicism. They point out that the prostitute bears full responsibility for this crime, but the client, as he is called, is not implicated in the guilt. A cartoon showing a woman being hauled off to jail while her client tiptoes away, shoes and shirt in hand, illustrates the article (Nuria). By removing the question from a moral category and addressing the financial exploitation of the woman by the pimp or by the client, this essay reiterates one of the most important and controversial points in the journal: revealing and challenging the role of women in a male-controlled economy. The consideration of women as a class and as a gender adds interesting Marxist dimensions to feminist theory, and the debates over class versus gender within feminist groups find their way into the pages of *Vindicación feminista.*

The conventional family structure discourages the wife from work outside the home and simultaneously depreciates her contribution within it. If the value of work is calculated in terms of income generated, then domestic tasks are low in the order of importance and therefore the housewife as worker is in an inferior position. Several articles suggest that real liberation would only be made possible by reconceptualizing the traditional Spanish notion of family. The most radical solution entails a complete redefinition of the family, so that it would no longer be what Falcón calls the primary structure for the economic exploitation of women (Levine and Waldman 72). Articles and case studies of exploitative family situations are not only consciousness-raising exercises; they also support the radical feminist position on the family. One issue devotes a large section to the topic "¿Es trabajo el trabajo doméstico?: De la explotación de 9.057.233 amas de casa" (Estany, Bayo, Falcón, and Alcalde) ("Is Housework Really Work? Concerning the Exploitation of 9,057,233 Housewives"). Another title reads, "Mi marido no me pega, pero tampoco me paga" (Hijar) ("My Husband Doesn't Beat Me, but He Doesn't Pay Me Either"). A regular column ("Recital de ama de casa" ["A Housewife's Speech"]) provides a humorous, ironic glimpse into the realities of domestic life. In one issue, the woman outlines a typical day spent in the car chauffeuring the children to and from their various schools and activities and complains after her husband suggests that she find something to fill her free time:

> ¿Horas libres? ¿Sabes quién hace la compra, limpia la casa, lava y plancha la ropa, y cuida de los niños al regreso del colegio? Yo, taxista sin carnet, ama de casa sin sueldo fijo pero con gastos varios, y compañera, por contrato irrevocable, del cínico de mi marido que me da consejos sobre mis horas libres. (Hijar 48)
>
> Free time? Do you know who does the shopping, cleans the house, washes and irons the clothes, and takes care of the children when they come home from school? Me! An unlicensed taxi driver, a housewife without a fixed salary but with various expenses, and, by irrevocable contract, the companion of that cynical husband of mine who gives me advice about my free time.

Not all articles are such direct calls for activism: some make the reader aware of subtle prejudices and stereotypes. One article, "Niños, a la guerra. Niñas, a la cocina" (Fuentes) ("Boys Go to War, Girls Go to the Kitchen"), details how the consumer society and the mass media reinforce stereotypes with advertising and gender-specific toys like nurse dolls or martial arts uniforms. Another study, "Erase una vez . . ." (Moix) ("Once upon a Time . . ."), analyzes analyzes children's literature during the Franco regime, demonstrating the ways in which behavior and values appropriate to each sex filtered into the tales of such books as *Mi libro rosa de cuentos* ("My Pink Story Book")—for girls—and for boys, *Mi libro azul de cuentos* ("My Blue Story Book"). The difference between expectations for boys and for girls is denounced in an article on women's education, entitled "La gran estafa" (Moreno) ("The Great Rip-Off").

One of the most innovative services that *Vindicación feminista* offers to the mid-1970s public is the open and frank discussion of subjects of a more delicate or private nature. "La terrible nostalgia de no ser ni joven, ni bella, ni lozana" (Sau) ("The Dreadful Feeling of Not Being Young, or Beautiful, or Energetic") compares the aging process and mentality in men and women. An interview with five housewives from different social classes shows that they are united in their loneliness and bitterness about their position in life. Other articles discuss alcoholism in women or spouse abuse ("Mujeres golpeadas: Tortura en el hogar" (Falcón, Bayo, and Sanahuja) ("Battered Women: Torture in the Home"). The thoughtful, direct presentation of subjects that were usually overlooked, or were even taboo in a conservative society, offer solidarity and practical resource information to women who may have been afraid to acknowledge their situation or to seek help. Other articles examine female sexuality, lesbianism, pornography, and prostitution, calling attention to topics relating to the woman's body and subjectivity in a patriarchal system.

Vindicación feminista provides a clearinghouse for meetings, activities, legislation, and publications relating to women's rights both inside and outside Spain. A resource section—"Women of the World"—lists women's organizations, including details of membership, purpose, and addresses. The first issue inaugurates this section by presenting descriptions of sixteen Spanish organizations. Subsequent numbers add to the growing national list, provide similar information about feminist groups outside Spain, and convey a sense of accomplishment and communality to readers who are aware of the isolation that had long characterized Spanish feminism.

Confrontational articles are only one facet of *Vindicación feminista*. Pride in women's accomplishments and recognition of excellence form another regular category. The portraits of noteworthy women, past and present, offer dramatic evidence that successful women do exist. The reclamation of the forgotten or unsung heroines of Spain provides a historical repertory of outstanding women. Various reports describe important contributions by individual women and by women's organizations toward the reforms enacted during the Second Republic or detail the heroic actions of women who took part in the fighting. Some women's names became household words—like Dolores Ibárruri, "La pasionaria"; others are less known, like Lina Odena, who, in 1936, led men to resist Franco's rebels and killed herself rather than be taken prisoner. The alternatives offered in the biographical information help counteract the institutionalized figure of the docile Francoist woman who is content to follow the leadership of men.

Interviews are a constant feature in this journal. Women of accomplishment share their opinions on their life and on feminist issues. The interview format itself creates a more direct and personal bond with the reader. Well-known subjects include the actresses Glenda Jackson and Nuria Espert, the singer Julia León, the French feminist Luce Irigaray, and the poet Gloria Fuertes. These women offer alternatives to traditional gender roles; their triumphs may inspire others to realize that gender does not have to be a barrier to advancement; their example and encouragement send a message of solidarity. A related section entitled "Sin miedo a volar" ("No Fear of Flying"), an obvious allusion to the Erica Jong novel, contains examples of women who were willing to take a chance, to be different, or to assert beliefs contrary to the prevailing ideology: among the roster of women who had no fear of flying are Sylvia Plath, Mary Wollstonecraft, Emma Goldman; and, from Spain, the novelist Emilia Pardo Bazán or the more modern political activist Victoria Kent.

From cartoons to columns, *Vindicación* relies on humor to provide criticism in a lighter vein.[12] By far the most original feature is "Nena no t'enfilis (Diario de una hija de familia)" ("Don't You Dare, Girl: Diary of a Daughter of a Bourgeois Family"), a regular column by the novelist Ana María Moix. Techniques of her fiction—narrative control and manipulation of point of view—spill into her column. Through the clever use of irony and humor, she conveys the feminist message in less harsh terms, insinuating with laughter and hyperbole what other articles accomplish with often strident criticism. The "entries" in the diary describe Ana María's relationship with her fictional family, which, to judge from other sources, is loosely based on her real family. Each month adds another episode in the serial of this amusing, dysfunctional group. With a quick sketch and a few incisive details, Moix creates a portrait that combines stereotype and caricature with human, even sympathetic, touches. The archconservative father, called "El capo," is an ardent admirer of Franco. If anyone could literally incarnate Jacques Lacan's Name-of-the-Father, this would be the man. One brother is a politically active Marxist who despairs because he cannot persuade his sister to read Sartre and Marx but who willingly compromises his lofty principles if it suits his convenience. A second brother is an artist who is blissfully unaware of political or social issues. The mother is a traditional housewife who defers to her husband; though as the series progresses, she develops into a person in her own right and even sneaks off to read a copy of *Vindicación feminista,* much to the exasperation of El capo. An old-style grandmother and a liberal female cousin on a visit from Holland complete the picture of this quirky family at perpetual cross-purposes. Ana María spends her time picking her way through the minefield of family relationships.

Moix's column is appealing because the broad strokes of caricature provoke such a humorous response. But each column has a sketch of a young girl in a birdcage, a reminder that under the veneer of this amusing diary are serious implications: the exposé of a problematic social and cultural history at its most basic level. In this way, the diary joins *Vindicación* in its complaint against the traditional family unit for being oppressive to women's rights. It moves from humorous parody to a sociological editorial by ridiculing Spanish values as represented by a so-called typical bourgeois family.

To provide a forum for discussion and a mechanism for airing differences, the journal's reports of meetings and feminist events, the round-table discussions, and the editorials allow an inside view of the debates that concerned and divided Spanish feminists. The first issue reports on the Jornades Catalanes de la Dona, briefly describing and summarizing—often in unfavorable terms—the conference's papers and sessions, deploring the loud, interruptive display of dissension by men in attendance and particularly by hostile feminist groups. The report ends on a disillusioned note concerning those women who would oppose radical feminism and defend "the interests of men" (Colectivo 21). The confrontational tone of the report illustrates the no-holds-barred policy of addressing questions bluntly and forcefully.

Vindicación feminista keeps its readers current on platforms, changes, and debates, constantly reiterating its commitment to provide "una plataforma de los distintos movimientos e ideologías feministas que luchan actualmente por la liberación de la mujer" (Editorial) ("a platform for the various feminist movements and ideologies that are now fighting for women's liberation"). "Los colectivos feministas se definen" ("Feminist Associations Define Themselves") describes a press conference on feminist theory; an article on neighborhood associations shows still another side of the feminist movement (Pineda).

The issue of 1 March 1977 contains a typical roundtable discussion format that *Vindición* uses to air various perspectives among groups. The piece begins by viewing philosophical differences in a positive light, as a sign of the growing pressure that feminism is exerting on society ("Militantes" 16). Prominent intellectuals and activists, such as Falcón, Nuria Pompeia, and Carmen Alcalde, express their varying positions on women, class, and politics. After considerable disagreement, Empar Pineda and representatives of Mujeres Libres acknowledge, "En cierta forma es imposible meternos todas en una organización feminista, con F mayúscula, porque nuestras creencias difieren" (18) ("In a certain way, it is impossible to fit us all into one feminist organization, with a capital *F,* because our beliefs differ"). But several women, particularly those opposed to radical feminist autonomy, advocate double militancy: they insist that working within a political party to achieve their goals would not vitiate their feminist project (19). Toward the end of the discussion, Falcón sounds a positive note, recognizing that even small groups have differences of opinion: "Nosotras estamos dispuestas a aceptar que dentro del feminismo habrá cinco corrientes, seis, veintiséis [. . .] como hay veintiséis sectores diferentes de proletariados y veintiséis maneras de entender la vida y la lucha" (18) ("We are willing to accept that there might be five, six, twenty-six tendencies within feminism [. . .] just as there are twenty-six different proletariat sectors and twenty-six ways of understanding life and the fight for freedom").

In one of the last issues of *Vindicación feminista,* Falcón wrote an article in which she publicly came to terms with the irreconcilability of so many feminist and antifeminist positions. In "El feminismo ha venido y se ha ido, nadie sabe cómo ha sido" ("Feminism Has Come and Gone and No One Knows What Happened") Falcón's disillusionment is obvious as she outlines the trajectory of feminism in her country. The use of the past tense is significant in this lamentation of lost ideals: "La idílica unión de todas las mujeres en lucha por su emancipación [. . .] resultó mucho más útopica que deseada" (30) ("The idyllic union of all women fighting for their freedom [. . .] turned out to be much more utopian than desired"). Falcón notes the dissolution of various independent groups and bitterly records the ingratitude that she perceives as coming from all sides of the political spectrum (30). The sense of isolation has grown as the number of feminist groups decreases, and political parties do not play an active part in the struggle for women's rights. Finally, Falcón sums up general public opinion in an incident that took place during a speech she was delivering: the audience was discourteous and someone shouted out, "¡Tú a fregar platos!" (34) ("Go home and wash dishes!"). She finishes on a dispirited note with a blow-by-blow description of a case in which she unsuccessfully tried to get political parties and various feminist groups to help a woman who was fined and briefly imprisoned because she attempted to get back her children after their father (to whom she was not married) had taken them from her.

Vindicación lasted only three years in part because, according to Falcón, it was not a profitable venture. In fact, it was never solvent and continued only at the personal expense of a few committed individuals. Another important reason for its termination was the lack of protection or encouragement on the part of individuals and institutions. The journal's radical and confrontational tone alienated those in authority; a considerable percentage of the female population was also disaffected. Not surprisingly, this included the traditional Spanish women of the silent majority. It is rather surprising, though, that some feminists were not supportive because of disagreement with the theoretical bases or the direction of the journal.[13]

For its duration, *Vindicación feminista* provided a challenge to the mainstream social and political pressures on women; it offered Spanish women access to a range of ideas and examples that encouraged critical thought through feminist models, and it enabled identification with feminism in the rest of the world. But if Falcón's aim was to offer *Vindicación* as a permanent forum for a Spanish feminist community, she was unsuccessful. Despite all her efforts, she finally acknowledged the failure of her project:

> [L]as mujeres no se unieron. Siguieron las consignas del poder, de los sindicatos, de los partidos políticos. Cuando llegó la crisis económica, cuando el salvamento de *Vindicación* hacía urgente la ayuda solidaria, el sacrificio económico, los partidos, los sindicatos, las mujeres esperaron con una evidente alegría, su hundamiento. Negaron su colaboración económica, su firma, su solidaridad.
> (“*Vindicación*” 64)

> [W]omen didn't unite. They took their cues from those in power, from the unions, the political parties. When the economic crunch occurred, when solidarity, help, and economic sacrifice were necessary to save *Vindicación*, the parties, the unions, the women waited for it to fail with obvious glee. They refused to help with money, with their name, with their solidarity.

Whatever its value may have been to feminism in the 1970s, for historians of Spanish society the twenty-nine issues of *Vindicación feminista* are a priceless time capsule of information about Spain and about the various directions that feminism was taking during the period immediately following Franco's death. The journal's contents allow a glimpse into Spanish social and political history from the minority perspective of feminism. Indeed, *Vindicación* is valuable because of its role in redressing Spanish history—particularly Spanish women's history—boldly and unsparingly. Despite its limited readership,[14] in providing an open forum and rallying point for many feminist ideologies in the post-Franco years perhaps *Vindicación* served its purpose better than its disillusioned founders believed.

Notes

I would like to thank the University of Kentucky Research Foundation for the fellowship that made research on the subject of this essay possible.

1. Accounts of the injustice of the double standard range from individual testimonials and memoirs to scholarly works on history and sociology. See, for example, Lidia Falcón's discussion in *Mujer y sociedad* (306).
2. Obedience was high on the list of feminine virtues touted by the Sección Femenina (see Scanlon 331–38).
3. Unless otherwise noted, all translations are mine.
4. Martín Gaite says her character "jamás se dio tregua, jamás dudó. Orgullosas de su legado, cumpliríamos nuestra misión de españolas, aprenderíamos a hacer la señal de la cruz sobre la frente de nuestros hijos [. . .] a sonreír al esposo cuando llega disgustado [. . .] a preparar con nuestras propias manos la canastilla del bebé destinado a venir al mundo para enorgullecerse de la Reina Católica, defenderla de calumnias y engendrar hijos que, a su vez, la alabaran por los siglos de los siglos" (*Cuarto* 96) ("never gave herself a moment's respite, never doubted. Proud of her legacy, we would fulfill our mission as Spanish women, we would learn to make the sign of the cross on our children's foreheads [. . .] to smile at our husband when he came home in a bad mood, [. . .] to prepare with our own hands the layette for the baby destined to come into the world to be proud of the Catholic queen, defend her from calumny, and engender children who in turn would extol her, till the end of time") (*Back Room* 89–90).
5. Regarding the Sección Femenina, María Teresa Gallego Méndez commented on "su influencia en las generaciones siguientes y en la pervivencia de valores sociales rígidos y antidemocráticos" (195) ("its influence on following generations and on the survival of rigid, antidemocratic social values").
6. Scanlon's chapter entitled "La 'España Nueva' " (320–56) ("The 'New Spain' ") offers excellent examples of the negative campaign. Martín Gaite protests this antifeminist campaign in her novel *El cuarto de atrás*: "La retórica de la posguerra se aplicaba a desprestigiar los conatos de feminismo que tomaron auge en los años de la República y volvía a poner el acento en el heroísmo abnegado de madres y esposas, en la importancia de su silenciosa y oscura labor como pilares del hogar cristiano" (93) ("Rhetoric in the postwar era was devoted to discrediting the feminist stirrings that had begun in the years of the Republic and stressed once again the unselfish heroism of wives and mothers, the importance of their silent and obscure labor as pillars of the Christian home and family") (*Back Room* 87).
7. The nineteenth century was excised from serious historical consideration because it represented the "anti-Spain," that is—in Franco's words—the "bastardized, Frenchified, Europeanized Spain of the liberals" (Arango 206).
8. See Antonio Castro Villacañas's untitled article in *La hora* (14 May, 1948, n.pag.), quoted in Martín Gaite, *Usos* (29).
9. Martín Gaite (*Usos*) also describes the unrealistic picture of love found in the movies and "women's literature." See her chapter entitled "Nubes de color de rosa" (139–61) ("Pink Clouds").

10. Lidia Falcón's bitter description of the return to traditional values sums up the state of affairs: "El papel de la mujer española volvió a centrarse en el hogar y en los hijos [. . .]. [L]as esforzadas sufragistas que acababan de obtener el voto, de entrar en las universidades, de ver abrirse ante sus ojos las puertas de la diplomacia, de la política [. . .] debieron abandonar sus aspiraciones varoniles para seguir a pies juntillas los dictados de la última moda" (Falcón, *Mujer y sociedad* 310) ("The role of the Spanish woman again centered on home and children [. . .]. [T]he energetic suffragists who had just obtained the vote, entered the university, seen the doors to diplomacy, to politics [. . .] open before their eyes had to abandon their male-oriented aspirations in order to follow firmly the dictates of the latest fashion").
11. Scanlon's comments concern the workplace but are equally applicable to women's attitudes in general.
12. One cartoon underscores the unconscious hypocrisy of progressive men who have no problem separating theory from practice. In the first frame, a young couple takes part in a demonstration for freedom and amnesty; in the second, the husband expansively states, "Juntos, contra el opresor" ("You and me together against the oppressor"); the final frame shows the couple back at their apartment, where the tired demonstrator puts up his feet and reads the newspaper while his disgruntled wife prepares his supper ("Lola").

    "Pepitina," the heroine of a regular comic strip, is a stick-figure sketch of an ill-humored young person who has a habit of taking words, phrases, and cultural codes in their literal sense, then exploding their significance by outrageous reactions. She exasperates her mother by questioning authority and accepting nothing at face value; she gets her friends to rebel against playing with dolls and confuses her teachers with illogical arguments. Her behavior recalls the French feminist practice of deconstructing patriarchal discourse with playful jibes and laughter.
13. Even after the journal ceased publication, Falcón continued her activities on behalf of women. The same year that *Vindicación* stopped, she began another publication, *Poder y libertad,* and founded the Partido Feminista, which was legalized in 1981 and is still in existence. She founded the Vindicación Feminista clubs in Barcelona, and later in Madrid, as places where "women could attend lectures, seek psychological and legal counseling, and simply gather" (Waldman 170). She continues to be a tireless writer, lecturer, and social and political activist.
14. As alluded to previously, Falcón laments that they never averaged the monthly sale of the fifteen thousand issues necessary to be self-supporting ("*Vindicación*" 57).

Works Cited

Arango, E. Ramón. *Spain: From Repression to Renewal.* Boulder: Westview, 1985.

Beltrán, Nuria. "El derecho a: El adulterio." *Vindicación feminista* 1 Aug. 1976: 21–22.

Colectivo Feminista de Barcelona. "Report on the Jornades Catalanes de la Dona." *Vindicación feminista* 1 July 1976: 20–21.
"Los colectivos feministas se definen." *Vindicación feminista* 1 Sept. 1976: 15–17.
Editorial. *Vindicación feminista* 1 June 1977: 5.
Estany, Ana, Regina Bayo, Lidia Falcón, and Carmen Alcalde. "¿Es trabajo el trabajo doméstico? De la explotación de 9.057.233 amas de casa." *Vindicación feminista* 1 Oct. 1976: 29–32.
Falcón, Lidia. "El feminismo ha venido y se ha ido, nadie sabe cómo ha sido." *Vindicación feminista* Sept. 1978 (nos. 26, 27): 29–42.
———. *Mujer y sociedad: Análisis de un fenómeno reaccionario.* 1969. 3rd ed. Barcelona: Fontonella, 1984.
———. "La ofensiva contra el feminismo." *Vindicación feminista* 1 Apr. 1977: 17.
———. "*Vindicación feminista* o el ideal compartido." Introd. Linda Gould Levine. *Revista de estudios hispánicos* 22 (1988): 53–65.
Falcón, Lidia, Regina Bayo, and María Encarna Sanahuja. "Mujeres golpeadas: Tortura en el hogar." *Vindicación feminista* 1 Apr. 1977: 44–46.
Folguera, Pilar. "De la transición política a la democracia: La evolución del feminismo en España durante el período 1975–1988." Folguera, *Feminismo* 111–31.
———, ed. *El feminismo en España: Dos siglos de historia.* Madrid: Iglesias, 1988.
Franquet, Rosa. "Evolución de la programación femenina en la radiodifusión (Los medios electrónicos en la configuración del estereotipo de mujer)." *Literatura y vida cotidiana: Actas de las cuartas jornadas de investigación interdisciplinaria.* Zaragoza: Universidad de Zaragoza, 1987. 396–402.
Fuentes, Gumar. "Niños, a la guerra. Niñas, a la cocina." *Vindicación feminista* 1 Feb. 1977.
Gallego Méndez, María Teresa. *Mujer, falange y franquismo.* Madrid: Taurus, 1983.
Hijar, Marisa. "Mi marido no me pega, pero tampoco me paga." *Vindicación feminista* 1 Mar. 1978: 40.
———. "Recital de ama de casa." *Vindicación feminista* 1 Oct. 1977: 48.
Levine, Linda Gould, and Gloria Feiman Waldman. *Feminismo ante el franquismo: Entrevistas con feministas de España.* Miami: Universal, 1980.
"Lola." *Vindicación feminista* 1 July 1976: 26.
Martín Gaite, Carmen. *The Back Room.* Trans. Helen R. Lane. New York: Columbia UP, 1983.
———. *El cuarto de atrás.* Barcelona: Destino, 1978.
———. *Usos amorosos de la posguerra española.* 3rd. ed. Barcelona: Anagrama, 1987.
"Las militantes: Proceso a las partidos." *Vindicación feminista* 1 Mar. 1977: 16–19.
Moix, Ana María. "Erase una vez ..." *Vindicación feminista* 1 Nov. 1976: 28–39.
Moreno, Amparo. "La gran estafa." *Vindicación feminista* 1 Apr. 1977: 29–37.
Nuria. Cartoon. *Vindicación feminista* 1 Aug. 1976: 32.
"La oposición se reúne en Madrid." *Vindicación feminista* 1 Oct. 1976: 62.
Pineda, Amparo. "Por unas vocalías de mujeres auténticamente feministas." *Vindicación feminista* 1 Dec. 1976: 64.

Sardá, Amparo Moreno. "La réplica de las mujeres al franquismo." Folguera, *Feminismo* 85–110.

Sau, Victoria. "La terrible nostalgia de no ser ni joven, ni bella, ni lozana." *Vindicación feminista* 1 Feb. 1977: 49–51.

Scanlon, Geraldine M. *La polémica feminista en la España contemporánea (1868–1974)*. Trans. Rafael Mazarrasa. Madrid: Akal, 1986.

Voltes, María José, and Pedro Voltes. *Las mujeres en la historia de España*. Barcelona: Planeta, 1986.

Waldman, Gloria Feiman. "Lidia Falcón O'Neill." *Spanish Women Writers: A Bio-Bibliographical Source Book*. Ed. Linda Gould Levine, Ellen Engelson Marson, and Waldman. Westport: Greenwood, 1993. 167–80.

Montserrat Roig: Women, Genealogy, and Mother Tongue

Christina Dupláa

Translated by H. Patsy Boyer

Montserrat Roig (1946–91) has been, without a doubt, one of the Catalan intellectuals most widely known and admired by women who grew up in Spain during the 1970s and 1980s. Her premature death deeply affected several generations of women and men who will remember her always as a great fighter for and defender of all political causes related to human rights.

Roig gave meaning to her everyday life through the art of writing, an art that she used not only to enjoy the play of words but also, fundamentally, to denounce the injustice under which the greater part of humanity lives. She devoted twenty-five years of her brief life to the creation of a complex literary universe made up of feminist essays; woman-centered fiction; the constant presence of her city, Barcelona; and the use of a minority language, Catalan. Like many other women, Roig's participation in the feminist movement of the 1970s shaped her response to androcentric discourse. She was highly conscious of her own marginalized status as a woman and a Catalan in the patriarchal and

Castile-centric society of twentieth-century Spain. She was aware that women are devalued by the dominant culture and that Catalan, like other minority languages of the nation (such as Galician and Basque), exists on the edge of dominant Spanish culture. Roig's solidarity with the marginalized led her to confront the necessity of recovering the memory of women who lived their own reality based on myths and social models that had been created to deny women, in their daily lives, freedom in the world. Such social models and cultural traditions relegated women to the domestic sphere and to absolute silence.

To give voice to so much silence, Roig converted women into protagonists: she interviewed them, researched their lives, and depicted them in her fiction. In a woman-centered modality and through a dialectic of memory and oblivion, Roig created over time a genealogical discourse that gave active meaning to woman's gaze and to the previously obscured importance of women's protagonism in history. As the philosopher Fina Birulés points out in *El género de la memoria* ("The Gender of Memory"), the effects of discrimination against women "se aprecian mucho más en la minusvaloración—cuando no en el olvido—de sus acciones y de su palabra (en su exclusión de la cronología) que en una menor presencia de las mismas en el ámbito público" (10) ("are much more noticeable in the undervaluing—if not in the ignoring—of their deeds and their words [in their exclusion from written history] than in their lesser presence in the public sphere"). The following consideration of the thematic issues at work in Roig's oeuvre demonstrates the author's dedication to reinserting women into history, to recognizing the need to value women's deeds and words, and to validating intellectual production in her mother tongue of Catalan.

Sexual Difference and "The Word's Recovery"

Roig's literary career can be understood in terms of her devotion to creating a genealogy of women's voices. For feminists, the creation of a genealogy represents a striking way to acknowledge the many roles women have played in the shaping of history. Women's authority, according to the philosopher Luisa Muraro, is not synonymous with power but, rather, is present in the politics of women "como principio de orden simbólico" ("as a principle of symbolic ordering") ("Sobre la autoridad femenina" 58) ("On Woman's Authority"). Thus one objective of the creation of a genealogy is to supplant the "victimization" of those who are unaware of women's political presence and symbolic subjectivity both past and present.

"La recuperación de la palabra" ("The Word's Recovery")[1] is the title of the prologue Roig wrote for Antonina Rodrigo's *Mujeres de España (las silenciadas)* ("Women of Spain [the Silenced]"), published in 1979. At that time, Roig had already completed various journalistic pieces collected into a book, testimonial novels, and other narrative fiction. This prologue deserves special attention because, within the general framework of all Roig's work, it could be considered a bridging text between her concern for national identity and her concern for sexual identity. While focused on journalism and on women's personal testimonies in the 1970s, Roig devoted herself to reinserting women into history. Through interviews and conversations with various women, Roig rescued many women's stories from oblivion. In anticipation of later work, some of Roig's publications from this period specifically center on current feminist issues.[2] In her essays from the early 1980s, her reflection on feminism comes to the fore in analyses of the hidden or seemingly invisible reality of women. In 1980, for example, she brought together the interviews conducted in the seventies and published them in *¿Tiempo de mujer?* ("A Woman's World?").

Roig, who understood history as a genealogy and genealogy as a testimony based on remembered reality, saw in Rodrigo's writing the same process of consciousness-raising she herself had experienced. In "La recuperación de la palabra," Roig establishes a point of contact between the discourse of sexual marginalization and that of national (and political) marginalization. She identifies with the women to whom Rodrigo gives voice in her text and especially with the ideological project this text represents. Referring to Rodrigo, Roig writes:

> Es una andaluza que vive en Cataluña, una mujer que ahora escribe sobre dieciséis mujeres. Primero fue la granadina que reflexionó sobre su propia tierra. Luego tuvo que comprender un país bien

> distinto, Cataluña. Y ahora es la mujer que bucea en su propia condición a través de la historia de otras mujeres. (15)
>
> She is an Andalusian who lives in Catalonia, a woman who is now writing about sixteen women. First, the woman from Granada reflected on her own land. Then she had to understand a very different land, Catalonia. Now she is a woman who searches for her own condition in the history of other women.

The genealogical parallelism between Roig and Rodrigo in the evolution of their national consciousness (Catalonia-Andalusia) to a different, more universal one (Catalonia plus Andalusia and Andalusia plus Catalonia) to reach finally a global ideology of feminist thought could be extended to a whole generation of women from the 1970s. As democracy gradually took hold in Spain, those women who at first began with personal identity in relation to their culture then sought it in relation to their gendered reality. The following quotation from the above-mentioned prologue is typical of this leap toward sexual consciousness and the ideological acceptance of feminism's interclass foundations:

> Dieciséis mujeres que saben muy bien que sólo la libertad colectiva les va a liberar como mujeres. Pero que no ignoran que incluso los hombres que más aman la libertad se azoran y se quedan perplejos al descubrir en sí mismo, gracias a la lucha de las mujeres, un buen tanto por ciento de opresor. (16)[3]
>
> Sixteen women who know well that only a collective freedom will free them as women. But they are not unaware that even the men who most cherish freedom are perplexed and astonished to find in themselves, thanks to the women's struggle, a significant amount of the oppressor.

In theoretical and analytical terms, the recuperation of women's words leads Roig to consider women's role in their own oppression and silence. Insofar as the author deals with historical material, feminist concerns, and the intersection between complicity and oppression, the prologue is emblematic of much of Roig's other work.

The lack of a complete history in which women can find their space and speak in the first person is what leads Roig and Rodrigo to write testimonial texts. The hegemony of the patriarchy falters and gives way to a different voice and to a new reality in these texts: both writers concern themselves with their perception of history as a genealogical process and devote themselves to making connections among the heretofore silent, marginalized voices. As Roig points out in "La recuperación de la palabra," "nuestras vidas ya no parecen tan efímeras. Con la recuperación de la palabra de los demás nuestra vida es menos muerte" ("our lives no longer seem so ephemeral. With the recovery of the word of others, our life is less dead"). To which Rodrigo adds, "Si no hablamos nosotras de nosotras, ¿quién lo va a hacer?" (12) ("If we women do not speak about ourselves, who is going to do it?").

It is very honest for Roig to indicate in her prologue that "Antonina, esta vez, ha escogido muy bien las palabras para contarnos 'su' verdad" (12) ("Antonina has, in this instance, chosen the words to tell us 'her' truth well"). It is evident that the voice we are reading is Rodrigo's and not that of the women she presents as examples of sexual marginalization within the patriarchal paradigm. As revealed in Roig's careful choice of words, this appropriation of others' stories allows Rodrigo to give voice not only to herself and her interpretation of women's reality but also to many women's voices.

The women in Rodrigo's text are presented as individual subjects and also—and this is the most important aspect of the testimonial nature of the work—as spokespersons for a silenced collectivity that is seeking a space for its own voice in Spain's public sphere. Roig addresses the issue of women's subordination to a dominant "History" in these words:

> Para superar nuestra incapacidad para expresarnos, para dominar la "sabiduría" de los hombres, la ciencia, para dominar, en suma, el universo, hacen falta años, quizás siglos, y sobre todo, las palabras de las que nos han predecido, de las grandes olvidadas, de las que descubrieron mucho antes que nosotras que la Historia ha sido fabricada por los hombres [. . .]. (13)

> Overcoming our inability to express ourselves, mastering the "wisdom" of men, the knowledge, in short mastering the universe, will take years, maybe centuries, and especially necessary are the words of those women who preceded us, the great forgotten ones, who

> discovered long before we did that History has been constructed by men [. . .].

This paragraph captures Roig's belief in the authority and influence of the women who preceded her. Like Rodrigo, Roig recognizes the importance of these women through her advocacy of the establishment of a specifically feminine genealogy that will help restore women to historical memory. As Montserrat Otero Vidal points out, we need to recognize other women's "capacity and power to grow and to create" ("Autoritat femenina" 113) ("Feminine Authority"). This desire to speak in the first person and to describe the world from the feminine perspective is fundamental to feminist thought on sexual difference; to recover the word is to accept an existence explained by its protagonists.

The question of what it means to speak from a feminine perspective is fraught with issues of national and sexual politics for Roig. As I discuss at length in the latter part of the essay, Roig reveals throughout her work that she is speaking as a woman as well as a Catalan, although she never develops this thinking at a theoretical level. Specifically, her work rebukes any definite duality in identity politics, explaining her belief in sexual difference as "[d]ejar de existir para lo uno, siendo lo otro" (*¿Tiempo?* 154) ("ceasing to be the one while being the other"). She posits this "being the other" through the acceptance of difference rather than an androgynous equality. Roig's model of equality involves a critique of patriarchy's requirement that to participate in the public sphere women must be virile. That is, she sees patriarchy as forcing women to strip themselves of their femininity and of their private life to serve in the public sphere: "En el mundo de los hombres, a esas mujeres se les acepta que desarrollen un rol tradicionalmente definido como 'masculino' mientras renuncien a ser 'mujeres' " ("Recuperación" 18) ("In the world of men, those women are accepted who play a role traditionally defined as 'masculine' while renouncing their identity as 'women' "). A firm believer in women's fundamental difference from men, Roig is fiercely critical of the sacrifices required of women to gain acceptance in the dominant culture.

In her essays and in her fiction, Roig stresses that there is a way of seeing and a way of being a woman that distances her from the symbolic order created by androcentric thought. In *L'hora violeta* ("The Violet Hour"), the last novel in her trilogy focused on women (the other two are *Ramona adéu* ["Farewell, Ramona"] and *El temps de les cireres* ["Cherry Season"]), the plot is based on a discussion of feminism by two of the three primary female characters. By 1980, in other words, the scales of Roig's consciousness had clearly tipped toward the identity expressed by her own body. It is when she discovered this reality that she became explicitly concerned with giving voice to other women.

Women Speaking for Themselves

Roig's concern for the specificity of women's experiences is a guiding force in the volume of collected essays, also published in 1980, *¿Tiempo de mujer?* As the question marks indicate, the author expresses her doubts about women's continued marginalization. A later expression of this problem appears in her 1991 essay *Digues que m'estimes encara que sigui mentida* ("Tell Me You Love Me Even Though It Is a Lie"):

> El ojo exterior de la mujer ve un mundo con la ilusión de que es el mundo. Con la ilusión, también, de que ella es "libre e igual." Ve lo mismo que los demás, ya no se la margina de la cultura, ya no se le prohibe la entrada a la universidad. La televisión ha democratizado el espectáculo. Pero, ¿Quién construye el espectáculo? (89)

> The external eye of a woman sees a world with the illusion that it is the world. Also with the illusion that she is "free and equal." She sees the same thing everybody else does, no longer is she on the margins of culture, no longer is she denied access to the university. Television has democratized the show. But who constructs the show?

As the allusions to contemporary culture and society suggest, Roig's probing critique of women's place in a changing world found its roots in women's everyday experiences. In *¿Tiempo de mujer?*, as indicated on the book jacket, "se recopilan artículos, entrevistas y reflexiones que constituyen datos, pistas y testimonios acerca de cómo es este tiempo para las mujeres, y de cómo son las mujeres de este tiempo" ("articles, interviews, and reflections are collected that provide information, clues, and testimonies about what these times are like for women and what the women of these times are like"). Roig relies on the support of another intellectual, Laura Tremosa, who, beginning with her own personal experience and a narrative "I," will legitimize Roig's text in the prologue. The relationship previously described between Roig and Rodrigo is being repeated. It is a relationship that, in ideological terms, confirms the understanding of history as testimonial genealogy and, in textual terms, affirms the formal need to direct the testimonial reading. Roig plays with the intertextuality of the prologue and with a preestablished goal: to make male and female readers reflect on the text and recognize that they, as modern men and women, are part of the story.

In explaining her experience, Tremosa reviews the stages that marked her own life and that, as the feminist historian María-Milagros Rivera Garretas points out in her study on feminist thought, helped her "pensar en otros términos la experiencia personal de vivir en un cuerpo sexuado en femenino" (*Mundo* 62) ("to think in other terms the personal experience of living in a body sexed as female"). Tremosa's life moves through the stages of confronting the option to be "superwoman"; acknowledging the lack of women's history and of a gendered memory; and reflecting on one's genealogy and coming to an awareness of "being a woman," of "being different" (15–16). Tremosa describes this awareness about her connections with women in her family in the prologue:

> A mis treinta y cuatro años, una noche, sola en mi dormitorio, se desmoronó el mito de la supermujer y me di cuenta de que era una más, atrapada por el rol que me correspondía en este mundo de fuertes y débiles, tan exiliada del mundo de fuera como lo fue mi madre, mi abuela y las mujeres que me habían precedido y que había llegado a odiar. (16)

> At age thirty-four, one night, alone in my bedroom, the myth of superwoman collapsed and I realized that I was one more woman, trapped by the role given me in this world of the strong and the weak, just as exiled from the larger world as my mother, my grandmother, and all the other women who lived before me and whom I had come to hate.

This silenced history and this sense of alienation of life for many women, combined with their ongoing frustrations down through the generations, offer an informative vision of a reality from which social history as well as women's history can benefit. Tremosa describes reality from a female perspective, showing as constants the lack of connection with masculine public life and especially the boredom and lack of love that many women endure. Not surprisingly, Tremosa's and Roig's narratives are difficult to characterize and study from the standpoint of traditional literary criticism. The way in which these women and their sisters and foremothers, who remain anonymous in patriarchal history, are given a voice suggests that new kinds of women-centered discourses are needed to break down the barriers that separate women's history from men's and, more immediately, that silence women's experiences.

Like Roig, Tremosa accepts the feminist challenge to politicize personal experience, and she praises the fact that Roig's interviews are based on speaking from the feminine "I" to recover the silenced word. For theoretical analysis of literary texts, this implies the recovery of oral discourse and of forms of expression based on alterity. Jean Franco recognizes this implication and poses the problem from the position of the intellectual devoted to gathering information. Franco speaks of the value of the testimonial as the discourse of the subaltern: "The question implicit in these texts is how to make the subaltern or marginalized woman speak within the hierarchy inherent in the position of the interlocutor" (109).

In *¿Tiempo de mujer?* there are various interviews and articles related to women and their struggle to achieve egalitarian treatment without giving up their feminine identities.[4] This mix represents, perhaps, a healthy effort to combine the feminine with the feminist, although this effort on the part of 1980s feminists was not well understood. Unlike France, where body-focused feminism was advocated by feminists in the 1970s, in Spain it took more than twenty years for feminists to overtly reinsert the feminine in feminism and to be able to speak of both terms in a climate of freedom. Since the 1990s the power of the connection between the feminine and the subversive capacity of a woman's body in the patriarchy has been widely recognized. Indeed, many women in the

1990s pointed out that this connection had a political value of unimaginable consequences. The implications of calling attention to women's difference had once again become part of the political scene, as we saw in the winter of 1995 when the Algerian Jalida Toumí, president of Triunfo de las Mujeres (Triumph of Women), protested the assassination of women in Algiers by Islamic fundamentalists and issued the following international call to denounce the murders: "mientras la persecución de mujeres no sea considerada una persecución política, el mundo será cómplice de los gobiernos que instauran el terrorismo de Estado" (qtd. in Mederos) ("as long as the persecution of women is not considered political persecution, the world will be an accomplice to those governments that practice state terrorism"). The connection between body and politics has also been made by the sociologist Marina Subirats, who asserts that "todas las mujeres conservamos en nuestro cuerpo (física y psíquicamente) las marcas de la discriminación") ("all women bear in our bodies [physically and psychologically] the marks of discrimination").[5]

Roig also grounds her perspective on women's worth in bodily difference, as she makes clear in her position on the dangers of androgynous egalitarianism in *¿Tiempo de mujer?* As a writer she struggles to find her language and her woman's gaze in fiction and in life. She intuits the need to create a different symbolic order, and she appreciates the conciliatory capacity offered by feminism as a theoretical position:

> El feminismo te reconoce el trabajo que has hecho como mujer durante siglos. Le da prestigio. Te reconoce la edad de oro, el reposo del guerrero. Has acumulado virtudes desprestigiadas socialmente, pero envidiadas por los humanistas: el desamor al poder, por ejemplo. Dicen que siglos de acumular sacrificio y resignación han hecho emerger la ternura. Te dicen, la ternura es gratuita. ¿Perderemos estas "virtudes" con la lucha feminista? ¿son corrupción la historia y la cultura? El *tempo* de las mujeres no es el *tempo* de los hombres. La historia de las mujeres no pasa por los mismos hitos cronológicos que la de los hombres. (27)
>
> Feminism recognizes the work you have done as a woman over centuries. It gives it prestige. It recognizes your golden age, the

> warrior's repose. You have accumulated virtues socially devalued but lauded by humanists: disinterest in power, for example. It is said that centuries of sacrifice and resignation have given rise to tenderness. They say tenderness is free. Are we going to lose these "virtues" in the feminist struggle? Are history and culture corrupt? The *time* of women is not the *time* of men. The history of women does not go through the same chronological stages as men's history.

One indisputable point of difference between the stages of men's and women's lives, of course, is the role of motherhood in women's experience. On this subject, Roig has always been very eloquent in affirming that "ellos tienen tanta envidia de nuestra maternidad que han fabricado la guerra y la muerte. Ellos dependen de nuestro cuerpo" (*¿Tiempo?* 28) ("men are so envious of our maternity that they have invented war and death. They depend on our bodies"). Of course, this statement is tantamount to saying that one way of controlling women's work (i.e., reproduction) is to perpetuate war (i.e., destruction of that work). These positions explain Roig's grave concern about women who reject their biology and who do not accept their bodies:

> Mujeres que no quieren oír hablar de un parto, de un embarazo. Que se marean al oír hablar de ovarios o de matriz. Hay mujeres que creyéndose "liberadas" se transforman y son incapaces de hablar de esos temas con objetividad. Otras que creen haber superado la biología a base de olvidarla. Que han renunciado a los hijos por disfraces culturales, cayendo en la trampa tendida, la que nos obliga constantemente a elegir entre ser "mujer" y ser "persona." (82)

> Women who refuse to hear about birth, about pregnancy. Who get sick at the mention of ovaries or the uterus. There are women who, even believing they are "liberated," change completely and are incapable of discussing these topics objectively. And others who believe they have overcome biology by ignoring it. Who have given up their children for cultural disguises, falling into the trap that makes us constantly choose between being a "woman" and being a "person."

With regard to this process of feminist consciousness-raising and acceptance of the female body, Roig herself acknowledges that at first she wanted to have a baby boy because she believed that this would help her achieve (by proxy) some of the power denied to women. Thanks to her reading of feminist texts, she soon realized that "al no querer una hija, lo que hacía era despreciarme terriblemente a mí misma, a mi sexo" (*¿Tiempo?* 75) ("by not wanting a girl, what I was doing was devaluing myself and my sex terribly"). The symbiosis between being a "person" and being a "woman," that is, between being equal but different, is pervasive in *¿Tiempo de Mujer?* and in all of Roig's work. It is, perhaps, in the chapter titled "¿Por qué no ha habido mujeres genio?" ("Why Haven't There Been Women Geniuses?") where we can see a clear intellectual and political defense of difference.

For Catherine Davies in *Contemporary Feminist Fiction,* Montserrat Roig and Rosa Montero support a feminism that is not radical, which, according to Davies, is the equivalent of saying that they do not favor a feminism of difference:

> Nor is their feminism overtly psychological, nor the feminisms associated with the better known French theorists, nor lesbian feminism. Generally speaking, they tend towards hetero, socialist, and political feminist positions. (10)

But Davies also recognizes there are works of fiction published in 1980, like Roig's "Mar" ("Sea"), that can be read from the perspective of sexual difference. Once again it is clear that our reading of Roig's texts is a reading that derives from our own subjectivity, which can be as contradictory as the author's.

Regardless of how one might classify or define Roig's feminist positions, there can be no doubt that the collection of texts compiled in *¿Tiempo de mujer?* (where Roig mentions women of varied feminist or political positions, including Juliet Mitchell, Adrienne Rich, Simone de Beauvoir, and Kate Millett) had strong ideological influence on the Spanish women of her generation. Because of its direct engagement with feminist ideology and its concern with women's past, present, and future roles in society, this book forms an important part of the history of late-twentieth-century Spanish feminism.[6]

Women and Humanism: A History of Feminism

Roig's direct engagement with feminist issues and the construction of female genealogies continued well beyond *¿Tiempo de mujer?* In 1981, for example, she published a history of feminism entitled *Mujeres en busca de un nuevo humanismo* ("Women in Search of a New Humanism").[7] This text is part of a series designed for the general public and is strictly informative and historicist. The first chapter generally explains the logic underlying feminist thought so as to rid it of the taboo that might make it seem dangerous to ordinary men. It is a text, according to my reading, intended for newcomers to the subject and also meant to demystify the grotesque views of feminism and of feminists created by the dominant, patriarchal culture. Roig's knowledge of the theoretical and political debates of the 1970s allows her to speak of topics that, even today, continue to be debated: the recovery of the word, of individual and collective history—that is, women's testimonial voice—of knowledge about one's own sex, and of a profoundly different reality that belongs to women's historical memory (*Mujeres* 5).

Again Roig insists on highlighting the importance of being aware of a female reality that legitimizes a historical past lived by women but silenced by the history "written by men," and supported from ancient times by certain groups of women who have refused to accept their position (*Mujeres* 8). Using informative documents and supporting photographs to accompany the text, the Catalan writer presents an essay based on what women who have accepted their identities as women have accomplished and continue to accomplish. The chapters, organized into five parts that study the history of feminism, the world of ideas, and contemporary women, are based on recognition of the political work and "vindication of the rights of women," as some would have it, down through history. Clara Zetkin, Aleksandra Kollontay, Rosa Luxemburg, Betty Friedan, and once again Millett and Beauvoir are cited in this construction of a genealogical memory.

In 1981 Roig identified the limits of the feminist struggle for equality, stressing those elements that go beyond and challenge every aspect of the patriarchy. Nevertheless, for Roig, this questioning still does not imply the need to think of a symbolic world at the margins of the patriarchy, but rather it is an effort to make hegemonic discourse accept otherness, a category that includes sex, race, class, and national identity. By now, some of the chapters in Roig's history of feminism may have been superseded by such decisive political events as the fall of Communism in Eastern Europe or the evolution of Spanish law and its effects on equality between the sexes. If some political and social change has occurred since Roig first began writing, one area of her ideological framework that continues in its importance and must be taken into account is the ongoing struggle for recognition of writing in the minority language of Catalan.

Minority Language and Feminism

The schizophrenia of writing narrative fiction in Catalan and editorials in Castilian constituted a significant dimension of Roig's professional development. Given that journalism written in Catalan was virtually nonexistent during the 1970s and was still limited during the 1980s, Roig's language choice can be seen as being imposed on her by necessity. The writer's preference was to write in her mother tongue, the language she learned from her family. As Roig explained in an interview with Geraldine Cleary Nichols in *Escribir, espacio propio* ("Writing, One's Own Space"): "he pertenecido a una familia muy catalana en donde desde los cuatro años he leído en catalán" (147) ("I belonged to a very Catalan family, where I read in Catalan beginning at age four"). From early childhood, Roig viewed Castilian as the language imposed in the public sphere (school) and as a language required by her professional life (journalism). Catalan was used by choice, however, for the more intimate communications of her life, both with her family and in her literature.

Interestingly, when Roig turned to Catalan as her language of choice, she recognized that her hold on the language had lost the written vigor of spontaneity because of the lack of intellectual continuity it had suffered for decades. Roig was aware of this reality. In her first book of short stories, *Molta roba i poc sabó . . . i tan neta que la volen* (1971) ("Lots of Clothing, Very Little Soap . . . and They Want It So Clean"), she points out this problem in the prologue: "Escric en una llengua a mig néixer i visc entre el caos i la solitut" (7) ("I write in an emerging language and I live between chaos and solitude"). Finding modern literary models was not an easy task either, since literature in Catalan preceded the Spanish Civil War. And with regard to the reception of her works, the choice of writing in a minority language poses a great risk since the generations born during the Franco period are illiterate in Catalan. Roig's ability to learn to write the language at an early age in her family environment is an exceptional case. What was more common during Roig's childhood was the oral transmission of Catalan between parents and children, but this remained far from achieving linguistic normalization at all levels. In the area of literature, such normalization comes from intellectuals who combine their literary activities with movie reviews, translations, conferences, and interviews, for example.

After having been asked repeatedly in many interviews why she used Catalan in her literary pursuits and in some newspaper articles, Roig roundly states in her essay *Digues que m'estimes* that she writes in Catalan for three reasons: "Primer, perquè és la meva llengua; segon, perquè és una llengua literària; i tercer, escric en català perquè em dóna la gana" (28) ("First, because it is my language; second, because it is a literary language; and third, I write in Catalan because I feel like it"). It is important to highlight this defense of Catalan because scholars of Hispanic literature, in general, read Roig in Castilian translation. She is studied as part of the generation of women writers of contemporary Spain, and seldom is the linguistic aspect mentioned. The abnormality suffered by minority languages without the protection of the state takes the form of an exaggerated insistence on the subject or of overlooking its significance altogether. Just as no one questions why a French, English, or Spanish woman writes in French, English, or Spanish, neither is a Norwegian, Swedish, or Danish writer asked why she uses her own language. The first group writes in majority languages, and the second in minority languages protected by state boundaries. But what unites most writers (including the Catalans) is that they write in their mother tongue.

In Nichols's book of interviews, authors address the topic of bilingualism or, more aptly, the linguistic choices in the literature written by

Catalan women. In the case of Roig it is important to stress that her literature connects with a Catalan literature written by men and by women—which demonstrates that the linguistic element is key—and not with a tradition of women's literature written in Castilian. This raises the question of what is more powerful for Roig: the reality of being a Catalan woman or the reality of being a woman? The following excerpt from Nichols's *Escribir, espacio propio* is illustrative:

> NICHOLS: "¿Cómo te ves en relación a una escritora en castellano contemporánea tuya como Esther Tusquets?"
>
> ROIG: "[. . .] generacional o temáticamente puedo estar más cerca de una Esther Tusquets que de una Mercè Rodoreda. Aunque tenga diez años más que yo Esther Tusquets vivió una influencia parecida a la mía; vivimos una Barcelona, un entorno parecido. [. . . L]o que pasa es que literariamente yo he buceado siempre en unas preocupaciones lingüísticas muy esctrictas, que no eran lógicamente las mismas que las de ella." (147)
>
> NICHOLS: "How do you relate to a contemporary Catalan writer like Esther Tusquets, who writes in Castilian?"
>
> ROIG: "[. . .] both generationally and thematically I feel closer to an Esther Tusquets than to a Mercè Rodoreda. Even though Esther Tusquets is ten years older than I am, she lived in an environment similar to mine; we lived the same Barcelona, the same events. [. . . W]hat is going on is that literarily I have explored clearly defined linguistic concerns that have not been the same as hers."

In literary terms, the ones who had the most impact on her were Mercè Rodoreda and, to a lesser extent, but often mentioned by Roig, Josep Pla. Regarding personality and ideology, Maria Aurèlia Capmany was her great teacher.

In the issue of *Catalan Review* that Jaume Martí-Olivella dedicated to Capmany and Roig, the editor published one of the more illustrative studies of the catalanism-feminism question as markers of a double marginalization and difference in Catalan women writers. In "L'escriptura femenina catalana: Vers una nova tradició?" ("Catalan Women's Writing: Toward a New Tradition?"), Martí-Olivella reviews the works by Nichols,

Kathleen McNerney, and Anne Charlon together with the feminist theorists who defend the concept of "l'écriture femenine." He raises the following question about the need to respect differences among writers:

> Vet aquí, doncs, la contradicció com pot mantenir-se viva una llengua minoritària, la catalana, si hom assumeix la "indiferència" d'escriure en català o en castellà en nom d'una nova tradició—la feminista—que, insisteixo, està basada en el concepte del respecte a la diferència? (207–08)
>
> This, then, is the contradiction: How can a minority language, Catalan, be kept alive if one is "indifferent" about writing in Catalan or in Castilian in the name of a new tradition—feminism—which, I insist, is based on the concept of respect for difference?

The question raised by Martí-Olivella has been present in the reflections of Roig, Carme Riera, Maria-Antònia Oliver, and other women writers throughout their careers. That they have chosen their mother tongue to give voice to women's previously silent stories and that this mother tongue was silenced by the Spanish state show, as I see it, that it is hard in certain historical periods to find a single definition of one's personal and political identity. During those years of transition to democracy in Spain, what is more decisive: identification with the struggle for national freedoms in Catalonia or the struggle for women's liberation? Perhaps they are struggles that arose simultaneously and that over the years have come to occupy a specific place in the identity of each of these women writers. Even understanding the problem of double marginalization that it implies, these women have made the choice to write in Catalan, purely and simply because it is their mother tongue.

Along with other women writers in Catalan of this century—such as Dolors Monserdà, Carme Karr, and Capmany—Roig sought in history and in everyday life a specifically female reality that would redress the narrow feminine models promulgated by Catalan nationalist discourse and by Francoism.[8] The testimonies of these writers and of the women whom they wrote about and interviewed are clear proof of this effort. For the philosopher Françoise Collin, the unification of past and present feminisms "al conceder a las mujeres el estatuto de agentes de su propia existencia y de la existencia colectiva, ha modificado las condiciones y el sentido de la transmisión que éstas asumen" (155) ("on granting women the status of being agents of their own existence and of a collective existence has changed the conditions and the meaning of the transmission that these have taken on"). Calling on another woman to participate and intervene is to accept the symbolic authority of women of the past; it is also an acknowledgment that we are not beginning at ground zero in the present. Like many authors before her, Montserrat Roig recognized that women have a genealogical chain that legitimizes our intellectual production, political engagement, and personal struggles.[9]

Notes

This essay is dedicated to Rosa, a dear friend.

1. Most of the translations of Roig's titles are taken from Geraldine C. Nichols's entry on Montserrat Roig in *Spanish Women Writers: A Bio-Bibliographical Source Book.*
2. An example is Roig's great testimonial novel, *Els catalans als camps nazis* ("Catalans in Nazi Camps"), published in 1977.
3. The women Antonina Rodrigo treats in her text are Dolores Ibárruri, María Goyri, María Blanchard, Victoria Kent, Antonia Mercé, Zenobia Camprubí, Margarita Xirgu, María de Maeztu, Federica Montseny, María Luz Morales, Margarita Nelken, María Teresa León, María Casares, Enriqueta Otero Blanco, Maruja Ruiz, and Carmen Conde.
4. The Jornades Catalanes de la Dona held in 1976 following Franco's death are without a doubt one of the most important events in the Spanish, and especially the Catalan, feminist movement. Symbolically this event marked the beginning of a new stage in the modernization of Spanish society, particularly of the legislation that still relegated women to a position clearly inferior to men's. As evident in *¿Tiempo de mujer?* this event and these years were decisive in the development of Roig's own feminist awareness and her essays on the subject.
5. Subirats's words were cited in the closing remarks of the Women, Work, Health Conference in Barcelona, 24–25 February 1995.
6. Some of the texts included in *¿Tiempo de mujer?* had appeared during the 1970s in such diverse publications as *Vindicación feminista, Penthouse, La vanguardia, Cuadernos para el diálogo, Tele-eXpres, La calle,* and *Mundo.* As to Roig's influence, in Almería I witnessed one example of the intellectual and human legacy Roig left to many women of her own and subsequent generations. In February 1995 the Assembly of Women of Almería filled a local theater for an act of homage to Roig.

7. The 1984 edition of *Mujeres* is entitled *El feminismo* ("Feminism").
8. In 1910 Monserdà wrote *Estudi feminista.* Karr was the original editor of *Feminal,* which was founded in 1907. Capmany published *El feminisme a Catalunya* in 1973.
9. Parts of what I have written in this essay correspond to the ideas dealt with in my book *La voz testimonial de Montserrat Roig: Estudio cultural de los textos* ("The Testimonial Voice of Montserrat Roig: A Cultural Study of Her Texts").

Works Cited

Birulés, Fina, ed. *El género de la memoria.* Pamplona-Iruña: Pamiela, 1995.

Capmany, Maria Aurèlia. *El feminisme a catalunya.* Barcelona: Nova Terra, 1973.

———. "Montserrat Roig, ofici i plaer de viure i escriure." *Cultura* (1991): 14–26.

Charlon, Anne. *La condició de la dona en la narrativa femenina catalana (1900–1983).* Barcelona: Edicions 62, 1990.

Collin, Françoise. "Historia y memoria o la marca y la huella." Birulés 155–70.

Davies, Catherine. *Contemporary Feminist Fiction in Spain: The Work of Montserrat Roig and Rosa Montero.* Oxford: Berg, 1994.

Dupláa, Christina. *La voz testimonial en Montserrat Roig: Estudio cultural de los textos.* Barcelona: Icaria, 1996.

Franco, Jean. "Si me permiten hablar: La lucha por el poder interpretativo." *La voz del otro: Testimonio, subalternidad y verdad narrativa.* Lima: Latinoamericana Editores, 1992. 109–16.

Martí-Olivella, Jaume. "L'escriptura femenina catalana: Vers una nova tradició?" *Catalan Review* 7.2 (1993): 201–12.

McNerney, Kathleen, ed. *On Our Own Behalf: Women's Tales from Catalonia.* Lincoln: U of Nebraska P, 1988.

Mederos, Alicia. "Los integristas consideran el cuerpo de la mujer un símbolo de oposición." *El País* 20 Mar. 1995: 6.

Monserdà de Macià, Dolors. *Estudi feminista: Orientacions pera la dona catalana.* Barcelona: Gili, 1910.

Muraro, Luisa. "Sobre la autoridad femenina." Birulés 51–63.

Nichols, Geraldine Cleary. *Escribir, espacio propio: Laforet, Matute, Moix, Tusquets, Riera y Roig por sí mismas.* Minneapolis: Inst. for the Study of Ideologies and Lit., 1989.

———. "Montserrat Roig (1946–1991)." *Spanish Women Writers: A Bio-Bibliographical Source Book.* Ed. Linda G. Levine, Ellen E. Marson, and Gloria F. Waldman. Westport: Greenwood, 1993. 429–40.

Otero Vidal, Montserrat. "Autoritat femenina i participació política." *DUODA: Revista d'Estudis Feministes / Revista de Estudios Feministas* 7 (1994): 111–17.

Rivera Garretas, María-Milagros. *Nombrar el mundo en femenino: Pensamiento de las mujeres y teoría feminista.* Barcelona: Icaria, 1994.

Roig, Montserrat. *Els catalans als camps nazis.* Barcelona: Edicions 62, 1977.

———. *Digues que m'estimes encara que sigui mentida.* Barcelona: Edicions 62, 1991.
———. *L'hora violeta.* Barcelona: Edicions 62, 1980.
———. "Mar." *Carnets de mujer.* Barcelona: Argos Vergara, 1981. 13–35.
———. *Molta roba i poc sabó . . . i tan neta que la volen.* Barcelona: Edicions 62, 1971.
———. *Mujeres en busca de un nuevo humanismo.* Barcelona: Salvat, 1981.
———. *Ramona, adéu.* Barcelona: Edicions 62, 1972.
———. "La recuperación de la palabra." *Mujeres de España (las silenciadas).* By Antonina Rodrigo. Barcelona: Plaza and Janés, 1979. 11–20.
———. *El temps de les cireres.* Barcelona: Edicions 62, 1977.
———. *¿Tiempo de mujer?* Barcelona: Plaza and Janés, 1980.
Tremosa, Laura. Prólogo. Roig, *¿Tiempo?* 11–18.

Maria-Mercè Marçal: The Passion and Poetry of Feminism

Joana Sabadell

Translated by H. Patsy Boyer

Las mujeres han constituído la imagen especular, el "otro" del "uno" coherente y poderoso del sistema patriarcal que ha servido como fundamento a la racionalidad occidental; un "speculum," como lo llamó la teórica francesa Luce Irigaray, permitiendo así perpetuarse la "lógica de lo semejante," el igual a sí mismo en la ideología dominante.

—Giulia Coiliazzi

Women make up the specular image, the "other" of the powerful and coherent "self" of the patriarchal system that has served as the base of Western rationality; a "speculum," as French theorist Luce Irigaray termed it, that reflects and gives substance to an uncontradictory, unitary image, thus allowing the perpetuation of the "logic of similitude," the equal to oneself, that characterizes the dominant ideology.

These words of Giulia Coiliazzi from "Mujeres y escritura: ¿Una habitación propia?" (114–15) ("Women and Writing: A Room of One's Own?") apply to all writing by women but most particularly to works produced in Spain's non-Castilian historical regions, which, when taken into account, have been considered marginalized and peripheral and not just in a geographic sense. Those who equate the Spanish language or Spanish literature with literature in Castilian define themselves through their difference from the other. Even today we find a situation of marginal, excentric literary minorities that, in the case of literature written by Catalan, Galician, or Basque women, makes it a "double minority" literature as described in Kathleen McNerney and Cristina Enríquez de Salamanca's felicitous title *Double Minorities of Spain: A Bio-Bibliographical Guide to Women Writers of the Catalan, Galician, and Basque Countries.*

The poetic, narrative, and essay universe of Maria-Mercè Marçal is inscribed in this *double marginalization*, a term that is well known in Catalonia and that continues to be relevant in understanding Catalan women's writing, as we can see from the tendency to exclude women from general (i.e., androcentric) anthologies of Catalan poetry.[1] This exclusion is even more acute with regard to Spanish anthologies of poetry or histories of literature, which seldom include Catalan writers, let alone any women poets from Catalonia.

Marçal, who was born in Ivars d'Urgell in 1952 and died in Barcelona in July 1998, is probably the best-known contemporary Catalan woman poet. She published seven books of poetry, all well received by critics and public. She also wrote short narrative works; one long novel, which won the Premi Carlemany; essays, literary criticism, and several translations. Besides her work as a poet—she is considered by many to be the best Catalan poet of the century—and her critical studies and translations, she promoted Catalan poetry by establishing the publishing house Llibres del Mall, by giving papers and lectures, and by organizing cultural groups to present poetry written by women. Other proof of her tireless efforts in advancing women writers are two projects she worked on to the end of her life with her characteristically unswerving commitment: the first is the publication of *Cartografies del desig* ("Desire's Cartography" [1998]), a book-length collection of the lectures that took place in 1997 at the Casa Elizalde de Barcelona. This anthology, like her other accomplishments, reflects Marçal's and the other collaborators' plan to create a women's literary genealogy. The second, *Paisatge emergent: Treinta poetes catalanes del segle vint* ("Emergent Landscape: Thirty Catalan Women Poets of the Twentieth Century") is an anthology she was working on and that was completed after her death by Montserrat Abelló, Neus Aguado, and Lluïsa Julià (1999).

Marçal's work is concertedly woman-centered, dealing with a female subject whose gynocentric and feminist perspective can never be doubted. That is how we as readers perceive it and the way Marçal herself acknowledges her work as woman's writing. When I commented to Marçal on the many poets who do not consider their writing gender-marked, she responded with her own position and roundly opposed the "logic of similitude" (the legitimization of uniformity in which women disappear) denounced by Luce Irigaray (qtd. in Coiliazzi 115). In my interview with her in 1998, she said:

> Moltes escriptores creuen que si defineixen la seva obra com a femenina es quedaran fora del circuit.
>
> Aquesta es la paradoxa. Perquè si ets igual ets supèrflua, prescindible, tan se val que hi hagi homes o dones. Si el noranta per cent són homes, es l'atzar, una casualitat que, d'entre els homes que escriuen, el noranta-nou per cent ho faci millor que les dones i que per això se'ls publiqui. Si som iguals, per què ens hem de fixar en el sexe de qui escriu? (Sabadell 15)

> Many writers believe that if they define their work as women's writing it will remain out of the mainstream.
>
> But that is the paradox, because if you don't recognize difference, if you are like everybody else, you are superfluous, dispensable; either way, it's all the same. If we are equal, and ninety percent of anthologized poets are men, does that mean that it just so happens that ninety-nine percent of men who write do it better? If we are equal, why pay attention to the gender of the author?

In these words, Marçal echoes how often people fear the stigmatization that punishes difference. But, as she concludes, if all men and all women were equal, we would be interchangeable and, consequently, expendable. And so we would get to the point, not far from current reality, where the feminine would disappear because it is unnecessary.

Buried at the heart of this issue is that most people still adhere to the notion that being a woman is less than being a person; however, as Marçal has stated, difference has a positive value: "jo considero que el fet de ser dona (o home), és més, afegeix alguna connotació, alguna coloració al fet de ser persona i, per tant, no és una restricció, sinó una addició" (Sabadell 15) ("I believe that being a woman [or a man] adds connotations to the fact of being a person and therefore is not a loss but a gain"). This defense of difference as necessary, positive, and desirable led the poet to stand up for her conviction in her political activity, professional work, and personal life, thereby achieving a markedly feminist work, unique in both the Catalan and the Spanish literary contexts.

Marçal's writing is grounded in "writing the female body": "el cos hi és en tot, en definitiva no som res més. Per això, si ets al text, el teu cos hi és d'alguna manera i, quan no hi és, també aquesta absència és una manera de ser-hi" (Sabadell 15) ("The body is in everything; in fact, we are really nothing else. It is no different in the literary text, and when it appears not to be present, this absence also is a way to be present there"). French feminism and theories of sexual difference assert that a woman's body is the very source of her experience of the world, and so Marçal, through her long meditation on this experience, inscribes this feminism in her work.

The same attitude that we read in her poetry, her narrative, and her essays characterizes her work as teacher, as editor (let us remember her work as founder and promoter of the key publishing house Llibres del Mall), as author of numerous critical studies on other women writers, as translator and organizer of symposia and roundtables, and as a member of Dones del Pen Club de Catalunya (Women of Catalonia's Pen Club). In this way, what Marçal expresses in the intimacy of her poetry, she translates into professional activity: she must be remembered as a public figure committed to the development and recognition of women's literature and, more generally, to women's sociopolitical causes.

In a more detailed analysis of her work than this brief study permits, we would focus on various levels in Marçal's work—the traces and representations of her own body and the body of others in a text—and on the semantic evolution, the words and expressions that are particular to her poetic voice. All of this would be contextualized within and compared to tradition—that is, to the ways in which Marçal uses particular techniques and themes to position herself within different literary and cultural traditions. In this essay I clarify some of these points and demonstrate that Marçal's writing is always feminine and often feminist. Marçal's voice reveals a subject who makes being a woman and being Catalan her central focus by continuously questioning all preestablished categories.

Marçal's complete poetic opus has been published in *Llengua abolida: 1973–1988* ("Abolished Language"), and some of her poems have been translated into other languages, but no complete work has ever been translated, not even into Spanish.[2] You can deduce from this lack of translations that her work suffers from its double minority status, making Marçal practically unknown to non-Catalan-speaking audiences (except for feminist literary circles where there is heightened awareness of works written by women). Within Catalonia, however, she enjoys a less marginal status. Among the numerous awards for her poetry, prose, and translations in Catalan, the most distinguished is the Carles Riba poetry prize, probably the most prestigious award for poetry in Catalonia. Her second book, *Bruixa de dol* (1979) ("Mourning Witch"), was such a success that its sales far exceeded expectations.

Marçal's name is linked to feminism through her activity in women's groups, through inscribing herself as a woman in her poetry, and through her active participation in the Catalan cultural scene. The poet herself conceded that a more defining marker even than social class "és tenir un cos, una situació, una història de dona, o l'altre element, que continua sent molt important, el lingüístic. No puc establir una separació entre aquests elements i jo" (Sabadell 16) ("is having a woman's body, position, and history. Yet another facet that is exceedingly important is the linguistic element. I cannot separate myself from these"). Nevertheless, and despite what her now famous proclamation of class, nation, and gender in *Cau de llunes* ("The Hiding Place of Moons") might lead her critics to think, Marçal's ideological aesthetic is not closed. It is just the opposite: she proposes to seek out and practice flexibility within seemingly fixed categories.[3] In the most fundamental sense, Marçal's poetry represents conceptual and verbal risk.

The poems echo Marçal's priorities: given that Catalan is fundamental to her, she makes it the subject of exhaustive study and uses a wide variety of expressive registers and elements from the popular tradition, which she recovers by adapting it to contemporary needs. And, since she sees the world "with the eyes of a woman," to use her own words, Marçal constructs an autobiographical poetry, granting to the feminine world and to the feminine imaginary a central rather than an auxiliary position. In this sense, Marçal's work develops on the border that separates the "I" from the "other" in a way that is characteristic of feminism as well as of other minority literatures. Writing in a language that is the other to Castilian, she gives written voice to a body that likewise is no longer the other to the masculine body.

Referring to Montserrat Roig's narrative, Catherine Bellver has observed insightfully the importance of writing in Catalan. The following statement clearly is applicable to other Catalan women writers:

> What her use of Catalan indicates is the close relationship between the vindication of her language and her sex. As Geraldine C. Nichols points out, today's Catalan women writers were brought up with the notion that both as females and as Catalans they were inferior. Thus the use of a previously repressed language has both personal, psychological implications and a collective, political purpose. (219)

Despite the pointedly political statement made by simply writing in Catalan, choosing to write in her marginalized language does not solve all problems of identity. Marçal faces the difficulty common to women writers: she writes in a language she loves but that does not represent her. For this reason she struggles to fill it with new meanings more suitable to her own expressive needs as a woman, always affirming the symbiosis of belonging and not belonging that defines her. The prologue to *Llengua abolida,* entitled "Sota el signe del drac" ("Under the Dragon's Sign"), is a reference, as the poet makes clear, to the dragon slain by Catalonia's patron saint as well as to his rescuing of damsels who then become subject to his lance. Marçal dedicates her complete works "sense paraules, a la memoria del meu pare, perqué ell fou qui, paradoxalment, m'obrí portes qu'em durien a questionar la seva llei" (11) ("to my father's memory, without words, because, paradoxically, he was the one who opened doors for me that made me question his own law"). That "petita esbojarrada" ("little crazy woman") she recognized in Clementina Arderiu's work is no longer the daughter obedient to her father in her own work, a rupture she expresses through complexity and ambiguity rather than through Manichaean dualisms. Thus she writes the contradictions of a complex female subject who is the center of a poetic universe, a subject who negotiates the differences of class, gender, and language that define her as other.

The poem "Daddy" (*Llengua abolida* 432) reveals a daughter's conflicted emotions as she grieves for her father. The subject recognizes her love for him and also distances herself. What results is an unresolvable fragmentation:

Cada dona adora un feixista . . . —*Sylvia Plath*

Aquella part de mi que adoraba a un feixista
    —o l'adora, qui ho sap!—
    jeu amb tu, jau amb tu.

No l'espanta la tomba. Cridada des de sempre
al domini més fosc,
mor amb tu, i viu de tu.

Ofrena remolosa, no sap sinó seguir-te
i arrapar-se al teu mal
com al port més segur.

Medusa desossada, alló que de mi resta
Malda per completar-se
Sense tu, lluny de tu.

El bisturí vacil.la. Qui em viu a l'altra banda?
I com podré pensar-te
com si jo no fos tu?

Every woman loves a fascist . . . —*Sylvia Plath*

That part of me that adored a fascist
    —or still adores one, who knows!—
    lies with you, lays with you.

It is not afraid of the grave. Summoned forever
to the darkest domain,
it dies with you, and lives off you.

Tremulous offering, it only knows to follow you
and cling to your hurt
like a safe harbor.

Deboned jellyfish, what remains of me
strives to complete itself
without you, far away from you.

The scalpel hesitates. Who is living me from the other side?
And how will I think of you
as if I were not you? (Abrams, "Five Poems" 69)

Marçal emphasizes the understandable pain and separation following her father's death, as well as the binary of rupture and symbiosis, which is a fundamental part of her own poetic subject. Here I look back to show the distance, temporal and linguistic as well as gendered and ideological, that separates the famous elegy by Jorge Manrique—a man who in remembering his father, like his homonym Saint George, invokes a shared history and tradition—and Marçal's elegy. Marçal's own poem recalls the irreconcilable difference in a history she belongs to but at the same time abhors, the fragmentation that defines her subjectivity. It is precisely with regard to that molecular subjectivity that the poem "Daddy" represents a notable evocation or homage, adaptation and personalization of the poem with the same name by Sylvia Plath, a woman admired by Marçal and a fellow poet much closer to Marçal both in time and in spirit than Jorge Manrique.

Marçal reopens communication with women's voices that have disappeared from histories of literature in poems where the ancient voice of the popular lyric (*jarchas*, Galician-Portuguese *cantigas de amigo*, Provençal *albadas*) resounds, rejuvenated but still recognizable.[4] She also establishes dialogues with the voices of women from a variety of traditions through references that she incorporates into her own poems or through translations or through critical studies of their works. This interconnectivity can be seen in her essays on the contemporary Catalan poets Arderiu, Rosa Leveroni, and Isabel de Villena and in her translations of Colette, Marguerite Yourcenar, Anna Akhmatova, Leonor Fini, Marina Tsvetayeva, and others.

In an effort to create an intimate language that better reveals the contradictions in her poetic subject and its relationship with the world, Marçal relies on the motifs so characteristic of her work: the moon, salt, and blood. This leads Marçal to a search for her own language that shows how she molds language to her needs as a woman, to the expression of her sexuality, and to pregnancy and the experience of maternity. These two latter topics are probably the most notable examples of women's mystification, which the poet from Ivars d'Urgell endows with an importance that far surpasses the predictable stereotypes.[5]

The moon motif is symbolic of Marçal's desire to deeply inscribe the feminine in all her writing, for the moon represents the traditional feminine in a satellite that passively reflects the sun's borrowed light.[6] Commenting on this in an interview, Marçal described some of the devices she uses to build her own language. She gave examples and referred to a procedure that had been very useful in creating a female language that codified or decodified her experience:

> Sobre la lluna hi ha diverses possibilitats: la del rebuig d'aquest femení tradicional, d'allunyament i abandonament, o la d'adonarte, de manera intuïtiva primer i després més conscientment, que aquesta idea et surt molt sovint i que el que jo feia era prendre un dels referents d'aquest femení tradicional i forçar-lo fins que aquella mateixa imatge s'anés transformant i carregant de connotacions diferents.
>
> I d'aquesta manera m'he anat fent una mena de diccionari propi en el qual aquesta paraula s'anava tornant molt important, perque s'havia anant omplint i enriquint, i cada vegada que la utilitzaba en un context diferent hi donava un nou espai.
>
> (Sabadell 18)

> With the traditional image of the moon, there are several alternatives: giving it up, rejecting it, or reusing it until it is transformed, until it acquires a different meaning. I have chosen the second because, as I got into it, the moon began assuming different connotations.
>
> In this way, I started building up a sort of personal dictionary where this word was acquiring a central importance as it was becoming gradually fuller and richer. Every time the moon was used in a different context, it would reach a new space as well.

When she uses these images her voice is at its most powerful. Just as diverse communities in the United States (e.g., African American, gay, lesbian) have appropriated and adapted the pejorative terms that traditionally characterized them as other, Marçal has assimilated and regenerated images that have traditionally represented the feminine, transforming them by means of a feminist language.

Marçal's voice is the lyric voice of Catalan feminism. Being a Catalan woman and writing about oneself as such means being simultaneously outside and inside a complex net of inclusions and exclusions—some imposed, some chosen—but it also means making one's own options. In this sense, one of the most remarkable characteristics of her art is perhaps her constant dialogue with the literary voices both feminine and feminist that she responds to or assimilates.

By placing female and Catalan identities at the poetry's center, Marçal questions the meanings and limits of all categories and the dichotomy between the center and the margin. Along this line we find some poems that are clear vindications, such as *Bruixa de dol* and the following verses from "Vuit de març" ("March 8th"), which commemorates International Women's Day:

> Vindicarem la nit
> i la paraula DONA.
> Llavors creixerà l'arbre
> de l'alliberament. (*Lengua abolida* 169–70)
>
> We will take back the night
> and the word WOMAN.
> Then the tree of liberation
> will grow.

In this as in other poems, the marginal, the others in the patriarchal system—the *night/nit* and the word *WOMAN/DONA*—constitute the center of Marçal's discourse and her cause for celebration. Another example of the fusion of her feminist and leftist militancy can be found in the heterogeneous poems written between 1980 and 1982 for the antinuclear demonstration of 1980 under the title "Els pasquins per a la revolta vegetal" ("Flyers for a Vegetable Revolution"). As the author explains in *Llengua abolida* (276), one of these poems, "Baixeu, veniu a la dansa futura" ("Come Down, Come to the Future Dance"), was actually printed and distributed as a lampoon by Women for the Antinuclear March. In a call for unity and for celebration of the alliances among women, the poet writes:

> Aviarem coloms
> per encetar la festa
> i inventarem camins
> en cels sense fronteres.
> Arreu tindrem hostal,
> farem convit arreu,
> amb la fruita de l'arbre
> de l'alliberament. (*Llengua abolida* 280–81; *Escarsers*)

> We will release doves
> to start the celebration
> and we'll invent roads
> in skies without borders.
> We will find lodging everywhere
> and have continuous banquets,
> with the fruit from the tree
> of liberation.

As in the poems already cited, where the alliances between women are expressed in a militant tone, one of the most personal poems is dedicated to Maria-Antònia Salvà, who was born in Palma, Majorca, in 1889 and died in Llucmajor in 1958. Salvà was perhaps the first modern Catalan woman poet, and her work was rediscovered by Marçal, Lluïsa Julià, and other specialists in Catalan literature. In the adaptation of the Majorcan poet's "D'un cactus" ("On a Cactus") in Marçal's "Furgant per les llivanyes i juntures" ("Searching in Cracks and Corners"), we again find the woman/dragon surviving in Saint George's Catalonia. Here Marçal connects with the woman's voice of her predecessor and recognizes that by means of her difference, her words, her poems, she is recovering her own genealogy, a history shared despite their distance in time. Marçal uses a quote from Salvà's "D'un cactus" as an epigraph to her own poem: "Furgant per les llivanyes i juntures / trobí el vell drac, encara aferrissat" ("Searching in cracks and corners / I found the old dragon, still fierce"). Then Marçal's poem begins:

Furgant per les llivanyes i juntures
d'aquesta paret seca, entre mac
i mac d'oblit, entre les pedres dures
de cega desmemoria que endures
et sé i saber-te em dóna terra, arrel.
Et sé . . . I em sé, en el mirall fidel
del teu poema, aferrissadement
clivellar pedra de silenci opac
—dona rèptil, dona monstre, dona drac
com el cactus, com tu, supervivent. (*Dotze sentits*)

Searching in cracks and corners
of this arid wall, among pebbles
of oblivion, between the hard stones
of blind forgetfulness that you endure
I know you and knowing you gives me land, roots.
I know you . . . And I know myself, in the faithful mirror
of your poem, fiercely
cleaving stone of opaque silence
—reptile woman, monster woman, dragon woman
like a cactus, like you, a survivor.

When Marçal asserts that recognizing herself in her predecessor gives her roots, she is clearly articulating the importance of the gynohistory in which she defines herself. We should read the valuable study the poet dedicated to the work of Clementina Arderiu in the same way. In the introduction to *Contraclaror* ("Backlightning"), Marçal pays particular attention to the incorporation of elements of risk in Arderíu's poetry, elements that have been least studied, and those with which she herself identifies.

And it is precisely in this personal search for the expression of risk and limit that Marçal connects with poetry from the United States:

> De les lectures de Plath i de Rich, encara que llegides en traducció, m'ha arribat una força—una mena de risc en el cas de Plath, i una visió política, en el de Rich—que no puc trobar a l'obra d'altres poetes catalanes de quina obra, de vegades, és més dificil trobar resultats concrets a la meva poesia que els produïts per la lectura de les poetes americanes. (Sabadell 16)

> From my readings of Plath and Rich, even though I read them in translation, has come a power—a kind of risk in Plath and a political vision in Rich—that I have seldom found in the work of other Catalan poets. Sometimes it's harder to find traces of them in my work than it is to discover evidence of my readings of the North Americans.

It is the intensity, the verbal and ideological risk, together with an impressive lyrical charge, that make Marçal's poetry so original and such a notable example of feminist poetry. For these reasons and because it is written in Catalan, her work is distinctive. It thus presents problems of classification not addressed in general studies or in anthologies that, by trying to be inclusive, exclude what is different in Spanish literature.

In conclusion, diverse but complementary modern theoretical perspectives—Lacanian psychoanalysis, feminism, and gender and race studies—focus attention on the same subject as Marçal's work: on the processes of exclusion. When Frantz Fanon, in *Black Skin, White Masks,* studies the way racism works, he insists on the idea that the black man is other to the white, who establishes himself as the only point of reference in a system in which the other is marginalized. Fanon shows that in each country described as civilized, the connection between family and nation is so close that family seems a miniature of nation, reproducing it on a small scale. Reading Fanon's study raises the ghost of Franco's Spain, of the dictatorship that saw itself as an organism in which each individual part fulfilled its mission. If we do not want to add the university to the sinister trilogy of "family, city hall, and labor union," which in the Franco organic state sought to reproduce the centralization of authority, we need to reexamine our way of seeing and reading ourselves, the myriad ways, in the case of literary studies, we look at ourselves without seeing each other. If Spanish literature alone is the literature of Spain, we either have to redefine the notion of state, or we will have to recognize the literature produced by Spaniards who neither speak nor write as men or who speak and write in a language other than Castilian. We also have to expand our tried and true canon so that it accommodates our reality and fills in the gaps of the millions of citizens whose history, literature, and identity have no real representation to date.

Marçal's poetry and prose is a good example of a fundamental opus that has been excluded from Hispanic studies. Indeed, her poetry ought to be studied in its dialectical relation to the work of other Catalan, Spanish, European, and North American women writers. By doing that, we would avoid repeating the historical errors we have been criticizing. As long as Marçal's poetry, like that of other Catalan, Basque, and Galician women, is not included in courses of study, we continue to perpetuate the idea that the Castilian literary canon represents all of Spanish literature and that the masculine gender includes and represents the feminine. We continue to legitimize the synecdoche as the only valid rhetorical and ideological figure in which the evocation and the existence of the unnamed is relegated to the shadows and difference is condemned to oblivion.

Maria-Mercè Marçal dedicated her energy and her life to validating women's intellectual and cultural production and to celebrating women's individual and collective difference. As I have demonstrated, overlooking her work would mean missing a vital link in Catalan, Spanish, and women's histories. On the occasion of her premature death, newspapers and cultural publications, mostly Catalan, published necrologies and other articles describing the work and biography of the great feminist writer of Catalonia. Rather than end this study with her absence, it is more in keeping with Marçal's spirit to celebrate her literary presence, the passion of her feminism, her tireless promotion of women's causes. Her work will be remembered for its lyric intensity and for the coherent way she joined feminist theory and practice by opening up space for the expression of the feminine. Her narrative, her essays, and especially her poetry represent the celebration of a universe written about voice and about the word that she, the splendid conjurer of words, cared about most passionately: *dona/woman.* To paraphrase the title of her novel, this word sums up "passion according to Maria-Mercè Marçal."

Notes

1. Marta Pessarrodona is the other great woman poet who was a contemporary of Marçal's and is often remembered and anthologized. Usually a choice is made of one or the other, but sometimes both are included. Seldom do any of the varied women poets of the present day appear.
2. José Agustín Goytisolo has translated fifteen of her best poems in *Veintiún poetas catalanes para el siglo XXI.* Other selections from her work have been translated into English by D. Sam Abrams in *Survivors,* and into Italian by Rosa Rossi and Valenti Gómez Oliver in their multilingual anthology. Except where otherwise noted, all Catalan poems and titles in this essay were translated into English by Kathleen McNerney and Joana Sabadell.
3. Among the works considered the best in Marçal's oeuvre, the epigraph to her book *Cau de llunas* stands out for its potent summarization of Marçal's philosophy: "Divisa / A l'atzar agraeixo tres dons: haver nascut dona, / de classe baixa i nació oprimida. / I el terbol atzur de ser tres voltes rebel" ("Motto / I am grateful to fate for three gifts: to have been born a woman / from the working class and an oppressed nation. / And the turbid azure of being three times a rebel"). This is Abrams's translation (available at www.intercom.es/folch/poesia/nov_gen.htm and previously published in his *Survivors*). The subsequent translation of "Daddy" is also taken from Abrams ("Five Poems" 69).
4. The linguistic renovation Marçal effects in her poetry has a dual origin. First it rises from within her connection with popular culture, which the poet identifies with the maternal and locates in a state before her acquisition of a written or literary culture. In Marçal's poems this culture is always present and in constant evolution. The second avenue to linguistic renovation and acquisition comes from her reading other women writers and from her desire to create a language that stems from women's experience.
5. Marçal's poetry is particularly moving for its dual eroticism, as we can see in "Amic, et citaré": "Amic, et citaré al cor d'una petxina. / Petit ocell, ajoca't en el pit de l'onada. / Dóna'l la llengua, amor. / Dóna'm la sal. / I dóna'm també / aquest dolç llangardaix que em duu follia / quan s'enfila per l'herba. / Ben a pleret, que ens hi atrapi l'alba" (*Llengua abolida* 110) ("Friend, I'll meet you in the heart of a shell. / Little bird, nest in the breast of the wave. / Give me your tongue, love. Give me the salt. / And give me too / that sweet lizard that makes me crazy / when it threads through the grass. / Slowly, let us catch the dawn there"). Marçal is equally moving when she writes about her lesbianism in "Solstici" ("Solstice"): "El teu sexe i la meva boca viva, / a doll, trenats com si fossin dos sexes" (*Llengua abolida* 298; originally published in *La germana l'estragera*) ("Your sex and my live mouth, / flowing, braiding together as if they were two sexes"). Again, with a blues cadence, she melancholically expresses the impossibility of the domesticity of her love in "El meu amor sense casa" (*Llengua abolida* 499) ("My Love without a Home").
6. The sun is usually depicted as the epitome of masculine self-sufficiency, of action, as the center of energy.

Works by Maria-Mercè Marçal, in Chronological Order by Genre

Poetry

Cau de llunes. 1977.†
Bruixa de dol. 1979.†
Escarsers, 1980–1982.†
Sal oberta. Barcelona: Mall, 1982.
Terra de mai. Valencia: Cingle, 1982.
Desglac. 1984–1988. *Llengua abolida* 417–518.
La germana, l'estrangera. Barcelona: Mall, 1985.
Llengua abolida: 1973–1988, 1989.†
Desglac. Barcelona: Edicions 62, 1998.

Narrative

"Viratges, reminiscències." *Barceldones.* Barcelona: Eixample, 1990. 51–63.
La passió segons Renée Vivien. Barcelona: Columna, 1994.

Essays and Criticism

Introduction. *Contraclaror: Antologia poètica.* 1985.†
"Per deixar d'ésser supervivents." *Dona i literatura.* Barcelona: I.C.E. de la Universitat de Barcelona, 1986. 33–37.
"Rosa Leveroni, en el llindar." *Literatura de dones, una visió del món.* Ed. Isabel Segura et al. Barcelona: La Sal, Edicions de les Dones, 1988. 97–120.
"El feminisme literari d'Isabel de Villena." *Revista de Catalunya* Sept. 1990: 120–30.
Cartografies del desig. 1998.†
Abelló, Montserrat, Neus Aguado, Lluïsa Julià, and Maria-Mercè Marçal. *Paisatge emergent: Treinta poetes catalanes del segle vint.* 1999.†
Marçal, Maria-Mercè, and Lluïsa Julià. "Diferencia y/o normalización: La poesía catalana de los últimos treinta años." *Mosaico ibérico: Ensayos sobre poesía y diversidad.* Ed. Joana Sabadell Nieto. Gijón: Júcar, 1999. 153–80.

Works Cited

Abelló, Montserrat, Neus Aguado, Lluïsa Julià, and Maria-Mercè Marçal. *Paisatge emergent: Treinta poetes catalanes del segle vint.* Colliure: Magrana, 1999.
Abrams, D. Sam. *Survivors.* Barcelona: Institut d'Estudis Nord-Americans, 1991.
———. "Five Poems by Maria-Mercè Marçal." *Homenatge a Maria-Mercè Marçal.* Ed. Montserrat Abelló et al. Barcelona: Empuries, 1998. 69–73.
Bellver, Catherine G. "Montserrat Roig and the Creation of a Gynocentric Real-

† See Works Cited.

ity." *Women Writers of Contemporary Spain: Exiles in the Homeland.* Ed. Joan L. Brown. Newark: U of Delaware P, 1991. 217–38.

Coiliazzi, Giulia. "Mujeres y escritura: ¿Una habitación propia?" *Mujeres y literatura.* Ed. Angels Carabí and Marta Segarra. Barcelona: Promocions i Publicacions Universitaries, 1994. 109–23.

Dotze sentits: Poesia catalana d'avui. CD-ROM. Barcelona: Universitat Pompeu Fabra, Edicions Proa i Institut d'Edicions de la Diputació de Barcelona, 1996.

Fanon, Frantz. *Black Skin, White Masks.* Trans. Charles Lam Markmann. New York: Grove, 1967.

Goytisolo, José Agustín. *Veintiún poetas catalanes para el siglo XXI.* Barcelona: Lumen, 1996.

Manrique, Jorge. "Coplas por la muerta du su padre." *Antología Cátedra de las letras hispánicas.* Ed. J. Francisco Ruiz Casanova. Madrid: Cátedra, 1998. 149–65.

Marçal, Maria-Mercè. *Bruixa de dol.* Barcelona: Mall, 1979.

———, ed. *Cartografies del desig.* Barcelona: Proa, Col. La mirada, 1998.

———. *Cau de llunes.* Barcelona: Proa, 1977.

———. *Escarsers, 1980–1982.* Marçal, *Lengua abolida* 275–89.

———. Introduction. *Contraclaror: Antologia poètica.* By Clementina Arderiu. Barcelona: La Sal, 1985.

———. *Llengua abolida: 1973–1988.* València: Tres i Quatre, 1989.

McNerney, Kathleen, and Cristina Enríquez de Salamanca. *Double Minorities of Spain: A Bio-Bibliographical Guide to Women Writers of the Catalan, Galician, and Basque Countries.* New York: MLA, 1994.

Rossi, Rosa, and Valenti Gómez Oliver. *Antologia della poesia spagnola, castigliana, catalana, galega, basca dal 1961 ad oggi.* Padova: Citadella (Amadeus), 1996.

Sabadell, Joana. "Allà on literatura i vida fan trena: Conversa amb Maria-Mercè Marçal sobre poesia i feminisme." *Serra d'or* (1998): 12–19.

Voice, Marginality, and Seduction in the Short Fiction of Carme Riera

Kathleen M. Glenn

A professor, scholar, and creative artist, Carme Riera (b.1948) is an important figure in the contemporary literary world, and her works of fiction have been awarded a number of prizes. Her insistence that she is not a feminist writer, although she is a feminist "citizen" ("Conversation" 55), reconfirms that *feminist* is a very problematic term in Spain, where most serious women authors argue that there is no relation between being a feminist and being a writer. In a May 1991 conversation that took place at the University of California, Los Angeles, Soledad Puértolas rejected the idea that as a female author she should shed light on the world of women, and Mercedes Abad insisted that she is not a "portavoz de [su] sexo" (Carmona, Lamb, Velasco, and Zecchi 158) ("spokesperson for [her] sex").[1] Cristina Fernández Cubas was more blunt, affirming that "[n]inguno de nuestros libros se puede considerar feminista. [. . .] Y es que literatura y feminismo no tienen nada que ver" (158) ("none of our books can be considered feminist. [. . .] The fact is that literature and feminism have nothing to do with each other"). The conversation is intriguing because it shows the American questioners returning again and again to the issue of feminism and feminist writing and the Spanish authors growing increasingly annoyed. Implicit, and at times explicit, in their responses is the conviction that critics try to force writing by women into a specific framework or straitjacket. Fernández Cubas used the feminine image of a corset to describe this situation: "[H]ay un corsé e intenta[n] que nuestro texto encaje en el corsé. Es como un corsé de talla única y que, sea una señora oronda o una señora delgadísima, pues a todas nos tiene que ir" (162) ("There is a corset and people try to make our text fit within it. The corset comes in only one size and it has to fit all of us, fat or thin").

Similar protests have been voiced by Paloma Díaz-Mas, Rosa Montero, Marina Mayoral, Riera, and others. Behind their statements lies the identification of feminist writing with advocacy and the assumption that it lacks literary worth. These writers want their work to be taken seriously, to be valued for its artistic merit—not for the sex of its author—and to be read by men and women alike. They resist being relegated to the ghetto of literature by and for women. It is within this context that we should evaluate Riera's declaration that she is not a feminist writer.[2] From this side of the Atlantic, however, she indeed looks like one. Well read in French feminist theory, she chose for her 1980 book the title *Palabra de mujer* ("Woman's Word"), reminiscent of Annie Leclerc's *Parole de femme.* She has explored the thorny question of *difference* in women's writing, has written brief articles on Santa Teresa and María de Zayas, has expressed admiration for the work of Mercè Rodoreda and Carmen Laforet, and has acknowledged that for the women of her generation Virginia Woolf is almost an idol. This essay reviews Riera's connections with several of these writers and her disagreements with others and discusses the manifestations of feminist consciousness in her short fiction.

Shortly before the fourth centennial of the death of Santa Teresa, Riera sets out to re-vision a figure alternately praised as a model of Spanish femininity and dismissed as a hysteric.[3] Riera turns directly to the saint's writing and what is novel about it in sixteenth-century Spain: that it is by a woman and intended for other women with whom Santa Teresa shares a manner of expression, an approach to certain themes, and an interest in scrutinizing personal experience. Inasmuch as Santa Teresa wishes to engage in conversation with her audience, she adopts a colloquial style characterized by repetitions, anacolutha, ellipses, and proverbs. Her persistent allusions to the weakness, clumsiness, and even inferiority of women and to her own lack of education and ability are a deliberate strategy, aimed at disarming male critics of her writing and the fact that she is writing.[4] The title of the article, "Vindicación de Teresa de Cepeda" ("Vindication of Teresa de Cepeda"), underscores that Riera's goal is to vindicate not a saint but a female writer who took up the pen to defend the spiritual rights of women and who did so with courage and skill.

If Santa Teresa has a distinctive voice, so too does María de Zayas. In "Los personajes femeninos de doña María de Zayas, una aproximación" ("The Feminine Characters of Doña María de Zayas: An Approach"), Riera and Luisa Cotoner suggest that it is anger at men's abuse of women that impels Zayas to write and that in *Novelas amorosas y ejemplares* (1637) (*The Enchantments of Love*) and *Desengaños amorosos* (1647) (*The Disenchantments of Love*) the seventeenth-century feminist presents various alternatives to accepting male mistreatment. The most interesting alternative, in the opinion of Riera and Cotoner, is taking refuge in a convent, where women could enjoy the company of other members of their sex. Riera and Cotoner, themselves close friends, emphasize the importance in Zayas's work of a theme that continues to interest Riera, friendship among women.[5]

Sandra Gilbert and Susan Gubar, in their classic *The Madwoman in the Attic*, maintain that the woman writer searches for female models to legitimize her revolt against patriarchal literary authority; she needs sisterly precursors as well as a female audience (50). While this is certainly true of the nineteenth-century women writers Gilbert and Gubar discuss, it is less applicable to Riera, who has written about other female artists not to validate or authorize her own work but—as a literary critic—to illuminate theirs. She suffers less from the "anxiety of authorship" Gilbert and Gubar attribute to women writers than from the "anxiety of influence" Harold Bloom detects in the work of male artists who must wage war against their literary fathers. Privileged by family background and education, Riera has distinguished herself as a professor at the Universitat Autònoma of Barcelona, as a scholar, and as a creative writer. From the beginning of her career, she has been confident of the merit of her work and has not hesitated to criticize established writers.

A case in point is her relationship with Rodoreda, the grande dame of twentieth-century Catalan literature. Riera's "Bisti de Càrrega" ("Beast of Burden") stories, in *Jo pos per testimoni les gavines* ("I Call on the Seagulls as Witness"), are reminiscent of narratives by Rodoreda. Riera has explained that her literary education was strictly Castilian, as was customary for the time when she was growing up, and that she read Rodoreda after she had composed the stories in question. Impressed and fascinated by the older woman's work, Riera wrote to her, declaring her admiration, but Rodoreda apparently thought that Riera had imitated her and so stated in an interview. Riera's reply was swift:

> I sent her a furious letter, which she didn't answer. I told her that I had written my stories before I read her work, but that she was free to believe whatever she wanted to, and that if she didn't respond, I would be convinced she had indeed made the remark attributed to her and that it was not a journalist's mistake. [. . .] I can be sarcastic, and I'm sorry for what I later said: that Rodoreda's problem was that she planted flowers and they turned out to be made of plastic. ("Conversation" 54)[6]

Riera has been even more outspoken in her criticism of Spain's most polemical feminist, Lidia Falcón, who is perceived by many critics as being "too radical, too strident, too bombastic" (Vosburg 210). In 1981 Riera contributed an article on sexist language to *Poder y libertad: Revista teórica del partido feminista de España* ("Power and Freedom: Theoretical Journal of the Feminist Party of Spain"), the successor journal to *Vindicación feminista* ("Feminist Vindication"), and she was involved in the founding of the Partido Feminista in Spain. Riera, however, in 1999, considered Falcón's attitude to be totally out of data and *machista* ("chauvinistic"):

> It consists of being just as intransigent as the most intransigent of men and insisting that if you don't believe as she does and act as

> she acts, you have no right to exist. [. . .] Lidia Falcón wants power. What I want is authority, which [. . .] is granted among equals, whereas power signifies the oppression of one group by another. Lidia Falcón's attitude is one of control, of domination, which doesn't interest me. I believe that what feminists ought to do is implant different social values. That there be women in power [. . .] is less important than that these women act in a different way and that their attitude not be machista.
>
> ("Conversation" 55–56)

Riera thus distances herself from both Rodoreda and Falcón and in the process positions herself as a writer who deserves respect for the quality of her writing and the independence of her thought.

In her female-centered narratives Riera foregrounds issues of voice, marginality, and seduction. These texts include "Te deix, amor, la mar com a penyora" ("I Leave You, My Love, the Sea as a Token") and "Jo pos per testimoni les gavines," stories of lesbian love published in 1975 and 1977, respectively; the "Bisti de Càrrega" stories of *Jo pos per testimoni les gavines,* whose female heroes are working-class women; "Estimat Thomas" ("Dear Thomas") from *Epitelis tendríssims* ("Most Tender Epithelia") (1981), a collection of irreverent, erotic tales; "Octubre, octubre" ("October, October"), a different kind of love story, published in 1992; and the novella *Qüestió d'amor propi* ("A Question of Self-Love") (1987), whose central character, a victim of male seduction, artfully plots an act of counterseduction against a background of many instances of literary seduction.

Riera, who was born in Palma de Mallorca in 1948, has described herself as "the margin of the margin of the margin" ("Conversation" 53). This triple marginalization is due to the fact that she is a woman, that in Spain she forms part of a minority literature (Catalan rather than Castilian), and that within this minority literature she is not from the center (Barcelona) but from an island. Riera's personal experience has made her especially sensitive to marginality and silencing, and she has repeatedly given a voice to those who have not had one, be they the crypto-Jews of *Dins el darrer blau* ("In the Furthest Blue") or the desiring, despairing, demented, and designing women of a host of shorter works.

Her focus upon the "ex-centric"—and I here borrow Linda Hutcheon's term (57–73)—highlights what is off-center and makes us reexamine the notions of margin and center, of outside and inside, of frame and framed, of what is excluded by or included within borders. The Cuban American writer Cristina García declares, "What's considered the fringe is, I think, redefining what mainstream literature and culture is, and it's not so marginal anymore. [. . . P]eople on the edge see more" (24). And, I would add, they often see differently.

If a concern with voice and marginality is a distinguishing feature of Riera's fiction, so too is the importance of seduction. She and the writer characters she has created insist that seduction is an absolute necessity. Pablo Corbalán, of *Joc de miralls* ("Game of Mirrors"), declares that it is his primary obsession:

> M'interessa d'entrada seduir el lector perquè segueixi llegint. Mitjançant l'aparença de la meva escriptura, mitjançant els signes, les ambigüitats i connotacions que li ofereix el meu discurs, envoltar-lo, conduir-lo i atracar-lo cap a mi, fer-lo meu, això vol dir seduir. (23–24)
>
> I'm interested in seducing readers from the outset so that they will continue reading. Through the appearance of my writing, through the signs, ambiguities, and connotations that my discourse offers them, [I wish] to besiege them, to lead them, and to draw them to me, to make them mine, that is to seduce.

Riera has made similar comments in various interviews, emphasizing that the first thing a writer must do is to seduce her readers, because without this seduction they will not continue reading; after all, life is short and the world is full of books. The crux of the matter is to seduce without resorting to cheap tricks and without deceiving; misleading, however, is permissible. The word *seduce*, after all, comes from the Latin *seducere*, meaning "to entice, to lead astray." Riera maintains that writers must provide sufficient data so that readers can make certain assumptions, but they need not show all their cards.

To establish contact with readers, awaken their interest, and ensure their continuing attention, Riera frequently resorts to ambiguity and surprise. In an interview with Geraldine Nichols, she underscored the significance and the interrelationship of both elements: "Lo que no puede ser objeto de sorpresa o de misterio, lo que es obvio, no tiene interés. [. . .] Si algo no resulta sorprendente—no en cuanto a maravilloso, sino en cuanto a oculto, no patente—entonces, no funciona" (216) ("What cannot be an object of surprise or mystery, what is obvious, holds no interest. [. . .] If something does not turn out to be surprising—not in the sense of marvelous but in the sense of hidden, not evident—then it does not work"). Acknowledging that she is delighted when a writer surprises her, Riera returns the favor when she writes. Her fiction is filled with narratives of seduction that illustrate the seductions of narrative. Seduction is both theme and strategy. It is not coincidental that the letter is one of Riera's favorite literary forms, inasmuch as epistolary literature abounds in stories of seduction and underscores the relation between seduction, narration, and love. As the fictional Angela Caminals of *Qüestió d'amor propi* is fond of affirming, "Qualsevol escriptura és una carta d'amor" ("Every piece of writing is a love letter") and "El text no és més que un pretext amorós" (24–25) ("The text is nothing but an amorous pretext").

That the epistolary form precludes the possibility of an omniscient narrator's interjecting explanations increases its ambiguity. Letter writers relate only what they choose to relate, passing in silence over those matters that it is to their advantage to conceal. They resort to the letter to make a case for a particular course of action, to justify their behavior, to overcome the resistance of their addressees, who must strive to decipher the words on the piece of paper they hold in their hands and determine how much confidence should be placed in them. Representations of the acts of writing, reading, rereading, and interpreting, which are typical of epistolary fiction, are a paradigm of our experience as readers. The epistle is a narrative vehicle that permits Riera to play with textual and sexual norms and to subvert our expectations, as she does with particular skill in one of the stories of *Epitelis tendríssims,* a book in which eroticism and humor are intertwined.[7]

Erotic literature has typically been written by and for men and has been taken quite seriously by them. The ludic spirit and irreverent tone of *Epitelis* and its author's gender represent departures from the norm.

"Estimat Thomas" is a good example of how Riera utilizes our expectations regarding erotic writing to mislead and surprise us. The story is composed of the nine letters that young Montse writes to her love while she is vacationing with her family. She stresses how much she misses Thomas, swears eternal fidelity to him, dreams of him at night, recalls his bewitching golden eyes, and fantasizes about the feel of his tongue "quan es posa en contacte amb la meva pell i puja per les cames, genolls amunt" (84) ("when it comes in contact with my skin and moves up my legs, above my knees"). Since we are reading an erotic text, we give a sexual interpretation to phrases that in a different context could be perfectly innocent, such as the closing "Un petó llarg, llarg, on més t'agradi" (81) ("A long, lingering kiss where it most pleases you") and the description of the bathroom tub, which makes Montse remember "els nostres jocs sota l'aigua" (81) ("our games under the water"). When we learn in the last letter that Thomas is the family's German shepherd, we are abashed as well as amused by what we have imagined, seduced by the suggestive wording of the letters.

Seduction and a surprise ending are also found in "Octubre, octubre," published in an anthology of stories that deal with love. The title of the book, *El primer amor* ("First Love"), conditions our expectations concerning its content. References to "aquell desig desbocat" (93) ("that wild desire"), to the transgressing of "totes les prohibicions" (94) ("all prohibitions"), and to "les meves mans lliscant pel teu cos joveníssim" (94) ("my hands sliding over your very young body") lead us to assume, as is logical, the existence of a flesh-and-blood lover. The revelation that he is of "cel-lulosa premsada" (96) ("compressed cellulose"), a notebook, takes us by surprise. Writing, Riera shows us, is a voluptuous act, an expression of an uncontrollable desire, and the pen that pours its ink onto a sheet of white paper can gently caress or can rip and tear with frenzy the body of the beloved.

Two of Riera's seductive, transgressive short stories deal with issues of marginality and framing. Distinctions between outside and inside tend to be particularly problematic in framed texts. Mary Ann Caws points out, "To frame in is also to frame out, so that the notions of grid and selection, of inclusion and exclusion, are constantly in play, as well as those of border and of centering or focus" (3). Riera has often utilized narrative frames, and I include under this heading introductory letters, preliminary notes, and prologues, all of which pique our interest, awaken expectations—which may or may not be fulfilled—and remind us how fluid margins can be.

"Te deix, amor, la mar com a penyora" (19–36) and "Jo pos per testimoni les gavines" (9–19) are companion pieces. Each is the opening and titular story of the volume in which it was first published. The two are the first and second tales of *Palabra de mujer*, the Castilian version of the Catalan originals, and both reappear in *Te dejo el mar* ("I Leave You the Sea"), Luisa Cotoner's Castilian translation of the 1975 and 1977 collections. "Te deix," which received the 1974 Recull Prize for short fiction in Catalan, exemplifies the importance of seduction as theme and narrative technique. The story consists of a letter written by a young married woman days before the birth of her child, a letter in which she takes leave of her first love, her high school math teacher. In the last paragraph we discover that the addressee is not a man but a woman, Maria. (In Catalan the feminine name Maria is written without an accent; the masculine name is Marià.) What is curious is that a good many people, including a male critic who shall remain nameless, have read Marià for Maria. Since what is natural from a heterosexual point of view—perhaps even more so in 1974—is that a young woman should fall in love with a young man, it is apparently inconceivable for some readers that the lover could be another woman. Furthermore, it's taken for granted in this (mis)reading that math teachers are men. Annette Kolodny has observed that we read well what we already know how to read, and what we know how to read depends in large measure on the works that have shaped our expectations and interpretive strategies. Texts that represent a break with our experience are uncomfortable, even incomprehensible (154–55). "Te deix" is doubly transgressive in that the lesbian relationship described contravenes social and religious codes and the narration of this relationship constitutes a further act of aggression against society.

While "Te deix" presents the other side of the traditional, heterosexual romance plot (girl loves boy, boy loves girl), "Jo pos per testimoni les gavines" presents the other side of "Te deix." What was recounted in the first story is now seen through the eyes of a former math teacher. Her version coincides in various respects with the version given us by the person she believes to be her former student; a number of the same incidents are mentioned and described in identical or similar terms. We do not know if what she tells us is true, for her words may be no more than the ramblings of a deranged woman. "Madness" is, of course, a convenient label for behavior that does not adhere to masculine norms; it can also be a means of escaping those norms. The structure of "Jo pos per testimoni les gavines" foregrounds the question of exclusion and inclusion, of what is outside and what inside, of what is marginal and what is central, of what is acceptable and what is not, in texts and in personal relationships, in literature as in life.

The story is introduced by two brief letters, the first of which is addressed to the director of the publishing house Laia and requests that he forward the enclosed missive and manuscript to Carme Riera, author of *Te deix, amor, la mar com a penyora,* which Laia had published. In the second letter, addressed to Riera, the writer confesses her amazement on reading a story that has so many points of contact with her own life:

> No es pot imaginar la sorpresa enorme que em causà veure'm gairebé retratada, retratada però, per un esguard generós i benevolent... No sé qui pogué contar-li amb detalls de miniaturista uns fets, esmicolant sentiments amb tanta precisió, escamotejant-ne a la vegada uns altres, canviant-ne l'acabament. Pens que tal volta l'atzar féu que vostè imaginàs una història que s'assemblava a la meva. (10)

> You can't imagine how surprised I was to see myself almost portrayed, portrayed, however, by a generous and benevolent gaze . . . I don't know who could recount events to you in such fine detail, examining certain feelings with such precision, at the same time skirting others, changing the ending. I think perhaps chance made you imagine a story that resembles my own.

The passage illustrates what Cotoner describes as Riera's "reveal-and-conceal" technique (21). The "almost portrayed" and the references to chance and imagination imply that the resemblance between the story and the writer's life is strictly coincidental, but the assumption that someone has related to Riera the most intimate details of the writer's existence argues otherwise.

We are offered two conflicting explanations—sheer invention versus factual testimony—and the resultant ambiguity is sustained in the closing paragraph of the letter: "Pens que tal volta aquesta història meva, corregida per vostè, reescrita si vol, pot interessar a la gent que ha llegit el seu llibre, com a testimoniatge d'uns fets reals" (10) ("I think that perhaps this story of mine, corrected by you, rewritten if you wish, may interest people who have read your book, as a testimony of real events"). The possibility that a woman who may be a character in "Te deix" has written to Riera because she believes that her history may interest readers of that story has Cervantine overtones and hints at a violation of the laws of fiction and a crossing of the boundary between the real and the imaginary, between the extratextual world of Riera and the intratextual world of the characters created by her. These framing documents with their metafictional border crossing not only awaken our curiosity but, equally important, point to the centrality of the marginal and emphasize that "Jo pos" presents the other side of the "Te deix" story, a fact obscured in the *Palabra de mujer* version, which omits the two introductory letters. That omission has led some to read the two tales as if they were unrelated to each other, which they are not. Both speak of transgressive desire, both transform the canonical heterosexual love plot with its conventionally happy ending, both remind us of the importance of that which is pushed to the margins of texts and of society, and both recount histories of seduction.

In "Te deix, amor, la mar com a penyora," "Jo pos per testimoni les gavines," "Estimat Thomas," "Octubre, octubre," and many other texts, Riera has a woman character tell her story. Instead of being spoken for, she speaks and makes herself heard; instead of being the object of a masculine narration, she is the subject of a feminine one. Making oneself heard is especially noteworthy in four tales that Riera describes as a tribute to women of Majorca. The female figures once again take shape through the device of the first person, as each woman tells her story, recounting in matter-of-fact fashion how she has been mistreated by the men in her life. The protagonists of "Noltros no hem tengut sort amb sos homos..." (109–13) ("We've Not Been Lucky with Men . . ."), from the collection *Te deix,* and "Te banyaré i te trauré defora" (73–77) ("I'll Wash You and Hang You Out"), "Es nus, es buit" (79–82) ("The Knot, the Void"), and "De jove embellia" (87–90) ("I Was a Beauty When I Was Young"), from the "Bisti de Càrrega" section of *Jo pos,* are women who, because of a series of circumstances—too much work; too little education; and a lack of self-confidence, free time, and practice with writing—would find it impossible to set their experiences down on paper but are able to speak of them. (And the texts impress us as being spoken, not written.)

These "beasts of burden," who have worn themselves out with hard work, are now elderly, alone, and accused of madness by greedy relatives. They speak from a position of sexual, social, and economic inferiority, and the language they employ is colloquial. Accustomed to playing a secondary role and to obeying rather than being obeyed or imposing their own will, they demonstrate a resigned passivity toward their lot. They do not openly criticize or protest their oppression; it is left to the readers to do that. The stories can be seen as an example of what King-Kok Cheung terms "double-telling," which conveys two tales in the guise of one (29), the first manifest, the second veiled. Each woman releases a torrent of words, and her interlocutor—a doctor, a fellow passenger on a bus, an unidentified "you"—listens without saying anything. That their interlocutors are silent while the women come to voice inverts the normal situation in which the latter are silent. Their speech is vacillating and digressive rather than lineal and monolithic, and the use of suspension points, indicating that sentences are incomplete and meaning interrupted, draws attention to what is not said. Riera allows anonymous, invisible beings, who usually go unheard, have no power, and are excluded from the dominant discourse, to express themselves. Each protagonist, very possibly for the first time, seizes the word. Cheung notes that "words spoken by the powerless have no impact" (138), but literary discourse can convey power and make a lasting impression.

The last narrative to be explored, with its references to a host of other works, is a critic's delight, and in it Riera utilizes intertexts to call attention to voices that traditionally have been silenced and to figures that, according to masculine norms, are unworthy of starring roles. It has been said, with notable condescension, that while men write books, women scribble letters. But Riera, like a number of her female contemporaries, including Rodoreda, Mayoral, Montero, Carmen Martín Gaite, Montserrat Roig, and Ana María Moix, vindicates the letter as a literary form.

Janet Altman has observed that epistolary literature is unique in that it makes the reader ("narratee") almost as important an agent in the narrative as the narrator: "The letter writer simultaneously seeks to affect his reader and is affected by him" (88). The comment, once we replace the masculine "his" and "him" with "her," is an apt description of what takes place in the novella *Qüestió d'amor propi*. Its protagonist, Angela Caminals, after Miquel terminates their brief affair, writes to her Danish friend Ingrid and requests that when Miquel travels to Scandinavia, Ingrid feed him false information for use in one of his future books. The maneuver would convert Miquel into a laughingstock and dash his hopes of being nominated for the Nobel Prize. Apropos epistolary novels of seduction, Altman notes that "the letter is an insidious device used by the seducer to break down his victim's resistance" (15). Angela attempts to forestall whatever objections Ingrid may have to being cast in the ignominious role envisioned for her. Although Angela postpones her request until the end of the letter, every page is designed to entice Ingrid into seducing Miquel. Angela's strategies include repeated references to the long-standing friendship and shared experiences that link the two women and a self-deprecating portrayal of herself as timid, foolish, and insecure in contrast to her Danish friend, who has greater self-assurance and more extensive sexual experience.

Miquel's initial seduction of Angela is staged against a backdrop of other literary seductions, such as that of Ana Ozores by Alvaro Mesía in the nineteenth-century novel *La regenta* ("The Judge's Wife"), Melibea by Calixto in the fifteenth-century *Celestina*, and Gretchen by Faust. Unlike the male authors Leopoldo Alas, Fernando de Rojas, and Goethe, Riera breaks with literary tradition and chooses for her protagonist a forty-eight-year-old woman. One of Angela's conversations with Miquel revolves around the curious fact that when male novelists portray a heroine who is in love, she is rarely over thirty. Older women are usually confined to secondary roles as mothers, aunts, grandmothers, and mothers-in-law and are depicted as ill-humored, hypocritical, avaricious, and antagonistic to the young. While Riera does not portray Angela as an admirable or heroic figure, she does give her a voice, a voice that Angela uses to dominate and control the text from beginning to end.[8] It is significant that the writing implement she employs is a pen given to her by her woman friend and that Miquel, apart from a few grandiloquent and obviously untruthful remarks, is silenced and pushed to the margin of the text. Instead, it is the person he regards as over-the-hill and washed-up, both as a woman and as a writer, who "lleva la voz cantante," a figurative expression that can be translated as "is the boss, has the chief say." The tables have been turned.

Elaine Hedges and Shelley Fishkin remind us in *Listening to Silences* that Tillie Olsen termed "unnatural" those silences that result from "being born into the wrong class, race, or sex, being denied education, becoming numbed by economic struggle, muffled by censorship, or distracted or impeded by the demands of nurturing" (3). One way to remedy those silences is to endow the marginalized—be they aging, uneducated, mad (in both senses of the word), or lesbian—with a voice and to allow them to speak up and speak out. By focusing on these ex-centrics, Riera draws them out of the shadows into the limelight. Her powers of seduction are manifest in the deftness with which she captures the attention of her readers and entices them to listen to voices of marginality, to the voices of women. Although Riera refuses to be categorized as a feminist writer, the issues of marginality and voice that are central to her fiction are primary concerns of feminism.

Notes

1. All translations are my own. Although there exists an English version of Riera's *Joc de miralls* translated as *Mirror Images* by Cristina de la Torre, I refer to this title as "Game of Mirrors." I wish to express my appreciation to my colleague Ton Pujol for his assistance with my translations of the Catalan quotations.

2. Riera's stance differs from that of Montserrat Roig and Maria-Mercè Marçal, both of whom identified themselves as feminist authors and were committed to the feminism of difference.
3. To re-vision, for Adrienne Rich (90), is to look back, to see with fresh eyes, to enter an old text from a new critical direction.
4. For more on the saint's rhetorical dexterity, see Alison Weber.
5. Riera dedicated *Joc de miralls* to Cotoner, who collaborated in preparing the Castilian version of the stories contained in *Palabra de mujer* and translated the narratives published in *Te dejo el mar,* for which Cotoner also wrote an excellent introduction. In a tribute written to commemorate the fortieth anniversary of the awarding of the Premio Nadal to Carmen Laforet's *Nada,* Riera voiced her admiration for the book and described it as a novel about female friendship.
6. Rodoreda was known for her love of gardening and the frequent use of flowers in her fiction.
7. See Riera's "Grandeza y miseria" on the use of letters as a literary device.
8. In a 1990 conversation I had with Riera, she described Angela as "quite odious" (Personal interview).

Works Cited

Altman, Janet Gurkin. *Epistolarity: Approaches to a Form.* Columbus: Ohio State UP, 1982.

Bloom, Harold. *The Anxiety of Influence: A Theory of Poetry.* New York: Oxford UP, 1973.

Carmona, Vicente, Jeffrey Lamb, Sherry Velasco, and Barbara Zecchi. "Conversando con Mercedes Abad, Cristina Fernández Cubas y Soledad Puértolas: 'Feminismo y literatura no tienen nada que ver.' " *Mester* 20.2 (1991): 157–65.

Caws, Mary Ann. *Reading Frames in Modern Literature.* Princeton: Princeton UP, 1985.

Cheung, King-Kok. *Articulate Silences.* Ithaca: Cornell UP, 1993.

Cotoner, Luisa. Introduction. Riera, *Te dejo el mar* 11–34.

García, Cristina. "People on the Edge See More." *Lectora* 1 (1995): 19–24.

Gilbert, Sandra M., and Susan Gubar. *The Madwoman in the Attic: The Woman Writer and the Nineteenth-Century Literary Imagination.* New Haven: Yale UP, 1979.

Hedges, Elaine, and Shelley Fisher Fishkin, eds. *Listening to Silences.* New York: Oxford UP, 1994.

Hutcheon, Linda. *A Poetics of Postmodernism.* New York: Routledge, 1988.

Kolodny, Annette. "Dancing through the Minefield." *The New Feminist Criticism.* Ed. Elaine Showalter. New York: Pantheon, 1985. 144–67.

Nichols, Geraldine C. *Escribir, espacio propio: Laforet, Matute, Moix, Tusquets, Riera y Roig por sí mismas.* Minneapolis: Inst. for the Study of Ideologies and Lit., 1989.

Rich, Adrienne. "When We Dead Awaken: Writing as Re-Vision." *Adrienne Rich's*

Poetry. Ed. Barbara Charlesworth Gelpi and Albert Gelpi. New York: Norton, 1975. 90–98.

Riera, Carme. "Conversation with Carme Riera." With Kathleen M. Glenn. *Moveable Margins: The Narrative Art of Carme Riera*. Ed. Glenn, Mirella Servodidio, and Mary S. Vásquez. Lewisburg: Bucknell UP, 1999. 39–57.

———. "Estimat Thomas." *Epitelis tendríssims*. Barcelona: Edicions 62, 1987. 79–95.

———. "Grandeza y miseria de la epístola." *El oficio de narrar*. Ed. Marina Mayoral. Madrid: Cátedra/Ministerio de Cultura, 1989. 147–58.

———. *Joc de miralls*. Barcelona: Planeta, 1989.

———. *Jo pos per testimoni les gavines*. Barcelona: Laia, 1977.

———. *Mirror Images*. Trans. Cristina de la Torre. New York: Lang, 1993.

———. "Octubre, octubre." *El primer amor*. Barcelona: Columna, 1992. 91–97.

———. *Palabra de mujer*. Barcelona: Laia, 1980.

———. Personal interview. 26 May 1990.

———. *Qüestió d'amor propi*. Barcelona: Laia, 1987.

———. *Te deix, amor, la mar com a penyora*. Barcelona: Laia, 1975.

———. *Te dejo el mar*. Trans. Luisa Cotoner. Madrid: Espasa Calpe, 1991.

———. "Vindicación de Teresa de Cepeda (En vísperas de un centenario)." *Quimera* 12 (1981): 4–7.

Riera, Carme, and Luisa Cotoner. "Los personajes femeninos de doña María de Zayas, una aproximación." *Literatura y vida cotidiana*. Actas de las Cuartas Jornadas de Investigación Interdisciplinaria. Ed. María Angeles Durán and José Antonio Rey. Zaragoza: Seminario de Estudios de la Mujer, 1987. 149–59.

Vosburg, Nancy. "On Post-transition Politics, *Picardía*, and Power: Lidia Falcón's *El alboroto español* (The Spanish Uproar)." *Spanish Women Writers and the Essay: Gender, Politics, and the Self*. Ed. Kathleen M. Glenn and Mercedes Mazquiarán de Rodríguez. Columbia: U of Missouri P, 1998. 198–211.

Weber, Alison. *Teresa of Avila and the Rhetoric of Femininity*. Princeton: Princeton UP, 1990.

Notes on Contributors

María Isabel Barbeito Carneiro holds a doctorate in Hispanic philology with a focus on Hispanic language and literature. Her extensive critical, bibliographical, and historical work on women in Golden Age Spain includes essays on María de Agreda, Sor Marcela de San Félix, María de Guevara, Mariana de San José, and María de Zayas. In addition to her two-volume doctoral thesis, *Escritoras madrileñas del siglo XVII* (1986), Barbeito Carneiro has written several books, including *Cárceles y mujeres en el siglo XVII* (1991), *Mujeres del Madrid barroco: Voces testimoniales* (1992), and *María de Orozco* (1997). Barbeito Carneiro directs the *Horas y Horas* collection "Mujeres en Madrid" and is a founding member of the Asociación Española de la Bibliografía.

Maryellen Bieder is professor of Spanish and adjunct professor of comparative literature at Indiana University, Bloomington. She has written widely on issues of gender and narration in Emilia Pardo Bazán, Carmen de Burgos, and contemporary Spanish women novelists.

H. Patsy Boyer, professor emerita at Colorado State University, wrote scholarly studies of a variety of Spanish seventeenth- and nineteenth-century Spanish writers. Her publications included the first complete English translations of María de Zayas's double masterpiece *The Enchantments of Love* (1990) and *The Disenchantments of Love* (1997).

Lou Charnon-Deutsch is professor of Hispanic languages and literature at the State University of New York, Stony Brook. She is the editor and author of numerous books and articles on women in nineteenth-century Spanish culture, including *Gender and Representation: Women in Nineteenth-Century Spanish Realist Fiction* (1990), *Narratives of Desire: Nineteenth-Century Fiction by Women* (1994), and *Fictions of the Feminine in the Nineteenth-Century Spanish Press* (2001).

Anne J. Cruz received her AB, MA, and PhD from Stanford University. She is professor of Spanish at the University of Illinois, Chicago, and previously taught at the University of California, Irvine, and, as visiting professor, at Stanford University. She has written over fifty essays on Spanish Golden Age literature and culture from feminist, historicist, and psychoanalytical perspectives. She edited, with Carroll B. Johnson, *Cervantes and His Postmodern Constituencies* (1999) and wrote *Discourses of Poverty: Social Reform and the Picaresque Novel in Early Modern Spain* (1999). She was awarded, in 1999, a Mellon Foundation Fellowship at the Newberry Library to complete a study on female subjectivity in early modern Spain.

Catherine Davies is professor of Spanish studies and head of the Department of Spanish and Portuguese at the University of Manchester. She has written extensively on nineteenth- and twentieth-century Spanish and Latin American literature and film. Her most recent publications include *Latin American Women's Writing: Feminist Readings in Theory and Crisis,* edited with Anny Brooksbank Jones (1996); *A Place in the Sun? Women's Writing in Twentieth-Century Cuba* (1997); *Spanish Women's Writing, 1849–1996* (1998); and an edition of Gómez de Avellaneda's *Sab* (2001). She is currently working on Hispanic feminist thought in nineteenth-century Latin America.

Christina Dupláa was associate professor of Spanish at Dartmouth College. Author of many articles about women and Catalan nationalism, including "La voz testimonial de Montserrat Roig," she coedited *Las nacionalidades del estado español: Una problemática cultural* (1986) and *Spain*

Today: Essays on Literature, Culture, Society (1995). Coordinator of the section on Catalan women authors for vol. 6 of *Breve historia feminista de la literatura española,* she also worked on the topic of memory as resistance in the narrative of Josefina R. Aldecoa.

Kathleen M. Glenn has written on a number of twentieth-century Castilian and Catalan women writers. She is an editor for the journal *Anales de la literatura española contemporánea* and has coedited *Spanish Women Writers and the Essay: Gender, Politics, and the Self* (1998) and *Moveable Margins: The Narrative Art of Carme Riera* (1999).

María Asunción Gómez is assistant professor of Spanish at Florida International University. She is the author of the monographic study *Estrategias metatextuales en el teatro y cine españoles* and the book *Del escenario a la pantalla* (2000). Her articles have appeared in *Journal of Interdisciplinary Studies, Estreno, Explicación de textos literarios, Letras peninsulares,* and *Bulletin of Hispanic Studies.* She is currently writing a book on the representation of women in film adaptations of literary works.

Margaret E. W. Jones is professor and chair, Department of Spanish and Italian, at the University of Kentucky. In keeping with research and teaching interests in twentieth-century literature, women's writing, and Spanish feminism, she has written articles and books on Spanish drama, the contemporary novel, and women's fiction. She has contributed studies on Paloma Díaz-Mas, Ana Diosdado, Carmen Laforet, Ana María Matute, Marina Mayoral, Dolores Medio, Ana María Moix, Ramón Sender, Esther Tusquets, and Antonio Buero Vallejo. In addition to writing literary criticism, Jones has translated Esther Tusquets's *The Same Sea as Every Summer* and Ana María Moix's *Dangerous Virtues.*

Josebe Martínez-Gutiérrez is assistant professor of Spanish at California State University, Fresno. Author of several articles on twentieth-century women, feminism, and film, she also wrote *Margarita Nelken: La lealtad del intelectual* (1997) and *Escritoras españolas en el exilio de 1939* (2000).

She is currently editing the volume "Women Intellectuals and Contemporary Nationalisms in Spain."

Joana Sabadell-Nieto received her doctorate from the University of Pennsylvania and is associate professor of Spanish at the State University of New York, Albany. A specialist in twentieth-century poetry in Catalan and Castilian, Sabadell has published many articles in Spain and in the United States. Her books include *Mosaico ibérico: Ensayos sobre poesía y diversidad* (1999) and *Fragmentos de sentido: La identidad transgresora de Jaime Gil de Biedma* (1997). She also coedited *Spain Today: Essays on Literature, Culture, and Society* (1995).

Teresa S. Soufas earned her doctorate at Duke University and is a professor in the Department of Spanish and Portuguese at Tulane University, where she is also dean of the Faculty of the Liberal Arts and Sciences. Her scholarship has been devoted to topics in Spanish Golden Age literature. In addition to many articles, she has written two books, *Melancholy and the Secular Mind in Spanish Golden Age Literature* (1990) and *Dramas of Distinction: A Study of Plays by Golden Age Women* (1997), and is the editor of the anthology *Women's Acts: Plays by Women Dramatists of Spain's Golden Age* (1997).

Constance A. Sullivan is associate professor of Spanish literature at the University of Minnesota, Twin Cities. While she has written on various topics related to Spanish literature, her recent work focuses on issues of gender and women writers in eighteenth-century Spain.

Joyce Tolliver is associate professor of Spanish and an affiliate of women's studies at the University of Illinois, Urbana. She has contributed many articles on Spanish and Latin American women writers and linguistics-based narrative theory and is the author of *Cigar Smoke and Violet Water: Gendered Discourse in the Stories of Emilia Pardo Bazán* (1998). She also edited and introduced critical editions of Emilia Pardo Bazán's collection *"El encaje roto" y otros cuentos* and its translation, *"Torn Lace" and Other Stories* (1996).

María Cristina Urruela received her PhD from the University of Texas, Austin. She is currently a lecturer in the Department of Spanish and Portuguese at Stanford University. Urruela's most recent translation is "*Torn Lace" and Other Stories,* by Emilia Pardo Bazán (1996). She is preparing a manuscript entitled "Spanish Scribblers: Nineteenth-Century Women Writers in Spain."

Lisa Vollendorf is assistant professor of Spanish at Wayne State University. She has written *Reclaiming the Body: María de Zayas's Early Modern Feminism* (2001), a study of Spain's only best-selling seventeenth-century woman author. In 1999 she was awarded a Monticello College Foundation Fellowship at the Newberry Library, and in 2000 she received an Ahmanson-Getty Postdoctoral Fellowship at UCLA's Clark Library to work on her current project, "Women's Self-Representation in Early Modern Spain," on women's literature and Inquisition trials.

Nancy Vosburg is professor of foreign languages and director of the Women and Gender Studies Program at Stetson University. She has written articles on many twentieth-century Spanish women writers and coedited *The Garden across the Border: Mercè Rodoreda's Fiction.* She is preparing a manuscript on the women writers who were exiled in the aftermath of the Spanish Civil War.

Alison Weber is associate professor of Spanish at the University of Virginia. From 1998 to 1999 she was research associate in women's studies in religion at Harvard Divinity School. The author of *Teresa of Avila and the Rhetoric of Femininity,* she writes about issues of gender and religious expression in early modern Spanish literature and culture. She is currently working on a book about the followers of Santa Teresa and the fortunes of the Carmelite Reform. She is also preparing, in collaboration with Amanda Powell, an introduction and translation to María de San José Salazar's *Libro de Recreaciones.*

Barbara F. Weissberger received her PhD from Harvard University and has taught at Brown University, Randolph Macon College, and Old

Dominion University. She is associate professor of Spanish at the University of Minnesota, Twin Cities, and a member of the MLA Executive Committee of the Division of Medieval Spanish Language and Literature. She has written on a wide range of topics related to sexuality, women, and readership in medieval Spain. Currently, she is completing a book on gender ideology in the literature of the reign of Isabella I.

Index of Names